I0814316

"This engaging and highly readable commentary will become a standard resource for preachers, teachers, seminary students, and anyone looking for deeper insight into Matthew's Gospel. Especially helpful is the introduction in which Powell lays out 'themes' of the Gospel that are woven throughout. Powell brings together a wealth of recent scholarship and shows how new perspectives are helpful for reflection, interpretation, and application."

—Cynthia M. Campbell, President Emerita, McCormick Theological Seminary, and retired pastor of Highland Presbyterian Church

"Powell's lifetime of studying Matthew's Gospel culminates in this thoughtful and well-informed study. Readers will find much that is helpful in this commentary, provoking many insights and further engagement with the Gospel's text."

—Warren Carter, LaDonna Kramer Meinders Professor of New Testament, Phillips Theological Seminary

"Powell is a masterful interpreter and guide. First-time students of the First Gospel will appreciate his conversational tone, honesty, and ability to move between the past and the present. Preachers and teachers will find fresh, perceptive insights. Powell summarizes Matthew's key themes in the introduction and references them throughout the commentary, taking deeper dives in timely excursuses. By the end of the journey, readers will have a deep appreciation for both the Gospel and the guide who led them through it."

—R. Alan Culpepper, Dean Emeritus, McAfee School of Theology, Mercer University

---

"As did its illustrious forerunner, the new Interpretation Bible Commentary series offers clergy, teachers, and students one of the richest interpretive resources for biblical inquiry and homiletical engagement. Integrating literary, historical, theological, and pastoral insights from an inclusive group of preeminent scholars and teachers, these volumes reflect the major shifts in interpretive strategies for a dramatically changing contemporary context. Whether one is leaning into research or preparing to preach, these volumes are a replete resource."

—Brian K. Blount, General Editor of the Interpretation Bible Commentary series, and President Emeritus, Union Presbyterian Seminary

Matthew

An Interpretation Bible Commentary

Interpretation Bible Commentary

Brian K. Blount, *General Editor*
Beverly Roberts Gaventa, *Associate Editor*
Jacqueline E. Lapsley, *Associate Editor*
Samuel L. Adams, *Associate Editor*

Volumes in the Series

Old Testament

Genesis 1–11
Genesis 12–50
Exodus
1 Samuel
Esther
Psalms
Isaiah 1–39
Isaiah 40–66
Ezekiel
Daniel
Hosea–Malachi

New Testament

Matthew
Mark
Luke
John
Acts
Romans
1 Corinthians

Matthew

An Interpretation Bible Commentary

MARK ALLAN POWELL

First Edition
Published by Westminster John Knox Press
Louisville, Kentucky

23 24 25 26 27 28 29 30 31 32 33—10 9 8 7 6 5 4 3 2 1

Cover and book design by Allison Taylor

Library of Congress Cataloging-in-Publication Data is on file at the Library of Congress, Washington, D.C.

ISBN: 9780664264291

With grateful appreciation for
Lenny†, Dylan†, Cyrus†, Cleopatra†, Bonnie, Collar†,
No Collar†, Augustine Flynn, Mango†, Apollo, Aztec†,
Amelia Bedelia, Dahlia, and others still to come.

CONTENTS

SERIES FOREWORD

The work of biblical interpretation is ever-changing because the art of reading and understanding is profoundly shaped by the lives of interpreters and their communities. The original Interpretation series was designed to meet the needs of clergy, teachers, and students as a resource that integrates literary, historical, theological, and pastoral insights. The decision to extend and reframe that series as the Interpretation Bible Commentary reflects awareness of the vast historical, cultural, and ecclesial changes that have occurred since the last volume of the previous series was published in 2005. These new volumes reflect the major changes in interpretative strategies as well as a keen awareness of a dramatically changing contemporary context.

Prominent among the significant changes in the interpretive landscape is the expanded range of voices in biblical scholarship. Biblical interpretation has always been a diverse, vibrant undertaking, but that breadth has not been reflected in publications. The diversity of contributors in this renewed series reflects respect and appreciation for a broad array of witnesses.

The primary focus of the Interpretation Bible Commentary series remains unchanged from its predecessor: to invite its readers into the lively work of careful biblical interpretation for the purpose of faithful exposition. Preachers and teachers seeking reflective guidance from the biblical texts will find these volumes an illuminating and highly accessible resource. This Interpretation Bible Commentary series will tend to the needs of its twenty-first-century audience while maintaining the priorities of its creators. The words of the original editors—James Mays, Patrick Miller, and Paul Achtemeier—still ring true: "What is in mind is the work of an interpreter who brings theological and pastoral sensitivity to the task and creates an interpretation which does not stop short with judgments about the text but is engaged in a dialogue of seeing and hearing with it as a contemporary believer."

Emphasizing both sound critical exegesis and strong theological sensibilities, these new volumes employ innovative approaches that allow for fresh readings of biblical texts, including difficult passages.

The series empowers readers to engage God's creation and our place in it with fresh eyes. Through their engagement with Scripture, the commentaries illumine our relationship with God, each other, and creation so that readers are propelled with new understanding and energy for fulfilling God's claims upon us in our rapidly changing global context.

Using several interpretive methodologies that are appropriate for the varying biblical texts, these volumes promise a compelling interpretation for the church and world today. Each exposition will situate the respective biblical books historically, theologically, literarily, and socially, providing a rich resource for unleashing the homiletical and formational potential of the text.

The text on which the commentary is based is the New Revised Standard Version Updated Edition (NRSVue). Because this translation is widely available, the printing of a text in the commentary itself is unnecessary. Each commentary is divided into sections appropriate to the particular book. Instead of offering a verse-by-verse interpretation, the commentary deals with passages as a whole. Thematic topics that are especially pertinent or have great bearing on the biblical book are addressed in excursuses. A "For Further Reading" section provides resources that are instructive for broadening the reader's hermeneutical horizons and diversify the reader's understanding of how to approach the text.

The writers and editors hope these volumes will explain and apply the meaning and significance of the biblical texts while addressing key contemporary issues. The Interpretation Bible Commentary series is intended to draw the reader into an interpretative community where, collegially, reader and interpreter can more fruitfully engage these ancient texts for present living.

The Editors

Introduction

Popular Christian tradition ascribes this Gospel to the tax collector named Matthew; according to this book, he became one of Jesus' twelve disciples (9:9; 10:3). Modern scholars, however, regard the book as written by an unknown Christian in an urban setting (possibly Antioch) around the year 85 CE. He was almost certainly a Jewish Christian (or perhaps better put, "a Christian Jew") who for some time had led a congregation of Jewish believers in Jesus, a community that had probably been ostracized by other Jewish groups and had experienced an influx of gentile converts. So, the Gospel was written for a community in transition and experiencing something of an identity crisis.

Further, it is widely (though not universally) believed that Matthew had two primary sources for his work: the Gospel of Mark, which he edited in accord with his interests and theology, and the early collection of Jesus' teachings that scholars call "the Q source" (cf. German, *Quelle*). In this commentary, we note the likely source for Matthew's material in italics at the beginning of each set of texts to be discussed. Sometimes we will also identify significant redactional changes that Matthew appears to have made in the material used (e.g., when he changes a story taken from Mark so that it now means something quite different). We do not dwell on such matters, however, because the primary goal of this commentary is to elucidate how Matthew's readers would be expected to understand or respond to the narrative that we now possess. Thus, we are interpreting the text of Matthew in what is conventionally called its "finished form," with only slight attention to the book's compositional history. For the most part, we do not ask what material might have meant in a prior context, before it was incorporated into Matthew's Gospel. Rather, we will look at the book as we now have it and attempt to understand it from the perspective of its implied readers or assumed audience: What are readers supposed to get out of this book? How are they expected to be affected by it and respond to it?

MATTHEW'S GOSPEL THEN AND NOW

Like all volumes in the new Interpretation Bible Commentary series, this commentary will keep two questions in the background at all times.

1. *What did Matthew's Gospel offer its original readers?* Obviously, Matthew's Gospel provided its original readers with a coherent account of the ministry, death, and resurrection of Jesus the Christ, the Son of God. But we can answer this question with greater specificity. Matthew's readers already had the Gospel of Mark (and probably a collection of Jesus' sayings). Apparently Matthew intended his book to replace those documents as his church's sacred text (otherwise, we would expect him to explain or defend some of his redactional changes). So the question might be considered in terms of what Matthew's Gospel offered its readers that the other documents did not. We will consider that question throughout the commentary, but at the outset we can state that Matthew probably found the Gospel of Mark to be inadequate in at least four ways: (a) Mark does not present Christ as currently present among his followers, and thus the locus of God's continuing presence in the world is ambiguous. (b) Mark offers little insight with regard to the discernment of God's will for new contexts or changing situations. (c) Mark's portrait of discipleship does not address the possibility of progress and thus it provides little hope or incentive for improvement. And (d) Mark's Gospel does not present the messianic movement of Jesus' followers as a faithful (perhaps the only faithful) expression of traditional Israelite (Jewish) religion. All these points may be gathered under one umbrella observation: from Matthew's perspective, the Gospel

of Mark contains no effective doctrine of the church. Addressing this concern may have been Matthew's major incentive for producing a replacement Gospel.

2. *What does Matthew's Gospel offer readers today?* Matthew's Gospel tells the story of Jesus, with emphasis upon his teaching and on his mission as the Son of God, who came to fulfill the Law and the Prophets (5:17), call sinners (9:13), build a church (16:18), and give his life as a ransom for many (20:28). This story is almost two thousand years old and is told in ways that can be mystifying (testing our knowledge of ancient Roman customs and Jewish practices) or off-putting (portraying opponents of Christianity in ways that are grossly stereotyped and unfair); it is told from a perspective that assumes we espouse beliefs and values we might not actually espouse (e.g., that demons are literally real and dangerous, or that slavery is an acceptable social institution). Still, the book offers much that allows for engagement with contemporary issues and concerns: (a) As indicated in the preceding paragraph, Matthew's Gospel is a highly significant book for developing a biblical understanding of the church—not so much as an institution, but as a movement of people who are carrying out the mission of God and manifesting the presence of God in the world. (b) Matthew's Gospel is the most important book in the Bible for Christian ethics, not only because of its emphasis on the moral teaching of Jesus but also because of its sustained hermeneutic of "binding and loosing," by which faith communities might interpret Scripture to discern the will of God in diverse circumstances and ever-changing contexts. (c) Matthew's Gospel offers a realistic but inspiring appraisal of human potential: steering a middle path between Mark's "disciples as failures" and Luke's "disciples as heroes," Matthew tells a story of how fallible people of "little faith" can nevertheless be the salt of the earth and light of the world. (d) Matthew's Gospel provides a compelling portrait of a world (or, at least, of a countercultural community) in which compassion and mercy are prime virtues, forgiveness and justice are top priorities, children are valued, outcasts are accepted, enemies are loved, and all people are treated with unselfish benevolence. (e) Matthew's Gospel is one of the most important texts in the Bible for Jewish-Christian dialogue—in spite of (or perhaps because of) its harsh rhetoric against the Jewish leaders who are said to have opposed Jesus. And (f) Matthew's Gospel offers one of the most devastating critiques of coercive

power and systemic injustice to be found anywhere in the Bible or, for that matter, in all of world literature.

The point might also be stated thus: Matthew's Gospel offers modern readers a paradigmatic pathway for understanding the benefits and deficits of Christianity. When Christians have gotten things wrong (Crusades, colonialism, divinely sanctioned sexism or racism, anti-Semitism), they have almost always cited Matthew's Gospel in support of their beliefs and actions. But when Christians have gotten things right (empowering the weak; protecting the vulnerable; opposing any and all forms of violence; striving for peace, justice, responsible stewardship, and radical inclusivity), they have likewise almost always cited Matthew's Gospel in support of their beliefs and actions. The book has a complicated legacy: understanding Matthew is the best way to grasp and evaluate that legacy.

READING MATTHEW

For the most part, this commentary serves as a guide for reading Matthew in a way that would be expected of its implied readers or assumed audience. At a basic level, this simply means understanding the Gospel on its own terms, as a literary work in its finished form (see Powell 2009). Still, this Gospel was written almost two thousand years ago in a world very different from our own. Some might ask, Is it possible for readers today to understand such a book the way its readers were expected to understand it? I think we can come pretty close, but I grant that for us to do so perfectly, three things would have to happen:

1. We would have to *receive* the story the way the author assumed we would receive it: out loud, in Greek, and as a continuous narrative that unfolds from beginning to end.

2. We would have to *know* everything the author assumed we would know, but no more than this. Thus, we would know the Hebrew Scriptures and many things about the Roman and Jewish worlds of the late first century, but we probably would not know other writings of the New Testament, nor doctrinal propositions from later Christianity, nor anything about the world that has come to light only as a result of scientific research or intellectual study in the years since this Gospel was written.

3. We would have to *think* the way the author assumed the book's readers would think, coming to the story with the beliefs and values expected of us, but not with beliefs or values that the author never would have anticipated his readers might espouse. So, we would accept that angels are actively involved in human affairs and sometimes guide people through dreams, but we would not believe that democracy is a preferred form of government or that capitalism is a desirable economic system.

Actually doing these three things could be arduous if not impossible, so we must use our imagination: we may need to pretend that we are hearing the story out loud from beginning to end; we may need to pretend that we know nothing about Luke's alternative Christmas narrative; we may need to pretend that we harbor a patriarchal mindset that allows (or even endorses) social inequities defined by an outmoded concept of gender.

I know this can be difficult, but we are only pretending—and this is only a first step. Eventually, of course, we will want to interpret Matthew in light of other information, and we will want to evaluate Matthew in light of our preferred and no doubt more enlightened ideologies. I trust that you will do that—and help others to do it. I make suggestions here and there along those lines, but this commentary is primarily concerned with the indispensable first step: determining how Matthew's readers would be expected to understand the Gospel. My job is to serve as your guide in this regard. I know that you are not actually hearing the Gospel read out loud in Greek from beginning to end, so I will sometimes indicate how a reader who was doing that might get something out of the text that you are likely to miss. And I will sometimes provide information about things you might not know if and when I'm pretty sure that the author assumed you would know these things. And, yes, there will be times when I try to unravel tendencies to read texts in light of modern knowledge and contemporary values rather than understanding them in light of the knowledge and values readers were assumed to possess. This last point becomes especially significant when the narrative seeks to *challenge* an anticipated value system. Jesus' words to Peter regarding forgiveness (Matt 18:22) will only be shocking to a reader who believes Peter's offer to forgive someone seven times was extraordinarily generous (18:21). Likewise, a modern reader may be inclined to think that the Canaanite woman in Matthew 15:21–29 is assertive or bold when she shouts after Jesus in public, but I suspect the reader is expected to regard her as obnoxious: the question then becomes, how would a reader who thinks this woman is obnoxious be affected by what follows, when Jesus praises the "obnoxious" woman for her great faith? Appreciating the narrative's rhetorical moves demands that we (temporarily) adopt the perspective of the narrative's implied readers or assumed audience.

A subtle but important part of reading the Gospel in this way entails recognizing that it is in fact a *story*: a narrative employing literary devices and rhetoric that are expected to guide or affect readers in particular ways. Most of the time we get this: when Matthew writes, "The disciples said . . . ," we know that the twelve men did not all speak in unison. But sometimes a historical interest in events that lie behind this story leads readers to miss the *fictive* (fiction-like) nature of the discourse. For example, many of the characters in Matthew's story are "flat characters," embodying only one or two basic traits; in this way they are not like the real flesh-and-blood people on whom they might be based. The Pharisees who are characters in this story are hypocrites—and almost nothing else. In reality, it seems unlikely that all Pharisees at the time of Jesus were hypocrites, or that any of them were hypocrites all the time. Even if they were, they would have had other traits as well. But in Matthew, the character group that we identify as "the Pharisees" functions to personify a characteristic: hypocrisy essentially becomes a character in the story. As a result, if we read Matthew in order to learn about first-century Pharisees, we may be misled or disappointed; but if we read Matthew to learn about hypocrisy, we may be treated to some rewarding insights.

THEMES IN MATTHEW

Most people who use this commentary will probably turn to individual sections to see what is said about selected passages. I hope it serves such purposes well, but its utility will be increased by noting how some matters are treated throughout the Gospel in ways that transcend individual pericopes. To that end, here I summarize some of the recurrent themes developed throughout the Gospel; I have numbered them for ease of reference. In the main body of the commentary, I often refer my readers to these summaries so that they can see how a subject in the text under discussion is featured in the Gospel as a whole. Themes specific to the passion narrative (Matt 26–27) are treated in a special section later in the commentary (see p. 281).

Theme 1. The abiding presence of God. From the virginal conception of Jesus onward, Matthew insists that "God is with us" (1:23), and numerous passages unique to this Gospel explore ways in which God's presence is manifest in the world. These include traditional affirmations of God's presence in the temple (23:21) and more innovative declarations of God's presence in Jesus as well as in his followers (10:40). Matthew also assumes that while the divine presence in our world is assured (18:20; 28:20), it may assume unlikely guises so as to go unrecognized by the righteous and the wicked alike (25:31–46). We may summarize his understanding of God's active presence in the world in terms of three propositions:

- God is present in Jesus
  - Jesus is born and, so, "God is with us" (1:23)
  - Jesus is worshiped (2:11; 9:18; 14:33; 15:25; 20:20; 28:9, 17)
- Jesus is present in the church
  - with little children (18:5)
  - with people who gather in his name to pray (18:20)
  - with needy members of his spiritual family (25:37–40)
  - with those who receive bread and wine in his name (26:26–28)
  - with people who baptize, teach, and make disciples (28:19–20)
- The church is present in the world
  - as salt of the earth and light of the world (5:13–16)
  - as sheep in the midst of wolves (10:16)
  - as victorious over the gates of Hades (16:18)
  - to make disciples of all nations (28:19)

These three propositions are expressed in a single verse when Jesus says to his followers, "Whoever welcomes you welcomes me, and whoever welcomes me welcomes the one who sent me" (10:40).

A few words of explication may fill out the points on the preceding list. First, Matthew's affirmation that God is present in Jesus goes a shade beyond mere insistence that God *acts* through Jesus. For Matthew, the reality of God's presence is tied to the very existence of Jesus, which is why the affirmation that "God is with us" only becomes true when Jesus physically enters the world (1:23). Of course, Matthew must believe that God has been present with the people of Israel in the past, before Jesus was born, but the presence of God manifested now in Jesus is something unprecedented and superlative. God may have dwelt in the Jerusalem temple, but the coming of Jesus represents "something greater than the temple" (12:6). Just how far Matthew is willing to take this becomes evident when we trace the theme of worship in this Gospel: worshiping Jesus apparently counts as worshiping God (see Excursus: Worship in the Gospel of Matthew, p. 51).

Still, if Jesus were regarded only as a figure in the past, the notion that God was once present in him would have little relevance. So, Matthew goes on to emphasize that Jesus is not merely a past figure but also a lively present one who is still active. The continuing presence of Jesus is most clearly evident in the community of his followers, which Matthew calls "the church" (16:18; 18:17). Given this, we might suppose that Matthew's answer to someone seeking the presence of God would be, "Go to the church, and there you will find the God who is present in Jesus." But Matthew does not really expect seekers to do this. Thus, a third proposition: the church is present in the world. For Matthew, the church is not a static institution but a dynamic movement, an assembly of missionaries who go out into the world willing to suffer in order to bring good news, healing, and life (10:7–8). The world may not appreciate them, but it will be a better place because of them.

Theme 2. Reign or rule of God/heaven. Jesus frequently speaks about what the NRSVue and other English Bibles call the "kingdom of God" or "kingdom of heaven." The two terms are synonymous though Matthew seems to prefer the latter, which avoids use of God's name in deference to certain Jewish pieties (cf. Exod 20:7). As is well known, the Greek word *basilea* (NRSVue, "kingdom") is a cognate noun that expresses verbal action. Almost all scholars agree that "reign" or "rule" would be a better translation because those are cognate "action nouns" in English (while "kingdom" is not). Thus the word does not refer to a place that can be located in space and time, but to the phenomenon of God's ruling: the reign of God, or rule of heaven, is found whenever and wherever God is in charge. This is easily illustrated by considering two famous lines from the Lord's Prayer. In English, we often pray, "Your kingdom come, your will be done" (cf. 6:10), but what does it mean for God's "kingdom" to come? Scholars recognize an instance of Hebraic parallelism here;

the same request is made in slightly different words: God's "kingdom" comes when God's will is done—or better, God's reign or rule may be seen as becoming effective whenever and wherever what God wants to happen takes place.

Still, Matthew does affirm both present and future expressions of this reality: people experience the benefits of God's rule already (12:28) even though the full consummation of that rule is still to come (6:9–10, 33; 16:28; 26:29). This theme has obvious connections to the preceding one: the reign of God (like the presence of God) is manifested through Christ's abiding presence, which is manifested in and through the church's activity in the world.

Here is a partial list of Matthew's fifty references to the reign of God or rule of heaven (in all cases, NRSVue uses the word "kingdom"):

- John the Baptist (3:2), Jesus (4:17), and the apostles (10:7) all proclaim that "the rule of heaven has come near."
- Jesus proclaims the good news of God's reign in Galilean synagogues (4:23; 9:35; see also 24:14).
- Jesus says the poor in spirit (5:3) and the persecuted (5:10) are blessed because heaven rules them.
- Jesus indicates that faithfulness to Torah will determine who is called least or great in the rule of heaven (5:19), but the scribes and Pharisees will never enter the rule of heaven (5:20; see also 23:13).
- Jesus teaches his disciples to pray, "Your rule come. Your will be done, on earth as in heaven" (6:10).
- Jesus says to seek first the reign of God and God's righteousness, and all else will be added to you (6:33).
- Jesus says that not those who call him "Lord," but those who do the will of the Father will enter the rule of heaven (7:21).
- Jesus says that people from east and west will eat with Abraham, Isaac, and Jacob when God's reign is finally manifested, while some of the "heirs" originally intended to benefit from that reign will be excluded (8:11–12; see also 21:43).
- Jesus says that John the Baptist was the greatest man ever born, but the least in the rule of heaven is greater than he (11:11).
- Jesus says his exorcisms are evidence that the reign of God has come (12:28).
- In parables, Jesus compares the rule of heaven to various types of seed (13:19, 24, 31), to yeast (13:33), to a treasure (13:45), to a valuable pearl (13:45), and to a net (13:47). See also 18:23; 20:1; 22:2; 25:1.

- Jesus says that every scribe trained for the rule of heaven knows to treasure what is new and what is old (13:52).
- Jesus promises Peter the keys of the rule of heaven so he can bind and loose on earth what will consequently be bound and loosed in heaven (16:19).
- Jesus says that some of his disciples will live to see the Son of Man coming to reign over all (16:28).
- Jesus indicates that little children and people who become as humble (insignificant) as little children are the greatest in the rule of heaven (18:1–4; see also 19:14).
- Jesus says it is harder for a rich person to enter the rule of heaven than for a camel to pass through the eye of a needle (19:23–24).
- The mother of James and John asks Jesus to grant her sons the two best seats in the rule of heaven (20:21).
- At the Last Supper, Jesus says he will not drink wine again until he drinks it with his disciples when they are reunited after death in the Father's reign (26:29).

Theme 3. The mission of God. Matthew explicates God's mission in the world as being conducted first through the earthly Jesus and then through the exalted Jesus, who abides with his followers and remains active through the community called "the church" (16:18; 18:17). There is remarkable consistency between these two phases of the mission, as may be seen by describing them in parallel columns in the accompanying table. In each case, the basic mission can be summarized in a single phrase. The primary task of Jesus was to save his people from their sins. The primary calling of the church is simply "to bear fruit," which means to be the people who have been saved from their sins, people in whom and through whom the mission of God begun in Jesus continues to be manifested. In both cases the mission has a strong eschatological character (with emphasis on the rule of heaven and the cross), an ethical dimension, and a communal focus.

God's Mission through Jesus	God's Mission through the Church
To save his people from their sins (1:21)	To bear fruit (13:23; 21:43)

<table>
<tr>
<td>Eschatological Character
(Rule of heaven and cross)
• to preach the good news of the rule of heaven (4:17, 23; 9:35)
• to forgive sins (9:6; 26:28)
• to plunder the house of Satan (12:29)
• to die on the cross for the sake of many (20:28; 26:28)
• to be raised from the dead (16:21; 17:9, 23; 20:19)</td>
<td>Eschatological Character
(Rule of heaven and cross)
• to preach the good news of the rule of heaven (10:7; 24:14)
• to forgive sins (6:12; 18:21–25)
• to overcome the gates of Hades (16:18)
• to carry the cross in self-denial (16:24)
• to tell people Jesus has been raised from the dead (27:64)</td>
</tr>
<tr>
<td>Ethical Dimension
• to fulfill the Law and Prophets (5:17)
– by living as a servant (20:28)
– by interpreting the law with authority (5:21–48; 7:28–29)</td>
<td>Ethical Dimension
• to do the will of God (12:49–50)
– by living as servants (20:25–26)
– by binding and loosing the law with authority (16:19; 18:18)</td>
</tr>
<tr>
<td>Communal Focus
• to build the church (16:18)
– by making disciples (4:18–22; 9:9; 10:1–4)
– by calling sinners (9:9–13)
– by revealing the Father (11:27)</td>
<td>Communal Focus
• to increase the church (13:23)
– by making disciples (28:19)
– by seeking sinners (18:12–17)
– by confessing the Son (10:32–33)</td>
</tr>
</table>

Theme 4. A positive Jewish orientation. Many passages in Matthew's Gospel display a strong orientation toward the Jewish people and affirmation of Jewish tradition:

- The Gospel begins with a genealogy that presents Jesus as the culmination of promises made to the Jews through Abraham and David (1:1–17).

- The very reason Jesus is called "Jesus" (God saves) is because "he will save *his* people from their sins" (1:21): "his people" refers at least initially and primarily to "the Jewish people."
- Jesus' disciples are explicitly commanded during his earthly life, "Do not take a road leading to gentiles, and do not enter a Samaritan town, but go rather to the lost sheep of the house of Israel" (10:5–6; cf. 28:16–20).
- Jesus also insists that he has been "sent only to the lost sheep of the house of Israel" (15:24).
- Jesus respects Jewish institutions, paying the temple tax so as not to give offense (17:24–27) and deploring what he regards as desecrations of the temple (21:12–13).
- Jesus says that God dwells in the temple (23:21) and laments the destruction that he knows is coming upon Jerusalem (23:37–39).

Also note the emphasis on "fulfillment of prophecy" (Theme 6) and the insistence on the continuing validity of Torah (Theme 7).

Of course, this Gospel's concern for the Jewish people and general affirmation of Jewish religion are easily overshadowed by the narrative's extremely harsh and negative portrayal of the religious leaders of Israel (Theme 14). But Matthew's narrative distinguishes between Jewish *leaders* and Jewish *people*: the leaders are always opposed to God, but the people as a whole never are (though they can be misled by their leaders, 27:20; 28:15). In similar fashion, gentile *rulers* (like Herod and Pilate) are invariably opposed to Jesus, but gentiles in general (despite their many failings; see Theme 5) are not. In this Gospel it is the possession and use of worldly power rather than ethnicity that sets people in opposition to God (see Theme 16).

Theme 5. Condescending acceptance of gentiles. Matthew's Gospel concludes somewhat triumphantly with a commission to make disciples of gentiles ("all nations," 28:16–20). This will not come as a total shock to the reader because Jesus has already been impressed by the faith of individual gentiles (8:5–13; 15:21–28), and the gentile magi in the birth narrative have prefigured the manner in which pagans from many nations will come to worship "the king of the Jews" (2:1–12). Jesus has spoken of the good news of the rule of heaven being "proclaimed throughout the world" (24:14) and suggested that people from many nations (probably gentiles) will participate in the reign of God when some of those for whom it was intended (probably Jews) are shut out (8:11–12; 21:43; see also 22:8–9).

All this, however, seems to come with an attitude of condescension, a recognition that certain *atypical gentiles* will be counted worthy even though, generally speaking, gentiles are not the sort of folk with whom godly people would want to associate. Indeed, Jesus' words in Matthew often suggest that he doesn't think highly of gentiles:

- Jesus tells his disciples, "If you greet only your brothers and sisters, what more are you doing than others? Do not even the gentiles do the same?" (5:47).
- Jesus tells his disciples, "When you are praying, do not heap up empty phrases as the gentiles do; for they think that they will be heard because of their many words" (6:7).
- Jesus tells his disciples, "Do not worry about your life, what you will eat or what you will drink, or about your body, what you will wear. . . . For it is the gentiles who seek all these things; and indeed your heavenly Father knows that you need all these things" (6:25–32).
- Jesus sends his disciples out on a healing mission, telling them, "Do not take a road leading to the gentiles, and do not enter a Samaritan town, but go rather to the lost sheep of the house of Israel" (10:5–6).
- Jesus warns his disciples, "You will be dragged before governors and kings because of me, as a testimony to them and the gentiles" (10:18). Here "gentiles" are cited as one example of "wolves" into whose midst Jesus' disciples are sent as "sheep" (10:16).
- Jesus concludes his instructions to the disciples on how to deal with unrepentant sinners by saying, "If the offender refuses to listen even to the church, let such a one be to you as a gentile and a tax collector" (18:17).
- Jesus tells his disciples, "You know that the rulers of the gentiles lord it over them, and their great ones are tyrants over them. It will not be so among you" (20:25–26).

In many of these passages, notably, the word "gentiles" is used in parallel structure to "tax collectors" (5:46–47; 18:17), "hypocrites" (6:5–7), or "Samaritan[s]" (10:5–6). In broad terms, gentiles are associated with vanity, tyranny, and sin. Even their best behavior is self-serving. God does not want to hear their long-winded prayers or heal their diseases. Nevertheless, *some* gentiles exhibit faith and the potential to be made disciples of Jesus. I am only slightly embarrassed to report a comment I once made at a meeting that has been widely quoted by others who found it poignant: "Matthew may want to baptize gentiles and teach them to obey Jesus, but he wouldn't want his daughter to marry one."

Theme 6. Fulfillment of prophecy. Matthew's Gospel includes twelve "fulfillment citations," passages claiming that what is reported serves to fulfill sayings of biblical prophets:

- a virgin giving birth to a son called "Emmanuel" (1:22–23)
- birth of a shepherd king for Israel in Bethlehem (2:5–6)
- God's son being called out of Egypt (2:15)
- mourning the children of Rachel in Ramah (2:17–18)
- Jesus being called a "Nazarene" (2:23)
- people in Galilee (Zebulon/Naphtali) seeing a great light (4:14–16)
- Jesus taking infirmities and bearing away diseases (8:17)
- Jesus commending silence after curing many people (12:17–21)
- people not understanding the esoteric teaching of parables (13:14–15)
- Jesus speaking in parables to proclaim hidden truth (13:35)
- Jesus entering Jerusalem mounted on a donkey's colt (21:5)
- thirty pieces of silver being used to buy a potter's field (27:9–10)

The fact that there are twelve such occurrences is often thought to be significant, since the number twelve can be symbolic of Israel (12 tribes). Scholars sometimes struggle to explain Matthew's precise construal of these prophecies: the citation in 2:5–6 appears to add words to the text of Micah 5:2, and the passage presumably quoted in 2:23 cannot be found. Other anomalies occur, and it is not certain whether Matthew quotes from the LXX, offers his own translation of the Hebrew text, or simply relies upon his (somewhat faulty) memory.

Many more passages in Matthew could be understood in the manner of those above even though no explicit "fulfillment citation" is offered (e.g., the dividing of garments in 27:35 recalls Ps. 22:18, though Matthew does not call attention to this). Matthew's narrative also seems filled with subtle but sweeping allusions to biblical stories (e.g., a character named Joseph who is guided by God through dreams; cf. 1:20–2:20 with Gen 37–50). And Matthew is often seen as developing his Christology on a variety of Old Testament models, especially that of Moses (see Theme 10) and the Isaian Servant (cf. 12:18–21 with Isa 42:1–4; note the frequent allusions to Isa 53 in the passion narrative).

Basically, the Matthean Jesus claims that he has come to fulfill the Scriptures ("the Law [and] the Prophets," 5:17), and Matthew appears to regard his entire life as previewed or predicted in the Scriptures:

- conception (1:22–23)
- birth (2:4–6)
- upbringing (2:23)
- ministry (12:17–21)
- passion (26:54)

Theologically, this indicates that everything is going in accord with God's plan, a plan worked out long ago: there have been no unexpected developments, and nothing has been left to chance. At another level, many scholars believe that Matthew presents Jesus as fulfilling prophecies in hopes of converting Jews who see that their Scriptures clearly point to him. I personally think that is unlikely. For one thing, no discerning Jew would be inclined to believe that Jesus actually said or did these things just because Christians say he did. More likely, Matthew wants to show gentile converts that the Jewish Scriptures have relevance for anyone who believes in Jesus. In other words, his aim is not to persuade those who accept the Scriptures to believe in Jesus, but to get those who believe in Jesus to accept the Scriptures.

Theme 7. Continuing validity of Jewish law. The Matthean Jesus insists that "until heaven and earth pass away, not one letter, not one stroke of a letter, will pass from the law" (5:18). By "law," he means the Jewish law, or Torah, inscribed in the Jewish Scriptures (what Christians usually call the Old Testament). Paul and other New Testament writers indicate that many parts of this law no longer apply to those who are "in Christ" (e.g., required circumcision, dietary laws, purity codes, prescribed fasts and sacrifices, Sabbath practices, and other ritual observances). Matthew appears to have rejected that notion:

- Matthew omits Mark's interpretive comment that Jesus "declared all foods clean" (Mark 7:19; cf. Matt 15:17).
- Matthew also adds a comment that Christians undergoing tribulation should pray that they will not have to flee "on a Sabbath" (Matt 24:20; cf. Mark 13:18).

Apparently, as far as Matthew is concerned, dietary and Sabbath laws are still in effect, as much for Christians as for Jews. We may suppose that this position would have put Matthew at odds with other Christian leaders, and there are hints that this may be the case:

- Some people who call Jesus "Lord" will actually be excluded from the rule of heaven on account of behaving lawlessly (7:21–23).
- Others (perhaps including the apostle Paul) will simply be called least in the rule of heaven for obtusely relaxing what they thought were insignificant commandments and teaching others to do so as well (5:17).

These ideals, however, must be considered alongside the numerous instances in Matthew that appear to show Jesus setting aside what Moses or other traditional exponents of the law have said (e.g., 5:21–48). From Matthew's own perspective, there would be no discrepancy: Jesus never actually abolishes or sets aside the law; he simply practices the necessary interpretive task of binding and loosing it (see Theme 8). That principle would potentially allow for Matthean ethics to be in line with (or even more progressive than) other Christian voices, but for the author of this Gospel, such a possibility may have remained hypothetical.

Theme 8. Binding-and-loosing commandments. Both times that Jesus refers to "the church" in Matthew's Gospel, he tells those who will constitute the church, "Whatever you bind on earth will be bound in heaven, and whatever you loose on earth will be loosed in heaven" (16:19, sg. "you"; 18:18, pl. "you"). Throughout history Christian interpreters who did not know Jewish literature proposed various interpretations of these passages (often taking them as parallel to John 20:23), but it is now widely recognized that the terms *bind* and *loose* were used in rabbinic interpretations of the law to designate whether or not a specific scriptural admonition was applicable for a given circumstance. For example, some rabbis might insist that the law forbidding work on the Sabbath was binding with regard to travel on the Sabbath, since travel is a form of work. By the same token, they might also decide that this law should be loosed with regard to certain types of travel or with regard to travel for certain purposes. Such discussions were widespread within Pharisaic Judaism around the time Matthew's Gospel was written (and today many examples can be found in the Talmud, where decisions from a later time were recorded regarding application of Torah to aspects of daily life).

Throughout Matthew's Gospel, Jesus acts like a rabbi, declaring whether or not laws should be bound or loosed:

- *bound:* the commandment forbidding adultery *applies* to lustful thoughts (5:28).
- *loosed:* the law forbidding work on the Sabbath *does not apply* to healing the sick on that day (12:12).

Matthew's Gospel invariably presents Jesus as the good example of one who binds and looses the law in accord with God's will.

By the same token, the Pharisees are made to serve as bad examples of people who invariably get it wrong:

- *bound*: laws that prohibit harvesting a field on the Sabbath are extended to forbid people picking a few grains of wheat to satisfy their immediate hunger (12:1–2).
- *loosed*: requirements to care for elderly parents can be ignored if the money is given to God (religious institutions) instead (15:3–9).

Thus, the scribes and Pharisees bind what should be loosed and loose what should be bound: when they do the former, they are said to "have condemned the guiltless" (12:7); when they do the latter, they are said to "nullify the word of God" (15:6).

Many observations and implications follow:

- Understanding this practice of binding and loosing explains apparent discontinuities in Jesus' attitude toward the law (see Theme 7): Jesus says that the entire Jewish law remains in full force (5:17–19), but sometimes he seems to set legal prescriptions aside (5:38–39). In the latter instances, he is not abolishing the law but fulfilling it through an interpretation that brings out its true intent (5:17).
- Jesus binds laws more often than he looses them, demanding that his followers adopt standards of righteousness that exceed those of the scribes and Pharisees (5:20). Still, Matthew claims that Jesus' stricter interpretations of the law constitute a paradoxically light burden compared to the heavy burdens laid on people by the Pharisees' misguided judgments (11:28–30; 23:4).
- Although the instances in which Jesus looses the law are relatively few, his justifications for doing so set sweeping precedents, with potentially radical implications:
  - "It is lawful to do good on the Sabbath" (12:12).
  - "It is not what goes into the mouth that defiles a person" (15:11).
- Matthew presents Jesus as explicitly extending his authority to bind and loose commandments to Peter and the other disciples (16:19;

18:18). When Jesus promises that what the church binds and looses on earth will be bound and loosed in heaven, the clear implication is that God will hold people accountable for following the ethical decisions of the church.

- This ecclesial authority is grounded in Matthew's eschatological and christological propositions. Eschatologically, he believes that the rule of heaven has come near (4:17), that God's reign is in the process of being established so that God's will can now be discerned and followed in ways not previously possible. Christologically, he believes that Jesus, the Son of God, who previously manifested God's presence in his bodily form on earth, now continues to manifest that divine presence (and authority) through the community of his followers.

In short, Matthew suggests that ethical discernment is not simply a matter of "doing what the Bible says" but rather of arriving at a communal understanding of Scripture's relevance to specific situations in specific contexts. The Matthean Jesus, furthermore, articulates several principles that should guide the church in making such deliberations:

- The Golden Rule: doing the will of God always aligns with treating others the way one wants to be treated oneself (7:12).
- The double love commandment: doing the will of God always involves doing what expresses love for God and love for neighbor (22:34–40).
- Divine preference: doing the will of God always recognizes that God prefers mercy to sacrifice (9:13; 12:7; see Hos 6:6).
- Weightier matters of the law: doing the will of God always recognizes that concern for justice, mercy, and faith takes precedence over many other matters.

This theme of binding-and-loosing commandments is not only important for understanding much of Matthew's Gospel; it also is one of the most significant contributions that Matthew's Gospel has made to the Christian religion and to all cultures influenced by Christian thinking. In a sense, the entire field of Christian ethics owes its existence to this simple insight from Matthew's Gospel: doing the will of God requires discerning the contemporary relevance of biblical mandates in light of contextual considerations and hermeneutical priorities.

For a more comprehensive discussion of this theme, see Powell 2003.

Theme 9. Jesus as the Son of God. Matthew's Gospel places special emphasis on the identity of Jesus as the Son of God.

- God speaks twice from heaven (at Jesus' baptism and at his transfiguration), and both times God calls Jesus "my Son" (3:17; 17:5; see also 2:15).
- The story of the virgin birth presents Jesus as God's Son in an almost literal sense (1:18).
- The disciples worship Jesus as the Son of God (Matt 14:32–33; in contrast to Mark 6:51–52).
- Peter's confession at Caesarea Philippi says that Jesus is not only "the Messiah" (Mark 8:29) but also "the Son of the living God" (Matt 16:16).
- In Jesus' blessing upon Peter, we see how the confession that Jesus is the Son of God seems to be closely connected to the foundation of the church, the overcoming of Hades, the reception of the keys to the rule of heaven, and the binding and loosing on earth of what will consequently be bound and loosed in heaven (16:17–19).
- Jesus' identity as God's Son in Matthew is closely linked to the story of his crucifixion:
  - In one of his parables, Jesus hints that the reason his enemies want to kill him is because he is the Son of God (21:33–46).
  - He is later sentenced to death for claiming to be God's Son (26:63–66).
  - On the cross, he is mocked by opponents who claim that such a fate proves he is not the Son of God (27:40, 43).
  - Ironically, the manner of his death leads others to confess that he is indeed "God's Son" (27:54).

Theme 10. Jesus as the new Moses. Matthew's strong emphasis on the law (see Theme 7) and on the teaching of Jesus is seen as compatible with a presentation of Jesus as a new or second Moses (Deut 18:15). Here are just a few of the more striking similarities to support such a presentation:

- The infant Jesus is saved from a baby-killing monarch, just as the infant Moses was saved from the baby-killing Pharaoh (2:13–18; cf. Exod 1:22–2:10).

- Jesus (with his family) flees from Israel to Egypt and then returns, just as Moses fled from Egypt to Midian and then returned (Matt 2:13–21; cf. Exod 2:15; 7:6–7).
- Jesus fasts for forty days and forty nights, just as Moses did (Matt 4:2; Exod 34:28).
- Jesus goes up on a mountain to deliver his new Torah, just as Moses went up a mountain to receive the original Torah from God (Matt 5:1; Exod 19:3).
- Jesus miraculously feeds people with bread in a deserted place, just as Moses called upon God to feed people with manna in the wilderness (14:13–22; 15:29–39; cf. Exod 16).
- Through blood, Jesus is the mediator of a new covenant just as, through blood, Moses was the mediator of the old covenant (Matt 26:28; Exod 24:8).
- Jesus commissions his disciples to go to all nations and teach observance of his commandments, promising them his abiding presence, just as in the days following Moses's death God commissioned Joshua to go into a foreign land and observe all the commandments, promising him God's abiding presence (Matt 28:16–20; Josh 1:1–9).

Scholars have noted other parallels or allusions as well, some of which are drawn more closely to Jewish traditions regarding Moses than to what is found in the Scriptures themselves (for instance, some noncanonical Jewish writings report momentous occurrences at the death of Moses—lightning flashing, the heavens or earth being shaken, angels appearing, and so forth; cf. Matt 27:51–53; 28:2–3). Dale Allison says that, like Moses, Jesus is many things to God's people: leader and king, savior and deliverer, teacher and revealer, intercessor and suffering prophet (Allison 1993). Most important of all, perhaps, many interpreters still accept Benjamin Bacon's century-old suggestion that Matthew organizes the teaching of Jesus into five great speeches in a deliberate attempt to provide the church with a new Pentateuch (Bacon 1930). The five "books of Jesus" that mimic the original "five books of Moses" are these:

- Chapters 5–7 The Sermon on the Mount
- Chapter 10 The Missionary Discourse
- Chapter 13 The Parables of the Kingdom
- Chapter 18 The Community Discourse
- Chapters 24–25 The Eschatological Discourse

Theme 11. Disciples as people of little faith. Five times in this Gospel, Jesus describes his disciples as people who have only a little faith:

- Jesus tells his disciples not to worry about what they will wear. "Consider the lilies of the field," he says. "If God so clothes the grass of the field, . . . will [God] not much more clothe you—you of little faith?" (6:28–30; cf. Luke 12:27–28).
- Jesus is with his disciples in a boat when a storm comes up at sea. They are terrified. He asks them, "Why are you afraid, you of little faith?" (8:26).
- When Peter tries to walk on the water, he is afraid and begins to sink. He calls out for help, and Jesus grabs him. Lifting him up, Jesus asks, "You of little faith, why did you doubt?" (14:31).
- One day, after miraculously feeding the multitudes, Jesus is teaching his disciples and uses the metaphor of "yeast." They misunderstand the expression and think he is concerned about whether they will have enough real yeast to make bread when they need it. He asks, "You of little faith, why are you talking about having no bread?" (16:8).
- When Jesus' disciples ask him why they are unable to drive a demon out of a possessed child, he tells them that it is "because of your little faith" (17:20).

In Greek, the expression for "little faith" is a single word, *oligopistoi*, which serves almost as a nickname bestowed upon the disciples by the Matthean Jesus (like "Sons of Thunder" for two of them in Mark 3:17). Thus, his disciples are almost *definitively* people of little faith. By contrast, Matthew's narrative mentions two persons who have "great faith"—a gentile centurion (8:10) and a Canaanite woman (15:28)—but Jesus does not call either of these to become his disciples or commission them for ministry as his followers in the world. We may wonder why the mission of God (see Theme 3) is entrusted to people of little faith when people of greater faith are clearly available.

The simplest answer may be that the disciples are uniquely qualified for mission because they are given "understanding" by Jesus, and understanding is a more important quality than faith for the mission to which they are called (see Excursus: "Understanding" and Divine Revelation in Matthew, p. 158). But this observation begs a slightly different question: why does Jesus choose to give such understanding to people of little faith? As it turns out, a lack of faith can be unfortunate, but it is not a devastating fault. Jesus tells his disciples that only the tiniest speck of faith ("the size of a mustard seed") is necessary to accomplish the impossible (17:20). Likewise, Matthew's Gospel twice describes the disciples of Jesus as doubting (14:31; 28:17), though both of these passages occur in contexts in which they are also said to worship him (14:33; 28:17). So, people with little faith can work miracles, and people who doubt can worship: these concepts are not incompatible or antithetical for Matthew, and we should probably assume that they inform his vision of the church. In this Gospel, Jesus insists that he has not come to call the righteous but sinners (9:13), so it should not be surprising if his followers are inadequate people who often fail at fulfilling even their best intentions (26:41), people who need to be forgiven repeatedly and who, in turn, need to forgive others repeatedly as well (18:21–35). Indeed, the Great Commission in 28:16–20 is explicitly given to apostates (26:31, 56, 69–75), and the task of making disciples of all nations is entrusted to worshiping doubters (28:17), whom Jesus regards as people of little faith.

Theme 12. Prominence of Peter. The disciple Peter has a more active role in Matthew than in any of the other Gospels, being mentioned by name in numerous narrative episodes:

- Peter and his brother are called to follow Jesus and become "fishers of people" (4:18–19).
- Peter attempts to walk on water, with partial success (14:28–33).
- Peter asks Jesus to explain his teaching on true defilement (15:15).
- Peter confesses Jesus to be the Messiah, the Son of the living God (16:18).
- Jesus identifies Peter as the rock on which he will build his church, giving to Peter the keys to the rule of heaven, i.e., the authority to bind and loose commandments (16:17–19).
- Peter rebukes Jesus for saying he is going to be crucified, earning Jesus' stinging rebuttal, "Get behind me, Satan!" (16:22–23).
- Peter sees Jesus transfigured on a mountain and offers to build booths for Jesus, Moses, and Elijah (17:1–8).
- Peter rashly tells inquisitors that Jesus pays the temple tax, then is sent by Jesus to catch a fish with a coin in its mouth to make good on that pledge (17:24–27).
- Peter asks Jesus how many times he should forgive a sibling, suggesting a policy of seven times (18:21–22).

- Peter calls Jesus' attention to how much he and the others have given up, asking, "What then will we have?" (19:27).
- Peter says he will never desert Jesus (26:31–33) or deny him (26:34–35).
- Peter goes with Jesus to Gethsemane and falls asleep when told to stay awake and pray (26:40–45).
- Peter follows Jesus when he is arrested, but then denies three times that he is an associate of Jesus (26:58, 69–73).

Obviously, Peter is also included in dozens of other texts that refer to "the disciples," but these are ones that mention him by name (also 10:2). In several cases, the reference is unique to Matthew (14:28–33; 15:15; 16:17–19; 17:24–27; 18:21–22). If Matthew's Gospel was written in Antioch, as many suspect, then it was composed in a community in which Peter played a significant though controversial role some fifty years previous (Gal 2:11–14).

Theme 13. A community called "the church." Matthew's Gospel is the only one of the four to display Jesus talking explicitly about the "church," which is to continue after he is gone. He tells Peter, "I will build my church, and the gates of Hades will not prevail against it" (16:18). In another remarkable passage, he speaks of the church as though it already exists during his ministry, outlining a process by which disciples who have complaints against each other may bring their disputes to the church for resolution (18:15–18). Thus, according to Matthew's Gospel, the church did not simply come into being after Easter as followers of Jesus struggled to understand what had transpired. Matthew portrays Jesus as starting the church during his life on earth. This church, furthermore, possesses some level of organization, with rules and procedures for defining membership and conducting business.

Matthew's understanding of the church can be presented in the following propositions:

- The church is instituted by Jesus and sustained by his authority.
  - Jesus is the one who "builds" the church (16:18): establishing the church is part of his mission on earth.
  - Jesus grounds his "Great Commission" to the disciples on the fact that he has been given "all authority in heaven and on earth" (28:18).
  - Jesus also says that the church will have divine authority to "bind and loose" on earth what will consequently be bound and loosed in heaven (18:18; cf. 16:19).

- The definitive characteristic of the church is that it embodies and manifests the continuing presence of Jesus on earth.
  - Jesus promises that he will be present wherever two or three gather in his name (18:20) and be with his followers to the end of the age (28:20).
  - Special attention is given throughout the Gospel to characters said to be "with Jesus" (his mother, 2:11; outcasts, 9:11; a follower, 26:51; disciples, 16:21; 20:17–19; 26:37–38, 40, 69, 71). This is significant, since Jesus says in 12:30, "Whoever is not with me is against me" (see also 12:14; 26:59; 27:1).
- The church is more like a missionary movement than a localized institution (like a synagogue or temple).
  - Jesus depicts the church as overcoming "the gates of Hades" (16:18), suggesting that it is more like an army than a fortress (gates don't attack; they get attacked).
  - Jesus commissions his disciples to *go*—moving out into the world to make disciples (28:19).
- The church is a moral community, committed to keeping God's commandments as interpreted by Jesus:
  - The notion of the church being built on a rock (16:18) recalls the parable of Two Builders, in which the house built on a rock represents those who hear and do Jesus' words (7:24–25).
  - People are made disciples and become part of the church by being taught to obey the commandments of Jesus (28:18–19).
  - Community members hold each other accountable for their moral behavior, calling those who sin to repentance (18:15–18).
- The church is portrayed as the family of God:
  - Jesus, the Son of God, designates his disciples as his true family and says that whoever does the will of God is his "brother and sister and mother" (12:46–50). He also says that whatever is done to any member of his family is done to him (25:40).
  - Followers of Jesus are called "children of God" (5:9, 45; 13:38; 23:9) and "siblings" (my trans.; 18:15, 21, 35; 25:40).
- The church is an egalitarian and inclusive community.
  - Church members include people from all nations (28:18), from east and west (8:11), and from the whole world (24:14).
  - No one in the church will be regarded as "Teacher" or "Father" because all are disciples of Christ and children of God (23:8–10).
  - The church will regard the greatest in the community as those who serve (20:26–27; 23:11), will view little children as its most important members and role models (18:1–5; 19:14), and will

always remember that Jesus willed for his church to be founded by women (28:1–10; see comments on this text).

- The church is typified by limited faith and by understanding that is given by Jesus:
  - The disciples of Jesus are presented as people of "little faith" (6:30; 8:26; 14:31; 16:8; 17:20), but Jesus makes clear that this is sufficient (17:20) (see Theme 11).
  - The disciples are presented as people who "understand" Jesus (13:51; 16:12), but typically this is only after they have been given understanding by Jesus (see Excursus: "Understanding" and Divine Revelation in Matthew, p. 158).
- The church may be characterized by paradoxically ideal combinations of responses.
  - Fear and great joy (28:8)—joy is what turns fear into worship; fear is what prevents joy from being shallow (see comments on this verse).
  - Worship and doubt (28:17; see also 14:31–33); worship turns doubt into faith; doubt is what keeps worship from becoming self-assured and superficial (see comments on these passages).
- The church is a community that practices constant and limitless forgiveness.
  - Jesus' followers are all sinners, who relate to him as the sick to a physician (9:12–13).
  - Members of the community pray regularly to be forgiven their sins and commit themselves to forgiving the sins of others (5:23–24; 6:14–15; 18:21–35).
  - The communal meal the church observes involves drinking wine, which reminds them of the blood of Jesus poured out for the forgiveness of sins (26:28).

Theme 14. Religious leaders as enemies of God. In Matthew's Gospel, the religious leaders of Israel constitute a "character group": the Pharisees, Sadducees, chief priests, elders, and scribes all evince the same point of view, share the same character traits, and play the same role in the plot. They form a "united front" in opposition to Jesus; while Matthew occasionally recognizes historical differences between them (15:1–2; 22:23), they are essentially treated as a single character. The characterization of them, furthermore, is relentlessly harsh.

Both Jesus and Matthew (as narrator) describe them as "evil" (*ponēros*):

- Jesus to scribes: "Why do you think evil in your hearts?" (9:4).
- Jesus to Pharisees: "Brood of vipers! How can you speak good, when you are evil?" (12:34).
- Jesus to scribes and Pharisees (twice): "An evil and adulterous generation asks for a sign, but no sign shall be given to it" (12:39; 16:4).
- Jesus to scribes and Pharisees: "So shall it be with this evil generation" (12:45).
- When the Pharisees try to trap Jesus, he is "aware of their evil" (22:18; NRSVue, "malice"; Gk., *ponēros*).

Literary critics usually identify this as the "root" or defining characteristic of the religious leaders in Matthew's story: they not only think what is evil, speak what is evil, and do what is evil: they *are* evil (just like Satan, "the evil one," 13:19, 38–39):

- The epithets "brood of vipers" (3:7; 12:34; 23:33) and "child of hell" (23:15) identify them as offspring or children of Satan (as opposed to being "children of God").
- Jesus tells his disciples that the Pharisees are plants "that the heavenly Father did not plant" (15:13), identifying them as the weeds mentioned in a previous parable (13:24–30); these weeds, he says, "are the children of the evil one, and the enemy who sowed them is the devil" (13:38–39).

The religious leaders also evince two other traits, which might be regarded as consequences of being evil:

- Hypocrisy (6:2, 5, 16; 15:7; 22:18; 23:13, 15, 23, 25, 27, 29). In Matthew, "hypocrisy" refers to the quality of *deception*: presenting oneself to be something other than what one truly is.
- Blindness (15:14; 23:16, 17, 19, 24, 26). When used metaphorically, blindness in Matthew refers to the quality of *self-deception*: believing oneself to be something other than what one truly is.

Thus, the religious leaders are evil, but they present themselves to others as righteous (this makes them hypocrites), and they have come to believe themselves to be righteous (this makes them "blind"). For Matthew, self-deception is not an excuse for their behavior (as it is in Luke 22:34; cf. Acts 3:17), but a consequence of divine judgment: they are not *allowed* to see the truth (about themselves, Jesus, or anything else) because they are evil.

There are no exceptions in Matthew to his portrayal of the religious leaders of Israel as enemies of God:

- A friendly scribe who agrees with Jesus in Mark 12:28–34 is transformed into an enemy who tests Jesus in Matthew 22:34–40.
- Jairus, who is called "one of the leaders of the synagogue" in Mark 5:22, becomes simply a "leader" in Matthew 9:18.
- Joseph of Arimathea, who is called "a respected member of the council" in Mark 15:43, becomes "a rich man" in Matthew 27:57.

The redaction is consistent: individuals who are presented favorably cannot be included among the character group of the "religious leaders of Israel" in Matthew's story.

In Matthew's story, as indicated, these religious leaders are not just opponents of Jesus but also enemies of God. Matthew's readers are not expected to think they are opposed to Jesus because they misunderstand him or fail to identify him for who he is. Rather, they are opposed to him precisely because he *is* God's Son and they have rebelled against God (21:33–45). Of course, they do not realize this themselves: their self-deception prevents them from seeing the depths of their own depravity. This becomes evident in the climactic events of Jesus' passion:

- They pay "blood money" for Jesus' betrayal (26:14–16; 27:3–6).
- They suborn false testimony against Jesus (26:59–62).
- They seek to cover up the truth when they apparently know that God has raised Jesus from the dead (28:11–15).

In all these instances, they somehow continue to view themselves as being "in the right" even when they are doing what they themselves would regard as wrong.

But Jesus is aware of their true nature:

- He uses them as the paradigmatic example of people who will never enter the rule of heaven (5:20).
- He tells them that the reign of God will be taken away from them and given to a people for whom that reign may prove more fruitful (21:43; cf. 8:12).
- The last thing he ever says regarding them is that they will not escape being condemned to hell (23:33; cf. his final words regarding the religious leaders of Israel in Luke 23:34).

Most telling, perhaps, is that while Jesus condemns the religious leaders to their face, denounces them to his disciples, and warns the crowds about them, he never once makes any attempt to minister to them or to suggest that they might change their ways or behave differently. He does not call them to repentance, any more than he would try to reform the demons he exorcizes (contrast Luke 10:28, 37; 11:41; 14:14). In one terribly revealing passage, he counsels his disciples to "leave them alone" (Matt 15:14). Their situation is hopeless, their condemnation is assured, and that is all that needs to be said about them (or to them).

In considering such a portrayal, we need to remember that Matthew's Gospel is a story and that these religious leaders are characters in that story. In literary terms, the religious leaders are "flat characters," and the literary function of flat characters is never to present a realistic depiction of people who exist (or once existed) in the world outside the story. The literary function of flat characters is to provide personification of values. Stories that employ flat characters typically do so to comment on the values that those characters are made to embody. In this case, Matthew's readers are expected to recognize that what the religious leaders do in this story is what *evil* does: evil condemns the guiltless (12:7), blasphemes the Holy Spirit (12:31), neglects the weightier matters of the law (23:23), and so on. The religious leaders of Israel represent evil in this story; even if we question the Gospel author's choice of telling the story in such a way, we can still recognize how the story is expected to affect its readers. Matthew's implied readers would not be expected to draw historical conclusions regarding any people who inhabit (or once inhabited) the world outside this story. Rather, Matthew's readers would be expected to come to a deeper understanding of the nature of evil: it tends to be hypocritical, masquerading as good (23:27–28); it involves unwitting self-deception, failing to recognize its own duplicity (15:14; 23:16–22); it perverts what would be good, ignoring motives or outcomes (6:2, 5, 16), and so on. Finally, in the ironic resolution of the passion narrative, the reader learns something else about evil: God triumphs over evil, even when evil succeeds at doing its worst (see Theme 15).

It is a sad fact of history that Matthew's Gospel came to be interpreted in ways that support anti-Semitism; his portrayal of the religious leaders of Israel certainly contributed to that. Some scholars have speculated that his harsh characterization was driven by poor relations with non-Christian Jewish people in his own day, by animosity toward "the synagogue down the street." There is no way to know whether that was the case, but I suspect that, for the most part, Matthew just wanted to tell an apocalyptic tale of good versus evil, and in order for that to work, someone in the story had to represent evil. That said, I have no interest in letting this author "off the hook" for telling the story the way he did. At the very least, it was incredibly insensitive of him to use actual historical people (ones with whom he would have had differences) as symbols of demonic evil in his fictive tale. The result is a story that (whatever the author's intentions) lends itself easily to anti-Semitic interpretation. Given that, this is nevertheless the story we have, and I think it is possible to do two things: (1) Engage the story on its own terms, and discern what readers are expected to get out of it: nothing to do with anti-Semitism, but a message that, in spite of the mode of presentation, can be profound, provocative, and potentially transforming. (2) Critique the author's unfortunate decision to tell the story the way he did. In this commentary, we focus on the first step, but I do believe the second is appropriate and absolutely necessary, so we will not ignore it altogether.

Theme 15. Conflict along three plot lines. The basic plot of Matthew's Gospel is driven by conflict: two of the principal story lines involve conflict between Jesus and his own disciples and the much more serious conflict between Jesus and the religious leaders of Israel. In the background, however, the reader senses conflict at another level, one not narrated in the story as such but always just below the surface. This is the apocalyptic conflict between God and Satan: for Matthew and his readers, this is what ultimately counts; otherwise, the book would not be a Gospel, for its story would not be "good news."

The conflict between Jesus and his disciples hinges on the disciples' opposition to Jesus as one who insists upon suffering and servanthood as constitutive of discipleship. Within the story, the disciples demonstrate a failure to grasp this essential component of Jesus' teaching (19:13–14, 23–25; 20:20–28) and even rebuke him for thinking this way (16:22). The worst possible outcome for this conflict, the reader imagines, would be for the disciples to reject Jesus altogether and cease to follow him. This, of course, is exactly what does happen when the conflict is resolved in Matthew's passion narrative (26:56, 69–75).

The conflict between Jesus and the religious leaders is defined primarily in terms of the leaders' opposition to Jesus as one who exhibits or claims to have divine authority. As this conflict develops in the story, the religious leaders test Jesus (16:1; 19:3; 22:18, 34–35), challenge him (21:15, 23), make accusations against him (9:3, 34; 12:24), try to "entangle him in his talk" (22:15), and even plot to kill him (12:14; 26:3–4). The reader imagines that the worst possible outcome for this conflict would be for the leaders to be successful in turning the people against Jesus or in having Jesus put to death. Again, these worst-case scenarios come to pass when the conflict is resolved in Matthew's passion narrative.

The most interesting thing about these two conflicts is that Jesus apparently loses both. We must not imagine that these losses are simply overturned by the resurrection. For one thing, theologically, such a claim would trivialize the horrors of abandonment and crucifixion suffered by Jesus: the events of the passion were not *undone*, as though they never happened; Jesus will remain "the crucified one" forever. But even more to the point, in terms of Matthew's narrative rhetoric, no final resolution for the previous conflicts is found in the resurrection narrative. The disciples continue to respond to Jesus with a combination of worship and doubt (28:17), precisely as they did before (14:31–33). The religious leaders continue to oppose Jesus' claim of divine authority, dismissing him as an "impostor" (27:63); far from having been silenced or overcome, they continue to be successful in turning people against him (28:15). In a very real sense, they won! They wanted to remove Jesus from the scene, and they did so. He will no longer be doing the things that brought him into conflict with them: teaching in Galilee, healing in synagogues, overturning tables in the temple, and so on.

But for Matthew, the passion was not a temporary setback of what might have been (but wasn't), set right by the resurrection. Rather, it represented the purpose of Jesus' mission on earth, and the negative resolutions to his conflicts do not prevent fulfillment of the goal that brought Jesus to the cross. Jesus did not need to retain his disciples' loyalty or overcome the religious leaders' opposition in order to save his people from their sins. In fact, ironically, he was unable to do those things if that goal was to be fulfilled. In short, he had to lose the conflicts with his disciples and with the religious leaders in order for the hidden conflict between God and Satan to be resolved favorably. Thus, when Jesus dies on the cross, he fulfills the will of God (see 26:39, 42) and defeats the will of Satan (see 16:21–23). This is the greatest irony of all in a narrative noted for its ironic touches: the defeat of Jesus and the triumph of his enemies is what facilitates the defeat of Satan and the triumph of God. (For a more detailed explication of these plot lines in Matthew's narrative, see Powell 1992.)

Theme 16. Critique of power, wealth, and wisdom. Matthew's Gospel offers a stark critique of worldly power (much like what is found in the book of Revelation). "Worldly power" means power that coerces or dominates, as opposed to power that serves. Jesus, of course, is the most powerful figure in the story, but his power is employed in service to others, sometimes sacrificially (20:28). Otherwise, human characters almost always use power coercively (if they possess it). Accordingly, two implicit value judgments underlie the entire narrative: (1) Characters are "evil" to the extent that they possess power (since they almost always use it coercively). (2) Characters are "good" to the extent that they lack power (or use it to serve, though that remains, for the most part, a hypothetical option).

We may consider, first, those who possess power. Look at what Matthew's Gospel says about political rulers:

- Satan is able to offer Jesus "all the kingdoms of the world" because, apparently, they are under his authority (4:8–9).
- Jesus says to his disciples, "You know that the rulers of the gentiles lord it over them, and their great ones are tyrants over them" (20:25).
- King Herod (2:16) callously slaughters children in a manner like evil tyrants of old: the pharaoh in the days of Moses (Exod 1:15–22) and Nebuchadnezzar at the time of Jeremiah (cf. Matt 2:17–18 to Jer 31:15; 39:1–9).
- Herod's son Archelaus is as much to be feared as his father (2:22).
- Herod the tetrarch murders God's prophet (14:3, 10) and is perceived as a threat to Jesus as well (14:13).
- Pilate, the governor, reneges on his responsibility for administering justice by ordering the execution of a man he knows to be innocent (27:15–26).

Indeed, within the world of Matthew's story, we do not encounter a single political ruler who exhibits positive traits. And as indicated above (see Theme 14), the same holds true for *religious leaders*. In Matthew, religious leaders, without exception, are portrayed as evil enemies of God, aligned with Satan, the "evil one" (13:19). So it can probably be said that Matthew's antipathy for Jewish leaders owes less to the fact that they are *Jewish* than to the fact that they are *leaders*. The story's denunciation of worldly powers makes no ethnic distinctions. Jewish *leaders* and gentile *rulers* alike are condemned; but humble Jewish supplicants, as well as gentile ones (8:5–13; 15:21–28), are acceptable. The primary line of opposition in this story is not between Jews and gentiles but between the powerful and the powerless.

But now, as for the second "value judgment" indicated above: characters are "good" to the extent that they *lack* power. Throughout Matthew's Gospel, the powerless are presented as people with whom Jesus' followers must identify:

- The coming of God's reign will be a blessing primarily to the oppressed people of the earth and to those who align themselves with them (5:3–12; see comments on this text).
- In contrast to political rulers, the followers of Jesus will emulate enslaved persons, seeking not to be served but to serve (20:25–28).
- In contrast to religious leaders, followers of Jesus will be learners in a community of equals, refusing positions of leadership (23:1–12).
- Jesus himself is portrayed as a person who "has nowhere to lay his head" (8:20), and his disciples are required to renounce their possessions and go out into the world with no apparent means of support (10:9–10), helpless as sheep in the midst of wolves (10:16).
- Little children are regarded as the greatest in the rule of heaven and should serve as role models for all followers of Jesus (18:1–4; 19:14).
- In a surprising twist at the end of the story, the church that Jesus has promised to build ends up being founded by women (28:1–10; see comments on this text).

So, for the most part, the powerless are good and the powerful are bad. Yet this theme may become more poignant when we observe that Matthew's critique of power extends to suspicion of two primary sources for such power: wealth and education.

First, Matthew's Gospel is highly suspicious of wealth:

- Jesus' disciples are called to give up their material possessions when they follow him (4:20, 22; 19:27; see also 10:8–10).
- Treasure in heaven is preferable to treasure on earth, since one's heart will always be with one's treasure (6:19–21).
- One cannot serve both God and mammon (NRSVue, "wealth," 6:24).
- A rich young man with potential for discipleship cannot follow Jesus because of his many possessions (19:16–22).
- It is harder for God to rule the life of a rich person than for a camel to go through the eye of a needle (19:23–24).

Second, Matthew's Gospel also exhibits a lack of esteem for worldly wisdom and education:

- God creates or reveals what is needed, apparently preferring to write the divine will on almost blank slates.
  - John the Baptist claims that God is able to raise children of Abraham from stones (3:9).
  - Jesus thanks God for hiding the truth from the "wise and intelligent" and revealing it to infants (11:25).
  - Jesus says (quoting Scripture) that God brings forth praise from the mouths of nursing babies (21:16).
- Jesus' disciples exemplify ignorance:
  - They must be *given* understanding by Jesus (13:51; 16:12; 17:13; see Excursus: "Understanding" and Divine Revelation in Matthew, p. 158).
  - Never once in the Gospel are the disciples depicted as knowing the will of God or even the basic content or teaching of the Scriptures. The only time they come close is especially revealing: they know that "Elijah must come first" (17:10), but they do not know that this teaching comes from Scripture; it is only something that "the scribes say."
- By contrast, the religious leaders of Israel know a great many things:
  - The Christ is to be born in Bethlehem (2:4–6).
  - Elijah will come before the end arrives (17:10).
  - Moses commanded the giving of divorce certificates (19:7).
  - The Scriptures commend levirate marriage (22:24).
  - The Christ is to be the son of David (22:42).
  - It is unlawful to place blood money in the temple treasury (27:6).

Still, such knowledge does not aid them in doing the will of God; quite the contrary, it leads them to resist God's plan and oppose God's agents.

Surely Matthew would not want his readers to regard knowledge of Scripture as a bad thing. Still, Jesus' shocking words in 11:25 do seem to represent an underlying evaluation of education fundamental for the narrative as a whole. The problem is that wisdom and knowledge obtained through education can be a source of social power: in Matthew's vision, those who obtain power tend to use it coercively. The uneducated and the ignorant are special to God because they tend to be powerless.

In sum, Matthew's story world consists of those who are "first" but destined to be last, and those who are currently "last" but destined to be first (19:30; 20:16).

- Those who are "first" yet destined to be last include the following:
  - political rulers (20:25),
  - religious leaders (15:12–14; 23:13–36),
  - rich people (19:16–23), and
  - scholars (2:3–6; 16:12; 23:15).
- Those who are "last," destined to be first, include the following:
  - the meek (5:5),
  - servants or enslaved persons (10:24–25; 20:27; 24:45–46),
  - children (18:1–4; 19:13–15; see also 11:25),
  - little ones (10:42; 18:6, 10, 14),
  - the uneducated (11:25; 21:16),
  - the "least" (25:40, 45), and
  - women (28:1–10).

In the world of Matthew's story, the rule of God is presently challenged by the rule of Satan (12:24–29; 13:24–30, 36–43). Dynamics of literary conflict throughout the narrative turn on the fact that the "last who will be first" are aligned with the rule of God; and the "first who will be last" are aligned with the rule of Satan, opposed to God, and especially opposed to God's mission as it is manifested through Jesus and the church (see Theme 3). On the ultimate outcome of that conflict, see Theme 15.

Theme 17. Divine judgment and condemnation in Matthew. More than half of all references to hell in the Bible (NRSVue) occur in Matthew's Gospel. Motifs concerning the final judgment, condemnation of sinners, and eternal punishment run throughout the book, offering a counterpoint to emphases on mercy (5:7; 9:13, 27; 12:7; 15:22; 17:15; 18:33; 20:30–31; 23:23), compassion (9:36; 14:14; 15:32;

20:34); forgiveness (6:12, 14–15; 9:2–8; 12:31–32; 18:21–35; 26:28), salvation (1:21; 8:11; 10:22; 13:43; 16:25; 19:25–26; 21:31; 24:13, 22; 27:42), and rewards (5:12; 6:4, 6, 18; 10:40–42; 19:27–30).

Here is a representative (though not comprehensive) list of things Jesus says about divine judgment and condemnation in Matthew:

- Those whose righteousness does not exceed that of the scribes and Pharisees will never enter the rule of heaven (5:20).
- Those who insult their siblings or are angry with them will be liable to judgment and the hell of fire (5:22).
- Drastic measures must be taken (metaphorically, cutting off one's body parts or plucking out one's eyes) so as not to be thrown into hell (5:29–30; 18:8–9).
- God will not forgive the debts of people who do not offer such forgiveness to their fellow human beings (6:14–15; 18:23–35).
- Few find the hard road that leads to life; most follow the easy road to destruction (7:13).
- Many who seek entrance to the rule of heaven will be shut out on the last day because, even though they called Jesus "Lord," they did not do the will of his Father (7:21–23).
- Many of those whom God initially offered a place in the rule of heaven will be thrown into outer darkness, where there is weeping and gnashing of teeth (8:12; see also 13:42; 22:13–14; 25:30).
- Sodom and Gomorrah will fare better on the day of judgment than towns that fail to welcome apostles with the message of God's reign (10:15). Specific condemnations of Chorazin and Bethsaida are in 11:20–24.
- Do not fear those who kill only the body, but fear the one who can destroy both body and soul in hell (10:28).
- Anyone who denies Jesus before others will be denied by him before his Father in heaven (10:32–33).
- Those who find their life in this world will lose it in the next (10:39; 16:25–26).
- Those who speak against the Holy Spirit will never be forgiven in this age or in the age to come (12:31–32).
- On the day of judgment, people will need to account for their unguarded speech (i.e., words that reveal their true nature) and will be justified or condemned accordingly (12:36–37).
- At the end of the age, the Son of Man will send angels to collect all causes of sin and evildoers and throw them into the furnace of fire (13:41–42, 49–50).
- When the Son of Man comes with angels, he will repay everyone for what was done (16:27).

- People who do not become like little children will never enter the rule of heaven (18:3).
- A horrible fate awaits any who hinder little children from being the persons God wants them to be (18:6–7).
- It is essentially impossible for a rich person to enter the rule of heaven (19:23–24; but see 19:26).
- God's ruling presence and power will be taken away from the religious leaders of Israel and given to others (21:43).
- The scribes and Pharisees and their converts are children of hell (23:15) and will not escape being sentenced to hell (23:33).
- The coming of the Son of Man will overtake many like the flood in Noah's day, bringing destruction upon those who are not prepared (24:36–44).
- God may be likened to a householder who cuts an unfaithful steward to pieces (24:45–51), to a groom who shuts delayed bridesmaids out of the wedding feast (25:1–12), to a master who punishes an enslaved person who does nothing to increase the master's wealth (25:14–30), or to a king who condemns uncharitable subjects to eternal punishment (25:31–46).
- It would be better never to have been born than to suffer the fate of one who betrays Jesus (26:23–24).

We should note, however, a strong affirmation in Matthew that judgment and condemnation lie within the province of God alone: human beings must never judge one another (7:1–2) or presume to decide who is destined for heaven or hell (13:27–30).

Part One of Matthew's Gospel: Presentation of Jesus

Matthew 1:1–4:16

Matthew's story of Jesus begins with an extended prologue. The account of his ministry, with which the Gospel is primarily concerned, will not begin until 4:17 (with the words, "From that time, Jesus began . . ."; see also 16:21). More than forty years ago, Jack Dean Kingsbury developed the thesis that Matthew delays the start of the story proper so he can relate a number of pre-ministry anecdotes that address the question of Jesus' identity (Kingsbury 1975). In these introductory accounts, we learn that Jesus is the Messiah, the son of David, the son of Abraham (1:1), the king of the Jews (2:2), the powerful judge who will baptize with the Holy Spirit and fire (3:11–12), the "great light" promised by Isaiah (Matt 4:14–16; cf. Isa 9:1–2), and above all, the Son of God (3:17; 4:1–11; see also 2:15).

MATTHEW 1:1–2:23
Jesus Comes into the World

All this material is unique to Matthew's Gospel, though a different genealogy and a different account of Jesus' birth are found in the opening chapters of Luke.

Matthew traces the origin of Jesus in a manner that highlights his relationship to the Jewish people and his significance for them, while also foreshadowing his importance for all peoples of the earth.

1:1–17. Genealogy of Jesus (only in Matthew, but see Luke 3:23–38)

Matthew begins his story with a list of the ancestors of Jesus. Unlike Luke, who traces the human lineage of Jesus to Adam, Matthew is content to begin with Abraham, the patriarch of the Jewish people. This is in keeping with Matthew's emphasis on Jesus' close association with Israel (10:6; 15:24). Jesus belongs not only to the line of Abraham (God's chosen people) but also to the royal line of David. Since Israel made no distinction between adopted and procreated children, the virginal conception of Jesus would make him no less a legitimate son of Joseph and therefore a descendant of David.

Matthew says he is relating "the genesis [NRSVue: genealogy] of Jesus Christ" (1:1; cf. 1:18). The Greek word *genesis* has a range of meanings including "origin," "beginning," "genealogy," or "birth"; its usage here is probably intended to recall the first line of the Hebrew Bible (or even the name of the first book, already called Genesis by Greek-speaking Jews). Perhaps Matthew wants us to believe that the coming of the one who will save God's people from their sins (1:21) has significance equivalent to the origin of those people (and their sins). More generally, there is a subtle suggestion that he views his book as a continuation of Scripture, as a sequel to the Bible—almost as if he knows he is writing "a New Testament"; the author of the Fourth Gospel seems to have had the same idea (John 1:1). Less amenable to traditional Christian doctrine is Matthew's clear implication that Jesus Christ *had* an origin and that it was at a point relatively late in human history; there is no talk of preexistence (such as we find in John 1:1–2, 14; 8:58; Phil 2:6–7).

The purpose of a genealogy (in both Jewish and Hellenistic literature) was not to provide a historically precise listing of ancestors, but rather a testimony of lineage that gave context to the subject's identity. It was not considered strange or fraudulent for a genealogy to omit the names of unsavory persons, add names of revered ones, or substitute names of cities, tribes, or nations for those of individuals. Thus, we should not expend undue energy in attempting to resolve or explain the numerous problems that arise from taking the Matthean genealogy as a straightforward historical account. First, let us simply affirm that the Matthean genealogy cannot be reconciled with the one in Luke 3:23–38 (in tracing the thousand years from David to

Joseph, Matthew and Luke have only two names in common). Suggestions that one relates ancestors of Joseph and the other ancestors of Mary do not hold up and do nothing to ameliorate the fact that neither of the two genealogies compares well with what is found elsewhere in biblical history. Here are only a few of the more notable discrepancies pertinent to the first Gospel: (1) Matthew omits three generations after Joram (Ahaziah, Joah, Amaziah), thus ignoring four chapters of the Bible (2 Chr 22–25) and sixty years of Israel's history (842–783 BCE); (2) he lists Rahab as the husband of Salmon, though she lived two hundred years before the latter; (3) he lists Josiah as the father (rather than the grandfather) of Jeconiah; (4) he changes the names of two of Israel's less reputable leaders to suggest that they were actually different persons (Asa becomes Asaph, the psalmist mentioned in 1 Chr 25:1; and Amon becomes Amos, the prophet); (5) he lists only nine generations between Zerubbabel and Joseph, a period of five hundred years (Luke lists eighteen generations).

But all this comports with what we have already said: precision is not the point. Rather, since the entire first section of Matthew (1:1–4:16) is concerned with the *identity* of Jesus, the genealogy must be understood in terms of what it contributes to that identification. Here are two major points Matthew's readers are expected to realize from the outset: (1) Jesus must be located within the larger story of God's dealings with Israel, and (2) Jesus is someone more at home among those who are last or least than among those who are first or best.

First, Matthew wants to be certain his readers know that Jesus (whom they probably worship as "Son of God") is the son of David and the son of Abraham. Preserving the Jewish matrix of Christianity is extremely important to Matthew; the Jesus who is now worshiped by an increasingly diverse population is the *Jewish* Messiah, sent first and foremost to the *Jewish* people. Perhaps nothing would distress Matthew more than the notion of Christianity becoming a separate, primarily gentile religion, but he may see the threat of such a possibility on the horizon. So, through this genealogy, his readers are expected to realize that Jesus belongs to the Jews: he stands within the tradition of God's continuing action in the history of Israel; those who know him as "the Son of God" should realize that he is properly the son of "the God of Israel." This explains the text's fascination with the number 14 (1:17). According to the common practice of gematria, each letter in the Hebrew (or Greek) alphabet was assigned a numerical value, such that it was possible to add up the value of the letters in anyone's name and assign that person a number. The Hebrew letters in David's name (D+V+D) corresponded to the numerals 4 + 6 + 4, so the sum, 14, became a numerical symbol for "David" and thus for "the messiah." For an interesting comparison, we may note how *2 Baruch* (a pseudepigraphical work written around the same time as Matthew's Gospel) divides all of world history into fourteen periods from Adam to the messiah (see *2 Baruch* 53–74).

As for the second major point, the genealogy places Jesus within a lineage that is somewhat ignominious. His forebears include promiscuous liars, bullies, murderers, and thieves, but Matthew's readers are expected to know that God has often worked with and through persons whose character and lifestyle were far from exemplary. Many of the unscrupulous figures in Jesus' genealogy became heroes in the Israelite tradition, not because of who they were but because of what God did through them. One might argue that it would be difficult to construct a genealogy of famous biblical characters that did *not* include scoundrels, but Matthew seems to revel in the inevitably unseemly character of Jesus' ancestry, accentuating the point by listing four women, whom he certainly did not need to mention and whose appearance in the listing is so surprising that it cries out for an explanation. The women referenced are Tamar (Gen 38), Rahab (Josh 2), Ruth, and Bathsheba (2 Sam 11; here called "the wife of Uriah"). Given the patriarchal character of society at the time, it was rare for women ever to be listed in a genealogy, though it was occasionally done if the women were of stature to enhance the dignity of the person's lineage. That does not appear to be the case here: model matriarchs Sarah, Rebekah, Rachel, and Leah are not mentioned, but rather four women who were not obvious heroes or exemplars. Were they, perhaps, heroes or exemplars in some nonobvious sense?

A common suggestion is that Matthew includes these four women because they were gentiles, assuming that Bathsheba was either a Hittite like her husband, or regarded as such as a result of marriage (Tamar was a Canaanite; Rahab, a Jerichoite; Ruth, a Moabite). Then the point would be that Matthew is preparing for gentile inclusion in the church and alluding to the promise that God blesses all people through the descendants of Abraham (Gen 12:3): though Jesus is the Messiah of Israel, he brings light to the gentiles as well (3:15–16). An alternative suggestion holds that Matthew mentions these women because they were persons of questionable virtue; in a 1522 sermon, Martin Luther commented, "God loves sinners so much that [God] even put them in Christ's family tree." But the Bible does not really attribute immoral behavior to any of these women. Rahab could be denounced as a sex worker, but nothing in the biblical narrative indicates that prostitution was an illegal or unacceptable profession at the time. Bathsheba could be considered an adulteress, but it is just as easy to view her as a rape victim. Tamar and Ruth could be seen as seductresses (Gen 38:15; Ruth 3:9–10), but their stories present them more as clever women whose wiles helped them secure justice in a world where empowered men could not be counted on to grant it. Still, the varied prospect of viewing these named women as either gentiles or sinners (or both) points to what may be the essential point: they were all potentially marginalized people (a sex worker, an abandoned daughter-in-law, an abducted wife, a widow), possibly racial and/or moral outcasts, but certainly women who lacked social power and yet ended up in the family tree of the one who is called son of Abraham, son of David, and Son of God. The common denominator for these women is simply that they were persons through whom the plan of God was advanced despite circumstances that could appear anomalous or scandalous. This, of course, prepares us for mention of a fifth woman: "Mary, of whom Jesus was born" (1:16).

1:18–25. Birth and Naming of Jesus (only in Matthew, but see Luke 1:26–38; 2:1–20)

In obedience to God, Joseph accepts Mary, who has become pregnant through the agency of the Holy Spirit; by naming her child, he demonstrates that he accepts the boy into his own family line. Krister Stendahl once described this story as an "enlarged footnote" on 1:16 because it explains the anomalous reference there to Joseph as the "husband of Mary, of whom Jesus was born" (Stendahl 1968, 102). But the story also prepares implicitly for the explicit identification of Jesus as the Son of God in 3:17. The focus of Matthew's story is on Joseph, identified as a "righteous man" (1:19). This is in contrast to Luke's account, where the focus is on Mary (Luke 1:26–56; 2:1–20). In the latter story, furthermore, the human character is essentially passive (Luke 1:38); but in Matthew's account, Joseph must act: he needs to do what God (through an angel) directs him to do (1:20–21, 24–25). This is in keeping with Matthew's understanding of God's grace requiring human action to become effective (7:21, 24–27).

The NRSVue translation of 1:18, which describes Joseph and Mary as engaged but not yet living together, modernizes the story in a way that trivializes the moral quandary that righteous Joseph must face. Actually, betrothal in the ancient world was legally tantamount to marriage, and the verb translated here as "live together" refers to the sexual consummation of a marriage relationship. In the ancient world, it was common practice for a woman to be legally given in marriage to a man but then to remain in the house of her father until the man had paid her dowry in full. The scene in Matthew presupposes this situation. Joseph and Mary are legally wed but do not yet have sexual relations. Thus, when Joseph learns that his new wife is pregnant, he naturally suspects her of having had relations, willingly or unwillingly, with another man (a likely scenario for that world, sad to say, would have been impregnation by her father). Joseph is a righteous man because he is willing to do as the law requires in such an instance and divorce her (Deut 22:22–24 actually prescribes death for the unfaithful betrothed, though Roman law would not have permitted such action at this time). Still, Joseph's righteousness exceeds that of the Matthean scribes and Pharisees (5:20) in that his respect for the law does not cause him to lose sight of the divine quality of mercy (see Matt 5:7; 9:13; 12:7; 23:23). Instead of making a public spectacle of Mary, he resolves to settle the matter as quietly as possible (1:19). Furthermore, after Joseph learns (1:20–23) what the reader already knows (1:18), that this pregnancy is the work of God's Holy Spirit, he demonstrates his righteousness still further by being absolutely obedient to the direction of God (1:24–25).

Righteousness is a prominent theme in Matthew (5:10, 20; 6:33; 13:43, 49; 25:37, 46; 27:4, 19, 24), so it is significant that Joseph is the only character in the story ever explicitly identified as "righteous" (but see 21:32; 23:35). He demonstrates three qualities essential to Matthew's understanding of what righteousness entails: (1) a default willingness to do whatever God requires; (2) a disposition to temper one's actions and attitudes with mercy; and (3) a commitment to discerning God's will that transcends traditional thinking, including usual interpretations of Scripture (cf. 12:1–8). Since the interpretation and application of Scripture is a prominent theme in this Gospel, it is noteworthy that Matthew begins his story with an account of a righteous man who realizes that God does not want him to do what traditional interpretations of Scripture suggest he do. Matthew's hermeneutic of Scripture holds that, yes, God said it; yes, we should believe it; but, no, that does not settle it: what God wants must be determined through a process of discernment that considers but transcends direct or straightforward application of biblical mandates to contemporary situations (see Theme 8 "*Binding-and-loosing commandments*" in the introduction, p. 16). Mercy (and love) play the dominant role in such discernment: if a human action is not merciful or loving, then it is not the will of God.

The mere fact that Matthew reports Jesus' potentially scandalous birth is significant since he might easily have ignored this (as do Mark, John). In a culture that espouses honor and shame as pivotal values, Matthew portrays his protagonist as entering and leaving his earthly life in ways that virtually everyone would have considered shameful: born to a woman who became pregnant before she was taken into the home of her husband; dying by crucifixion in the most ignoble manner imaginable.

Theological studies regarding this text have focused primarily on the subject of the virgin birth, which in the entire New Testament is mentioned only here and in Luke 1–2. Neither Matthew nor Luke, however, share the fascination of modern theologians with the hows and whys of this event. With regard to "how," Matthew is content to say that it is the work of the Spirit (cf. Luke 1:35), who, after all, created life out of nothingness at the genesis (the word translated "birth" by the NRSVue in 1:18) of the world (Gen 1:1; cf. 2:7). As for "why," Matthew simply believes it was in accord with God's plan to mark Jesus as unique in this manner. A child being born to a virgin is a miracle that is in line with, but also greater than, the Old Testament miracles in which children are born to women who are barren or past the age of childbearing (Gen 21:2; 30:22–24; 1 Sam 1:19–20). In the same way, Matthew believes Jesus himself will be in line with, but also greater than, all the heroes of Israel's history. Jesus' status as God's Child is unique, distinct from the status of others who are called children of God (see Matt 5:45; 13:38), distinct even from the status of those whose election to God's work is "from the womb" (Isa 49:1; Jer 1:5; Gal 1:15). We should note, however, that although the virgin birth *demonstrates* this unique nature of Jesus for Matthew, it is in no way intrinsically necessary. Matthew has no interest in the miracle as a "proof" of Jesus' divinity, nor would he ever consider that Jesus had to be born of a virgin to be free of the effects of original sin. The notion that being born of a virgin renders Jesus more godlike or pure than persons conceived through sexual union would disparage God's intended order for creation (Gen 1:28); such thinking would have been offensive to Matthew and to most Jews and Christians prior to the influence of Gnosticism.

When viewed within the context of Matthew's Gospel as a whole, the virgin birth (which never comes up again) is a less significant theme than the naming of the child, which is used to introduce two prominent themes that will be dealt with repeatedly: salvation and the abiding presence of God. The name "Jesus" introduces the theme of salvation. Literally, "Jesus" (or "Joshua" in Hebrew) means "God helps" or "God saves." He is given this name because he will "save his people from their sins" (Matt 1:21). Thus we are told that Jesus' mission is to bring salvation, but this mission is limited in two ways. First, the salvation is for those identified as "his people," an expression that first seems to refer to the nation of Israel (10:6; 15:24) but eventually may be expanded to refer to a community known as "the church" (16:18). Second, while his Old Testament namesake (Joshua) earned his name by saving God's people from their *enemies*, this Jesus will save people from their *sins* (1:21). Many people might have preferred a messiah who would save them from Roman occupation or from high taxes to one who would save them from their sins—and there have been Christians ever since who have wanted Jesus to save them from one thing or another but to leave their sins alone. Still, Matthew defines Jesus' job description as Savior with precision: the one who saves his people from *their sins* (not necessarily from other people's sins). As Matthew's story continues, we realize that Jesus accomplishes this specific mission by authoritatively forgiving sins (9:5–8); by calling outcast sinners into a new community (9:9–13), where the discernment of God's will and restraint of sins will be a corporate responsibility (18:15–18); by giving his life as a ransom (20:28); and by pouring out his blood for forgiveness (26:28).

None of this is meant to imply that salvation is only a spiritual matter, divorced from sociopolitical realities. Rather, Matthew's readers would be expected to realize at this point that salvation in all its manifold dimensions (spiritual, social, political, and so forth) is obtained when God's people get right with God and with each other, not when extraneous threats are defeated or extinguished. Of course, ultimately, we will learn that salvation in an apocalyptic sense will include the destruction of evildoers and the extinction of "causes of sin" as well (13:41).

Matthew says this child will also bear the name "Emmanuel," which is derived from Isaiah 7:14. Although that passage no doubt suggested itself to Matthew on account of the catchword "virgin" used in the Septuagint translation, Matthew's appreciation for the text is based mainly on the name "Emmanuel" itself, for through this name he introduces a major motif for his narrative: God's abiding presence (see Theme 1 "*The abiding presence of God*" in the introduction, p. 7). At this point, readers are simply expected to recognize that the birth of Jesus into our world means that God is now "with us." Of course, readers would believe God has been with God's people in some sense throughout history (Num 23:21; Deut 2:7; Isa 43:5; Ezek 34:30; 37:26–27; Zech 8:23). Still, the presence of God becomes uniquely manifest through Jesus. Matthew's readers are to regard Jesus' entry into the world as a cataclysmic event: somehow God becomes present in a way that God has never been present before (cf. 12:6).

2:1–12. Visit of the Magi (only in Matthew)

When Jesus is born, God uses a star to guide magi from the East to the very house where Jesus lives so that they can come and worship him. Along the way, they encounter the evil king Herod; when they indicate that they have come to venerate a newborn "king of the Jews," he fears that the messiah may have been born.

The story recalls elements from the narrative of Balaam in the Old Testament (Num 22–24). According to Philo and the *Palestinian Targum*, Balaam and his two servants were regarded as magi. Like the magi in Matthew 2, they travel to Palestine from the east. A wicked king tries to use them for cursing and destroying God's people but, informed of God's will through the intervention of an angel, they offer blessing and worship instead. In Numbers 24:17, Balaam even refers to a star that he sees rising out of Jacob.

The story also foreshadows later developments in Matthew's narrative. Perhaps most obviously, it previews the faith of gentiles (8:5–13; 15:21–28; cf. 27:19) and the community's mission to make disciples of such persons (28:19). But in a broader sense, the story indicates that, even in his infancy, Jesus inspired both worship and hostile opposition, responses repeated throughout the narrative. The magi represent the first of many characters to worship Jesus in Matthew (2:11; see Excursus: Worship in the Gospel of Matthew, p. 51), a point that may be obscured in English Bibles that choose a soft translation here for *proskyneō* (NRSVue, "paid him homage"). For Matthew, Jesus' receiving worship here and elsewhere has christological significance, marking Jesus as the one in whom God is present (1:23). As for opposition, the religious leaders of Israel here do the bidding of a political ruler who wishes to destroy Jesus. Later the situation will be reversed: the political ruler (Pilate) will do the bidding of religious leaders who have decided that Jesus must die (27:1–2, 11–26).

As a literary masterpiece, this brief episode in Matthew's story has captured the imagination of Christians for centuries and inspired numerous legends. The magi came to be identified as kings, probably due to an association of this passage with Isaiah 60:3. They came to be called "wise men," an identification so pervasive that it was even used as an English translation of *magoi* in the NRSV (corrected now to "magi" in the NRSVue). In the Middle Ages, the Western Church decided there were three magi (cf. three gifts, 3:11; the Eastern church has 12) and assigned them names: Caspar, Melchior, and Balthasar. Such legends are significant for Christian piety, but they may distract us from the story Matthew tells. Matthew's account is indeed about kings and wise men, but these figures are people other than the magi. The *kings* in Matthew 2 are Herod and Jesus. Herod exemplifies the sort of king whom Jesus later denounces in Matthew 20:25. He is a tyrant, lording over those he rules rather than serving them. He is not a ruler who "shepherds" God's people (2:6). By contrast, the infant king Jesus is helpless and vulnerable, a ruler whose power is hidden in humility (cf. 21:5). The *wise men* in Matthew 2 are not the magi but the chief priests and scribes, who function as Herod's key advisers. Learned in the Scriptures, they possess scholarly knowledge that both Herod and the magi lack. But what good does it do them? It does not lead them to their messiah but causes them to become involved in a plot to kill him.

Responsible exegesis has always resisted the identification of the magi as kings. Calvin called it "dubious," and Luther polemicized against it in rare harmony with doctors of the Roman Church. The tradition seems to have begun with Augustine, who wanted to use the Day of Epiphany as an occasion for fund raising. In eight annual sermons, he compared the evil king Herod with Caesars of the past who persecuted the church; then he exhorted the current emperor to be a noble king like the magi, who demonstrate their devotion to Christ by opening treasure chests and bestowing gifts. Augustine knew magi weren't actual kings, but once they became metaphorical kings, Isaiah 60:3 was read in a way that facilitated a more literal identification. Although this tradition of "the kings" (especially popular in Hispanic culture) may seem harmless, even if historically wrong, it has had unfortunate consequences. First, it reduced the effectiveness of a prominent theme in Matthew, whose story is deliberately constructed so that all rulers of the earth are characterized as tyrants, excluded from God's favor (see Theme 16 "*Critique of power, wealth, and wisdom*" in the introduction, p. 31). Second, this identification facilitated use of the passage throughout history to support colonialism: the rulers of various pagan nations were expected to follow the example of the magi and give tribute to whichever Christian ruler or nation was viewed as a stand-in for Christ. Indeed, the reason Balthasar was traditionally African was not because the church wanted to be racially inclusive, but because the church wanted Africans to pay tribute to colonial overlords who had brought Christ to them.

The identification of the magi as "wise men" may ultimately be even more problematic. The tradition arose after the Renaissance period and became normative during the Enlightenment (18th c.), when theologians argued that secular science could lead people to discovery of divine truths. Of course, actual magi would have been astrologers, not astronomers, and Matthew's readers would not be expected to regard their "science" as knowledge worthy of attainment. Philo (in the passage cited earlier) refers to magi as "experts in nonsense" and calls them "the most foolish of all men." The only magi in the Old Testament are inept fools whose pitiful attempts at discerning divine truth are mocked by the godly (Dan 2:2–11; the LXX uses the word *magoi* where NRSVue has "sorcerers"). So, Matthew's readers would not be expected to regard these Persian astrologers as "wise men" any more than they would be expected to regard them as kings. This time the tradition may seem fortuitous, used for centuries to justify the church's support for education in general and of science in particular. But again, it conflicts with a Matthean motif: in this Gospel, educated people are just as likely to be opposed to God as are political tyrants (again see Theme 16 "*Critique of power, wealth, and wisdom*" in the introduction, p. 31). So, reading the passage in support of science comes at the cost of missing a point the story is intended to make. What Matthew's readers are expected to notice is that God has somehow revealed the truth about Christ to pagan fools, but *not* to Israel's finest scholars of Scripture. What is going on? Later in the narrative, Jesus will claim that God hides divine truth from "the wise and the intelligent" and reveals it to infants (11:25). That seems to be exemplified here since Matthew's readers would probably regard magi as persons infantile in their understanding: ignorant of the things of God and lacking wisdom that accords with "divine things" rather than "human things" (cf. 16:23).

In short, the central message of this text may be framed as an answer to a question: Whom does God favor? *Not* kings nor wise men, but foreigners who are neither powerful nor possessed of what the reader would be expected to regard as wisdom. Ironically, in recasting the story so that the magi actually become kings or wise men, readers subverted this message until the text seemed to support notions it was intended to suppress. Still, lest we be arrogant in judging these traditions too harshly, we should recognize what they tell us: such traditions arose because, apart from such elaboration, the message of the text is a hard one to hear. The Messiah comes as an antithesis to what the world regards as power and wisdom and finds welcome only among those whom Matthew's readers would be expected to regard as useless fools. (For a comprehensive discussion of magi traditions, especially their misidentification as "kings" and/or "wise men," see Powell 2001.)

2:13–23. Flight and Massacre (only in Matthew)

Guided by an angel, Joseph takes "the child and his mother" to Egypt, to escape the murderous wrath of Herod, who slaughters babies in Bethlehem. They remain until an angel tells them it is relatively safe, and then they settle in Nazareth.

The report of travels is recounted here with unusual attention to divine guidance (via angels and dreams). Matthew's readers are expected to realize that everything is transpiring according to God's plan. Further, the itinerary includes four geographical settings, all of which have scriptural significance: Bethlehem (Mic 5:2; cf. Matt 2:6); Egypt (Hos 11:1; cf. Matt 2:15); Galilee (Isa 9:1; cf. Matt 4:15); and Nazareth ("the prophets"; cf. Matt 2:23). The last reference is oblique because no one is sure what passage in the prophets Matthew has in mind: prominent conjectures involve references to the "shoot [*nezer*] of Jesse" in Isaiah 11:1 or to the Nazirite in Judges 13:5–7. In any case, when we note that Matthew 2:17–18 recalls Jeremiah 31:15, it can be seen that Matthew 2:13–23 is especially replete with scriptural allusions or citations. As indicated in the introduction, this may be because Matthew wants the increasingly gentile church to realize the extent to which the life of their Lord is grounded in Jewish experience (see Theme 6 "*Fulfillment of prophecy*," p. 14). Jesus comes as the culmination of a divine history concerning a chosen people: those who call him Lord must not separate him from that legacy.

Matthew's readers might be expected to notice other allusions to Scripture. The story of a man named Joseph being guided by dreams and bringing his family to Egypt certainly calls to mind the narrative in Genesis 37–50. Egypt serves as a place of refuge in other biblical accounts as well (1 Kgs 11:40; 2 Kgs 25:26; Jer 43:1–7). The most remarkable allusion, however, is ironic. In the well-known biblical story of the exodus, the Hebrew people had to flee Egypt and travel to Israel in order to escape a baby-killing monarch; now righteous Jews need to flee Israel and go to Egypt in order to escape a baby-killing king in their own land. But, as if that is not enough, Matthew's readers may also be expected to notice that all the Scripture texts cited as finding fulfillment in these events are ones that address restoration after the exile. Thus, Matthew supplements the story's obvious exodus motif with exilic nuance; one might even say he presents the infant Jesus as reprising key moments in the salvific history of the people he has come to save (1:21): descent into Egypt, exodus, exile, and return.

This portion of Matthew's narrative may also be viewed as presenting an unexpected turn in the career of Jesus the Messiah, a turn toward lowliness and humility rather than grandeur and greatness.

Previously, people came from far away to worship him; powerful people trembled at the news of his birth (Matt 2:3, 11); but now he is presented as a refugee and as a victim of social injustice. The early wanderings of the "holy family" and the ever-present danger they face from Herod and his descendants set a tone for the narrative to follow, a story that presents Jesus as one who has nowhere to lay his head (8:20) and whose disciples will be pursued from town to town (10:16–25). Interestingly, this is one feature that the quite different infancy narratives of Matthew and Luke have in common. Both Gospels report (in different ways) that the family of Jesus needs to undergo burdensome travel due to the oppressive or perilous nature of imperial authorities (cf. Matt 2:12–23 with Luke 2:1–5). And there is Christological significance in such a presentation. Some apocryphal gospels present the infant Jesus as possessed of incredible power, a tendency that would culminate in a sixth-century account of the flight to Egypt in which Jesus protects his holy parents by miraculously producing food and subduing lions, leopards, and dragons (*Gospel of Pseudo-Matthew*, a reworking of the second-century *Protevangelium of James*). But nothing like that is in our canonical account: here, Jesus himself is completely helpless and vulnerable; he must be protected (by God, his family, an angel, and the cooperative magi); and such protection is ultimately very costly to others.

Now that we have addressed Matthew's reports of the family's movements, let us turn to the central event (2:16–18) that is framed by those reports (2:13–15, 19–23). The most memorable feature of Matthew 2:13–23 is its horrifying mention of Herod killing all the children under two years of age in and around the area of Bethlehem (2:16). Matthew's readers are expected to regard such an action as unspeakably heinous, though they may also know that this same Herod murdered two of his own children when he feared they might be regarded as contenders for his throne (Josephus, *Antiquities* 16.11.1–8). The event reported by Matthew is usually called "the massacre of the innocents," though *innocence* would be less the point than *vulnerability*. Matthew tends to identify those who are "least" in this world (that is, least powerful) as ones most favored by God (19:30; 20:16; 20:26; 23:11; 25:40, 45), so the helplessness of children (their total lack of power) may be what makes them favored recipients of divine revelation (11:25), exemplars of "greatness" (18:1–2), role models for discipleship (18:3–4), incarnations of Christ's abiding presence (18:5), and paragons of true worship (21:15–16). In any case, it is certain that this Gospel evinces a deep and abiding concern for children and an awareness of their plight. Matthew believes that every child has an angel assigned to report to God every instance of disrespect or abuse that child suffers (18:10). Imagine, then, the fate that Matthew and his readers must assume awaits an earthly king who so casually murders those to whom the rule of heaven belongs (19:14).

EXCURSUS

Worship in the Gospel of Matthew

Several verses in Matthew's Gospel speak of worship, though English Bibles do not always make this clear: the NRSVue sometimes says that someone "knelt before" Jesus or "paid homage to him" in places where Matthew almost certainly means the Greek word (*proskyneō*) to be read as "worship" (as 4:10 makes clear, the word describes reverence or devotion that should only be rendered to God or to one regarded as God's equivalent). Instances of worship may be categorized under three headings:

First, we have worship as *reverence and submission*:

- A man with a skin disease worships (*proskyneō*) Jesus, desiring to be cleansed (8:2).
- A ruler worships (*proskyneō*) Jesus, wanting him to restore his daughter to life (9:18).
- A Canaanite woman worships (*proskyneō*) Jesus and asks him to heal her daughter (15:25).
- The mother of James and John worships (*proskyneō*) Jesus and requests special positions for her sons (20:20).

In all these cases, people show their reverence before the Lord when they have a request to make. Notably, the worship always *precedes* the request: Matthew wants to present worship as the proper context for prayer and to show that those who approach Jesus deem him worthy of worship regardless of whether their requests are granted.

Second, we have worship as *praise and thanksgiving*:

- Crowds glorify God after Jesus heals a paralytic (9:8).
- Jesus gives thanks to the Father for revealing to infants what is hidden from the wise and understanding (11:25).
- A crowd glorifies the God of Israel after Jesus heals many people (15:31).

In all these instances, notably, the ones who give thanks do so for what God has done for *others*, not for themselves.

Third, we have worship as *devotion and awe*:

- The magi worship (*proskyneō*) Jesus as one born King of the Jews (2:11; cf. 2:2).
- Disciples worship (*proskyneō*) Jesus as the Son of God (14:33).
- Children offer praise to Jesus as the Son of David in the temple (21:15–16).
- Two women worship (*proskyneō*) the risen Jesus (28:9).
- The disciples worship (*proskyneō*) the risen Jesus (28:17).

In these cases, people worship simply because they are aware of God's majesty and presence. They are awestruck and caught up in the splendor of a divine moment, worshiping God or Jesus for who they are, not for what they have done or might do. This seems to be worship in the purest sense, an expression of corporate love, with an element of mystery to it. Indeed, in two of the five cases, the worshipers are said to be people who experience fear and/or doubt (14:31–33; 28:17), indicating that the phenomenon owes more to the divine majesty that commends it than to the disposition of those who offer it.

We may also note two instances in which worship does *not* occur:

- Herod does not worship (*proskyneō*) Jesus, as he claims he will (2:8).
- Jesus does not worship (*proskyneō*) Satan, as he is tempted to do (4:9).

Finally, Jesus speaks about worship three times:

- Jesus quotes Scripture to Satan: "Worship [*proskyneō*] the Lord your God and serve [*latreuō*] God only" (4:10).
- Jesus tells his disciples: "Let your light shine before others, so that they may see your good works and glorify your Father in heaven" (5:16).

- Jesus applies to religious leaders the Scripture that says, "This people honors me with their lips, but their hearts are far from me; in vain do they worship me, teaching human precepts as doctrines" (15:8–9; citing Isa 29:13).

MATTHEW 3:1–4:16
Preparation for Ministry

Matthew now begins to follow his Markan source. For this portion of the narrative, he makes few redactional changes aside from the discussion of the appropriateness of Jesus' baptism at 3:14–15 and his transformation of a private revelation to Jesus ("You are my Son," Mark 1:11) into a public one ("This is my Son," Matt 3:17). He also inserts material from Q that deals with the preaching of John (3:7–10; cf. Luke 3:1–17) and the temptation in the wilderness (4:1–11; cf. Luke 4:1–13); he concludes the section with unique material that provides geographical detail and a lengthy citation of Scripture (4:13–16).

Matthew prefaces his story of Jesus with a prologue (1:1–4:16) that deals primarily with establishing the identity of the man whose ministry and passion will be recounted. He has related how Jesus came into the world and immediately inspired both worship (2:11) and hostile opposition (2:13–18). Now, without noting any passage of time, he turns to events that prepare the adult Jesus for his ministry to Israel. No clue to Jesus' age is provided (cf. Luke 3:23), and almost no information is given regarding his upbringing in Nazareth, though a later text indicates that this was so unremarkable that no one thought to expect much of him (13:54–57). Now, however, his significance will be recognized by the greatest of all God's prophets (11:11), and readers will see how his identity as the Son of God is what defines his relationship both with God in heaven and with Satan on earth (3:17; 4:3, 6).

3:1–12. Proclamation of John the Baptist (cf. Mark 1:2–6; Luke 3:1–9; John 1:19–23)

John the Baptist prepares the way for Jesus' ministry by calling people to repentance and baptizing them in the Jordan River. He deems the religious leaders of Israel ineligible for this baptism and claims that a "more powerful" one is coming, one who will enact destructive judgment on the unprepared (3:11).

This episode is the first of seven accounts in Matthew's Gospel dealing with John the Baptist:

3:1–12	The ministry of John is reported.
3:13–17	John baptizes Jesus.
9:14–15	John's disciples ask why the disciples of Jesus don't fast.
11:2–15	John questions Jesus' identity, and Jesus speaks of John's role.
14:1–12	John is executed by Herod.
17:10–13	Jesus speaks of John following the transfiguration.
21:23–27	Jesus refers to John when his own authority is questioned.

A study of these texts reveals that John is an unusually significant figure in this Gospel; he is very much the forerunner of Jesus, not only in the sense of preparing the people for Jesus' ministry, but also in the sense that his words and deeds parallel or foreshadow those later attributed to Jesus. We may note a few obvious similarities between John and Jesus in Matthew's story:

- The coming of both was foretold by the prophet Isaiah (1:23; 3:3; cf. Isa 7:14, 40:3).
- Key elements of John's speech are echoed by Jesus. John's message, "Repent for the [rule] of heaven has come near" (3:2), is identical with that of Jesus (4:17) and close to that of Jesus' disciples (10:7). Both John and Jesus use the epithet "brood of vipers" (3:7; 12:34; 23:33), both employ the metaphor of fruitless trees (3:10; 7:19), and both describe judgment in terms of harvest and fire (3:12; 9:37–38; 13:37–42).
- Both John and Jesus are initially well-received by the masses (3:5; 4:24–25), who regard them both as prophets (11:9; 14:5; 21:11, 26, 46). But in time, both are rejected (11:16–19; 27:20).
- Both John and Jesus are pictured as being at odds with religious leaders (3:7–10; 9:3), who are not willing to admit that either of the two derive their authority from heaven (21:23–32).
- Both are eventually arrested (4:12; 26:50) and put to death by the order of Roman-sanctioned authorities (Herod, 14:10; Pontius Pilate, 27:26).

Still, even though John is like Jesus in some respects, he is clearly subordinate to Jesus (3:14; 11:11). As John's own speech declares,

Jesus is the "more powerful" one, who will baptize with the Holy Spirit and fire (3:11). This image probably does not have anything to do with Christian Pentecost; instead, it connotes the refining and largely destructive judgment that is to come at the end of time (see Amos 7:4). In this case, fire and Holy Spirit are one: the fiery breath of God, which will consume the wicked. John's role is simply to offer the truly repentant symbolic protection from this conflagration by dipping them in water; Jesus' role will be to unleash the unquenchable fire itself. Top billing at the eschatological judgment should clearly go to him.

This is the Gospel's first use of the phrase *basilea tou ouranou* (NRSVue, "kingdom of heaven," 3:2); along with the synonymous phrase *basilea tou theou* (NRSVue, "kingdom of God," 6:33), the expression occurs fifty times in Matthew, usually on the lips of Jesus. The English word "kingdom" may not convey the full intent of this all-important concept since the Greek *basileia* refers to an *activity* rather than to a place (see Theme 2 "*Reign or rule of God/heaven*" in the introduction, p. 8). In any case, the essential meaning of John's declaration is that the absolute power and authority that God exercises in heaven are now close to being exercised on earth: the second and third petitions of the Lord's Prayer (6:10) are about to be granted. This makes repentance both possible and imperative.

The description of John's peculiar dress and diet (3:4) marks him as a person who is beholden to no human: he relies entirely upon God for life's necessities. Camel's hair and strips of skin can be found in the wilderness, as can locusts (possibly insects, but more likely bean pods from carob trees) and honey (likely date honey). Thus, John does not "sow nor reap nor gather into barns" but clothes and feeds himself with what is provided by the Creator (cf. 6:26). And, as often recognized, his dress alludes to a possible identification with Elijah (see 2 Kgs 1:8), a theme that will be taken up later in Matthew (11:9–14; 17:9–13).

We know of no precedent for the sort of one-time-only baptism that John is performing. It clearly resonates with certain Jewish ablutions or purification rituals, including ones practiced at Qumran, but it is distinctive. At any rate, Matthew indicates that many people seek this baptism, but it is only granted to those who confess their sins (3:6) and show evidence of a transformed life (3:8) in anticipation of eschatological judgment (3:10–12). As indicated, the primary meaning is probably that immersion in water offers symbolic protection from the coming fire, mentioned three times in 3:10–12. Perhaps it also symbolizes cleansing (hence, forgiveness), but that is not emphasized here (cf. Mark 1:4; Luke 3:3).

In any case, the religious leaders of Israel are deemed ineligible and turned away. In Matthew's Gospel, the "Pharisees and Sadducees" (a historically unlikely combination) are only loosely representative of actual people who lived fifty years before this Gospel was written; they are best regarded as characters in a story in which they are made to represent the forces of evil opposed to God's Son and God's purposes (see Theme 14 "*Religious leaders as enemies of God*" in the introduction, p. 25). The point here is simply that God's enemies often cite religious platitudes and seek to ingratiate themselves with those whose values they actually despise. Douglas Hare applies Matthew's intent to the modern day: "The Christian equivalent of 'We have Abraham as our Father' is 'We have Christ as our Savior'" (Hare 1993, 20). Matthew says as much in 7:21–23: those who think it will be sufficient merely to *confess* Jesus as Lord are in for a nasty surprise on judgment day.

Matthew's readers would be expected to hear the words in 3:9 as an allusion to one of the best-known stories that the Romans had inherited from Greek mythology. After the human race was wiped out (in a great flood, actually), the immortal beings Deucalion and Pyrrha walked through the land, casting stones over their shoulders: adult men sprang from the stones Deucalion cast and adult women from the stones Pyrrha cast; so the world was repopulated. The historical John the Baptist may not have intended any allusion to this tale by his claim that the God of Israel could raise a new race of "children of Abraham" from stones, but any Christian living in a Roman city around 85 CE would be likely to make the connection.

John's description of what Jesus will do when he arrives seems to clash with what Matthew's reader has been told previously, that Jesus will save his people from their sins (1:21). John does not present Jesus as Savior but as Judge, and the judgment he foresees is one of horrible finality (see Theme 17 "*Divine judgment and condemnation in Matthew*" in the introduction, p. 34). Jesus the Winnower (3:12) is such a threatening figure that one may wonder if John has identified the right person. Indeed, John himself will be led to wonder this in 11:2–3. But John's prophecies are true: only his timing is off. He speaks not of the earthly ministry of Jesus about to commence, but of the eschatological parousia, still in the future (13:37–43; 24:36–44; 25:31–46). Thus, ironic though it seems, the role of John the Baptist, according to Matthew's Gospel, is not to prepare people for Jesus' first coming but for his second. As the new Elijah, he prepares people for the "great and terrible day of the LORD" (Mal 4:5–6). Through John the Baptist, God sets in motion preparations for the final coming of Christ even before the earthly ministry of Jesus gets under way.

In this way, Matthew grants theological primacy to eschatology, recognizing the extent to which the present must be determined by the future. In an analogous way, liturgical churches always begin their observance of the church year with texts that focus on the end of time: even before they celebrate Jesus' first coming to earth at Christmas, Christians begin to make preparations for Christ's second advent. These preparations include baptism (3:6), confession (3:6), repentance (3:2, 8), and the bearing of fruit (3:9; see also 7:16–20; 12:33; 13:8, 26; 21:19, 41, 43).

3:13–17. Baptism of Jesus (cf. Mark 1:9–11; Luke 3:21–22; John 1:29–34)

After a brief objection, John baptizes Jesus in the Jordan River. The Holy Spirit descends upon Jesus, and a voice from heaven declares him to be the beloved Son of God with whom God is "well pleased." Notably, in this short passage, Jesus speaks for the first time in the Gospel (3:15), and God speaks for the first of what are only two times (3:17; cf. 17:5).

John the Baptist is a significant figure in Matthew's narrative (see the list of seven passages in comments on 3:1–12). But even if he is the greatest human being ever to have lived, he belongs to an old era being transformed by the arrival of God's reign (11:11–14). Thus, Matthew understands John to be a bridge figure between the old covenant and the new: he brings the era of promise to a close and initiates a new era of fulfillment. The story in 3:13–17 presents a "passing of the baton" from John to Jesus.

Why does John try to prevent Jesus from being baptized? Many Christians have probably thought that it is because his baptism was one of repentance (3:11) and thus would be superfluous for the sinless Jesus. But such thinking may be foreign to Matthew. John is calling *Israel* to repentance and, though individuals might have personal peccadilloes to confess (3:6), the primary focus would be on the sins of the nation. Jesus and others are baptized by John in order to proclaim and participate in a national movement of repentance for Israel and to symbolize a new birth for that nation, a cleansing for the people of God.

John's objection to baptizing Jesus is related to a difference in status. John recognizes Jesus to be the "more powerful" one, the eschatological figure he has been talking about for some time (3:11). He assumes that the time of messianic judgment has come, and he is ready to receive the baptism with the Holy Spirit and fire that he knows this entails (3:11); this is what he means when he says, "I need to be baptized by you" (3:14).

John's water baptism is one of repentance, which prepares the way for the messianic judgment that establishes God's righteousness. Jesus' response picks up on precisely that theme: they must do what is proper to "fulfill all righteousness" (3:15). This response is somewhat mysterious, but it contains two of Matthew's favorite words: "fulfill" (*plēroun*) and "righteousness" (*dikaiosynē*). The latter is used here and in 5:6, 10, 20; 6:33; and 21:32; the adjective *dikaios* (translated "righteous" or "just") is also used eighteen times. Without doing an in-depth word study (book-length monographs have been produced), we note that the word *dikaiosynē* describes appropriateness: "the way things ought to be." But Matthew uses the word with religious significance: "righteousness" happens when things are the way *God* wants them to be. Further, it is not primarily a moral term (though it may have moral implications) but a relational one: righteousness is the state of people being properly related to God and to each other. For more on the meaning of "righteousness" in Matthew, see comments on 1:18 (discussion of what Matthew means by describing Joseph as "a righteous man").

It is highly significant that the first thing Jesus ever says in Matthew's Gospel is that righteousness must be fulfilled. This will be the primary effect of God's rule being established (4:17) and of God's will being done on earth as in heaven (6:10); it is what Jesus says people should strive for above all else: indeed, it is the *only* thing they need to seek, since everything else will follow (6:33). The fulfillment of righteousness (restoration of relationships to the way God wants them to be) is the primary reason Jesus has come. As for *why* he must be baptized by John for this to be accomplished—well, that is left ambiguous; we may at least gather that God has a plan for making everything right and that Jesus is committed to being obedient to that plan. Perhaps what is needed is simply an occasion for Jesus to be publicly anointed and empowered as God's chosen representative. But the question "Why does he need to be baptized?" is only a minor conundrum that prepares us for a much bigger one: "Why does he need to die on a cross?" Matthew recognizes that neither Jesus' baptism nor his death makes sense from a human point of view: thus, John tries to prevent the baptism, and Peter tries to prevent the death (16:22). But both are required for righteousness to be fulfilled.

The real focus of this story, however, is on the descent of the apparent dove and especially on the voice from heaven. Church tradition is replete with explanations for why the Spirit would descend "like a dove," with frequent references to the dove that signaled the end of the deluge in Genesis 8:8–11. Tertullian and John Chrysostom both took it as a sign that, at least for now, God is coming to people in peace, not with the violence that John predicted in 3:11–12 (Tertullian, *On Baptism* 8; Chrysostom, *Gospel of Matthew* 12.3). There is also (unresolvable) debate as to whether the Spirit descended upon Jesus physically in the form of a literal dove or merely swooped down from heaven in a manner associated with doves. Of course, pagan literature is also filled with references to birds as omens associated with deities.

Matthew's Gospel is about God, but most of the time God is in the background. People talk about God, and the thoughts of God are often revealed through prophets or angels or through references to Scripture, which is "the word of God" (15:6). But only two texts in Matthew report God as actually speaking directly, as a character in the story (3:13–17; 17:1–9). For those in churches that use the Revised Common Lectionary, one is read for the Baptism of Our Lord, the *first* Sunday in the Epiphany season; the other is read for the Transfiguration of Our Lord, the *last* Sunday in the Epiphany season. The weeks the church designates as Epiphany are literally framed by two divine pronouncements, the only two such pronouncements in Matthew. What's especially interesting is that both times when God chooses to speak aloud from heaven, God says almost exactly the same thing: Jesus is God's beloved Son, and God is pleased with Jesus (3:17; 17:5).

The single most important thing that Matthew's Gospel wants to say about Jesus is this: *Jesus is the Son of God* (see Theme 9 "*Jesus as the Son of God*" in the introduction, p. 19). Although Matthew has dropped hints previously (1:16; 2:15), the baptism narrative offers the first direct acclamation of Jesus as the Son of God. Thus, the story is told such that God's own voice may be the first to proclaim this climactic designation, which, as Matthew's Gospel will make clear, can only be recognized by those to whom God reveals it (11:27; 16:17).

Why is this identification so important? It is the confession that gives birth to the church (16:16–19) because, for Matthew, the divine sonship of Jesus is what establishes him as one in whom God is present (1:23). Of course, God has been present through people before—through kings, judges, prophets—but not like this. God is present in Jesus in an *unprecedented and superlative* sense, so much so that people worship Jesus (see Matt 2:11; 8:2; 9:18; 14:33; 15:25; 20:20; 21:16; 28:9, 17; in all these verses, the Greek word is *proskyneō*). Radically monotheistic Jews, who believe that people should worship no one—no prophet, no king, no spirit, no angel, not even the messiah—*no one* but the Lord God (Matt 4:10), are now worshiping Jesus. How is that okay? Matthew would say, because Jesus is the Son of God, and God is so present in him that worshiping Jesus counts as worshiping God (see Excursus: Worship in the Gospel of Matthew, p. 51).

The acclamation at Jesus' baptism recalls the words of the coronation hymn in Psalm 2:7 but then continues with the words, "with whom I am well pleased," a definite allusion to the beginning of the Servant Song in Isaiah 42. Thus Jesus is presented as both royal Son of God and faithful Servant of the Lord, a collusion that continues to be developed in the temptation story following this passage. And as Matthew's story continues, associating Jesus with the Isaian Servant will be a significant motif (see 8:17; 12:17–21; cf. the passion narrative with Isa 53).

Finally, whatever the historical character of John's baptisms may have been, Matthew's readers would be expected to view the baptism of Jesus as a prototype for Christian baptism. Preachers often note analogies that were no doubt intended by Matthew: when we are baptized, we too receive the Spirit, and we too are identified as beloved children of God. We are baptized with Christ and into Christ, so that God's plan of righteousness might be fulfilled in us and through us. Further, Christian baptism is typically a Trinitarian exercise (owing to Matt 28:19), and this story of Jesus' baptism is regarded in church tradition as a prime instance of Trinitarian involvement: Jesus is explicitly identified as the Son, which implies that the heavenly speaker is the Father (or at least Parent), and the Spirit of God acts independently but in accord with both of these. The author of Matthew's Gospel did not espouse Nicene Trinitarian doctrine (and had no concept of a Three-in-One Godhead), but Matthew does provide the material on the basis of which such a doctrine could and would eventually be developed.

4:1–11. Temptation of Jesus (cf. Mark 1:2–3; Luke 4:1–13)

The Spirit, who has just come upon Jesus at his baptism, now leads him into the wilderness to be tested by Satan. Three tests follow, and Jesus responds to each by quoting Scripture, though (as the second test reveals) the devil too can cite the Bible (4:6). These tests, furthermore, come at the end of a time in which Jesus has fasted for forty days and nights, a period analogous to when Moses fasted on Sinai (Exod 34:28) as well as to the forty years that Israel was tested in the wilderness on the way to the promised land (Deut 8:2). Now Jesus proves more faithful than Israel, rejecting satanic suggestions that would interpret his identity as God's Son in ways that would not please God (cf. 3:17), that would involve his "being served" rather than "serving" (20:28). Jesus refuses to produce bread miraculously to satisfy his own hunger, though he will do so later to relieve the hunger of others (14:13–21; 15:32–39). He similarly rejects the ways of self-aggrandizement or compromise as shortcuts to manifesting his authority on earth. Already, Matthew's readers are being prepared to recognize as satanic any route to participation in the reign of God that bypasses the cross (cf. 16:21–23). Thus, as indicated at his baptism, Jesus is the Son of God, but his role as Son is to be exercised paradoxically as a Servant.

This account of the temptation of Jesus (from Q) is often cited as the clearest example in New Testament literature of a "myth." One common definition of that literary genre holds that a myth is a story that has a god (or divine being) as a character; in some sense the entire Gospel of Matthew could then be classified as myth, but 4:1–11 is a more blatant example because it tells of two divine entities interacting with each other in a context devoid of ordinary human beings. But genres are assigned by literary critics, with little attention to intentions of historical authors or perceptions of original readers. In terms of Jewish literature, Matthew 4:1–11 exemplifies "haggadic midrash," presenting an imaginative (and overtly fictive) tale woven from threads found in biblical narratives (in this case, the temptation of Adam and Eve, the testing of Israel, and the ordeal of Job—though, as we shall see, the second of these predominates).

Mark's Gospel probably wanted to use its brief temptation story to present Jesus as the "second Adam" (cf. Rom 5:12–21), and that motif has often dominated theological reflection on Matthew's narrative as well. But Matthew is more interested in presenting Jesus as "representative Israel," putting right what the nation did wrong. Earlier, Matthew noted that Jesus would fulfill the prophet's words, "Out of Egypt I have called my son" (2:15; cf. Hos 11:1). Those words originally referred to Israel, God's "son" who was brought out of Egypt via the exodus (cf. Exod 4:22), only to be found wanting when tested in the wilderness. Now Jesus delivers the faithfulness God expects. Thus, all three Scripture verses Jesus quotes during his temptation come from Moses' reflections upon the ignominious period of Israel's wilderness wanderings (Deut 8:3 in Matt 4:4; Deut 6:16 in Matt 4:7; Deut 6:13 in Matt 4:10). Jesus is doing what Moses said Israel should have done, evincing the attitude befitting a son with whom God is pleased (3:17).

To grasp the nature of the temptations, it is imperative to understand the premise explicitly stated for the first two: "If you are the Son of God . . ." (4:3, 6). This is an example of what Greek grammars traditionally called a "first-class condition," one in which the premise is assumed to be true. When Paul says, "If we live by the Spirit, let us also be guided by the Spirit" (Gal 5:25), he is not wondering whether or not people live by the Spirit and proposing that if it turns out that they do, they should be guided by that Spirit. No: he means, "It is a given that we live by the Spirit; *therefore*, we ought to be guided by the Spirit." Likewise, Satan does not wonder whether Jesus is the Son of God (nor is he prompting Jesus to prove this). In Matthew's Gospel, Satan and the demons *know* who Jesus is (8:29). Satan is suggesting to Jesus that *because* Jesus is the Son of God, he should not have to suffer want (hunger, injury) the way other people do; indeed, he should recognize that God is at his bidding to satisfy his every whim and/or to protect him from recklessness. It is possible that Matthew viewed Israel as failing God in precisely this manner, interpreting its favored status in terms of entitlement and privilege rather than duty and responsibility. But Matthew's readers would be expected to be more concerned with the attitude and behavior of Christians in the developing church. As suggested in the discussion of 3:13–17, Matthew's readers regard the baptism of Jesus as somewhat paradigmatic of Christian baptism. Like Jesus, they have been empowered with the Holy Spirit and, through baptism, declared to be the beloved children of God. Perhaps the fundamental temptation facing them is to interpret their new status as an entrée to power and privilege rather than as a call to suffering and service.

The third temptation, in essence, is to decide that a seemingly desirable end justifies obviously iniquitous means. Of course, some ethicists maintain that *sometimes* less-than-ideal means must be employed to achieve a greater good, but the story world of Matthew's Gospel does not allow for such nuances. In any case, the scenario here poses the "end-justifies-the-means" question in extreme terms: What if the only thing necessary for Jesus Christ to rule the entire world is for him to worship the devil? An adult forum in a modern church might have a lively discussion of such a question, but Matthew's answer would be that, then, the rule of heaven would no longer be at hand (4:17). If Jesus were to yield to this temptation, he would make Satan his god and, thus, could only announce or manifest the rule of hell.

Dostoevsky offers memorable comments on this text in "The Grand Inquisitor," a tale related by an atheist to a monk in the book *The Brothers Karamazov* (1880). In that story, Jesus visits the earth and is accosted by church officials who rebuke him for having rejected reasonable offers from "the wise and dread Spirit" (i.e., Satan), a mistake that the church has now labored for centuries to overcome. Indeed, these officials propose that the mission of the church can almost be defined as "correcting Christ," obtaining the power to conquer, coerce, and transform society in a manner that Jesus so blithely rejected. Dostoevsky, of course, intends this as pessimistic hyperbole (dismissed as "absurd" by the monk, the book's main protagonist); nevertheless, it seems to be presented in a manner suggesting that the tale's indictment of post-Constantinian Christianity is somewhat justified. Certainly, many potential targets of the fable's polemic have had the humility to grant that something trenchant is to be derived from it. (For more on Matthew's understanding of the church's mission and acquisition of power, see Excursus: "Christ beneath Culture" as a Paradigm for Mission, p. 229.)

Matthew's story assumes the legitimacy of Satan's offer; if not, there would be no real temptation. Satan *does* have authority over all the nations and governments of the earth (a premise stated explicitly in Luke 4:6). Those who consider this perspective extreme should remember that this is a story. We have no way of knowing what the Gospel's author thought about actual kingdoms or their rulers, but he has composed an apocalyptic tale in which all rulers of the earth (gentile and Jewish) serve as pawns of the devil. Thus the current episode (relating Jesus' temptations in the wilderness) is extremely important for the narrative because it reveals the true conflict that underscores the entire plot. On the surface, Matthew's story unfolds as a tale of conflict between Jesus and the power players of the world (gentile rulers and Jewish leaders); but in reality, it is indeed a story of the conflict between God and Satan: Jesus as God's agent versus the "powers," who serve as agents of the devil. As indicated in the introduction, the ironic genius of the story is that God wins this ultimate conflict in such a way that the earthly manifestations of satanic rule do not even realize they have been defeated (see Theme 15 "*Conflict along three plot lines*" in the introduction, p. 29). By presenting an overt encounter between Jesus and Satan in 4:1–11, Matthew helps readers recognize the apocalyptic (mythological) character of what is happening elsewhere in a story involving more conventional human characters.

So, even though Matthew concludes this episode by saying, "The devil left him," the reader will eventually realize that the departure of the devil was not absolute. Satan continues to plague Jesus throughout his ministry, most notably when he uses Peter to suggest that suffering and death ought not be the destiny of "the Messiah" (16:16–17, 21–23) and when he speaks through witnesses of the crucifixion with words that echo the first two temptations proffered at the outset: "*If you are the Son of God*, come down from the cross" (27:40; cf. 4:3, 6).

The ministration of angels recounted in 4:11 recalls how God provided for Elijah after the primary conflict of his career in 1 Kings 19:5–8. It is mentioned here with a note of irony, since Jesus has recently refused to regard the assistance of angels as something he should take for granted (4:5–7); such assistance is something he will refuse again, when it could matter most (26:53–54).

4:12–16. Jesus Moves to Capernaum (cf. Mark 1:14)

The narrative jumps ahead in time (from the account of Jesus' baptism and temptation) to some indefinite period after John the Baptist has been arrested. We do not actually hear the story of that arrest or its outcome until Matthew 14:1–12. Its mention now, however, offers ominous commentary on the world into which Jesus has come. As one who came to prepare the way of the Lord, call people to repentance, and indeed collaborate with Jesus in fulfilling all righteousness (3:15), John is a great prophet of God (see 11:7–15). Jesus' ministry is taking place in a world where such persons are arrested, where righteousness is resisted. Such a world may be described as a place of darkness, but Matthew concludes the first section of his Gospel on a hopeful note: a "great light" has dawned on the people who dwell in such darkness. Specifically, the citation here of Isaiah 9:1–2, with its reference to Jesus' homeland as "Galilee of the gentiles," indicates that the light will shine even for pagan peoples of this dark world, or even especially for them. There is hope even for the gentiles, that is, for the non-Israelites who have not traditionally been identified as belonging to God's chosen people. The visit of the magi has already foreshadowed some possible connection between the messiah of Israel and people from nations far away. Eventually Matthew's Gospel will conclude with a proclamation to make disciples of such persons (28:16–20).

Matthew notes that the man traditionally known as "Jesus of Nazareth" actually makes his home in Capernaum, which becomes the seat of his adult ministry. As with previous travels (2:15, 23), these movements follow a pattern that fulfills Scripture passages. Such fulfillment indicates that everything is going in accord with God's plan and demonstrates (for gentile believers?) that Jesus must be understood in light of sacred Jewish tradition.

Historically, the reference to Galilee as a gentile-infested region would have been more accurate in Isaiah's day than it was at the time of Jesus. In the latter period, the area had a heavily Jewish population: we will see that Jesus encounters very few gentiles as he moves about Galilee for the next nine chapters. In Jesus' day, however, Galilean

Jews did have a reputation for being a somewhat unsophisticated or low-class people. They were easily recognizable by their rustic dialect (26:73). For this reason, many scholars say that a Galilean Messiah fits well with Matthew's intention to identify Jesus with the marginalized (8:20; 25:31–46). There is something to this, but the point might have been lost on an urban Roman congregation consisting of post-70 CE Diaspora Jews and large numbers of recent gentile converts. More likely, Matthew's readers are just expected to realize that the God whom gentiles are now coming to know has been thinking about them all along.

Part Two of Matthew's Gospel: Jesus' Ministry to Israel

Matthew 4:17–11:1

The phrase "From that time [on] . . ." (4:17) signals the beginning of a new section of the Gospel (cf. 16:21). This second major portion of Matthew's Gospel describes the mission that first Jesus and then also his followers undertake on behalf of Israel. It is a ministry of word and deed, of preaching, teaching, and healing (4:23; 9:35; 11:1). Jesus instructs his disciples on how to live in accord with the will of God; together they announce the advent of God's reign and exercise authority over diseases and demons. In this portion of the Gospel, opposition to Jesus is somewhat muted. We discern some displeasure on the part of religious leaders concerning Jesus, and we hear predictions of persecution that is to come, but the conflicts reported here are less intense than the confrontations that erupt in the next section of the narrative.

MATTHEW 4:17–25
Jesus Calls Disciples and Begins His Ministry

Matthew derived most of this material from Mark 1:14–20, with the summary of Jesus' ministry in 4:23–25 offering a major expansion of Mark 1:39.

Before describing Jesus' ministry to Israel in detail, Matthew's Gospel offers an overview: a capsule report of his essential message, a paradigmatic account of how he called disciples, and a summary description of what he did for people and how they responded.

4:17. The Message of the Kingdom (cf. Mark 1:14–15)

The phrase "From that time [on] . . ." (4:17) signals the beginning of a new section of Matthew's Gospel, one that focuses on his ministry to Israel. The précis of Jesus' message to Israel is stated in one sentence: "Repent, for the [rule] of heaven has come near." Notably, this is the same message proclaimed by John the Baptist (3:2) and essentially the same message that Jesus' disciples will proclaim (10:7). The phrase "rule, or reign, of heaven" is synonymous with the phrase "rule, or reign, of God," which is used in the other Gospels and occasionally turns up here (6:33). Either phrase refers to the activity of God's ruling, a phenomenon not limited by space or time (see Theme 2 "*Reign or rule of God/heaven*" in the introduction, p. 8). To say that the reign of God, or rule of heaven, has "come near" implies that what God wants to happen is about to take place. Thus Jesus declares that there is a sense of imminence to the ultimate accomplishment of God's will; he indicates that the nearness of God's rule makes repentance both possible and imperative. Such repentance implies not simply minor alteration of habits but also a radical reorientation of life that allows for participation in God's reign, such that God's will might be done not only on the cosmological scale that Jesus has announced, but also in the particular lives of his hearers.

4:18–22. Call of Disciples (cf. Mark 1:16–20; Luke 5:1–11)

Immediately after announcing that the rule of heaven has come near, Jesus begins calling disciples to join him in the work of making this proclamation known. The call stories of two sets of brothers are related not only because these individuals prove to be among the most significant in the narrative that follows (Simon is later known as Peter; see Theme 12 "*Prominence of Peter*" in the introduction, p. 22), but also because their stories offer a paradigm for how other disciples presumably were called (see 9:9). Jesus initiates the relationship by summoning persons who apparently had no previous interest in him. They respond by abandoning their former way of life—family, possessions, and occupation—in order to follow him.

The stories bring out the authoritative nature of Jesus' person and word, which can inspire total allegiance. They demonstrate that Jesus himself is responsible for building the community that will eventually be known as his "church" (16:18).

Jesus appears to be unique among rabbis in inviting (or commanding) people to follow him. More often, a prospective disciple would approach a teacher and request permission to study with him (cf. 8:19). That said, there is precedent for call narratives such as this one in Greco-Roman literature, including Diogenes Laërtius's account of how Socrates summoned Xenophon (*Vitae philosophorum* [*Lives of Eminent Philosophers*] 2.48). Socrates bars the man's way in a narrow passage and inquires as to where various types of food are sold. Then he asks, "And where do men go to become good and honorable?" Xenophon does not know, and Socrates declares, "Follow me and learn!" So Xenophon becomes his disciple from that day forward. Matthew's readers might be expected to know that story, but they would also be expected to know tales from the Hebrew Scriptures that relate how God called Moses (Exod 3:13–4:19) and various prophets (e.g., Gideon in Judg 6:11–35; Isaiah in Isa 6:1–13; Jeremiah in Jer 1:1–10). As in those stories, Jesus summons with an authority that can hardly be resisted (at least not for long or effectively). Indeed, one notable feature of this call story is the absence of an "objection," which is a common feature in such narratives (it is present in Luke's version at 5:8). In any case, the call of Jesus' disciples resembles that of Moses and the prophets more closely than that of Xenophon or any rabbinic pupils because the call is to engage in mission directed to others. The disciples are not called primarily to be students of Jesus (though that is certainly part of it), but to be agents of God's mission in the world (see Theme 3 "*The mission of God*" in the introduction, p. 10). They will announce and to some extent effect the advent of heaven's rule (10:7–8). Personal growth (even in terms of gaining understanding or becoming good and honorable) is not the main goal: they are to be salt of the *earth* and light for the *world* (5:13–16).

The call to become "fishers of people" will assume prominence in Christian culture as a metaphor for mission and evangelism. Like most metaphors, it only works if you don't think about it too much. Fish are typically snared against their will and are seldom better off after they have been caught than they were before. Originally, of course, this was just a cute expression, playing on the individuals' original profession. A farmer might be called to "sow the gospel," a carpenter to "build God's community," or a dressmaker to "clothe people with righteousness." So, men and women who cast nets to catch large numbers of fish are now envisioned as casting light into a dark world so that those who see their good works might be gathered into a community defined by their awareness that the rule of heaven has come near (4:16; 5:16). Furthermore, as a later parable of Jesus indicates, one principal connotation of fishing is that of radical diversity (13:47–50): a net draws fish "of every kind"; the mission of God for which the disciples are commissioned will eventually be similarly indiscriminate. Some sorting will be necessary at the end of time, but that job is reserved for angels and denied to the disciples or missionaries themselves (cf. 13:27–30, 39).

4:23–25. Summary of Jesus' Ministry (cf. Mark 1:39)

This is the first of three passages in Matthew that summarize Jesus' work of preaching, teaching, and healing (see also 9:35; 11:1; cf. 8:16; 15:29–31; 19:1–2). Indeed, 4:23 is repeated almost word for word in 9:35, suggesting that Matthew 5–9 forms a unit presenting the ministry so described. Everything Jesus does proclaims the good news of God's reign: Matthew 5–7 shows how this is done through teaching, and 8–9 shows how it is accomplished through healing.

The focus of Jesus' ministry is clearly the people of Israel since most of the teaching takes place in synagogues (see 10:5–6; 15:24). We may note, however, that Matthew's use of the pronoun "their" to identify these synagogues (4:23) discloses some recognition that the locus for Jesus' work is a somewhat foreign environment for the Gospel's readers: it is happening in *their* synagogues, not *ours.* In any case, for the first time we are also informed that Jesus is working miracles, healing people who suffer from a variety of diseases or disabilities. Such works, furthermore, have made Jesus so famous that great crowds from a variety of locations are now following him (as he called the disciples to do, but generally with less commitment; see comments on 19:1–2).

We should also note that the message of the rule of heaven, stated in 4:17, is now designated as "good news" (4:23). This would not necessarily have been the case. Indeed, based on what John the

Baptist said in 3:10–12, Matthew's readers might be forgiven for thinking that when Jesus began preaching, "Repent, for the rule of heaven has come near," it could be the opposite of good news! But now, in 4:23, we discover that such a proclamation is "gospel," at least for some people. For one thing, it means that diseases *can* be cured: this is phenomenally good news for demoniacs, epileptics, and paralytics. Before long, Jesus will list others who should welcome the announcement of God's reign as good news: those who are starved for justice, who find no reason for hope, no cause for joy, . . . and, of course, the peacemakers, the pure in heart, the merciful, and the persecuted (5:3–12).

EXCURSUS

The Sermon on the Mount (Matthew 5:1–7:29)

The Sermon on the Mount represents the first of five great speeches given by Jesus, which, taken as a whole, may have been intended to provide the fledgling church with something like a Christian Torah (see Theme 10 "*Jesus as the new Moses*" in the introduction, p. 19). The overall theme of the sermon is *discipleship,* response to the call of Jesus. The sermon follows Jesus' announcement that the rule of heaven has come near (4:17) and explains the implications of this announcement for those who repent and follow Jesus.

More than half the material in the Sermon on the Mount finds a parallel in different sections of Luke's Gospel, much but not all occurring in a passage where Jesus instructs a multitude of people "on a level place" (Luke 6:17). This leads scholars to believe that much of the Sermon on the Mount (62 of 106 verses) derives from the lost Q document: Matthew has woven material from that source together to form a beautiful and relatively cohesive "sermon," adding additional material from Mark or unknown sources as seemed appropriate.

Be that as it may, attention must also be paid to parallels between passages in the Sermon on the Mount and New Testament epistolary literature. The following comparisons are especially noteworthy:

Matthew	Epistles
5:10	1 Pet 3:14

5:11–12	1 Pet 4:13–14
5:16	1 Pet 2:12
5:31–32	1 Cor 7:10–11
5:34–37	Jas 5:12
5:39	Rom 12:17; 1 Thess 5:15; 1 Pet 3:9
5:44	Rom 12:14; 1 Cor 4:12
5:48	1 Pet 1:15
6:19–20	Jas 5:1–3
6:25	Phil 4:6
7:1–2	Rom 2:1–3; 14:10
7:7	Jas 1:5; 1 John 5:14–15
7:16b	Jas 3:12
7:21–27	Rom 2:13; Jas 1:22

Such parallels are striking because the authors of these epistles are not thought to have had access to either Matthew's Gospel or the Q source. The common suggestion, therefore, is that such sayings were attributed to Jesus via oral tradition in various sectors of the church.

Despite its popularity in Christian tradition, the Sermon is often thought to present an impossible ethic. The history of interpretation amounts to an account of attempts to domesticate its radical demands. Proposals include (1) some mandates apply only to clergy or others who pursue religious vocations (Thomas Aquinas); (2) the ethical expectations apply only to personal and religious life, not to behavior within the social, secular sphere (Luther); (3) dictates that seem absolute within the Sermon itself may be recognized as situational or relative when considered within the broad context of Scripture (Calvin); (4) the main point of the Sermon is to form the "inner person" by inculcating a certain disposition within believers rather than by prescribing literal behavior (Zwingli); (5) radical demands of the Sermon represent an "interim ethic" that applies only for those who believe the end of the ages is imminent (Schweitzer); (6) the Sermon describes life and governance in a future dispensation when Christ establishes his millennial rule over the earth (Darby). Many or all of these ideas may help some believers make sense of Jesus' words for their own particular contexts, but our interest is in first discovering how Matthew's readers would be expected to understand these words and respond to them. It is unlikely that they would be expected to adopt any of the specific strategies proposed. Rather, they would be expected to receive the words as people who believe that (regardless of whether the end is imminent) the rule of heaven has come near but has not yet fully arrived. Given this, they hear the Sermon as an explication of ethics for the reign of God: people seek God's reign and God's righteousness by striving to live in compliance with the Sermon's demands (Matt 6:33). To the extent that the reign of God is already present, they will find some success, sufficient to be salt of the earth and light for the world (5:13–16). Their failures serve as reminders that God's reign is not yet fully established and that God's rule over their own lives remains incomplete. Thus the Sermon does not present an "impossible ethic" so much as an ethic that Christians are to live into, striving to live in the present as they are destined to live for eternity.

MATTHEW 5:1–2
Introduction to the Sermon on the Mount

These two verses may be considered unique to Matthew's Gospel, though there is a similar text in Luke 6:17–20 that specifies a different setting and audience for a similar sermon.

Jesus deliberately separates himself from the crowds to speak important words to his disciples on a mountain (cf. Mark 3:13; John 6:3). As far as we know, Jesus has only called four disciples by this point (4:18–22). Perhaps those four constitute his entire audience, or maybe we should not assume the narrative is that tightly plotted. In any case, by indicating that disciples are the intended audience, Matthew's Gospel presents the words that follow as Christian teaching, not as exposition of moral behavior that would be expected of, or imposed upon, the world at large. In time, people from all nations who are baptized and who become disciples (28:19–20) will be taught to obey these commandments of Jesus, which call for a greater righteousness than is exhibited by others (5:20), but at no time should the church expect such behavior from society as a whole. Nevertheless, at the conclusion of the Sermon, Matthew will indicate that people for whom the teaching was not intended have overheard his words and have been astonished by them. So, Matthew grants that people who are not followers of Jesus may be impressed or dumbfounded by his teaching, since he speaks with an authority that humans are not accustomed to hearing (see 7:28–29). Still, his words are intended for disciples, for people who have given up everything to follow him.

The location of this teaching on a mountain recalls the giving of the law to Moses in Exodus 19–31. Scholars typically view this as one more instance (perhaps the primary one) of Matthew presenting Jesus as the new Moses (see Theme 10 "*Jesus as the new Moses*" in the introduction, p. 19). There may be something of that here, but the analogy is more suggestive of something else. In Exodus, Moses goes up the mountain to receive Torah from God and then comes down to teach that Torah to the Israelites. In Matthew, the disciples (= the church) go up the mountain to receive Torah from Jesus and then come down to teach that Torah to all nations (28:19–20). So, to get the analogy correctly, we should view Jesus as standing in the role of God and the disciples in the role of Moses. Matthew may like the idea of Jesus as a new Moses, but he also seems to think that the church can have that role (especially when it is given the keys to the rule of heaven and authority to determine God's will on earth; cf. 16:18–19; 18:18).

MATTHEW 5:3–12
The Beatitudes

The text derives in part from the Q source and is paralleled by Luke 6:20–26, but all except the last of the nine Beatitudes in Matthew are either unique to that Gospel or differ significantly from their Lukan counterparts (e.g., compare Matthew's "the poor in spirit" with Luke's "you who are poor"; Matthew's "those who hunger and thirst for righteousness" with Luke's "you who are hungry now").

The Sermon on the Mount begins with a poetic prelude that presents Jesus' vision for what will happen when the rule of heaven becomes established. A two-stanza poem (5:3–10) is followed by direct comments offered to the disciples themselves (5:11–12). The poem, consisting of eight Beatitudes worded in the third person, has been read in two ways, which differ mainly on how the first four blessings are to be understood.

5:3–6. Reversals for the Unfortunate (cf. Luke 6:20–21)

A common, traditional view understands Matthew 5:3–6 as promising rewards to persons who exhibit various virtues: for example, the poor in spirit may be linked with the unpretentious, those who mourn with the penitent, the meek with the humble, and those who hunger for righteousness with those who earnestly desire to do what is right. Proponents of this view usually maintain that Matthew has spiritualized the Beatitudes found in the Q source, which are preserved more faithfully in Luke 6:20–22. About thirty years ago, however, I proposed an alternative reading that has been taken up by many (Powell 1996b). I suggest that the first stanza of the Beatitudes (the first four of the eight) does not name virtues to be rewarded, but rather unfortunate circumstances that will be reversed when God's will is done. According to this view:

- The poor in spirit are the despondent, people with no reason for hope.
- Those who mourn are the miserable, who have no cause for joy.
- The meek are dispossessed people, deprived of their share of the earth's resources.
- Those who hunger for righteousness are victims of injustice, longing to see God's righteousness prevail.

This interpretation makes better literal sense of the language that is used.

To be "poor in spirit" is not elsewhere considered to be a virtue. Literally, it would mean "those who are spiritually weak" or simply "not very spiritual"; yet the context suggests that Jesus is not referring to people who are intrinsically unspiritual but to people who have become that way due to hardship: the "crushed in spirit" or "brokenhearted" of Psalm 34:18 and Isaiah 61:1. Some interpreters move in this direction by suggesting that the "poor in spirit" are the pious poor among Israel who trust God in spite of their dreadful circumstances. But I think those people would be called "rich in spirit" (though poor in things). No, the poor in spirit are people on the verge of giving up, people whose dire circumstances have affected them spiritually so that they no longer see any reason to trust God. Why would Jesus call such people "blessed"? Because, he says, "heaven rules them" (a much better translation of 5:3b than "theirs is the kingdom of heaven"; the cognate noun *basilea* ("reign" or "rule"; NRSVue, "kingdom") is accompanied by two genitive terms, *heaven* and *them* (in such a construction, the genitive terms usually indicate the subject and object of the verbal idea expressed in the cognate). But would the Messiah bless people who (almost) gave up on God? The notion is somewhat counterintuitive but completely in sync with that same Messiah's claiming he has come to call sinners rather than the righteous (Matt 9:13) and telling chief priests they need to wait behind tax collectors and sex workers to receive God's favor (21:32). That is the type of Messiah that Matthew's readers would be expected to see in Jesus—much more so than a Messiah who blesses first and foremost people who are nice, submissive, and unassuming, people who keep decorum (as implied by the traditional interpretation).

The word translated "those who mourn" can indeed refer to persons grieving over the death of a loved one, but more broadly it simply refers to people who are unhappy, people who have miserable, terrible lives. This is never a virtue to be rewarded: it is an unfortunate condition that the advent of God's reign will remedy.

English Bibles persist in translating *praǘs* in 5:5 as "the meek"; a better rendering would be "the oppressed." It is true that in the Greek literature of the gentile world, to be *praǘs* means to be submissive, to know one's place in the world and not seek to rise above it. Thus, in that literature, the word does indeed describe a virtue, specifically one to be exhibited by women, children, and enslaved persons. We also find this usage in 1 Peter 3:4 (where the NRSVue translates it "gentle"). In the Septuagint, however, the word is used to translate *anawim*, a Hebrew word that often refers to the poor, the lowly, the neglected, and others on whose behalf the prophets often speak. Again, in Psalm 37, the closest analogue to Matthew 5:5, "the meek" (*praǘs* in the Septuagint) referred to in 37:11 are called "the poor and needy" in 37:14. In a book-length study of this term, Klaus Wengst determined that in the Septuagint the word refers not to "the humble" but to "the humiliated" (Wengst 1988, 36–41). My sense is that Matthew (unlike 1 Peter) would be more likely to use the word the way it was used in the Scriptures (LXX) than the way it was used in Greco-Roman literature: all three uses of *praǘs* in Matthew reflect Old Testament rootage (cf. Matt 5:5 to Ps 37:11; Matt 11:29 to Zeph 3:12; and Matt 21:5 to Zech 9:9). So, Matthew portrays Jesus as blessing the oppressed and, specifically, as promising them that they will "inherit the earth." An inheritance, of course, is not a reward but the granting of one's due. In short, what Jesus says in Matthew 5:5 is that when God's will is done, those who have been deprived of their share of the earth's resources will finally receive what they should have had all along. This is poetry, so we should perhaps avoid an overliteral interpretation suggesting that the meek will ultimately have the entire earth all to themselves. Rather, they will have their portion of what God provides: a generous creation and a promised land that abounds with more than enough for all.

Matthew 5:6 does not speak of those who yearn to be righteous people but, rather, of those who yearn for righteousness, that is, for the world to be a righteous place, or indeed, a place where they are treated righteously. In short, they are not people who yearn *to do* what is right, but people who yearn to have "what is right" *done to* them. Remembering that the Greek word *dikaiosynē* can be translated either "righteousness" or "justice," I suggest that people who hunger for righteousness may also be described as people who are "starved for justice."

In the first four beatitudes, Jesus describes the great reversal that the advent of God's reign will bring. He is not (yet) stipulating rewards for the righteous but articulating how God's rule will remedy unfortunate conditions. The point is not that people should be poor in spirit, mournful, meek, or hungry for righteousness; the point is that no one should ever be any of those things: when God's rule is established, no one ever will be so again. Almost as an aside, we can see the first four Matthean beatitudes as basically consistent in meaning (despite distinctive wording) with the Lukan Beatitudes, which explicitly promise reversals for the unfortunate rather than rewards for the virtuous (cf. Luke 6:20–22).

5:7–10. Rewards for the Righteous (only in Matthew)

The second stanza of Matthew's Beatitudes does promise rewards for people who are godly in their attitude and conduct, exhibiting mercy and integrity, actively working for peace, and displaying a willingness to suffer so that God's will might be done. Since these four beatitudes cannot reasonably be read as promises of reversal, some scholars think a more traditional interpretation of 5:3–6 than that described above has the advantage of exhibiting internal consistency within the Matthean poem, which has usually been read as offering eight blessings for eight virtues. But the alternative view that I am proposing provides consistency of a different sort: the virtues praised in 5:7–10 are specifically ones enacted on behalf of the unfortunate persons described in 5:3–6; thus, the advent of God's rule will be a blessing both to those who are suffering and to those who join God in alleviating such suffering. In either case, Jesus promises that the rule of God will come and that the things for which the faithful strive (peace, righteousness, mercy) will be realized: the coming of God's rule will itself provide the ultimate blessing for those who seek it.

The *merciful* (5:7; cf. Heb 2:17) are those who exhibit the divine quality of mercy. According to Matthew's Gospel, mercy is one of the weightier matters of the law; like *justice* and *faith,* it is something that one *does* (23:23). God desires mercy over sacrifice (9:13; 12:7; both times quoting Hos 6:6), and Jesus is often portrayed as responding to those who ask him to have mercy on them (9:27; 15:22; 17:15; 20:30–31). In part, being merciful means refraining from judgment (the context for both 9:13 and 12:7), such that the fifth beatitude states positively what Matthew 7:1 states negatively. It may also mean showing compassion and offering forgiveness: Jesus tells a parable in which an unforgiving person is described as failing to "show mercy" (18:23–34, esp. 33). Elsewhere in Matthew, however, a cognate for the word "mercy" (*eleos*) is used to describe the practice of giving alms to the poor (*eleēmosynē*, 6:2, 3, 4). In a literal sense, then, being "merciful" often means "giving money to the poor." Indeed, the person in the parable just mentioned fails to show mercy not by refusing to forgive another man's sins but by refusing to forgive his monetary debt. Also, several times in Matthew, "to show mercy" means to heal those who are sick (9:27; 20:30, 31) or possessed by demons (15:22; 17:17). As such, acts of mercy represent instances in which the rule of God comes upon people and the house of Satan is plundered (12:28–29). In a basic sense, then, the merciful (5:7) are healers, people who seek to put right what has gone wrong. They favor the removal of everything that prevents life from being as God intends: poverty, ostracism, hunger, disease, demons, debt.

The *pure in heart* (5:8) are those who practice their faith with authenticity and integrity. In Matthew (and elsewhere in the Bible) the heart (*kardia*) represents the true self, what one really is apart from pretense. To "understand with the heart" (13:15) is to understand truly; to "forgive from the heart" (18:35) is to forgive truly; and so on. Matthew does not think that any human being will be completely pure in the eyes of God or others, but those whom Jesus calls blessed do not make a show of purity (cf. 6:1–18), like those he will later liken to "whitewashed tombs" (23:27). For Matthew, hypocrisy is the chief bane of religion (7:5; 15:7; 22:18; 23:13–29; 24:51): hypocrites may worship

God with their lips while their hearts are far from God (15:8). So, in a fundamental sense, the pure in heart are simply not hypocrites: they store up treasure in heaven so their hearts may be there also (6:21), they bear fruit because their hearts provide good soil for the message about God's reign (13:23, cf. 13:19), and they love the Lord God with all their hearts and their neighbors as themselves (22:37–39). Further, to be pure in heart probably implies a singular focus: since no one can serve two masters (6:24), the pure in heart strive to live in the rule of God (6:33) with unalloyed devotion. But, again, the main point is authenticity: they are who they present themselves to be.

The *peacemakers* in 5:9 have often been identified with people who work for reconciliation either within the community of faith (5:23–24; 18:15) or in the world at large. Examples of the latter include those who come to terms quickly with their accusers (5:25) and those who love their enemies (5:44). The latter application is especially appealing because Jesus describes those who love their enemies as "children of your Father in heaven" (5:45), a phrase that parallels the apodosis of this beatitude. This is basically sound, but any interpretation that equates peacemaking with reconciliation must take into account Jesus' claim that he did not come to bring peace in that sense of the word (10:34); indeed, association with him may create divisions and evoke hostility (10:35–36; cf. 5:11–12; 10:21–22). We must seek a fuller meaning that views reconciliation as a good thing but not necessarily as an end in itself. The Greek word *eirēnopoioi* ("peacemakers" in 5:9) is not used elsewhere in the New Testament, but it does occur in Greco-Roman literature, where it applies to rulers who establish security and socioeconomic welfare. We may assume that this sense of the term would be intensified in a Semitic document such as Matthew's Gospel due to the influence of the Hebrew term *shalom*, which is typically translated as peace (*eirēnē*) in the Septuagint. As is well-known, *shalom* in the Old Testament is a parallel term for *mishpat* (justice): thus peace is not seen merely as an absence of conflict but more broadly as an absence of the inequities that make for conflict. The peacemakers whom Jesus blesses in 5:9 are actively working to make the world the safe, equitable, just, and wholesome place that God wants it to be.

The virtue commended in the eighth beatitude (5:10) is not persecution itself but the degree of investment that may be assumed for those so committed to God's cause that they are willing to suffer for it. Such people may be contrasted with those who receive the good news about God's reign with joy but quickly fall away when tribulation arises on account of this word (13:20–21). This eighth beatitude serves as a fitting conclusion to the second stanza of four and summarizes the basic thought of that unit. Those who show mercy and those who work to establish God's *shalom* are examples of people committed to *dikaiosynē* (righteousness/justice); if these people are pure in heart, they will not falter in the face of persecution.

5:3–10 as a Unit

As background for both stanzas of the Beatitudes (5:3–6, 7–10), we recall Jesus' announcing that God's rule has come near (4:17) and should recognize that this announcement will be identified throughout Matthew's Gospel as "good news" (4:23; 9:35; 10:7; 24:14). Now, at the beginning of his inaugural address, Jesus clarifies for whom the advent of God's reign is good news. He declares that it is good news for two groups of people: (1) those who lack resources, privilege, and power; and (2) those who are willing to give up their resources, privilege, and power for the sake of those who lack these things. In other words, he declares in his first four beatitudes that it is God's plan and desire to aid the dispossessed and disadvantaged people of the world: therefore the advent of God's rule is a blessing for such people. Then in the second four beatitudes, he declares that it is God's plan and desire to aid the disadvantaged *through* virtuous people who allow God to use them in this manner; therefore the advent of God's rule is also a blessing for these people, who will serve as agents in the accomplishment of God's mission.

5:11–12. One for the Disciples (cf. Luke 6:22–23)

Jesus appends to the Beatitudes a final (ninth) blessing in the second person, addressed directly to the disciples themselves. In this way, he offers a strong word of warning: any who join God in working for justice and righteousness will themselves become oppressed and persecuted. Still, it is to these that the establishment of God's rule will be a blessing.

Jesus has spoken the preceding eight beatitudes to disciples who presumably would not identify themselves as being among those described in the first stanza but who might view themselves as potential candidates for inclusion with those described in the second stanza. Now Jesus lets them know that those who seek to be among the second group (those who aid the oppressed) will ultimately find themselves among the first group as well (the oppressed themselves). But this is cause for rejoicing: those who suffer because of their voluntary solidarity with the oppressed share in the legacy of God's prophets and will have great rewards in heaven. This all comports with what Jesus says elsewhere in Matthew, that when God's will is done, "the first will be last, and the last will be first" (19:30; 20:16).

In a literary sense, Matthew 5:11–12 should be read not only as Jesus' words to his disciples but also as a direct address to the readers of Matthew's Gospel. The blessing and the warning are for "you." It is "you" who will exhibit qualities associated with both groups described in the Beatitudes poem. Even if "you" are not a person who suffers misery like those described in 5:3–6, "you" might end up like them when you are reviled, despised, and persecuted for becoming like the people described in 5:7–10. The promise/warning/blessing is simple: if "you" take the side of the disadvantaged, you will become one of them: the world does not discriminate between the oppressed and their advocates but curses both alike. Still, "you" are fortunate because God also does not discriminate between the oppressed and their advocates but blesses both alike: both come under the rule of heaven.

MATTHEW 5:13–16
Salt and Light

The main thrust of this text, designating disciples as "salt of the earth" and "light of the world," is unique to Matthew, but the follow-up points, on the ineffectuality of flavorless salt or a hidden light, derive from the Gospel of Mark (4:21; 9:50; cf. Luke 8:16; 11:33; 14:34–35).

Jesus uses two metaphors to describe the relationship his disciples are to bear to the world: they are to be its salt and its light. The precise meaning intended by the former symbol is hard to identify since salt was used for a variety of purposes: as seasoning, as a preservative, and in religious ceremonies involving sacrifices or covenants. What is certain is that Jesus' followers are not to withdraw from the world that persecutes them (5:11–12) but are to engage that world in ways that have a beneficial effect upon it. They are to do this through the performance of good works (5:16), which in context must be assumed to include acts of mercy and peacemaking performed from a pure heart and for the sake of righteousness (5:7–10).

Here Matthew's Gospel exhibits an unusually high evaluation of Christian potential. In designating Jesus' followers as the "light of the world," Matthew applies to Christians an acclamation usually reserved for God (Ps 27:1), for some special agent of God (Isa 9:2; 49:6), or for Jesus himself (Matt 4:12–16; John 8:12). There is, however, precedent for Israel being called a light to the nations (Isa 60:1–3); that could be especially relevant here since the pronoun "you" in Matthew 5:13–14 is plural. In Philippians 2:15, the apostle Paul indicates that individual believers may "shine like stars" in a dark world; but for Matthew, it is the community that serves as light for the world (or as salt for the earth). This is all in keeping with Matthew's view that the community of Jesus' followers embodies the presence of Jesus and of God in the world (10:40) and that this community becomes a primary agent for the mission of God (see Themes 1 "*The abiding presence of God*" and 3 "*The mission of God*" in the introduction, pp. 7, 10).

Both metaphors are offered with tacit recognition that the "high potential" may not always be fulfilled. If salt were not salty, it would be useless, as would be a lamp if it were put under a bushel basket. Such scenarios are ridiculous (the first impossible, the second improbable) but work to score the point in a humorous way. A church that did no good works to benefit the world around it would be like salt that had no flavor or a lamp that gave no light.

MATTHEW 5:17–20
The Greater Righteousness

The text is almost unique to Matthew, representing an expansion of a single Q saying also preserved in Luke 16:17.

Jesus declares that he has come to fulfill the Law and the Prophets, which will remain valid until heaven and earth pass away (though his own words will remain even longer than that; see 24:35). This is the first of four explicit "statements of purpose" in Matthew, passages in which Jesus states what he has come to do (see also 9:13; 10:34; 20:28). "The Law and the Prophets" could simply mean "the Scriptures": the whole of Matthew's Gospel presents Jesus as one who does indeed fulfill the Scriptures, often because details from his life match quotations from these revered writings (see Theme 6 "*Fulfillment of prophecy*" in the introduction, p. 14). But Matthew's main interest here seems to be with how Jesus fulfills the *law.* He could be said to do this by living in a way perfectly consistent with the will of God (cf. Gal 6:2: to "fulfill the law of Christ" means to live the way Christ wants people to live). In context, however, the point seems to be that he fulfills ethical mandates of the law by authoritatively interpreting them through his own teaching. It is the latter sense that will be most significant for what follows: in Matthew 5:21–48, especially, Jesus will fulfill the law by explaining what obedience to the law really means.

Jesus' endorsement of the entire law (see Theme 7 "*Continuing validity of Jewish law*" in the introduction, p. 15) has been considered problematic because it seems to contradict the more dismissive or relaxed attitude toward portions of Jewish law that would become typical of Christianity, an attitude that seems to find support elsewhere in the New Testament canon (e.g., Mark 7:20; Rom 10:4). Did the Matthean community continue to practice circumcision, observe strict Sabbath regulations (24:20), and adhere to various dietary requirements? Possibly; but the main point would be that Matthew's community accepts every detail of the law itself as valid while also allowing for a fairly generous program of "binding and loosing" the law (see Matt 16:19; 18:18; and Theme 8 "*Binding-and-loosing commandments*" in the introduction, p. 16). All Jewish parties known to us (Pharisees, Sadducees, Essenes, as well as the Messianists, or Christians) recognized that all of Torah was valid: disputes between such groups concerned when and how the Torah commandments should be applied. All the groups recognized that sometimes, in some cases, some of the commandments were not applicable. When they disagreed, the group with the stricter interpretation would accuse the others of "abolishing" the law. Jesus basically accuses the Pharisees of doing this in 15:3–6 (see comments on that passage). Thus we may surmise from Matthew 5:17 that someone has accused Jesus or, more likely, the Matthean community of abolishing the law by interpreting it in ways that allow for practices other groups thought were implicitly forbidden. We don't know which practices prompted such allegations, but the Gospel does reveal a relatively lax position regarding fasting (9:14–15) and labor on the Sabbath (12:1–13). So, Jesus responds in the classic manner, claiming that his supposedly lax interpretations of Scripture actually discern God's will in a manner that allows Torah to be fulfilled; that done, he moves rather quickly into demonstrations of how, most of the time, his interpretations are not lax at all (5:21–48).

First, however, he comments on two rival groups (5:19–20): (1) those who seek to live in accord with Torah but misinterpret it such that they do not actually live the way God wants: these will be called least in the rule of heaven (5:19); and (2) those who merely put on a hypocritical pretense of righteousness without any sincere effort at living the way God wants: these will never enter the rule of heaven (5:20).

We will say more about each of these. The people referred to in 5:19 are probably rival Christian communities: churches associated with the apostle Paul seem likely candidates. Matthew knows that many sincere followers of Jesus have loosed commandments of Scripture in ways that his church probably finds appalling. They have decided that many, if not most, "Jewish laws" no longer apply to gentiles who have been baptized into Christ, or even to Jews who are now "in Christ" and relate to God through grace apart from the law. Matthew thinks these Christians are wrong and that they will be embarrassed and ashamed when they get to heaven and find out this was the case. They will be called "least" in sharp antithesis to the more faithful followers of Jesus (= members of Matthew's church), who "will be called great" in the rule of heaven. Such a construal may strike us as chauvinistic but will probably not seem unfamiliar. For almost two millennia, Christians have disagreed as to how Scripture should be properly interpreted to reveal the will of God; all sides usually assume that they are right and that the correctness of their thinking will be vindicated in heaven. What is highly significant, however, is the Matthean Jesus granting that those who fail to meet his best expectations will still have a place in the rule of heaven: chagrined citizens of paradise are yet in paradise. And this Gospel will eventually reveal that people can be called "great" or "least" in the rule of heaven for reasons that have nothing to do with their perceptive interpretive skills (18:1–4; 20:26; 23:11). In any case, the homiletical potential here lies in recognizing that judgment on such matters is deferred (we cannot know *now* who is right and who is wrong about disputed matters) and that when the right answers are finally revealed this will happen within a context of ultimate inclusion.

[As a personal aside, I adopted the habit some years ago of looking in the mirror each morning and saying, "I am almost certainly wrong about some of the things that I believe." This is supposed to keep me humble. When it doesn't, I tell myself that, assuming I am right about everything, I will have so much time in heaven to tell people who disagreed with me, "I told you so," that I don't have to invest any of my time on earth in doing that now.]

Moving on, 5:20 indicates that a minimal level of righteousness must be met. This point is often missed because readers assume that the scribes and the Pharisees, despite their opposition to Jesus, were devout religious people whose behavior was exemplary for their day. To say that someone's righteousness must exceed that of the scribes and Pharisees would be like saying that someone must be "holier than the pope." But that does not work for Matthew's Gospel. To understand 5:20 (and many other passages), we should not identify the "scribes and Pharisees" in Matthew's Gospel with the historical persons who confronted Jesus in Galilee or even with their counterparts who may have been opponents of the Christian community in Matthew's own day. In either of the latter cases, those persons probably would have been exemplary in many behavioral matters important to Jesus and to Matthew. But the scribes and Pharisees who serve as *characters in Matthew's story* are an irredeemably evil brood of vipers (Matt 12:34; 23:33; cf. 9:4; 16:4) and implacable opponents of God (Matt 23:34–36; see Theme 14 "*Religious leaders as enemies of God*" in the introduction, p. 25). These scribes and Pharisees (as characters in Matthew's story) have no interest in true righteousness or the will of God: they desire only a facade that glorifies themselves and helps them maintain coercive power over others. As such, they practice selective adherence to highly visible but relatively insignificant matters while ignoring anything that really counts: justice, mercy, or faith (23:23). We may (I think we should) object to Matthew's selecting an actual historical group of people to personify "false religion" in his narrative; but once we realize that this is what he is doing, we can read the story as a literary reflection on "false religion" (of any type) rather than as an historical exposé of a particular group's views or practices.

Thus, Jesus does not indicate in Matthew 5:20 that a high standard of righteousness is required for admission to the rule of heaven; he only indicates that *something* is necessary (something beyond the nil level of righteousness associated with the evil scribes and Pharisees). Much of what follows in the Sermon on the Mount (esp. 5:21–48) indicates that Jesus does harbor unusually high expectations for his followers, but we should probably not assume that failure to meet those expectations implies exclusion from God's rule in any absolute or ultimate sense. Those who fail to act on his words may experience disaster in this life (7:24–27) and/or be regarded as "least" among those granted participation in the life to come (5:19), but this Gospel's strong emphasis on mercy and forgiveness suggests that those who exhibit only a little righteousness (like those who have only a little faith) will ultimately be reckoned among those whom Jesus saves from their sins (see 1:21). Further, the strong antipathy to hypocrisy in this Gospel leads me to believe that, for the Matthean Jesus, sincere effort may be what counts most (see 6:33).

MATTHEW 5:21–48
The Antitheses

As a unit, the text is unique to Matthew, though parallels exist for many of the individual verses. Here, we observe the evangelist's redactional skills at their best: texts drawn from diverse contexts in both Mark and Q are now woven together within a framework that lends coherence and thematic unity.

Jesus illustrates what he means by his summons to a greater righteousness (Matt 5:17–20) with six concrete examples of the moral behavior expected of his followers. These examples are traditionally called "antitheses" because in each case the expectation of Jesus contrasts with a more moderate or contradictory expectation indicative of what conventional wisdom may regard as scriptural teaching. In some instances, Jesus introduces his teaching with an actual quote from Scripture that he thinks is sometimes interpreted or applied in ways deserving of comment (e.g., 5:38); in other instances, he introduces his teaching with a paraphrase of an idea probably regarded by many as scriptural even though it is not found in Scripture as such (e.g., 5:43). In either case, Jesus' operating principle is that the goal of moral instruction should be nothing less than perfection: his followers should strive for the sort of righteousness exhibited by God (5:48).

Within the context of Matthew's Gospel, the antitheses may be best understood as examples of "binding and loosing," the principles for moral discernment that Jesus authorizes the church to practice during the era between his resurrection and parousia (Matt 16:19; 18:18; on this principle, see Theme 8 "*Binding-and-loosing commandments*" in the introduction, p. 16). Understood in this light, each of the antitheses reflects Jesus' authoritative decision regarding a quasi-rabbinic debate over application of Torah. In every instance, the starting point is Scripture, which prohibits three things (killing, adultery, oath-breaking), allows two things (divorce with proper documentation, appropriate retaliation), and requires one thing (love for neighbors).

In the first grouping, debates would concentrate on whether the prohibitions should be viewed as applicable to matters not specifically or literally referenced (murderous thoughts, adulterous fantasies, oaths not kept due to factors beyond one's control). Some might have argued that the law should be "loosed" or deemed inapplicable in such instances, but Jesus repeatedly insists that the law must be "bound" and given a broad sphere of application. Thus many things not specifically prohibited by Torah should by implication be recognized as contrary to the will of God.

A similar, reverse logic applies to the last category, matters that Torah requires. We have here but one example, the grandest of all: love for neighbor. Since it was generally assumed that Moses intended *neighbor* to mean "fellow Israelite," ethical debate could and did engage the question of whether the requirement should be given a broader sphere of application. Some might have argued that the commandment should be "bound" as applicable to "resident aliens" (see Lev 19:34) or righteous gentiles. Jesus is remarkable (though not unique) in binding the requirement as applicable to all human beings, including enemies.

A middle category concerns matters for which Torah offers neither a requirement nor a prohibition, but rather sets stipulations to govern "allowable conduct." Some might argue that one can with good conscience do anything that Scripture says is permitted, but Jesus vehemently disagrees, proposing a seemingly obvious yet revolutionary principle of ethics: biblical laws sometimes serve not to ensure that God's will is done but rather to preserve a reasonable degree of order in a world where God's will is often *not* done. Thus, what the Bible allows (but does not require) is not necessarily what God wants. Discerning what is most pleasing to God depends on spiritual and theological insight that transcends mere citation of Scripture passages.

The main value of the antitheses for the Matthean community, and their ultimate value for Christian communities today, lies in their examples of how Scripture must be interpreted (bound and loosed) to determine what is most pleasing to God. For Matthew's readers, the broad questions would be "Who has the authority to make such determinations?" and "On what basis are such determinations made?" As for the first question, Matthew wants to establish that Jesus has this authority as the Messiah and Son of God (thus "But I say to you . . ." is an authoritative proclamation, not just an expression of one person's opinion). Likewise, we eventually discover that the community in which Jesus continues to abide as a living presence has this authority (16:19; 18:18). As for the second question, the basis for determining what is most pleasing to God, that is more complex; but in the first, fifth, and sixth of the antitheses, the governing principle appears to be the primacy of the love commandment (22:37–40; cf. 7:12). A case might be made that this is true in the other instances as well.

5:21–26. Concerning Anger (cf. Luke 12:57–59)

Jesus expands upon the biblical commandment prohibiting murder (Exod 20:13; Deut 5:17) to indicate that harboring vicious thoughts against another person also violates the will of God. Though the commandment deals explicitly with only the most extreme case of a person doing harm to another, the logical implication is that God does not want people to harm each other in lesser ways either, or even in nonphysical ways. But the suggestion that anyone who gets angry with their (metaphorical) sibling or who calls such a person a fool will go to hell is obvious hyperbole: there would be little point in the Matthean Jesus insisting that his followers forgive each other repeatedly (18:21–22) unless he assumed they would sometimes abuse each other in ways necessitating such forgiveness.

Jesus uses the term *adelphos* (NRSVue, "brother or sister") four times in this passage, implying that the main concern is for community relationships. Notably, Jesus has no scruples about calling scribes and Pharisees "fools" (23:17) or venting anger toward them (23:13–36). Apparently Matthew's readers are expected to recognize that there are servants of evil in the world against whom angry reproach (though not violence) is justified. Still, Jesus' followers are not to insult *each other*, and reconciliation must be a first priority in the family of God's people, or else the worshiping community will be no different from the world at large, where festering pride and resentment lead people to drag each other into court and throw each other into prison. In that regard, the dictum to postpone sacrificial offerings in order to seek reconciliation with a sibling first (5:23–24) is especially striking but consistent with Jesus' citation of Hosea 6:6 in two later passages (9:13; 12:7) and with his characteristic tendency to subordinate ritual obligations to ethical ones (e.g., 15:16–20). More to the point, the call to seek reconciliation with one who justly or unjustly "has something against you" offers a practical strategy for avoiding anger and defusing conflict within the community of faith.

5:27–30. Concerning Adultery (5:27–28 only in Matthew, but cf. 5:29–30 with Mark 9:43–47)

Jesus likewise expands upon the prohibition against adultery (Exod 20:14; Deut 5:18) by insisting that even lustful thoughts and glances are unacceptable. Biblical interpreters often say that in the ancient world, adultery was primarily a sin against a man (husband), whose property (wife) was being used by another man to whom she did not belong. According to that view, Jesus would be saying that it is wrong for a man to use another man's wife for sexual gratification even if he does so only in his private thoughts and fantasies. That would be true as far as it goes, but careful reading reveals no mention of a husband here: there is no indication that the woman who becomes an object of male lust is married. The point, then, is simply that when a man looks lustfully upon a woman to whom he is not married, he is guilty of sexual infidelity: he has sinned against God, against himself (see 1 Cor 6:18), against his wife (if he has one), and, of course, against the woman he objectifies. Imaginative appropriation of a woman for sexual gratification is sinful regardless of whether or not that woman is subject to some man who resents the appropriation. Further, Jesus' words, while androcentric in perspective, allow no hint of condemnation for the victim in the imagined scenario: when a man looks lustfully upon a woman, the problem is not that she is a seductress who has induced him to lust, but that he is a faithless adulterer, with a corrupted heart. Of course, we know that these gender identities can be reversed or combined in a variety of ways (both men and women lust after both men and women), but the distinction between violator and violated remains. So, while Jesus' words on this topic often sound prudish to the modern ear, they actually evince a perception two millennia ahead of its time. The increased concern we are witnessing for appropriate "sexual boundaries" in the workplace and other sectors of society resonates with a concern Jesus expressed a long time ago but that was not given much consideration until recently. Even today, there is little appreciation for the idea that "boundary violations" can involve inappropriate *thoughts* as well as words, looks, or deeds.

Jesus punctuates his remarks on avoidance of lust with extreme statements about plucking out one's eye or cutting off one's hand to ensure righteousness (cf. Mark 9:43–48; see Matt 18:6–9, where the same action is recommended, if necessary, to avoid causing children to stumble). Church history records occasional tendencies to take these words literally, for example, by cutting out the tongues of blasphemers or chopping off the hands of thieves; as for lust, it was soon surmised that neither eyes nor hands were the primary culprits, and Matthew 5:29–30 was then allowed to justify castration (voluntary or involuntary) as an aid to holiness. Modern exegetes recognize the sayings as classic instances of prophetic hyperbole, intended to emphasize the necessity of forestalling temptation and of dealing with potential problems before they become actual ones. The Matthean Jesus believes and teaches that a defiled heart is the actual source of sin (15:18–30), not the eye, hand, tongue, or any other body part that might be employed in commission of a sinful act.

5:31–32. Concerning Divorce (cf. 19:3–9; Mark 10:11–12; Luke 16:18)

Jesus goes on to liken divorce and remarriage to a form of legalized adultery. He seems to grant that Scripture allows for such a practice, but he wants to maintain a distinction between what is merely *allowed* and what is truly pleasing to God. Jesus does, however, recognize one exception to his ruling: remarriage is not to be considered adulterous when the divorce is enacted because of *porneia* (translated "sexual immorality" in the NRSVue). Just what is envisioned by this exception clause has been a matter of discussion: some interpreters think it applies to a marriage in which one of the partners has been unfaithful; others believe the reference is to a marriage that involves incestuous union or some other arrangement that may have been condemned within Jewish circles but practiced among gentiles. Although it is impossible to determine with any certainty which of these is envisioned, my guess is that the latter suggestion is more likely: the concern here is not to identify what is permissible but what God most desires, and it makes more sense to think that God might desire termination of an illegitimate marriage than to imagine that God would desire termination of a compromised one. On the question of divorce and remarriage, see further comments on Matthew 19:3–9, where the matter resurfaces and is treated in more detail.

5:33–37. Concerning Oaths (only in Matthew)

Jesus radicalizes the traditional view regarding the swearing of oaths (see also 23:16–22). Conventional wisdom teaches that one must always carry out a vow; Jesus insists that it is wrong to offer vows in the first place. His reason is that the ability to fulfill the vow may depend on factors beyond one's control (cf. Jas 5:12). People should not promise what they might not be able to deliver. Moses said as much: "If you refrain from vowing, you will not incur guilt" (Deut 23:22), but that advice had been largely ignored in Israelite religion, as have Jesus' words on the subject in most expressions of Christianity to the present day.

5:38–41. Concerning Retaliation (cf. Luke 6:29)

Jesus repudiates vengeance and insists on a practice of nonretaliation. He recognizes that Scripture does allow for limited vengeance: the point of Exodus 21:24–25 was to prevent excessive retaliation (see, e.g., Gen 4:23–24). But (as with divorce) Jesus says that his followers should forgo their right to claim what the Scriptures allow. The apostle Paul understood this teaching of Jesus to mean that those who repay "evil for evil" are effectively overcome by evil, while those who respond to evil by doing "what is noble in the sight of all" are able to "overcome evil with good" (Rom 12:17, 21). So, followers of Jesus should be known as those who turn the other cheek, surrender the shirt off their back, and go the second mile.

As those examples indicate, the presumed contexts for Jesus' sayings were situations involving obnoxious domineering behavior (bullying) and/or religious persecution, but not outright violence. The humiliation of being slapped on the cheek, the aggravation of being deprived of clothing in payment for a debt, the annoyance of being conscripted by a soldier or nobleman to carry something for a mile—all these situations exemplify gross injustice, but none imply immediate violence to which acquiescence could be damaging to one's life or physical well-being. That has not always been recognized with regard to 5:39 ("if anyone strikes you on the right cheek"). Scholars now suggest that this does not refer to receiving a beating but, more likely, to a symbolic action expressing rejection or extreme disdain. In Matthew's day, it could have been part of a ritual in which Christians were expelled from synagogues, disowned (and disinherited) by their families, or cast out of professional trade guilds. In Jesus' Galilean setting, such a slap might have functioned as an extreme insult: a Jewish person slapping the right cheek of another Jewish man was tantamount to "giving someone the finger" or spitting on someone (cf. Matt 26:67) in our modern culture. Of course, Jesus' teaching on this point may have implications that go beyond those immediate contexts, but neither Jesus nor Matthew would have understood the sayings in 5:39 as forbidding self-defense, or as prohibiting punishment of criminals, or as inhibiting the constraint of evil in society as a whole. Preachers should realize that, when these verses are read aloud in almost any congregation in America, persons may be present for whom the words summon direct and vivid memories. There may be people (especially women and children) who hear the words "if anyone strikes you" with a poignancy that the preacher can scarcely imagine. To imply, even by silence, that Jesus counsels passive acceptance of one's fate in such circumstances would be an obscene misinterpretation of Matthew's intent.

Of course, we should observe that Jesus' subsequent passion does depict *him* as practicing nonretaliation in circumstances involving extreme violence. He also indicates that those who follow him will need to "take up their cross" (16:24), implying submission to metaphorical if not literal crucifixion (10:17; 24:9). Nevertheless, one can accept that faithfulness might occasion suffering or even lead to martyrdom without reconciling oneself to a position that tolerates abuse as inevitable. Dr. Martin Luther King Jr. exemplified this distinction well (and his primary inspiration for doing so were the very words we are considering now).

Jesus provides no rationale for his radical ethic of nonretaliation, at least not in these verses. We should not assume that he imagines such behavior will bring about the conversion of an oppressor or that the primary objective is spiritual self-improvement of the oppressed (though either of these could be a welcome by-product). In recent years, it has become almost axiomatic for scholars to claim that Jesus is offering a subtle strategy for allowing the oppressed to get the better of their oppressors in terms of honor and shame. Turning the other cheek, stripping naked in court, exceeding the demands of forced labor: all such actions expose the outrageous cruelty of the dominant party, bringing shame upon the one who would otherwise be the "winner" in the transaction and bestowing honor on the ostensible "loser." There could be something to this—most modern scholars endorse such an interpretation—but I think we will ultimately miss the point if we think we should practice Jesus' ethic in order to humiliate others and bring honor to ourselves. A better rationale for nonretaliation can be found in Matthew 7:12, the Golden Rule: the will of God is fulfilled not when we treat people the way they treat us, but when we treat people the way we *want* them to treat us. Also, a simple rationale is provided in the final antithesis: we are kind and generous to those who mistreat us because we love them (5:44).

5:42. Indiscriminate Giving (cf. Luke 6:30)

In Matthew's Gospel, Jesus' call to nonretaliation is followed by a seemingly random affirmation that Jesus' followers should give to anyone who begs from them and loan to anyone who wishes to borrow. As an independent saying from Q, the comment seems a bit out of context here, though it fits with the general idea that the greater righteousness encouraged by Jesus means going beyond usual expectations of Torah obedience. And of course, it could be read as an example of practicing the Golden Rule, toward which all these instructions are moving (7:12). But is it another instance of hyperbole? Should we indiscriminately give to any and all beggars, or should we simply be alert at all times for ways of providing effective assistance and of minimizing factors that create destitution and debt? I know of no Christian leader or church body that would advise adopting Jesus' counsel as a literal practice, but I have known individual Christians who have done so and who, after a lifetime of such practice, have no regrets.

5:43–47. Love for Enemies (cf. Luke 6:27–28, 32–35)

In the final antithesis, Jesus expands Scripture's call to love one's neighbor into a general proclamation to love all people, even (or especially) one's enemies. This was not a wholly new concept: love for enemies is taught in numerous ancient documents, including the Old Testament (Exod 23:4–5; Prov 25:21–23). Still, Jesus assumes his audience has heard it said, "You shall love your neighbor and hate your enemy" (5:43). That must have been a popular dictum of the day, an aphorism of sufficient stature that many people (including Matthew? including Jesus?) may have assumed it was found in the Scriptures. Some biblical texts could be read in support of such a sentiment (Deut 23:3–6; Ps 139:21–22; Sir 12:4–9), and a passage from the contemporary Dead Sea Scrolls encouraged community members to "hate all the sons of darkness, each according to his guilt" (Rule of the Community 1:10; cf. 1:3–4; 9:16, 21–22).

Thus, Jesus may be seen here as favoring one strand of tradition over another and accentuating it to an unprecedented degree. But he definitely thinks that practicing what he calls love for enemies will mark his followers as abnormal and distinctive. Even pagans and the worst of sinners generally care for friends and allies: the mark of having a life ruled by God is treating enemies with the same consideration. As is usually the case in biblical literature, *love* may be defined here as "unselfish behavior" (cf. 1 Cor 13:4–7); it has nothing to do with emotion or feelings and everything to do with action and conduct. To love one's enemy is to treat them in ways that one hopes will be to their benefit. In this regard, we may recall the age-old pastoral advice to one who says, "I know I *should* love my enemy (or neighbor), but I don't! What should I do?" The counsel consists of one word: "Pretend!" That is, if you don't feel like you love your enemy (neighbor), just act as though you do: treat the person the way you would treat them if you did love them (and then, biblically speaking, you will be loving them in reality).

The theological rationale for adopting such behavior is striking: it is what God is like. God shows kindness to good and bad alike (5:45). The sun does not shine only for people who are friends of God; rain does not fall only on God's devotees. If Jesus' disciples want to be called children of the heavenly Father, they should recognize that they are pledging themselves to emulate a God who famously blesses the ungrateful and the selfish. The reason God's people should love their enemies and bless their persecutors is, simply, because God does this. Being "godly" means taking God as one's ultimate role model.

According to the Chronicler, Jehu once asked King Jehoshaphat, "Should you help the wicked and love those who hate the LORD?" (2 Chr 19:2). He apparently thought this was a rhetorical question, but Jesus would not have regarded it as such; he would have surprised the zealous crusader by responding, "Yes! You should!" Why? Because the Lord would do so and in fact does do so—all the time, every day.

5:48. Be Perfect (only in Matthew, but cf. Luke 6:36)

When all six antitheses are considered together, Matthew's reader is presented with a consistent portrayal of the attitude and behavior that Jesus expects of his followers. The greater righteousness of which he has spoken previously (Matt 5:20) goes beyond superficial obedience to legal requirements; his followers will conform themselves inwardly to the will of God and seek what is ideal rather than settling for what is acceptable. They will not simply ask about what is required or what is allowed but will always seek what would be most pleasing to God. The goal is to be perfect (5:48); we must reject interpretive suggestions that dilute this expectation by saying what Jesus *really* means is to be sincere or complete or authentic or something else that seems more attainable (but probably isn't). Likewise, we should not ignore the Matthean text in favor of the Lukan parallel (6:36, "Be merciful, just as your Father is merciful"), which likewise counsels something that may seem more attainable (but probably isn't). The question of whether perfection is attainable in this life is irrelevant. It remains the goal of every Christian life regardless. Those who are not perfect have not reached the goal and continue to strive for it.

Thus, from Matthew's perspective, perfection may be what is called "an asymptotic goal." The term *asymptotic* refers to something that an entity constantly approaches but never reaches. In mathematics, the set of numbers beginning with 8 and divided by 2 would be "8, 4, 2, 1, 1/2, 1/4, 1/8 . . . and so on ad infinitum." The fractions could be listed forever, and they would never reach zero, though they would always be progressing toward zero, not regressing in the opposite direction. So, Matthew envisions Christian discipleship (seeking the reign of God, 6:33) as a progression *toward* holiness and godliness, becoming as perfect as the heavenly Father is perfect. Such progression requires not only a commitment to live in accord with the will of God but (as the antitheses reveal) an ability to discern God's will by knowing what Scripture implies and being able to recognize contexts for its application.

MATTHEW 6:1–8, 16–18
Practicing Righteousness

This text is unique to Matthew, though the Lord's Prayer inserted in the middle of the material (6:9–13) comes from Q; we will comment on that significant text separately in the next section.

Jesus declares that his followers are not to practice their righteousness in ways that call attention to themselves. If they do so, he says, that attention itself constitutes all the reward they will ever receive, for such is the way of hypocrites (6:2, 5, 16). Hypocrisy is a key theme in Matthew (see 7:5; 15:7; 22:18; 23:13–29; 24:51). In this instance, at least, the term is used in its purest sense as a synonym for "pretense": a "hypocrite" was literally a play actor (as on stage), but by Jesus' day the term had come to be employed metaphorically for a person (not on stage) who pretended to be someone they were not.

Let us back up a moment to see the full context. Jesus has told his disciples that a higher standard of righteousness will henceforth be possible (and expected) for those who join him as agents in fulfilling God's mission (5:17–20). Then in "the antitheses" (5:21–48), he contrasted the new norm for righteousness with traditional, diluted understandings. Now he makes a further, essential point: *motive counts!* It is not enough to go through the motions, to do what appear to be godly things for selfish reasons, to perform good deeds that should glorify God (5:16) in order to bring glory or honor upon oneself.

Three spiritual disciplines or pious practices are mentioned. *Almsgiving* (Matt 6:2–4) involved charitable contributions above and beyond the stipulated tithes and offerings that everyone was expected to make. *Prayer* (6:5–15) included the recitation of certain memorized or liturgical prayers at key times of the day (according to some authorities, the Shema was to be said twice and the Tefilla three times), but Matthew's readers would also be expected to think of unstructured communication with God, conversing with the heavenly Father as with an earthly parent, and seeking good things that Parent may wish to bestow (Matt 7:7–11). *Fasting* (6:16–18) meant going without food or, at least, restricting one's diet in penitence for sin, in observance of a holy day, as an expression of mourning, or simply as a way of strengthening one's communion with God.

Jesus assumes that his followers will do all these things. Almsgiving is commanded in Torah as a regular duty for all Israelites (Deut 15:11), and Jesus has just indicated that his followers should always give to anyone who begs (Matt 5:42; cf. 19:21). Likewise, Jesus urges his disciples to pray (7:7–11; 21:22), and while his disciples can be accused of laxity with regard to fasting (9:14), he makes clear that this is only a temporary situation: fasting will remain a prominent part of Christian spirituality in the era of the church (9:15). So the practices themselves are noble: the point is simply that people ought to practice such disciplines in a manner that does not call attention to themselves (Matt 6:4, 6, 17). To make this memorable, Jesus offers some hyperbolic and/or amusing "bad examples" of what *not* to do: don't sound trumpets in the synagogue to make sure everyone sees you deposit an offering in the box (6:2); don't choose a public street corner as the site for your personal prayer time (6:5); don't disfigure yourself when fasting in order to exaggerate the effects of abstention and impress people with your asceticism and selflessness (6:16). Perhaps some people really did such things: in any case these hypocrites (real or imaginary) have now become cartoons, and there is a degree of ironic satisfaction in seeing acts of pomposity generate the exact opposite response than was intended (mockery, not esteem).

The ostensible advice Jesus offers for avoiding such hypocrisy is to practice spiritual and religious disciplines with absolute secrecy. This could be mildly hyperbolic as well: "Do not let your left hand know what your right hand is doing" (6:3) essentially means, "Keep such matters a secret—even from yourself!" Still, common sense and Christian practice reveal that a concern for secrecy can be overstated. There is value, for instance, in Christians being examples or role models for one another: we benefit from knowing about the spiritual disciplines that others find meaningful, and we can be encouraged by the enthusiasm or level of commitment with which they embrace such practices. Stewardship leaders maintain that specific examples of generous giving can inspire others to be faithful in their contributions. Elsewhere in Scripture, Jesus publicizes the extravagant generosity of a widow (Mark 12:41–44), and the apostle Paul openly tells the Corinthians about the generosity exhibited by the Macedonian churches (2 Cor 8:1–6)—though neither the widow nor the Macedonians sought such recognition: they had not given money *in order to* obtain affirmation and praise.

In any case, our modern world is different from the religious society of Jesus: public displays of piety cannot be automatically dismissed as instances of someone seeking glorification. We should not assume that the couple who says grace before eating in a restaurant or the student who goes to class on Ash Wednesday with a dirty cross on her forehead is parading their religion in order to receive accolades; indeed, in our current society, they might be practicing their faith at risk of public scorn.

The point of Jesus' comments is not that religion should always be practiced in private and good deeds kept a secret, but that one should not practice religion or perform good deeds *in order to* attract positive attention to oneself. On this point, we should also note the apparent discrepancy between what Jesus says here about keeping acts of righteousness a secret and what he said a short time ago about not hiding one's light under a basket: "Let your light shine before others, so that they might see your good works!" (5:16). Wasn't that the exact opposite of what he is saying now? No, not quite. For one thing, all the second-person pronouns in 5:13–16 are plural while those in 6:1–8, 16–18 are singular. Thus, while individuals who act righteously should often remain anonymous (or at least wish to remain so) to avoid bringing glory to themselves, a community should want its good works to be public, since a good reputation for the people of God as a whole ultimately brings glory to the God who inspires them.

On the topic of prayer, Jesus also decries the pagan practice of babbling empty phrases under the misguided impression that one will be heard on account of speaking "many words" (6:7). This is not actually a condemnation of long prayers or of repetitive ones: Jesus himself can spend considerable time in prayer (14:23) and offer the same petition repeatedly (26:39–44). The point rather is to reject the concept of prayer as a strategy for manipulating God. Certain cults that were popular among gentiles attempted to control divinities by naming every power known to them and/or speaking every word or phrase associated with gaining influence in the spiritual realm. We have found liturgies that consist of long lists of gods, goddesses, angels, demons, or who knows what: the priest or congregation would rattle these off, not even knowing what they were saying or to whom they were praying, but believing that if they uttered the right magic word or name, the power in question would have to do their bidding (by the second century, the name of Jesus would be added to such liturgies). Matthew wants his increasingly gentile church to know that Jesus encouraged the Jewish concept of prayer, which begins with an assumption that God is already aware of (and always attentive to) our needs. The purpose of prayer is to commune with God and to be influenced by God, not to sway God to do whatever serves our interests (see comments on 7:7–11). As an illustration of such prayer, Jesus teaches his disciples the Lord's Prayer, on which we comment in a separate section below.

Three times Jesus declares that those who follow his counsel and practice righteousness appropriately will be rewarded by the heavenly Father (6:4, 6, 18). This theme of heavenly reward is present elsewhere in Matthew (10:41–42; 19:27–29) and is generally more prominent in this Gospel than in the others. The nature of the reward is not specified: it may be eschatological (e.g., elevation of one's status in the rule of heaven; see 5:19) or temporal, spiritual, or material. It may be nothing more nor less than hearing the words "Well done!" from the master one lives to please (25:21, 23). In any case, the promise of reward in one sense or another is extremely biblical; we should not shy away from proclaiming that promise simply because it can be abused. Of course, some preachers have tried to turn the promise into a crass investment strategy, insisting that Christians who give generously (especially of their money) will be enriched by God and enjoy almost immediate material prosperity. But anyone with a modicum of common sense should be able to recognize that this does not pan out existentially, and anyone with a shred of biblical insight should realize that God does not want people to be motivated by lust for wealth and material things (Matt 6:24; 13:22; 1 Tim 6:9–10). Granted, there are sheep lacking such sense and insight, and shepherds must protect them from the wolves—a point Jesus will make directly (7:15). But setting all that aside for a moment, let us admit that God does promise rewards to those who are faithful (and, often, specifically promises rewards for those who are generous with their money or material possessions: Luke 6:38; 1 Cor 3:14; 2 Cor 9:6, 11). People who know this should not be faulted for hoping to receive what the Bible promises. Yet there can be something wonderfully ironic about such hope, as captured in these words of Jesus from another Gospel: "Expect . . . nothing in return, and your reward will be great" (Luke 6:35).

MATTHEW 6:9–15
The Lord's Prayer

Matthew derived this text from Q; it is paralleled in Luke 11:2–4.

The teaching on practice of piety in Matthew 6:5–18 is interrupted by Jesus' presentation of a model prayer in 6:9–13 and a brief comment inspired by that prayer in 6:14–15. The model prayer has come to be called "the Lord's Prayer" or "the Our Father"; slightly different versions are also preserved in Luke 11:2–4 and in the *Didache* (8.2). The prayer is exceptionally Jewish in form and content; in Matthew, Jesus presents it in explicit contrast to the type of prayers said by gentiles (Matt 6:7). This is recognized today by numerous Jewish leaders who say there is nothing in the content of "the Lord's Prayer" that would exclude its usage in modern synagogues (though its association with Christianity makes such usage unlikely). The first few lines of the prayer are similar to the opening of the Qaddish, an Aramaic prayer of mourning, the antiquity of which is uncertain though some version of it was probably used in Galilee at the time of Jesus: "May (God's) great name be magnified and sanctified in the world which (God) created according to (God's) will; may (God's) kingdom rule and redemption take seed."

This prayer is typically understood to consist of a salutation ("Our Father in heaven") followed by three petitions that explicitly ask for what God would want, then four more petitions that ask for what would be to our benefit. This is somewhat artificial; in reality, all seven petitions ask for what God would want, and all seven request God to do what would be to our benefit. Still, the sequence of the petitions is noteworthy: *your* name, *your* rule, *your* will; then, give *us*, forgive *us*, lead *us*, deliver *us*. The *your, your, your* comes before the *us, us, us, us* (with no mention of *me, me, me*).

6:9a. Our Father in Heaven (cf. Luke 11:2a)

The metaphorical identification of God as *Father* is typical for Matthew, occurring ten times in Matthew 6:1–18 alone (see also Matt 5:16, 45, 48; 6:26, 32; 7:11, 21; 10:32, 33; 12:50; 15:13; 16:17; 18:10, 14, 19, 35; 20:23; 23:9; 24:36; 25:34; 26:29, 42, 53; 28:19). For Matthew, this image presents God as both a caring parent and an authority figure, as the one whose unilateral decisions are to be respected by the whole family of believers (Matt 23:9). By encouraging his followers to call God "Father," Jesus urges them both to respect God's authority and to trust in God's generosity and providential wisdom. The word, of course, describes a role that need not be gender specific: women can be fathers in every sense except the procreative one, which is clearly not envisioned here. Since this has not been understood or proclaimed, many women and men have come to view "Father" language for God as reductive (attributing traditionally masculine attributes to God) or heretical (suggesting that God is male). Thus, recent decades have witnessed tendencies to avoid using the term altogether or to supplement it with metaphorical "Mother" language (which has some, albeit slight, biblical support; e.g., Deut 32:18; Isa 49:15; 66:13). Such tendencies, to my thinking, are helpful insofar as they move in the direction of expansive inclusivity, but they do not transcend the binary conception of gender that lies at the root of the problem. I hope for a day when all can pray to God as "Father" without assuming the name designates anything associated with any particular expression of gender.

6:9b–10. God's Name, Rule, and Will (cf. Luke 11:2b)

The prayers for God's name to be revered, for God's rule to come, and for God's will to be done are parallel petitions, stating the same basic request three times in slightly different words (only one of the three,

"Your [rule] come," is included in Luke). For Matthew, the essential request is for God to bring to fulfillment what has begun with Jesus. The rule of heaven has already come near (3:2; 4:17; 10:7), Jesus and his followers are bringing God's will to accomplishment (4:23–25; 10:8; 11:4–5), and God's name is being glorified on account of them (5:16; 9:8; 15:31). Jesus' followers are to pray for the mission of God begun in the ministry of Jesus to continue (see Theme 3 "*The mission of God*" in the introduction, p. 10).

All three of these petitions assume that God is the ultimate and final actor: God (not sinful human beings) is the one who will sanctify God's name, consummate God's rule, and accomplish God's will. One implication of this realization is that we are invited to pray every day for God to do what God has promised to do: we are invited, perhaps encouraged, to be a bit impatient with God (cf. Ps 13), to yearn for the culmination of what we are incapable of accomplishing. The entire Lord's Prayer is a model prayer for "the meantime," the difficult days of fasting and mourning that stretch between the first Easter and the parousia (9:15). During that period, we pray for God to feed us, forgive us, and protect us (6:11–13); but before we do any of that, we pray for the time to be shorter. So the first three petitions of the Lord's Prayer are essentially equivalent to another prayer of the early church: *Marana tha* (Aramaic, in 1 Cor 16:22, NRSVue), "Our Lord, come!" Jesus and Matthew (and Paul) wanted every Christian community and individual to be filled with this eschatological urgency, with a restless longing for God to put things right.

As such, the petitions also imply an eagerness to be vessels in which and through which God might act. As many pundits note, "It is better not to say 'God's church has a mission,' but rather 'God's mission has a church.'" So, God will do it all, but God might do some of it *through us*. Martin Luther expressed this well in famous quotes from his Small Catechism: "God's name is holy in itself, but we ask in this prayer that it may also become holy in and among us. . . . God's rule comes on its own without our prayer, but we ask in this prayer that it may also come to us. . . . God's good and gracious will comes about without our prayer, but we ask in this prayer that it may also come about in and among us."

Four more petitions make simple requests of God, ones that Jesus deems appropriate for people to make at any time.

6:11. Give Us Our Daily Bread (cf. Luke 11:3)

The request for "daily bread" flows from an assumption that all followers of Jesus embrace a simple lifestyle. We don't pray for a daily feast or banquet. Bread, of course, serves as a metaphor for life's necessities, but *basic* necessities are what Jesus has in mind. In 6:25–32, he will suggest that this means food and clothing. Paul seems to think that should be enough (1 Tim 6:8), but I might want to add a few more items: shelter, health care, sanitation, safety, clean air. In any case, in this prayer Jesus' followers ask that God provide them with what they need, no more, but also no less.

The word that is often translated "daily" (*epiousios*) is extremely rare: it appears nowhere in extant Greek literature except here and in parallel versions of the Lord's Prayer. As a result, no one knows what it means. For centuries, church leaders have realized with some embarrassment that Jesus told us to pray for something for which we are not quite able to pray. We are supposed to pray, "Give us today our [something] bread," and *daily* seems a good guess for filling in the blank. Others have suggested *epiousios* could mean "necessary," "nutritious," "sustaining," "for tomorrow," or something similar (Cyprian of Carthage anachronistically argued that it meant "eucharistic," such that Jesus was commending the daily mass; *On the Lord's Prayer* 18). But the bottom line is, nobody knows. This should serve as a (daily) reminder of our incomplete knowledge of biblical truth (cf. 1 Cor 13:12).

6:12, 14–15. Forgive Us Our Sins (cf. Luke 11:4)

The request for forgiveness of sins is traditional for Judaism, grounded in a conviction that the God of Israel is a forgiving God (Exod 34:7). Jesus attaches to the request a commitment to forgiving the sins of others: being forgiven and being forgiving are two sides of a coin; people cannot be one without also being the other. Although the Sermon on the Mount is replete with moral demands, the need to practice forgiveness is the only facet of Jesus' moral teaching deemed so important that his followers are to commit themselves to it every time they pray. To emphasize the point even further, Matthew quotes another saying of Jesus on this subject following the prayer (6:14–15). This saying seems to suggest that forgiveness is by nature reciprocal, such that it can only be received when it is practiced. But we ought not understand God's economy in simplistic terms of cause and effect. People do not earn God's forgiveness by forgiving others, nor is God's mercy doled out in terms proportionate to what we offer (as a parable in 18:23–35 will make clear). Rather, the entire Lord's Prayer is about communion with God, through which we participate proleptically in a transformed reality called "the rule of heaven." As God's name is revered, God's reign established, God's will accomplished, we discover a new identity as participants in mercy: forgiveness of sins is not only something that happens for us but also through us. All sin is against God, and all sin is forgiven by God. When we pray the Lord's Prayer, we recognize, first, that *our* sins have been forgiven; then, that people who we thought were sinning against us have also been forgiven: we acknowledge this in whatever ways are appropriate.

Actually, a similar postscript would fit the other petitions of the Lord's Prayer as well: Give us today our daily bread, as we give bread to those in need. Save us from the time of trial, as we save others from their times of trial. Deliver us from evil, as we deliver others from whatever evil assails them. Such addendums are implicit, insofar as the first three petitions ask for God's name to be revered as holy in and through us, for God's rule to come in and through us, and for God's will to be done in and through us.

But we cannot pass from this petition without noting with appreciation that the word the NRSV translated "sins" in 6:12 (*opheilēmata*) is more correctly rendered as "debts" in the NRSVue. Of course, the term is intended to have metaphorical meaning; in 6:14–15, the word "trespasses" (*paraptōma*) is used as a synonym, with obvious metaphorical sense. Still, literal financial debt was perhaps the single greatest social problem in the world of Matthew's first readers (and certainly in the world of the historical Jesus), so we should not suppose that the potential for metaphorical meaning eliminates immediate literal application. Notably, the parable Jesus tells in Matthew 18:23–35 uses remission of literal financial debt to illustrate the principle of living in a culture of forgiveness. Matthew's readers are probably expected to recognize the emerging rule of heaven as a reality that eschews all financial indebtedness; accordingly, they understand this line of the prayer as indicating that they should apply principles of remission they have already adopted in economics to broader, spiritual venues as well.

6:13. Protection from Trials and the Devil (cf. Luke 11:4)

The sixth petition is easily misunderstood when translated, "Lead us not into temptation," since neither Matthew nor Jesus would have wanted to imply the possibility that God might tempt people to sin (cf. Jas 1:13–14). Rather, the request is for God to guide Jesus' followers in such a way that they will not experience trials that could test their faith (cf. Matt 26:41). According to the parable of the Sower (Matt 13:2–9, 18–23), such trials might take the form of hardship ("trouble or persecution") or distraction ("the cares of this age and the lure of wealth"). Elsewhere, Matthew indicates that some trials are inevitable (18:7; 24:9–13), but we are nevertheless invited to pray this prayer, knowing that the request will not always be granted. Thus, this petition leads into a seventh, final one: "Rescue us from evil" (or, "the evil one"). Although this is missing from Luke's version of the prayer, it really gets at the heart of the matter. Jesus' followers are to ask that they be spared trials whenever possible and, when this is not possible, that they be protected from the potentially destructive consequences of such experiences (cf. Jas 1:2–4; 1 Pet 1:6–7).

A well-known conclusion to the Lord's Prayer ("For the kingdom and the power and the glory are yours forever. Amen") was not originally in the Bible. It was written by early Christians when the prayer came to be used in liturgical worship. Later, some copies of the New Testament began adding the conclusion to the text; as a result, it is found today in a few English translations (including KJV) and as a footnote in the NRSVue.

MATTHEW 6:19–34
Undivided Allegiance

This material derives from the Q source, though Matthew may be responsible for bringing the verses together in a manner that gives them thematic coherence (the parallel Lukan passages are found in disparate contexts).

The structure of the Sermon becomes somewhat looser after the segment on the practice of righteousness (6:1–18); still, many scholars detect seven distinct units of material in 6:19–7:11, which lead to a concluding affirmation that has come to be called the Golden Rule

(7:12). Here we will explore the first four units or groups of sayings, which all seem to address a theme of undivided allegiance to God.

6:19–21. Hearts and Treasures (cf. Luke 12:33–34)

By saying that his followers should store up "treasures in heaven," Jesus indicates that they are to value the things of God over the things of the earth. He will soon indicate, however (in 6:25–34), that birds, flowers, and other aspects of nature count as things of God (that is, as things cared for by God and valued by God), so the point cannot be simply to prioritize what is spiritual (heavenly) over what is physical (earthly)—or, at least, not to do so in a manner that despises the latter. More likely, "treasures on earth" should be identified with the "mammon" (*mamōna*) that Jesus identifies as an unworthy master in 6:24.

We will say more about that point momentarily; first, let us consider Jesus' affirmation "Where your treasure is, there your heart will be also" (6:21). This is one of the most important things Jesus ever says about spirituality, but the saying is often misread as though it states an opposite corollary (where your heart is, there your treasure will be). Then, Jesus is viewed as simply stating the obvious: people tend to invest their money or time or whatever in things they care about. Accordingly, stewardship sermons sometimes focus on how financial expenditures indicate where our true priorities lie: "Look over your check register at the end of the year: did you spend more on sporting events than you gave to the church? Then you must care more about entertainment than you do about God." There is much wrong with such proclamation, but for a start we should recognize that it is not what Jesus says. Jesus' point is not that where we put our treasure *reveals* what sort of people we *are*, but rather that where we put our treasure *determines* what sort of people we *become*. It is a promise, one that embodies what I call "the good news of biblical stewardship" (see Powell 2006b).

Simply put, Jesus says that what we do with our treasure (something we can control) affects the state of our heart (something we otherwise cannot control); this is phenomenally good news for anyone who wishes to grow spiritually. Perhaps we can read this as endorsement of what are sometimes called "spiritual disciplines"; Jesus is at least affirming the principle that sustains such disciplines.

When we invest our time, talents, or money in ways that are pleasing to God, our hearts are directed or redirected accordingly: we increasingly become people who *want* to please God (and who actually do so); we become more spiritually mature.

This is one reason why "it is more blessed to give than to receive" (Acts 20:35): generous giving can be a pathway to a deeper, more meaningful spiritual life. The church's traditional stewardship message is "Give from the heart!" That would be good advice if our hearts were pure. But what if they are not? What if we *wish* we were better people—more caring, more generous, more spiritual—but we have stingy hearts that care way too little for the things of God? Jesus would say, "Give according to where you wish your heart were—and your heart will catch up." Act as though you are the person you want to be, the person you think God wants you to be, and you may actually become that person. Perfection remains an asymptotic goal (see comments on 5:48), but growth is possible; there is something especially wonderful about realizing that one has changed not only outwardly but also within. Storing up treasure in heaven means using our resources (physical, mental, emotional, financial, and so forth) the way we believe God would want us to use them; the promise of Matthew 6:21 is that people who do this often become the sort of people they most want to be, people whose hearts are more easily and faithfully drawn to God. (For more on the topic of stewardship in Matthew, see Excursus: Stewardship and the Gospel of Matthew, p. 245.)

6:22–23. Lamp of the Body (cf. Luke 11:34–36)

The teaching on hearts and treasures is followed by an obscure group of sayings about a "healthy eye." In the biblical world, the eye was believed to function as a lamp, projecting light out from the body, rather than functioning as the receptor of light, as we know it to be today. A healthy eye could thus indicate whether the body was full of light or darkness—but Jesus clearly means this metaphorically: he is not commenting on the spiritual condition of people who are physically blind (or nearsighted). Some scholars think Jesus is alluding to superstitions regarding the "evil eye," but what sense that would give to the passage is unclear. The basic point may simply be that those whose allegiance to God is undivided have clarity of vision; those with divided loyalties have blurred vision. In context, the blurred vision of an unhealthy eye should probably be equated with storing up treasure on earth (6:19) or serving two masters, God and mammon (6:24).

6:24. Two Masters (cf. Luke 16:13)

This third comment on undivided allegiance is almost a parable: it would be easy to imagine a short narrative behind the moral that no enslaved person can serve two masters. Perhaps it was that once, and the Q source preserved only the punch line. In any case, the meaning of the saying is obvious, in keeping with what has just gone before. We should note, however, how Jesus assumes that "having *no* master" is not an option (cue the Bob Dylan song "You're Gonna Have to Serve Somebody"). Jesus and the Bible in general present "absolute freedom" in the sense of not needing to answer to anyone for anything (or of not needing to rely on anyone for anything) as illusory. Of course, people do not always realize this. Sheep do not necessarily want to have shepherds. But that is because they are sheep: they do not realize that green pastures and still waters sometimes need to be provided for them, and they may not give enough consideration to "the wolf factor." So, the point here is that given the inevitability of a master, people should identify who their master is—and then decide if that master is worthy or if, perhaps, they would benefit from switching allegiance to a different master. The story seems to assume that such changes are possible: unlike real enslaved people, metaphorical enslaved persons can reject metaphorical masters who are unworthy or cruel and be accepted into the servitude of a kind and gracious Lord. That, indeed, would pretty much define what Matthew's Gospel means by repentance: people are invited (urged) to repent when the possibility of being ruled by God becomes a viable option (3:2; 4:17); for that rule to be effective, they must give up being ruled by anyone or anything else.

Given all this, we must acknowledge that many modern readers have problems understanding our relationship with God in terms of master-and-slave imagery. Metaphors rarely work if one thinks about them too deeply (see comments on the "fishers of people" imagery in 4:19). In this case, the image is self-consciously flawed insofar as it assumes that enslaved people typically love their so-called masters and are devoted to them. So, let's not take the imagery too seriously or push the analogy too far. Matthew's readers are probably expected to evaluate this saying of Jesus with reference to the exodus tradition.

God brought the Israelites out of slavery, then took them to Sinai and announced, "I will be your God, and you shall be my people" (Lev 26:12; Jer 11:4; 30:22). This was not received as an onerous burden. No one (at that time) thought, "I knew there'd be a catch: God saved us, but now we have to be God's people!" No, being God's people was what redemption was all about: it wasn't payback for salvation; it *was* salvation. Likewise, the point in Matthew 6:24 is that we may take as our master the God who liberates. The parabolic language is meant ironically: we can be "enslaved" to the God who enslaves no one, belonging to the God who frees instead of belonging to something that subdues and shackles with illusions of liberty.

In any case, Jesus suggests that those who do not serve God will inevitably serve another master, often mammon (Greek, *mamōna*). The NRSVue's unfortunate translation of *mamōna* as "wealth" in 6:24 misrepresents materialism as a problem for rich people, even though in this passage Jesus is explicitly speaking to people who are inclined to worry about having food to eat and clothes to wear (6:25–32). The word *mamōna* was originally the name of a Syrian deity associated with profit and riches, but in broader contexts (as here) it simply came to mean "money and/or things that money can buy." People of diverse social classes must struggle not to prioritize acquisition of money and material things over serving God (though, of course, such wrong prioritization seems especially obnoxious when characteristic of those who have more than they need).

Hypothetically, Jesus might have made the point about two masters regarding any number of referents: "You cannot serve God and pleasure" or "God and politics" or "God and whatever." But he didn't. He said "mammon." Likewise, the apostle Paul could have identified many things as "a root of all kinds of evil" (1 Tim 6:10). He might have said "the love of status" or "the love of power," but he didn't. He said, "the love of money." This should tell us something about the single most prominent candidate for idolatry in biblical times and today (see Eph 5:5; Col 3:5). Money, according to Jesus, is something that should be *used* (Matt 25:14–30), not *served* or *loved.*

6:25–34. Learn from Birds and Lilies (cf. Luke 12:22–31)

Jesus launches into an extended address about anxiety. He warns that concern for such things as food and clothing may distract one from striving for what truly counts: God's rule and righteousness (6:33). According to Jesus, anxiety is a sign of "little faith" (Matt 6:30; cf. 8:26; 14:31; 16:8; 17:20) since God is generous and can be trusted to provide for those whose loyalties are undivided.

This section of Matthew offers the Gospel's finest example of teaching that is in line with Israel's wisdom tradition (Ecclesiastes, Proverbs). To put things simply, the *prophetic* tradition features declarations of divine truth that must be revealed to be apprehended: "the [rule] of heaven has come near" (4:17) is a good example; no one would ever have figured that out if a prophet had not been sent by God to reveal it. The *wisdom* tradition, by contrast, offers observations based on nature and the reality of the world: the sage is famous for common sense, pointing out what should be obvious (though it may have gone unnoticed). Jesus is typically associated with the prophetic tradition, but in the Sermon on the Mount and especially in Matthew 6:25–34, he appears to be more of a sage: if people just pay attention to the world around them (birds of the air, lilies of the field), they will recognize God's providence and be relieved of needless anxiety.

The passage would become one of the most popular texts in the Bible. Douglas Hare has asked why these verses have become so much better known than, say, Paul's advice in Philippians 4:6, which makes the same point in a more straightforward vein (Hare 1993, 73). Surely it is the poetic quality, which I think invites sentimentality. Consider the beloved poem of Elizabeth Cheney, "Overheard in an Orchard" (1859), which has been needlepointed and decoupaged on countless decorative items sold in religious bookstores:

> Said the robin to the sparrow,
> "I should really like to know,
> Why these anxious human beings
> Rush about and worry so!"
>
> Said the sparrow to the robin,
> "Friend, I think that it must be,
> That they have no Heavenly Father,
> Such as cares for you and me!"

Intellectuals and/or elitists might scoff at such "naive piety," but Jesus hardly avoided it: he affirms the underlying sentiment without embarrassment.

Still, we might wonder whether the counsel holds up existentially: many birds starve to death every winter, and many fields wither without having been beautified with flowers. Further, the notion that providence is offered to the idle, to those who "neither sow nor reap" (6:26), "neither toil nor spin" (6:28), seems to encourage a passivity that confuses faith with presumption. But it is the nature of Wisdom literature to offer general observations without the encumbrance of caveats and footnotes. Of course, sometimes some people probably should worry about what they will eat or wear. And even if creation is basically generous, this can be spoiled by human greed and injustice. Still, most of us, most of the time, enjoy the benefit of much that we did nothing to deserve. Generally speaking, the wiser course in life is to be thankful for what we have rather than anxious about we lack (or might lack). Embedded in the nature parable is a simple truism: you cannot "add a single hour to your span of life" (or possibly, a cubit to your height) by worrying about it (6:27).

Matthew 6:33 returns to the subject of priorities. Our primary concern should be the reign of God (NRSVue, "kingdom of God"): this does not mean that we should prioritize "going to heaven when we die" over this-worldly matters; it means that our first priority should be "living in the rule of God here and now" (see Theme 2 "*Reign or rule of God/heaven*" in the introduction, p. 8). If our number-one concern is doing God's will, allowing God to rule our lives, then many other things will fall in place (and our eternal destiny will be assured).

Matthew 6:34 sounds almost like Shakespeare in the KJV: "Sufficient unto the day is the evil thereof." Somehow, that seems more profound than "Today's trouble is enough for today." But the meaning is the same.

MATTHEW 7:1–11
On Judging, Waste, and Prayer

As with the previous material (6:19–34), these verses derive from the Q source, but Matthew may have brought them together from disparate contexts. The saying in 7:6 is unique to Matthew.

In the previous section we noted that Matthew presents seven distinct units of material in 6:19–7:11, leading to a concluding affirmation that has come to be called the Golden Rule (7:12). The first four units exhibit some coherence of theme (undivided allegiance to God); the next three units of material, discussed here, take up miscellaneous topics in what appears to be a random order.

7:1–5. On Judging (cf. Luke 6:37–38, 41–42; Rom 2:1)

Jesus warns his followers to leave eschatological judgment to God, refraining from speculation concerning the ultimate fate of any human being (cf. 13:27–30). Matthew makes clear elsewhere that he does not want these words of Jesus to discourage church members from holding each other accountable for their sins (Matt 18:15–18). He is commending compassion and empathy, not apathy or willful ignorance. Still, followers of Jesus are called to make self-improvement their first priority and to be merciful in their assessment of others. Jesus also indicates that people will end up being judged (by God or by other people) according to the standard they have applied when judging others ("measure for measure," the verse that gave one of Shakespeare's plays its name). But this should not be taken literally: Matthew did not believe in karma, nor did he want to suggest that human beings are role models for God, who voluntarily mimics their failings. As with 6:14–15, the saying is provocative in posing a "what-if" scenario: when tempted to judge others, Matthew's readers should ask themselves, "What if I were the one being judged?" The appeal is to the imagination, prompting potential judgers into applying the Golden Rule (7:12).

In any case, Matthew's readers should not let their concern for righteousness set them on a crusade to correct the faults of others while ignoring their own failings (7:3–4). The image of someone with a log stuck in their eye obsessing over the speck of sawdust in the eye of another is wildly hyperbolic and no doubt intended to be humorous. There is not a lot of obvious humor in the Bible, perhaps because what was once considered to be "funny" is not easily recognizable as such in a different culture and time. But this is one of the clearest instances we have of Jesus being a comedian, and it is enough to make us wonder whether some of his other hyperbolic sayings were intended as jokes as well (e.g., 5:29–30; 6:3; 17:20; 19:24; 23:24).

7:6. On Waste (only in Matthew)

The next set of sayings offers twin proverbs regarding waste. Just as one does not throw pearls into a pigpen or take sanctified food from an altar and toss it out in the street as scraps for dogs, so Jesus' followers ought not waste what God has given them. These proverbs could have numerous applications, and no specific reference point is provided within the Sermon itself. Later in Matthew's narrative, Jesus will urge his followers to show discernment in their proclamation of the good news: they should seek new audiences rather than wasting their efforts on the stubbornly unperceptive (10:5, 14, 23). This could be the sense in which Matthew wants the proverbs on waste in the Sermon on the Mount to be understood. Or they might be intended as further reflection on correcting the faults of others, to which he has just made reference: some people just are the way they are, and there is no point in wasting our breath in telling them their faults (over and over again).

7:7–11. Confidence in Prayer (cf. Luke 11:9–13)

A group of sayings urge Jesus' followers to be confident in prayer. Jesus encourages his followers to seek "good things" from God and to believe that God will grant their requests. Notably, the two examples he uses for God's gifts are bread and fish. Later in the Gospel story, Jesus will demonstrate quite literally how God provides these items (14:15–21; 15:32–39). Jesus says that prayer for such necessities is to be offered in the trust that God is like a parent who has both the means and the desire to provide for their children; this is consistent with the language of the model prayer he offered his disciples in 6:9–13. This teaching on "asking God for things" must be understood within a larger biblical context of prayer in general: the ultimate purpose of prayer is not to bend God's will to our design but to draw us closer to God until our will is bent to God's design. Note what we have observed on the chronology of the Lord's Prayer's petitions: the *your, your, your* comes before the *us, us, us* (without any *me, me, me*). That said, this passage does encourage us to ask for what we want.

Many books on prayer contain theologically sound suggestions on the appropriateness of prayer requests, so that we may ask for things that accord with God's will (1 John 5:14) rather than just seeking gratification of selfish pleasures (Jas 4:3). But here Jesus encourages us to approach God as a child approaches a parent, without being overly concerned with whether we are doing it right or asking correctly. Some people say, "Be careful what you pray for." I say, "Well, yes, but don't be *too* careful." We need not worry that God will punish us for praying wrongly. If your child asks you for bread, would you give him a rock to eat instead? Or if she asks you for a fish, would you give her a snake? Of course not. But I think that sometimes we are just dumb enough to ask for rocks and snakes—and then, God gives us bread and fish anyway.

MATTHEW 7:12
The Golden Rule

This single verse contains an ethical maxim that appears to be from the Q source (cf. Luke 6:31), but the claim that this maxim "is the Law and the Prophets" is unique to Matthew.

Jesus indicates that if people treat others the way they want to be treated themselves, their behavior will fulfill the Scriptures ("the Law and the Prophets") and thus be consistent with the will of God. Later, he will say the same thing about the two greatest commandments, the command to love God and to love one's neighbor as oneself (Matt 22:34–40). In some sense, then, people who love God may regard "treating others the way one wants to be treated" as a practical equivalent for loving one's neighbor as oneself. Such congruence is evident in the *Didache*, a first-century Christian writing that probably drew on Matthew's Gospel: "The way of life, then, is this: First, you shall love God who made you; second, love your neighbor as yourself, and do not do to another what you do not want done to you" (1.2).

This maxim has come to be called "the Golden Rule," a label that may derive from a 1750 sermon by John Wesley. Its basic sentiment can be found in many ancient writings (Homer, Herodotus, Seneca) and many religions (especially Confucianism). A negative formulation (similar to that in the *Didache*) is found in the book of Tobit, which was in wide use among Jews in the Second Temple period: "What you hate, do to no one" (4:15). What is almost unique and could be original with Jesus is the claim that keeping this Golden Rule is equivalent to doing the will of God. His words "For this is the Law and the Prophets" probably mean "For this fulfills the Law and the Prophets" (cf. 5:17–20). The sense, then, is that God really expects or demands nothing else—a proposition potentially controversial. The latter is clearly the idea in a version of the Golden Rule attributed to the Jewish teacher Hillel in the Babylonian Talmud, a sixth-century commentary on the Jewish Mishnah. According to that document, a lazy gentile approached Hillel and said he would convert to Judaism if the sage could teach him all that was required (in terms of moral conduct) while standing on one foot—that is, in a manner that would be quick and easy, not requiring years of study. Hillel did so, declaring, "Do not do to your fellow what you hate to have done to you. This is the entire Torah. The rest is explanation" (b. Shabbat 31a). Since Hillel taught in Jerusalem a few decades before Jesus, it is quite possible that Jesus (or Matthew) knew of Hillel's teaching and is simply endorsing what was already a prominent though contested notion. But since our record of Hillel's teaching dates from some centuries later, it is also possible that Jewish teachers liked this saying of Jesus and decided to ascribe it to a rabbi who had not become associated with a competing religion (no teachings of Jesus are found in the Mishnah, though many would be consistent with what is found there). As such, the question of originality is unresolvable; the more significant point would be that both Jews and Christians claim this is a matter on which Hillel and Jesus would have been in sync.

Pedantic ethicists have complained that the Golden Rule is egocentric, failing to discern that the wants and needs of the neighbor may be different from one's own. This notion is easily defeated: if I want you to respect my personal interests and treat me in accord with my particular needs and wants, then I should respect your personal interests and treat you in accord with your particular needs and wants. The essential point is simply that one should value other human beings, recognizing that they have worth equal to oneself. The rule proscribes naked self-interest, which takes no account of the interests of others; it prescribes a way of life that seeks what will be of most benefit to all.

In any case, the most notable feature of the Golden Rule in Matthew's Gospel is its treatment as a hermeneutical principle for determining right from wrong. To use Matthew's own language, the rule can function as a guideline for binding-and-loosing commandments, determining when, where, how, and to what extent biblical mandates apply to various situations (see Theme 8 "*Binding-and-loosing commandments*" in the introduction, p. 16). Matthew's story offers "bad examples" of how religious leaders get things wrong because they ignore this principle (12:1–8, 9–14; 15:3–6). Further, many of Jesus' unconventional legal interpretations can be justified in light of the principle (5:21–22, 38–47). Indeed, many of his sayings seem to assume it: you should forgive others their sins if you want to be forgiven your sins (6:14–15); you should not judge others if you do not want to be judged (7:1–2).

Nevertheless, the rule does not always indicate what is recommended, nor can it be trusted when applied in a naive or literalistic manner. Someone might reason, "If I were a criminal, I would not want people to report me to the police; therefore, I should not report criminals to the police." But this is hardly what Jesus or Matthew (or Hillel) intended. It may be better to say that the Golden Rule offers a hermeneutical *orientation* for doing ethics. It certainly does not substitute for ethical discussion and discernment but, in the words of Augustine, determines our *intention* for engaging in such discussion and discernment (*Sermon on the Mount* 2.22.75). Thus, the Golden Rule does not obviate or preclude the field of ethics; but within a Judeo-Christian culture (or a Confucian one), it may give rise to such a field or give it focus. Our goal is to behave in ways that benefit not merely ourselves but also others; given that, we still need to determine what kinds of behavior are most beneficial.

MATTHEW 7:13–27
The Two Ways

This material features passages from Q but adds a good bit that is unique to Matthew, including the image of wolves in sheep's clothing.

Jesus concludes the Sermon on the Mount by contrasting the way that leads to life with the way leading to destruction. The main content of the Sermon (instructions for living in accord with God's will, in a way that fulfills "the Law and the Prophets") came to a climactic end with the summary statement of 7:12. Now Jesus simply exhorts his followers to pay attention to his explanation of what faithfulness to God entails and to live accordingly. The Greek word *poieō* (do) occurs nine times in this short passage (translated "bear" or "bears" by the NRSVue in 7:17–19; "do" in 7:22; and "act" or "acts" in 7:24–26). The emphasis clearly is on *orthopraxis* (correct behavior), not on *orthodoxy* (correct thinking). The presumed context, furthermore, seems to be eschatological: "on that day" in 7:22 is a likely reference to the day of judgment, when Jesus returns. So, having explained in 5:17–7:12 what God wants of people now that the rule of heaven has come near (4:17), Jesus now proclaims that people will be held accountable for whether they live in accord with these instructions.

7:13–14. Two Ways (cf. Luke 13:23–24)

First, Jesus indicates that the way to life is like "a narrow way" or a rough road and that few find it. The imagery that Jesus uses here is conventional (Ps 1:6; Jer 21:8; Sir 21:10; 2 Esdras 7:1–19) and could be used in a secular sense to indicate that the most popular course of action is not always the wisest.

Matthew's original readers in a Roman city would certainly have been familiar with how this theme is treated in Greek mythology. First, there is the story of Heracles at a crossroads, which Xenophon recounts as a favorite parable of Socrates (Xenophon, *Memorabilia* 2.1.21–24). A young Heracles encounters the goddesses Arete (goodness) and Kakia (badness) at a juncture where he must choose which of two roads to travel. Kakia assures him that one road will lead him to a long and easy life, filled with pleasure but devoid of glory. Arete tells him the alternative will involve a lifelong struggle with evil and will lead to a life full of strife and hardship, but a life worthy of eternal renown. He chooses the latter (or else none of us would have ever heard of him). Likewise, in *The Iliad* (9.410–15), Homer recounts how the Nereid Thetis told her son, Achilles, that he could choose between two destinies: die young but with great glory, or live long but be forgotten when gone. Of course, he chooses glory. Scholars suspect one of these myths might have borrowed its theme from the other. And we might be excused for wondering if Matthew has not adapted a simple saying of Jesus (such as is found in Luke 13:24) in order to construct an updated Jewish reflection on one or both of the well-known tales.

In any case, the context in Matthew suggests that Jesus is applying the two-roads concept to ultimate participation in or exclusion from the rule of heaven (7:21): the "life" to which Jesus refers is probably the eternal life to be found in a blessed paradise after death, and the "destruction" to which he refers is eternal torment in hell (cf. 13:41–43; 25:34, 41, 46). Such theology may be out of vogue in some churches today, but we need not fudge exegesis to obtain a more palatable interpretation. We should accept as an almost indisputable fact that the historical Jesus and the author of Matthew's Gospel believed that hell was real and the great majority of people were going there (see Theme 17 "*Divine judgment and condemnation in Matthew*" in the introduction, p. 34). This does not prevent us from regarding apocalyptic elements of the biblical worldview as mythological so long as our Christology and hermeneutic of Scripture are mature enough to allow that the human Christ and the biblical authors made little distinction between myth and reality. And, of course, universalists can always appeal to Matthew 19:25–26; both the historical Jesus and the Matthean evangelist would have granted that God can defy their expectations regarding widespread damnation should God choose to do so.

That said, our focus should probably be on the affirmation that the narrow gate and the road that is hard lead to life. The Greek words here are somewhat distinctive. The term for "narrow" (*stenos*) is not only spatial but also has a general sense of "troubled" or "beset with difficulty," and the word for "hard" (*tethlimmenē*) usually means "oppressed" or "afflicted" (cf. 2 Thess 1:6–7). The positive point, then, is that eventual participation in a blessed life makes the enactment of self-discipline and the bearing of present hardship and persecution worthwhile (cf. Rom 8:18).

7:15–23. False Prophets (cf. Luke 6:43–44, 46; 13:25–27)

Having made this initial distinction of two ways, Jesus says more about those who will *not* enter the rule of heaven; he warns his followers that false prophets will come among them to lead people astray. Such persons "behave lawlessly" (7:23); they are people who ignore or violate Torah as explicated in the Sermon on the Mount; perhaps, given the immediate context, they are simply persons who do not keep the Golden Rule (7:12). Unfortunately, they are also like "wolves in sheep's clothing" (7:15), bearing a superficial resemblance to true followers of God. They may use Jesus' name, call him their Lord, and even work miracles or drive out evil spirits in spectacular ways (7:22; cf. 24:24). Still, if one knows what to look for, the false prophets can be detected as surely as a tree may be identified by its fruit: they are people who do not live in accord with the will of God as explicated by Jesus in this sermon. We note only in passing that Jesus' statement that wolves in sheep's clothing may be known "by their fruits" is perhaps the single most egregious example of a mixed metaphor in world literature. If Jesus had written the Sermon on the Mount for my eighth-grade English class, Mrs. Jackson would have made him do it over.

Since a wolf would have to don a sheep's fleece knowingly to deceive the flock, Jesus' image suggests con artists who knowingly use religion as a facade that helps them exploit the gullible. But that may be pressing the point too far. The protest in 7:22 seems sincere, so we should perhaps assume that many wolves in sheep's clothing are not aware of their disguise: there are active, dynamic church leaders who think Jesus is their Lord but are in for a nasty surprise on judgment day (cf. 25:44). Other interpreters have suggested that both forms of deception are dealt with, successively: 7:15–20 tells us of frauds who try to deceive the faithful, and 7:21–23 tells us that some who think they are being faithful are actually deceiving themselves. To determine if either type of deception is operative, we need only compare the lifestyle of our leaders or of ourselves with the type of conduct Jesus espouses in the Sermon on the Mount.

Modern collections of Aesop's *Fables* feature a tale in which a wolf disguises itself in *shepherd's* clothing, an image that is more outlandish but would have made the point Jesus intended to make better than his figure of "sheep's clothing." I have never found a date for this fable and cannot determine whether it might have influenced Jesus or vice versa (though Aesop lived 600 years before Jesus, many stories attributed to him come from much later times, and some probably depend on the New Testament). In Aesop's version, the scheme fails when the wolf tries to imitate the shepherd's voice (cf. John 10:2–5).

In the history of interpretation for Matthew 7:21 23, commen tators frequently call the false prophets "charismatics" who make a great show of spirituality (miracles and exorcisms) while neglecting the more important work of moral development. In recent decades, the text has often been used to attack Pentecostalism, claiming that Jesus denounced charismatic displays in favor of promoting down-to-earth religion concerned with righteousness and justice. This is not only unfair but also highly unlikely. Matthew probably assumed that all true apostles or prominent church leaders would be "charismatics," working miracles and performing exorcisms and other deeds of spiritual power (10:7–8). The point is that even those who do such things, thus appearing to be qualified church leaders, may lack obedience to Jesus' words, which is ultimately more important. What we call charismatic manifestations are "sheep's clothing": completely appropriate (indeed, expected) for sheep, but sometimes donned by wolves as well.

7:24–27. Parable of the Two Builders (cf. Luke 6:47–49)

The two ways described by Jesus in 7:13–14 are further elucidated by his brief parable of Two Builders. Those who act on his words (live in accord with what is presented in the Sermon on the Mount) will have a sure foundation for life, while those who do not so act will see the collapse of all they hoped to accomplish. Notably, the two houses in the parable suffer the same tribulations, but only the house on rock survives (cf. 16:18). Thus, Jesus does not indicate that his faithful followers will be spared adversity, but rather maintains that they will endure such trials and ultimately be saved (cf. 24:13).

The focus now seems to have shifted from eschatological salvation to accomplishment of mission (see Theme 3 "*The mission of God*" in the introduction, p. 10). Jesus is talking to people he has called to be agents of God's work in the world (4:18–22; 5:13–16), and now he explains whose work will *last.* Here is a potential promise and a warning. With regard to the latter, those who ignore the teaching of Jesus in this Sermon may find that everything to which they dedicated their lives (what they "built") can come tumbling down. Sadly, we may note that many pastors, church leaders, and others who sought to do God's work have found this to be true: what might have been worthy achievements were obscured or undone because they did not practice a life marked by the moral integrity and spiritual authenticity championed by Jesus in Matthew 5–7. That's the bad news. But there is also gospel: the good news revealed in this parable is that people *can* build houses that last. Mere mortals (people of little faith and limited understanding) *can* make a difference in this world. This should be our primary takeaway from the parable that concludes the most famous sermon ever preached: we can expect what we do for God to be of lasting value. Our lives can count for something. The world can be a better place for having had us in it.

MATTHEW 7:28–29
Response to the Sermon on the Mount

This text combines a verse from the Markan source (Mark 1:22) with Matthew's own formulaic conclusion to Jesus' great speeches (cf. "finished" in 11:1; 13:53; 19:1; 26:1–2).

The Sermon on the Mount concludes with a note that the crowds were astonished at Jesus' teaching since he taught "as one having authority and not as their scribes." The point is not simply that he teaches in an authoritative style, but that his teaching reveals him to be a person authorized to speak for God in a way that other religious teachers were not (cf. 8:5–13; 9:8; 10:1; 21:23–27; 28:18). From now on, the crowds will regard him as "a prophet" (14:5; 16:13–14; 21:11, 46; but see 13:57).

The revelation that crowds are hearing the sermon at all is surprising because Matthew indicated earlier that Jesus was speaking to his disciples apart from the crowds (5:1–2). The Sermon presents teaching intended primarily for followers of Jesus: the disciples who have heard his words are to act on them (7:24); in time, baptized persons who want to be made disciples will be taught to do so as well (Matt 28:19–20). But now we discover that other people have eavesdropped, overhearing words not intended for them. For Matthew's readers, "the crowds" may represent the unbelieving world in which the church is situated, persons who have not experienced Jesus' call but have heard snippets of his message (see comments on 19:1–2). Although they do not know what to make of Jesus or his message, such people may be astonished at the authority evident in his words (to be "astonished" is a basically positive but somewhat confused and uncertain response: cf. 8:27; 12:23; 22:33, where synonyms are used with the same sense). Thus Matthew's Gospel presents the Sermon on the Mount as teaching that is explicitly intended for the church, but it does so with an awareness that people outside the church might find these words stimulating as well. The words of the Sermon possess an inherent wisdom capable of impressing or challenging anyone who hears them.

MATTHEW 8:1–17
Healing Miracles

The stories of Jesus healing a man with a skin disease and, later, the mother-in-law of Simon Peter derive from Mark's Gospel, but the report of Jesus healing a centurion's "boy" is one of a few narratives believed to derive from the Q source (which mainly has sayings material).

Picking up on the theme of *authority* sounded at the conclusion of Jesus' most famous sermon (7:29), Matthew's Gospel continues for two chapters with a section narrating events in Galilee that further display the authority that the crowds heard in Jesus' voice. Thus, the Messiah is presented as one mighty in word (chaps. 5–7) and deed (8–9). In all, ten miracle stories are reported in these two chapters; some scholars see a parallel to the ten miracles of Moses in Egypt (Exod 7:8–11:10). Further, the stories of Jesus' miracles in this section are interspersed with episodes that introduce conflict between the religious leaders and both Jesus and his disciples.

In 8:1–17, Matthew relates three healing miracles of Jesus in quick succession, concluding with a formula citation that identifies him as the one spoken of by Isaiah.

8:1–4. Healing of a Man with a Skin Disease (cf. Mark 1:40–44; Luke 5:12–14)

A man with a skin disease is healed by Jesus and told to offer the sacrifices for purification prescribed in Scripture (Lev 14:1–32). In Matthew's narrative, this account serves as the Gospel's first miracle story (though general references to Jesus' healing activity were made in 4:23–24). Specifically, the healing of a man with a *skin disease* presents Jesus as one in line with the great prophets of old (2 Kgs 5:1–20; cf. Matt 11:5).

We should not imagine that the man in this story suffered from what is now called leprosy (Hansen's disease). The NRSV and most English translations of the Bible do refer to the man as a "leper," but the NRSVue renders the Greek word *lepra* more accurately as "skin disease." The word *lepra* is used throughout the Bible to refer to a variety of blemishes or disfiguring marks that might appear on human skin (Lev 13:2–44), clothing (13:47–59), or other surfaces (including the walls of houses, 14:34–53). In many instances, such a condition was not permanent, but Scripture advised quarantining afflicted persons from regular society for as long as the effects were evident (Lev 13:45–46; cf. 2 Kgs 7:3–5). Thus, such persons could be treated as social outcasts, but Christian preachers must be careful not to attribute such ostracism to the defects of Jewish religion. Far more drastic and cruel treatment of people identified as "lepers" was practiced in the gentile world (and indeed, would later be practiced in the "leper colonies" of Christendom). In fact, the social distancing expected of people with skin diseases in the Jewish world appears to have been voluntary, as indicated by the variety of occasions in which Jesus and his followers encounter such persons (10:8; 11:5; 26:6; Luke 17:12). Of course, isolation from human community may nevertheless have been one of the more distressing aspects of having such a disease.

In particular, Christian interpretation should not play up the plight of the man in this story by emphasizing how Jewish purity codes labeled such persons "unclean" and brought public shame that exacerbated their suffering. For the most part, purity codes were observed with a high degree of compassion and common sense (as they are today). Persons could be "unclean" for a variety of reasons that did not bring humiliation or shame. Notably, Jesus never criticizes the codes as harsh or unjust. That said, one can detect a motif of ironic reversal in this story. Normally, what was unclean was thought to have power to pollute whatever was clean. But when Jesus touches this man (8:3), he does not become unclean. Instead, the afflicted man is cleansed. This is a dramatic signification that God's rule has come near, that purity is now more powerful than impurity. Similar thinking will govern his association with sinners in 9:11–12.

The man cleansed of a skin disease worships Jesus and displays the ideal attitude elsewhere identified as "faith." He is thus the first character in the narrative to worship the adult Jesus, echoing the response of the magi to the infant in 2:11. In both those instances, Matthew deliberately uses the word *proskyneō* to designate the sort of devotion that Jesus and the Scriptures indicate should be shown only to "the Lord your God" (4:10; cf. Deut 6:13). The NRSVue veils this "high Christology" by translating the word "paid him homage" in 2:11 and "knelt before him" in 8:2, but Matthew means for his readers to recognize Jesus being treated as one in whom God is so present that worshiping him is essentially equivalent to worshiping

God (see Excursus: Worship in the Gospel of Matthew, p. 51). The man's faith, however, is best demonstrated in his words: "If you are willing, you can make me clean" (8:2). For Matthew's Gospel, such an affirmation is perfect, revealing full confidence in Jesus' ability but making no presumption regarding the divine will.

Jesus sends the healed man to the priests for verification of his cleansing in accord with Leviticus 14:1–9. This will facilitate the man's full integration back into human society. Further, the healed man's sacrifice is to be "a testimony" to the priests, serving as evidence that Jesus does in fact observe the law and also that he has power to accomplish what the law cannot. But Jesus instructs the man not to tell anyone else what has happened (8:4). This is the first instance of a secrecy motif inherited from the Gospel of Mark (see further 9:30; 12:16; 16:20). In Mark's Gospel, the "messianic secret" is a controlling motif, though scholars continue to debate just what theological significance should be attached to it. Matthew preserves some of the calls to secrecy but does not appear interested in developing the theme to serve any particular agenda. Here, the admonition to silence presents Jesus as humble (not seeking glory for what was a glorious deed) and as eager to avoid publicity that could attract undue attention and cumbersome crowds.

8:5–13. Healing of a Centurion's Boy (cf. Luke 7:1–10; John 4:46–54)

A centurion comes to Jesus and asks him to heal a member of his household who is paralyzed and "in terrible distress." The Greek word *pais* in 8:6 (NRSVue, "servant") means "boy" and could be used for either a son or an enslaved person. Most scholars think the latter is meant here (cf. Luke 7:2, where the word is *doulos*, "enslaved person"; but if John 4:46–54 recalls the same historical incident, the sick person would be the Capernaum official's son). In any case, Jesus is amazed at the faith of the centurion, who knows Jesus can heal the boy from a distance by merely speaking a word. This time "faith" is couched in terms of a recognition of Jesus' authority, a point that picks up a dominant theme in this portion of the narrative (see 7:29; 9:8). The centurion believes Jesus can give orders to the spiritual powers that keep this boy paralyzed just as surely as he himself can give orders to soldiers and enslaved people on more mundane matters.

That such faith is found in a gentile prompts Jesus not only to perform the healing but also to declare that the advent of God's rule will indeed transcend all social and ethnic boundaries. Jesus alludes to the great banquet expected to celebrate God's final victory, when God's rule is fully established (see Isa 25:6; Rev 19:9). The thought here is not that gentiles *as such* will be favored at this banquet and Jews *as such* excluded, but that people will come into the sphere of God's presence and power from unexpected quarters, while many thought to be insiders find themselves shut out. Lineage is no longer what counts (3:9). This theme of reversal has already been sounded in the Beatitudes (5:3–9) and in the warning about false prophets (7:21–23); it will be sounded again (see 19:30; 20:16; 25:31–46).

There is some question as to how Jesus' words in 8:7 should be translated. The Greek can be read either as a statement ("I will come and cure him") or as a question ("Should I come and cure him?"). The NRSVue prefers the former, but many have noted that a question might make more sense. That would, at least, make the story more consistent with the later narrative of Jesus' encounter with a Canaanite woman (15:21–28). Jesus would then be presented as hesitant in both stories, not because he is reluctant to help outsiders, but because he is attentive to God's timetable: the time for the gentiles has not yet come—but then, in both instances Jesus is moved to make exceptions for individual gentiles with extraordinary faith.

For some reason, this text has been subject to two quite different novel interpretations in recent years. First, a few scholars have argued that this centurion is actually Jewish and that the reference to many who "come from east and west" (8:11) is to Diaspora Jews, not to gentiles. I grant that a case might be made for this in terms of a historical encounter between Jesus and a Jewish centurion (they did exist) in Galilee. But we are interpreting the story as presented in Matthew, and I think that Matthew's readers are almost certainly expected to receive it as a preview of the church's gentile mission (28:19). Second, a popular interpretation making the rounds in recent years holds that the centurion's "servant" is actually a male sex partner so that, in healing the boy, Jesus was implicitly approving same-sex relationships. I have been a prominent affirmer of same-sex relationships for decades, but I still have to say that I find that interpretation of this story to be somewhat ludicrous. The only thing it seems to have going for it is the troubling fact that (normally heterosexual) Roman commanders did sometimes keep young boys for sexual purposes. But that would hardly be the sort of same-sex relationship that anyone today is suggesting should find approval. Nor is it clear to me why healing a person who is in terrible distress would constitute approval of that person's lifestyle.

The problematic aspect of the text for modern readers should be its assumption that slavery is a socially acceptable institution. Apart from the question of whether the sick boy is a son or an enslaved person, the centurion proclaims his authority by openly boasting of how the people he regards as his slaves show him unquestioned obedience. Still, Jesus points to the centurion as a role model of faith, without saying a word about how horrible it is for anyone to own human beings and to regard other people as property. What do we do with such a story? In the introduction (under "Reading Matthew," pp. 4–6), I suggest that acceptance of biblical authority does not mean we need to think the way the Gospel's readers are expected to think; but *understanding* the Gospel story may necessitate *pretending* to think that way. We do not need to approve or excuse slavery in any form that it has ever existed to recognize that readers of Matthew's Gospel are not expected to question the legitimacy of the institution. We will, of course, ultimately reject the implicit value system that assumes we are not troubled by things that are actually horrific; but first, we accept the terms of the story (including its flawed value system) long enough to discover what meaning it intends to convey. We need to do something similar with texts that are highly patriarchal or apocalyptic: all that is required is imagination, though I grant that this is harder with some texts than with others.

8:14–17. Healing of Peter's Mother-in-Law (cf. Mark 1:29–34; Luke 4:38–41)

Jesus goes to Peter's house in Capernaum and, at his own initiative, heals Peter's mother-in-law of a fever. In contrast to the two preceding stories, nothing is said of this healed person's faith or confidence in Jesus' power. Instead, Matthew reports that after the healing, she "served" Jesus. Many people *follow* Jesus in this Gospel, but Peter's mother-in-law and another unnamed woman in 26:10 are the only people who *serve* him. They are, in that sense, the two persons in the story whose attitude is most like that of Jesus himself (20:26–28).

Matthew then notes that many people are healed by Jesus (4:23–25; 9:35; 14:35–36; 15:29–31; 19:1–2). A special emphasis is given to those possessed by demons (see comments on 8:28–34). Further, Matthew notes that, through such actions, Jesus fulfills the prophecy that a true Servant of the Lord would take away human suffering in a way that would ultimately involve suffering himself (see Isa 53:4). That Jesus not only takes away infirmities but also "bears" them is one of the first (subtle) indications in the Gospel that the benefits he brings humankind come at a cost to himself.

MATTHEW 8:18–22
Would-Be Followers

Matthew begins this episode with a geographical notation from Mark 4:35 and then relates a story of would-be disciples taken from the Q source (paralleled in Luke 9:57–60).

Jesus determines to expand his ministry to the foreign area on the other side of the lake. Before he leaves, two encounters, juxtaposed for comparison, highlight the demands of being his follower.

A scribe states, "Teacher, I will follow you wherever you go." The claim is certainly bold, but we are probably to take it as naive if not presumptuous. Jesus has not called this scribe to be his disciple, and Matthew's Gospel does not suggest such a position is open to volunteers. Further, in Matthew only outsiders or unbelievers address Jesus as "Teacher" (8:19; 9:11; 12:38; 17:24; 19:16; 22:16, 24, 36); the only disciple to do so is Judas (26:25, 49, NRSVue, "Rabbi"; otherwise, disciples and those whom readers are to view favorably call him "Lord"). In any case, Jesus' enigmatic response, "The Son of Man has nowhere to lay his head" (8:20), indicates that the rigors of discipleship may be beyond what the eager scribe has calculated. Matthew does not actually indicate whether the scribe thinks twice about his allegiance or not, so we should not overstate the case as an outright rejection by Jesus. Yet again, it is sometimes noted that, in Matthew, Jesus typically refers to himself as "the Son of Man" only with a view to the unenlightened general public, not in reference to how he is to be perceived by believers (cf. 16:13–15).

After apparently rebuffing the overweening scribe, Jesus ironically learns that one of his own disciples, whom he *has* called, now wants to turn back from following him to fulfill an important family obligation. He wants to provide his father with an appropriate burial, as social custom and most interpretations of the law would demand (Exod 20:12; Tob 4:3; Sir 38:16). Jesus' harsh response takes the form of a proverb ("Let the dead bury their own dead," 8:22). The exact meaning of this aphorism is unclear, but certainly the disciple's request for a leave is denied. If this seems cruel, we should at least not make it worse with anachronistic assumptions. It is unlikely (though not impossible) that the disciple's father has just died and that this disciple wants a day off to attend the funeral. Either of two different scenarios is more probable: (1) the father is still alive; the disciple promises to follow Jesus sometime in the future, after his father has died; or (2) the father died a year ago, and now it is time to re-inter the body, moving the bones from an ossuary to a family tomb—a sacred task that needs doing but one that lacks immediate urgency (and could be performed by any family member). Still, Matthew does intend for Jesus' rejection of the request to be shocking, requiring a brutal assessment of priorities. Elsewhere, Jesus insists on the importance of keeping family obligations (15:4–5), but he will not allow devotion to family (10:34–37) or any "good cause" (26:8–11) to become an excuse for letting the reign of God become a secondary concern (6:33; cf. 22:1–10). On this, see further the comments on 10:34–37.

Taken together, the two encounters make the same point: home and family are principal sources of comfort and security, as well as essential foci of obligation. By making them secondary concerns, Matthew does not intend to de-emphasize their importance: rather, he chooses these matters as examples of the penultimate precisely because they are so significant. The mission of God to which Jesus and his followers are committed is more important than what would otherwise be the most important things in the world.

MATTHEW 8:23–9:8
Deliverance from Nature, Demons, and Paralysis

Matthew derived all this material from his Markan source, but he abbreviated the accounts considerably, leaving out numerous colorful details (e.g., the demoniac's shackles and wild activity, Mark 5:4–5; the unroofing of tiles to lower the paralytic, Mark 2:4).

After a brief interlude on the harsh demands of discipleship (8:18–22), Matthew continues his narration of ten miracle stories (Matt 9–10) that present Jesus as one who acts with divine authority (just as the Sermon on the Mount in chaps. 5–7 presents him as one who speaks with divine authority). These three stories are especially dramatic; they conclude with an affirmation that his authority is recognized as coming from God (9:8; cf. 9:34; 12:24).

8:23–27. Stilling of a Storm (cf. Mark 4:35–41; Luke 8:22–25)

On the way to the other side of the lake (8:18), a storm comes up, frightening Jesus' disciples. They awaken him and appeal for help in language that sounds liturgical ("Lord, save us"; cf. Mark 4:38, "Teacher, do you not care that we are perishing?"). He chides them for their "little faith" and miraculously makes the storm stop. The disciples' incredulous response (8:27) shows that they do not yet know that Jesus is the Son of God (cf. 14:33).

Matthew is relating stories that reveal Jesus to be "one having authority" (7:28–29). We (and the disciples) have observed that he shows authority not only in teaching but also in healing and casting out demons; soon he will demonstrate that he even has authority to forgive sins (9:2–6). In this episode, his authority is established over the natural world, the created order, which frequently seems prone to chaos. In Israelite tradition, such chaos is often associated with the sea (cf. Pss 65:5–7; 89:9–11; and consider the Noah story, Gen 6–9, and the Red Sea miracle, Exod 14–15). To our thinking, stilling a storm at sea might ratchet "miraculous power" up a few notches from merely healing diseases or exorcising demons, but the biblical world would not have made such a distinction. Matthew's readers would not be expected to think that Jesus did anything supernatural (that is, contrary to laws of nature) here or anywhere else. No such category existed: in that world, at that time, what we deem "impossible" would have been considered "extraordinary." Further, when Jesus "rebuked the winds and the sea" (8:26), he probably performed an exorcism not too dissimilar from the ones he had been performing regularly. Matthew's readers would not be expected to consider the exorcism of a lake to be a greater (or lesser) miracle than the exorcism of a human being.

For those who like verisimilitude, the drama of this episode has been enhanced somewhat by the 1986 discovery of a first-century fishing boat submerged on the northwest shore of the Sea of Galilee. Dubbed the "Jesus boat" and now a tourist attraction, study of the 8-×-26-foot craft did grant insight into the nature of a typical vessel used by fishermen during the Gospel period. The boat was poorly crafted, constructed from various materials (some recycled from previous projects), and had undergone numerous repairs. The most startling discovery, however, was that the boat had a smaller draft than anyone would have supposed and it would have floated much lower in the water than anyone previously would have thought advisable. Presumably, this lack of depth was intentional, to facilitate hauling nets filled with fish into the vessel—but this also meant that the boat could be easily swamped by waves and would have been unusually vulnerable to sinking in a storm. Further, the Sea of Galilee (which is actually a lake) sits six hundred feet below sea level and is subject to frequent unexpected storms when unforeseen winds rush abruptly through ravines from the surrounding hills.

So, storms on the Sea of Galilee were both common and potentially devastating (this is the first of two stories in Matthew in which Jesus stills a storm on that troubling sea; cf. 14:22–33). The fear of the disciples is real, especially given that many people in that time and place, including fishermen, were not able to swim (though John 21:7 suggests that Peter could). In any case, Jesus styles such fear as exemplary of "little faith," a descriptor that Matthew considers especially apt for followers of Jesus and, no doubt, the church (see Theme 11 "*Disciples as people of little faith*" in the introduction, p. 21). People of little faith can accomplish incredible things (17:20), but their fear and doubt prevent them from experiencing the peace that imbues those who trust more fully in God. Such trust is modeled by Jesus here: he sleeps peacefully in the midst of danger (cf. Pss 3:5–6; 4:8). In Mark's Gospel the disciples of Jesus apparently have no faith at all (Mark 4:40). In Matthew, they have a little—enough to be salt of the earth and light of the world (5:13–14)—but if only their (our) faith were greater, they (we) would not worry about trivial matters like having food to eat and clothes to wear (6:30–31), nor would they (we) fear such inconveniences as drowning in the midst of a storm-tossed sea.

Throughout church history, the story has been read as a sort of parable or allegory: the boat is the church, and the storms are all the cultural and spiritual forces that would destroy it. Peter Chrysologus (Bishop of Ravenna, ca. 433–450) is typical: "Christ gets into the vessel of his church, always ready to calm the waves of the world. He leads those who believe in him through safe sailing to the heavenly homeland" (*Sermons* 50.2). And preachers have found other applications: What are the storms that would destroy our nation? Our families? Our schools? The story invites diverse interpretation: it practically begs for ever-new applications for ever-changing contexts. The boat can be lots of things, as can the wind and waves, but the constant message is that "trust in God is what keeps us afloat."

Matthew also has a christological interest here, ending the narrative with a question to which his readers know the answer. "What sort of man is this . . . ?" the disciples mutter, and we want to shout, "The Messiah, you fools! . . . The Son of God! . . . How can you not know that . . . ?" It is a remarkably effective literary device for reader engagement, foreshadowing the discussion of identity in 16:13–17.

8:28–34. Exorcisms at Gadara (cf. Mark 5:1–17; Luke 8:26–37)

As Jesus enters gentile territory for the first time since the commencement of his ministry, he encounters two demon-possessed men who live in a cemetery near a drove of pigs and are apparently insane. The demons know what no human character in the story has yet discerned, that Jesus is the Son of God (8:29; see also 4:3, 6). They fear that he has come to them "before the time," that is, before the end of all things, when heaven and earth will pass away (24:35) and God's rule will come in all its fullness (6:10). They think their spree on earth should last longer but, as Jesus will later explain, Satan has already been bound, and his legions are being routed (12:28–29). The rule of heaven has "come near" (4:17) and, in some sense, already arrived in the person and work of Jesus (12:28). At their own request, the demons are cast into the pigs, which then plunge off a cliff and drown. Far from being grateful, the townspeople beg Jesus to leave.

Matthew's readers are not expected to be familiar with the parallel story in Mark's Gospel (from which this one was derived), but modern readers who do know that story want to ask, "Why *two* demoniacs when Mark's version has only one?" (Mark 5:2). Redaction critics have come up with a number of explanations for this curious doubling; none is satisfactory, though the best may be the simple suggestion that since Matthew omitted the story of a demoniac in Mark 1:23–26, he added a demoniac here by way of compensation. That does not, however, explain his doubling of characters elsewhere (one blind man in Mark 10:46–52 becomes two blind men in Matt 20:29–34; one steed in Mark 11:7 becomes two steeds in Matt 21:6–7). It is possible that each instance of such doubling would require a separate explanation. In any case (leaving that unresolved), we may note the literary effect for readers who simply take the story as it is without wondering about editorial innovations. A story featuring *two* men suffering the same malady (as opposed to just one) is imbued with a new element: the danger of contagion. In this case, it is not biological or even psychological contagion (insanity is not "catching") but, rather, the possibility that the demons who inhabit this region are expanding their influence by increasing the number of their victims. If they have possessed two men in this particular way, why not three? Or four? Or five? These appear to be unusually greedy, imperialistic demons, and the townspeople seem to have lapsed into a compact of colonial appeasement: life is pretty good, thus far the demons have only wanted two of us, and we can keep those two in the cemetery where they do little harm (except to themselves). This is the strongest image Matthew has given us so far of "the gentile world" into which Jesus' followers will ultimately be sent (28:19). The pagan character of the setting would be disturbingly offensive for any Jewish reader (including members of Matthew's predominantly Christian Jewish community): tombs and swine are the epitome of ritual impurity, and demons are "unclean spirits" (10:1; 12:43).

Readers may also ask, "Why would demons want to enter pigs? Why would Jesus let them do so?" A comical negotiation appears to be assumed. The demons and Jesus know that, come judgment day, they will be cast into eternal fire (25:41) and suffer everlasting punishment (25:46). This is a given, but the demons fear that the arrival of their eschatological Judge means that their torment is going to begin early, ahead of schedule, and that does not seem fair. On the other hand, Jesus cannot just cast them out of these demoniacs and leave them be, knowing their reputation as repeat offenders (12:43–45). So they try to make a deal: they will enter *pigs*, not *people*, and be content to inhabit those animals until the day of reckoning comes.

Jesus grants the request either because he agrees that it is fair or (more likely) because he knows what will happen. Pigs are not easy to possess, and the demons discover too late that their plan was ill-advised. They end up loose in the sea, consigned to a realm over which Jesus has just demonstrated his authority (8:26–27). This account is, of course, intended to be humorous; Matthew's readers would never be expected to worry about the loss of property experienced by filthy rich pagans whose unclean mammon perishes at a word from one more worthy of their devotion (6:24). That loss, however, could be what prompts the townspeople to insist that Jesus leave: perhaps they have been okay with demons driving a man or two (or three . . .) into cemetery-embracing insanity if it meant they could keep their hogs. Or perhaps they simply prefer evil powers with which they are familiar to divine ones about whom they know nothing.

This is the most dramatic story of demonic possession in Matthew's Gospel, though there are numerous other accounts of Jesus battling unclean spirits and releasing people from the possession by demonic beings that cause so much misery (4:24; 8:16; 9:32; 12:22; 15:22–28; 17:18; see also 7:22; 10:8). Such presentations seem out of sync with modern views of reality, though we should recognize that depictions of demons in the Bible differ from many popular conceptions. For one thing, demons are never associated with immorality in the Bible. Demons do not cause people to sin, but make people sick or afflict them, usually in physical ways. Demons are held to be responsible for fever, skin diseases, epilepsy, deafness, blindness, muteness, paralysis, and other such ailments—but also, as here, for what we would probably diagnose as mental illness (perhaps a bipolar condition or schizophrenia or multiple personality disorder). By attributing such maladies to demons, the ancient world affirmed three things: (1) What has happened to this person is not good; it is unfortunate, if not evil, certainly not life as it ought to be. (2) God is not responsible for what has happened to this person: there is no divine retribution here; rather, this person's condition represents an occasion in which God's will has *not* been done. (3) The person suffering from this condition is also not responsible for what has happened. In short, attribution of a malady to demons was a way of affirming that someone was the victim of an unfortunate circumstance that had nothing to do with God and in no way was that person's own fault.

9:1–8. Healing of a Paralytic (cf. Mark 2:1–12; Luke 5:17–26)

Returning to Capernaum, which is now called Jesus' "own town" (9:1), Jesus tells a paralytic that his sins are forgiven. He is apparently prompted to do this by the faith of the man's associates; as with the story of the centurion's "boy" (8:5–13), it is the faith of others (not of the infirm) that facilitates a divine blessing. The story also presents Jesus as possessing unusual mental powers: he is somehow able to "see" the faith of the paralytic's companions (9:2). He is also able to know the evil thoughts of the scribes (9:4), who believe he is already guilty of blasphemy, the charge for which he will ultimately be condemned to death (26:65–66). In this case, the charge would be that he is acting as someone who has been authorized to speak for God, like the prophets of old (2 Sam 12:13; Isa 40:2); there is no suggestion that he is claiming to *be* God, though of course Matthew's Christian readers may have found such a distinction to be tenuous. Jesus responds by healing the man of his paralysis, which prompts the crowds to glorify God (see also 5:16; and Excursus: Worship in the Gospel of Matthew, p. 51). Notably, the crowds are now impressed by the authority evident in Jesus' actions just as they were previously by the authority evident in his speech (7:28–29). On the role the crowds play as a character in Matthew's narrative, see comments on 19:1–2.

The story is not intended to imply a causal connection between sin and disease, as though the man's paralysis has been caused by his sin; if that were the case, we would expect to see Jesus pronouncing forgiveness as a prelude to every healing. That said, there is a symbolic aspect to this healing: sin *can* have a "paralyzing effect" on people's lives: forgiveness is essential to holistic treatment, allowing people to get out of whatever bed (or rut) is confining them. Further, Jesus leads with forgiveness when the man obviously needs physical healing to indicate how divine priorities may differ from human ones. From a human perspective, enabling a paralytic to walk is certainly a more difficult, greater miracle than simply telling someone their sins are forgiven (9:5); but from God's point of view, spiritual welfare is far more important than one's physical condition (see also 5:29–30).

We also note that what elicits praise is the revelation that God has given the authority to forgive sins not just to the Son of Man

(9:6) but also to "human beings" (9:8). We know that Matthew believes people need to forgive those who sin against them (6:14–15; 18:21–35), but the suggestion here is that *human beings* can forgive people who sin against God. Matthew probably thinks that offering such forgiveness will be a part of the mission of the church (though it is never spelled out as clearly as in John 20:23). Further, he probably thinks that the indisputable success Christian leaders display in healing ministries (10:8) stands as evidence to the world that such leaders have the authority to pronounce forgiveness as well. Such a supposition, however, would require caveats since lawless leaders and false prophets can apparently perform mighty works as well (7:22–23; 24:24).

MATTHEW 9:9–17
The Call of Matthew and Two Occasions for Controversy

Matthew is following his Markan source, deriving all this material from Mark 2:14–22, with little editing.

This section of the Gospel reveals escalation of conflict between Jesus and the religious leaders of Israel (who have already suspected Jesus of blasphemy in 9:3). Such conflict will come to a head in 12:1–14, where some Sabbath controversies motivate those leaders to plot his death.

9:9–13. Call of Matthew and Meal for Outcasts (cf. Mark 2:14–17; Luke 5:27–32)

Jesus summons a tax collector called Matthew to follow him in a manner reminiscent of his call of four other disciples in 4:18–22. In the other Synoptic Gospels, this tax collector is named Levi; the name change may be due to the fact that no "Levi" is ever included among later lists of the Twelve, though an otherwise unknown person named Matthew is (Matt 10:2–4; Mark 3:16–19; Luke 6:13–16). For some reason, a tradition arose in the church that this tax collector-cum-disciple became the author of this Gospel: that does not seem likely, though it is possible that the disciple Matthew wrote down some material about Jesus (e.g., sayings incorporated in the Q source?) and thus became associated with a Gospel containing that material.

A short time later, Jesus hosts a group of "tax collectors and sinners" for a meal at Peter's house in Capernaum—not, as is often supposed, at Matthew's house. The house would have been too small for the guests to be indoors, so the party must have overflowed into the courtyard or street, attracting considerable public attention. That may have been intentional if, as is often supposed, Jesus hosted the meal as a prophetic act, a public demonstration of what he had been teaching regarding the rule of heaven. Prophets often did such things: Isaiah walked around naked for three years (Isa 20:3); Jeremiah wore a yoke (Jer 27:1–7) and broke a pot (19:1–13). Jesus staged a banquet (symbolizing the great banquet at the end of time) and filled the tables with outcasts who exemplified some of the people he had claimed in the Beatitudes would be blessed when God's rule was established (5:4–6, see comments on those verses).

Tax collectors were regarded as wicked people, whose occupation violated God's law and constituted treason. Recent studies, however, have revealed that the tax collectors with whom Jesus typically fraternized were probably not the wealthy bosses of tax-collecting enterprises (Zacchaeus, called a "chief of tax collectors" in Luke 19:1–10, would be the only exception) but, rather, low-life "thugs" such bosses used for doing the grunt work of shaking people down for their money. Universally unpopular, these tax collectors were often men who had something wrong with them: mild mental challenges, speech impediments, physical deformities, and the like (Roman documents characterize tax collectors in the provinces as "large," "stupid," and "ugly"). They were often enslaved persons or, at least, were people who for some reason could not find work in a more desirable profession. The man called to follow Jesus was obviously not an enslaved person (since he left his position), but he was probably representative of a class of people considered pathetic, despicable, or both. The same would be true of the "sinners" in attendance at Jesus' house party. That term is probably used here in a specific sense, as a euphemism for sex workers, and we now know that all sex workers in Palestine at the time of Jesus were enslaved (which is why we never hear of ex–sex workers). Further, given high mortality rates, almost all were teenagers (daughters were sold into slavery as soon as they reached puberty, and no reference to sex workers over the age of 18 can be found in extant Roman records). (On this understanding of "tax collectors and sinners," see Powell 2015; and further comments on 11:19 and 21:31–32.)

Thus, Jesus calls a tax collector to follow him and then hosts a party for a motley sampling of misfit hoodlums and adolescent sex workers, many of them enslaved persons, none with prospects for a future existence that would qualify as "life" in anything but the most naked biological sense. These were the most pitiable people of his world, though of course it may have been difficult to pity them when they were robbing you, or physically assaulting you, or tempting your husband to spend grocery money on adultery, or infecting your sons with venereal diseases. In Jesus' day as in ours, pathetic individuals were both easy to pity and easy to despise. Although Jesus was certainly not the only compassionate Jew in Galilee, he did earn a reputation for *extreme* compassion, showing mercy (a step up from pity) to these outcasts. But in Jesus' day, as in ours, such compassion for the undeserving could evoke dismay and disdain, and more so among religious people than among people in general. So, historically, it would not be surprising if Jesus' fraternity with such people offended the pious. In terms of Matthew's story, however, that doesn't really matter: the Pharisees and other religious leaders of Israel who are characters in Matthew's story think and act the way they do because they are evil, and being evil doesn't require much of a rationale (see Theme 14 "*Religious leaders as enemies of God*" in the introduction, p. 25).

The objection to Jesus' conduct prompts his memorable proverb regarding a physician serving those who are sick, not those who are well. The proverb asserts Jesus' commitment to welcome rather than shun sinners while also affirming his intention to heal them. He also quotes Hosea 6:6 to indicate that his policy of prioritizing mercy reflects the preferences of God (see also 12:7). But we might ask, what would healing entail in such an instance? It almost certainly does not imply conversion since, for enslaved persons (or people without options), "repentance" or a change in lifestyle would not have been existentially possible. Further, the objection to Jesus' conduct would not make much sense if Jesus was converting tax collectors and sex workers (note that there is no objection to a *former* tax collector joining his disciples). No, the offense is that Jesus is welcoming *current* tax collectors and sex workers, people regarded as "traitors" and "harlots," who are probably not going to change their ways. The healing that he brings such people must typify what we might call "care of souls": he can assure them that they are accepted by God and will enter the rule of heaven in spite of current circumstances that reflect nothing of God's reign or righteousness. By welcoming them and hosting them in his house, he honors them: in a culture for which honor and shame are primary values, he bestows honor on those who otherwise live in shame.

9:14–17. Question about Fasting (cf. Mark 2:18–22; Luke 5:33–39)

A query from the disciples of John the Baptist as to why Jesus' disciples do not fast (cf. 11:18–19) prompts an enigmatic response from Jesus. He compares himself to a bridegroom and cites or coins two proverbs regarding patches on cloth and wine in wineskins. The incident hints at tension between Jesus and the Baptist, or at least between their followers (see 11:2–19 for later development and possible resolution of this tension). Surprisingly, here, in contrasting themselves with the followers of Jesus, the Baptist's disciples group themselves with followers of the Pharisees, who are elsewhere presented in opposition to John (3:7; 21:23–32).

The bridegroom theme picks up an image that became popular in early Christianity (John 3:29; Eph 5:22–33; Rev 21:9; 22:17), but it is used here in a double sense. On the one hand, the nearness of God's reign (4:17) calls for celebration, specifically a celebration of love similar to that of a wedding. On the other hand, the bridegroom will be taken away, initiating a time when joy and celebration are not yet complete. Matthew 9:15 may be a veiled reference to the passion, but beyond that it is the first of two significant passages in Matthew that speak of the "absence of Jesus" during the time of the church (see also 26:11). These sayings must be held in tension with assurances of Jesus' continued presence (18:20; 28:20). Jesus *is* still with us, this evangelist wants to say, but not as he once was and not as he will be: that distinction is significant for piety, theology, and ethics (see Excursus: Presence and Absence of Jesus in Matthew, p. 139).

The following two proverbs or parables (9:16–17) indicate the good news about God's reign that Jesus brings cannot simply be added to an already-existing system or lifestyle. It changes everything and demands total transformation, which is why the announcement of that good news is typically preceded in Matthew by the word "Repent" (3:2; 4:17). Not only individual lives but also religious and social systems must be changed to accommodate this good news. So, in the previous verses (9:10–13), repentance is a more appropriate theme for the *society* that traps people in evil from which they cannot escape than it is for the *people* so trapped. In general, the question of fasting becomes paradigmatic for how all behavior must be reevaluated in light of the gospel: Jesus has come to fulfill the law, not abolish it (5:17), but sometimes fulfillment requires reassessment and transformation (5:21–48).

EXCURSUS

Presence and Absence of Jesus in Matthew

Matthew's Gospel proclaims that Jesus remains present with the contemporary community of his followers but retains the Markan insistence that Jesus is now absent. The eternal, abiding presence of Jesus is emphasized in a number of passages (10:40; 18:5, 20; 25:37–40; 28:20; see Theme 1 *"The abiding presence of God"* in the introduction, p. 7), but the absence theme is maintained in these two instances:

- When people wonder why his disciples are not more diligent with regard to fasting, Jesus says it is because he (the bridegroom) is still with them; but then he adds that a time will come when he (the bridegroom) will no longer be with them, and then they will fast and mourn (9:15; cf. Mark 2:19–20).
- When disciples complain that ointment used to anoint Jesus could have been sold to make a donation to the poor, Jesus tells them that they will always have the poor with them, but he will not always be with them (26:11; cf. Mark 14:7).

Thus Matthew can insist that Jesus is with us always in many remarkable ways while also recognizing that he is no longer with us *as he once was* and that he is not now with us *as he will be.*

Elsewhere I have discussed the significance of these congruent themes for spiritual formation (Powell 2004, 51–59). In brief, recognizing the absence of Jesus allows for the Christian life to be marked by (1) confident sadness and (2) urgent anticipation.

Confident sadness means that, while there may be joyful moments in the Christian life, followers of Jesus do not expect to be happy all the time: on the whole, this life is less like a "wedding feast" than it is like a time of fasting and mourning. The Matthean Jesus says that those who receive the word "with joy" but without understanding have no root but endure only for a little while, without bearing fruit (13:21–23). By contrast, recognizing the absence of Jesus allows us to face the reality of life in a way that avoids what Martin Luther called a quixotic "theology of glory." Luther warned against an overly enthusiastic piety by which persons think that faith will enable them to rise above problems in life and enjoy a trouble-free existence. Confident sadness allows us to live with faith that does not deny reality, faith that recognizes that life in this world is hard, indeed, not as it should be.

Urgent anticipation means that, while we are not in glory yet, we do expect the one now absent to return. Matthew's readers are expected to long for the return of Christ and to look for him to return very soon. Modern believers often have trouble doing this (perhaps because so much time has already passed), but healthy spirituality resists satisfaction with what is currently available. So, Matthew's Gospel contains passages in which Jesus seems to indicate he will return within the lifetime of his disciples (10:23; 16:28; 24:29–31). By the time this Gospel was written, that had not occurred, but Matthew retains the passages so that readers who empathize with the disciples in his story might hear those sayings as addressed to them: clearly, Matthew would hope that readers in his own day or in any future generation would expect Jesus to return within their own lifetimes.

The themes of presence and absence come together in the community meal Jesus institutes in 26:26–29. On one hand, the elements consumed by believers at this meal are to be identified as the body and blood of Jesus, implying some symbolic or mystical connection through which they experience his abiding presence among them. But, on the other hand, the meal is fundamentally a commemoration of his *last* supper with his followers, in recognition that he would no longer be with them, that he would never again share a cup with them until they were all together in the reign of God (26:29). Even so, in most Christian churches today, the Eucharist is identified as "a foretaste of the feast to come." It is good, but not as good as it gets. Appetizers are supposed to do what the name implies: stimulate our appetite to want the feast itself. We appreciate what we have but yearn for something better—and fully expect to receive it!

So the twin motifs of the presence and absence of Jesus invite Matthew's readers to experience Christ in their lives here and now, yet with full awareness that such an experience is only a bridge between remembrance and anticipation. Jesus is with us, but not as he once was and not as he will be.

MATTHEW 9:18–34
Three Healings and a Resurrection

For this section, Matthew took the intercalated stories in 9:18–26 from Mark's Gospel and added two additional healing stories, both of which appear to be doublets of stories he will tell later.

These stories present Jesus' miraculous power to overcome disease, disability, and death, bringing to conclusion the two chapters (8–9) Matthew has devoted to the divine authority evident in Jesus' deeds (just as 5–7 showed the divine authority in his teaching). In all, he will have related ten miracles of healing or deliverance in these chapters, which some scholars suggest present a parallel to the ten miracles of Moses recounted in Exodus 7:8–11:10.

9:18–26. Ruler's Daughter and Hemorrhaging Woman (cf. Mark 5:21–43; Luke 8:40–56)

A pair of miracle stories presents Jesus as one who restores life and health to two unnamed women: the daughter of a leader (called Jairus in Mark 5:22 but nameless here) and a woman who has suffered from a hemorrhage for twelve years. Matthew does *not* say the "leader" in 9:18 is a leader "of the synagogue," as Mark 5:22 styles him. The NRSV was misleading on this point; the NRSVue has corrected the NRSV's bizarre inclusion of words found in a different Gospel, words that Matthew had deliberately omitted. Matthew's reluctance to identify this man, whom Jesus helps, with a synagogue is congruent with the disturbing fact that in his Gospel all religious leaders are evil (see Theme 14 "*Religious leaders as enemies of God*" in the introduction, p. 25). On another point, note that in Matthew the omniscient Jesus knows who touched his garment and need not query the disciples or crowd about that matter (9:22; cf. Mark 5:30–32).

Both stories are reported matter-of-factly, with an emphasis on faith. Like the man with a skin disease in 8:2, the girl's father worships Jesus (see Excursus: Worship in the Gospel of Matthew, p. 51) and demonstrates complete confidence in his power. The hemorrhaging woman is so confident of this power that she knows she need only touch Jesus' garment to be healed (cf. 14:36). Lest this be interpreted as magic, Jesus affirms that it is her faith in his power that has brought about the healing. Such examples of faith are contrasted with the ridiculing laughter of the crowds at the young girl's funeral (9:24).

We ought not read these stories as critiques of Jewish purity codes. Even though there is no mention of ritual "cleanness" or "uncleanness" in the text, Christian preachers have often explained that the hemorrhaging woman would have suffered from years of ostracism and shame due to her perpetual uncleanness; but this is probably not true and is at least potentially anti-Semitic. In Jesus' day, as in our own, most Jews who observed ritual purity did so in ways that were not oppressive or onerous: observance was voluntary, strictness of application varied, and states of uncleanness were regarded as completely natural and respectable (no cause for shame). We do better to keep the focus where Matthew puts it: on faith, wholeness, and restoration to life. These are previews of the coming rule of heaven, demonstrating what life is like when God's will is done (and what life will always be like when God's will is always done).

9:27–31. Healing of the Blind (cf. Matt 20:30–34; Mark 10:46–52; Luke 18:35–43)

Jesus opens the eyes of two blind men who address him as the Son of David. The use of the title "Son of David" probably indicates that these men think Jesus is the Messiah (see 22:42; cf. 1:1; 12:23; 15:22; 20:30, 31; 21:9, 15). If so, they may also believe that Isaiah identified the healing of the blind as a sign of the messianic age (Isa 29:18; 35:5–6; 42:7; cf. Matt 11:5). Once again, faith is emphasized (cf. 8:10; 9:2, 22), though here it is Jesus' mercy rather than his power that is sought (9:27); this appears to prompt Jesus to ask whether they have confidence in his power as well (9:28; cf. 8:2, 8; 9:18, 21). As before (8:4), Jesus wants the matter kept secret for reasons never explained (see also 12:16; 16:20; 17:9). But this time, his wish is ignored, and the incident becomes one more occasion for his fame to spread (9:31; cf. 4:24; 9:26). Notably, Matthew does not fault the healed men for disobedience in making the matter known. The point for Matthew's readers may be to realize that even though Jesus did not seek "celebrity status" for his miraculous powers, the effects of his works were simply too marvelous to be kept a secret. A story similar to this one is told in Matthew 20:29–34. Despite the difference in geographical location, the two stories are usually regarded as "doublets": two versions of what was once a single story. Matthew does have a habit of telling the same story twice (see 5:31–32//19:9; 9:32–34//12:22–24; 12:38–42//16:1–4).

9:32–34. Exorcism of a Mute Demoniac (cf. Matt 12:22–24; Mark 3:22; Luke 11:14–15)

Jesus casts a demon out of a man who is mute, enabling him to speak (on demonic possession, see comments on 8:28–34). The man is probably also deaf; the Greek word used for his condition (*kōphos*) is identical to that translated "the deaf" in 11:5. This brief incident elicits contrasting responses from the crowds and the Pharisees. The crowds proclaim, "Never has anything like this been seen in Israel." Such acclaim may seem exaggerated in light of the healings and miracles worked by such ancient prophets as Elijah and Elisha, but Matthew wishes to stress that something unique has come in the person and work of Jesus. The Pharisees dismiss the exorcism as the work of the devil, an accusation that prepares for the larger discussion of this charge in 12:22–32.

Earlier, Matthew concluded the Sermon on the Mount with an acclamation by the crowds concerning the authority of Jesus evident in his teaching (7:28–29); so now he concludes two chapters devoted primarily to miracles with an acclamation by the crowds, recognizing the unique authority evident in his deeds. In both instances, furthermore, the tension and potential conflict between Jesus and the religious leaders of Israel are evident.

MATTHEW 9:35–11:1
Plentiful Harvest and Missionary Discourse

This long text is unique to Matthew as a unit in its present form, though most of the verses are paralleled elsewhere. The missionary discourse that takes up most of chapter 10 especially exhibits Matthew's editorial skill, weaving material from Mark and Q together (with some new material as well) to form a cohesive "speech" out of what had been disparate sayings found in different contexts.

The Missionary Discourse is the second major speech that Jesus gives in this Gospel (the first was the Sermon on the Mount in chaps. 5–7). It is ostensibly addressed to the twelve persons called "apostles" (10:2) and is predicated by Jesus' compassionate realization of Israel's great need (9:36). The discourse concerns the work that the Twelve are to perform as missionaries to Israel. In fact, however, some content of this speech appears to be addressed to Christians of a later time and place, when the good news about God's rule would be taken to all nations (10:18; see also 24:14; 28:19); in fact, much of it presumes a situation of violent persecution that the church would not know for decades after Jesus' death. In any case, the speech describes the work of God conducted through Jesus' followers as closely paralleling the work of God accomplished through Jesus himself; it indicates that the fate his followers may suffer as a consequence of doing God's work will also parallel that which will befall Jesus (10:24–25; see Theme 3 "*The mission of God*" in the introduction, p. 10).

9:35–38. Summary of Jesus' Ministry (cf. Mark 6:6b, 34; Luke 8:1; 10:2; John 4:35)

This is the second of what are usually called the three "summary passages" in Matthew, describing Jesus' ministry (the others are 4:23–25 and 11:1; but see also 8:16; 14:35–36; 15:29–31; 19:1–2). Scholars note that 9:35 repeats 4:23 almost word for word, forming something of an *inclusio* around chapters 5–9 and setting that entire section of Matthew apart as a recognizable unit: the theme of those five chapters is the divine authority of Jesus, evident in his teaching (5–7) and deeds of power (8–9). The schemata basically works if applied without concern for absolute consistency.

The full summary offered here, however, is unique in that it concludes with an emphasis on Jesus' compassion and on the need for more workers to take up the sort of ministry he performs. The Greek word for feeling compassion is *splanchnizōmai*, deriving from the word "intestines" (*splanchna*, as in Acts 1:18; hence the KJV's "bowels of mercies," Col 3:12), and implies emotional distress: here Jesus is portrayed as not only merciful (cf. 9:27–30; 15:22–28; 17:14–18; 20:30–34; see also 5:7; 9:13; 12:7; 23:23) but also empathetic, identifying emotionally with those who suffer, feeling what they feel (cf. 14:14; 15:32; 20:34). In English, we might describe a powerful emotional experience as "gut-wrenching." Notably, Jesus' compassion for the people is aroused not by the degree of sickness or suffering they experience, but by something more fundamental: a lack of leadership that leaves them harassed and helpless, like "sheep without a shepherd" (9:36; cf. Num 27:17; 2 Chr 18:16). This theme of lost or scattered sheep looms large in Matthew (10:6; 15:24; 18:12; 26:31); here it is linked to the even more prominent indictment of Israel's unfaithful leaders (see Theme 14 "*Religious leaders as enemies of God*" in the introduction, p. 25). The work that needs to be done on behalf of these sheep is described as a "harvest" (another mixed metaphor; cf. comments on 7:15–16), but this does not signify eschatological judgment as in 13:39–42. Rather, this use of the harvest metaphor points to what is envisioned in the parable of the Sower, as explained in 13:18–23. Jesus says to pray for persons like his disciples to sow the message of God's rule through preaching and healing (10:7–8) so that some, at least, may bear much fruit (13:23). Aside from what is presented in the Lord's Prayer, this is one of the few things that Jesus ever explicitly tells people to pray for (cf. 26:41).

10:1–4. Twelve Apostles Chosen (cf. Mark 3:16–19; 6:7; Luke 6:13–16; 9:1; Acts 1:13)

Jesus has been calling disciples all along (4:18–22; 9:9), but it is only now that we hear that there is a total of twelve and only now that we get a list of names. The number twelve is itself significant as a symbolic reconstitution of the twelve tribes of Israel (19:28). Matthew emphasizes that Jesus gives these twelve disciples power over unclean spirits so that they will be able to conduct a ministry of healing similar to his (see Theme 3 "*The mission of God*" in the introduction, p. 10). He also refers to them (only here) as "apostles," a term indicating that they are commissioned for a specific task. The people to whom Jesus gives authority over every disease and sickness are the same ones elsewhere described as having "little faith" (6:30; 8:26; 14:31; 16:8; 17:20; see Theme 11 "*Disciples as people of little faith*" in the introduction, p. 21). Indeed, they include Peter, the future denier; Judas, the future traitor; and ten future deserters. Still, Judas, Peter, and the other apostate apostles are apparently successful in fulfilling their commission. Matthew's readers are expected to realize that the mission of God is accomplished by God acting through woefully inadequate people.

10:5–15. Instructions for Missionary Work (cf. Mark 6:8–11; Luke 9:2–5)

Jesus gives specific directions regarding the mission to the lost sheep of Israel (10:5–6 is unique to Matthew). Identifying Israel rather than the gentile nations as a mission field implies a certain ironic reversal since the people of Israel have typically regarded themselves as God's chosen ones, who are to become a light to the (other) nations. Jesus has not abandoned this ideal, but he believes that first Israel itself needs enlightenment (28:19 reveals that 10:5 is not meant to imply exclusion of non-Israelites in any ultimate or final sense). Jesus' followers are to preach the good news of the rule of heaven (10:7; cf. 3:2; 4:17) and conduct a ministry of healing remarkably like that of Jesus himself. In short, they are to continue doing what he did, multiplying his work quantitatively without substantially changing it qualitatively. Like him, they are to accept no payment for their preaching and healing. This will be possible if they adopt his ideal of an austere lifestyle, requiring no more of their hosts than the basic hospitality (food and shelter) due to any traveler. Echoes of the Sermon on the Mount are found here, for by their carefree, unburdened existence, Jesus' disciples are to demonstrate what it means to put God ahead of material things (6:24) and to seek the reign of God above all (6:33). Jesus notes, however, that some will prove unworthy of their ministry, refusing even to acknowledge their greeting of *shalom*. They ought not waste their time on such as these (7:5), but instead move on, shaking the dust from their feet: a traditional prophetic sign that warns of divine judgment to come (cf. Acts 13:51). The seeming inability of some to receive the word is a theme elsewhere in Matthew (see 7:6; 13:19; 15:12–14).

10:16–23. Certainty of Persecution (cf. Mark 13:9–13; 12:11–12; Luke 21:12–19)

Jesus intensifies the warning he has been giving his disciples, indicating now that some will be not only inhospitable to them but will actively seek to demean them, betray them, and persecute them violently. The demands of Jesus (as stated, for instance, in 5:43–48) make them vulnerable to such abuse. Their position will be like that of sheep in the midst of wolves; many of them will suffer, and some will die. Even members of their own families will turn on them (10:21; cf. 24:10), which will require radical assessment of loyalties (see 10:34–39). Still, Jesus counsels them not to be anxious but to trust in God. They are to "beware" of tyrants and oppressors (10:17), but this only implies reasonable caution and realistic appraisal of the situation; it does not imply fear (see 10:26–31) or even anxiety (10:19). Wisdom and innocence become especially important virtues in such a context: they are to be "wise as serpents" so as not to provoke their enemies and bring persecution upon themselves unnecessarily; they are to be "innocent as doves" (10:16), living publicly in such an exemplary fashion as to give the lie to whatever slanderous accusations may be made against them. If they do this, they might not be spared suffering, but their persecutions will serve the cause of God: the Spirit will give them words to say even in situations into which they are dragged against their will, and they will find themselves bearing testimony for Jesus' sake (10:20). This is, incidentally, the only reference in Matthew to the activity of the Spirit in the lives of Jesus' followers (but see 3:11; 28:19). Jesus insists that such persecution, although unfortunate and undesirable, is inevitable and pervasive: "You will be hated by all because of my name" (10:22; see also 24:9). Nevertheless, he promises that, in the end, the Son of Man will come and save those who have endured such suffering and indignity. They need not worry about satisfactory completion of the mission. The goal is simply to do what can be done as the occasion arises; the work, Jesus knows, will still be incomplete when the Son of Man returns. For more on the seeming nonfulfillment of 10:23, see comments on 24:29–31.

10:24–42. Promises and Threats (cf. Mark 4:22; 9:37, 41; Luke 6:40; 8:17; 10:16; 12:2–9; John 13:20)

Jesus continues his warnings about coming persecution in a way that broadens the topic into a general discussion of assurances and rewards that may or may not be granted. He begins by explaining that the persecution coming upon his followers needs to be considered in light of the suffering that he himself is bearing and will bear on their behalf. Though Matthew may well have the ultimate suffering of "the cross" in view here (10:38), the specific reference is to the more immediate indignity Jesus endures when Pharisees malign his healing ministry as demonic (9:34; 12:24). Remembering this, Jesus thinks, will be one source of comfort for his beleaguered followers: when they are unjustly slandered, they can at least know that their Lord was slandered as well (cf. John 15:20). Another source of comfort will be the realization that, eventually, everything will come out and the truth will be known (10:26–27). Still another will be the awareness that, even at its worst, human suffering is limited and finite. The God who knows the fate of every sparrow and the number of hairs on every head is the one who determines the ultimate fate of human beings, who have been created to be more than just flesh and blood. Realizing this trivializes, or at least de-emphasizes, the threat of anyone or anything that can, at worst, destroy only "the body."

Yet Jesus lets it be known that the rewards he promises are not automatic. Those who deny him, who put earthly concerns (such as family ties) ahead of him, who refuse to take up the cross that following him requires them to bear (10:38; see also 16:24), who are concerned only with preserving their own lives (10:39; see also 16:25)—such disciples (10:24) risk missing the blessings of God's reign. The threats Jesus makes are daunting: Jesus will deny such people before the Father, they will be found unworthy of him, and they will lose "life" in its ultimate and fullest sense. By contrast, rewards will come to those who acknowledge Jesus before others and are willing to lose their lives for his sake. Indeed, these blessings will also come to all who are receptive of his followers or who show even the slightest kindness to "the little ones" he calls his own (10:42; see also 18:6, 10; 25:40). This is in keeping with Matthew's view that Jesus himself—and therefore God, who sent Jesus—remains present on earth in and through the community of people who are his followers (10:40; see Theme 1 "*The abiding presence of God*" in the introduction, p. 7).

Jesus' words in 10:34 ("not peace, but a sword") have nothing to do with endorsement of armed conflict, an unthinkable proposition for this, the most pacifist book in the Bible (see 5:38–41, 44–45; 26:52). The word "sword" was often used as a metaphor for "something that divides," and Jesus is using it here to reference the divisions that will become evident when people are forced to decide for him or against him (see 12:50). In doing so, he draws heavily on the prophet Micah's description of the folly of trusting in human beings when only God can offer salvation (Mic 7:6–7). On the need to love Jesus more than parents or children, see the comments on 8:18–22 regarding how home and family are chosen to exemplify the penultimate precisely because they are otherwise the most important things in the world. Obviously, Jesus does not want his followers to neglect their parents (15:3–6) or children (18:1–5; 19:13–15) any more than his call to "deny oneself" (16:24) implies neglecting appropriate self-care. Rather, loving Jesus more than family or self means that one should not prioritize what will benefit one's own interests or the interests of one's friends or family (or church or town or country) over the interests of Jesus, which is to say, over that which will benefit all people, the entire earth (5:13–14). Of course, for Jesus' disciples in the immediate context of these sayings, the priority was what would bring healing and deliverance to the lost sheep of Israel (10:6–8), but Jesus has already indicated that eventually their concern will be for whatever might lift the spirits of the despondent (5:3), benefit the meek and miserable (5:4–5), satisfy the hunger of those who are starved for justice (5:6), or simply bring the blessings of God's rule to all, including one's enemies (5:7–10, 43–47).

11:1. Conclusion

With a final sentence, Matthew concludes not only Jesus' missionary discourse to his disciples, but also this broad section of the Gospel in which the dominant motif has been his ministry to Israel (4:17–11:1). This is now the third "summary passage" (see also 4:23; 9:35) that describes Jesus' work of preaching and teaching (the other summaries also mention healing) throughout the land of Israel. The ministry to these "lost sheep" (10:6) is not complete (10:23), but it has now been described sufficiently for Matthew to turn his attention to the matter of their response.

Part Three of Matthew's Gospel: Israel's Repudiation of Jesus

Matthew 11:2–16:20

The mood of Matthew's narrative shifts from a concentration on the glorious works of God being done in Israel to a focus on Israel's failure to respond to those works. From the sincere questioning of John the Baptist (11:3) to the conspiratorial plotting of the Pharisees (12:14), the tenor of the story becomes unmistakably negative. Jesus speaks oracles of judgment upon the unrepentant (11:20–24; 12:39–42), publicly condemns the religious leaders (12:34; 15:3–9), and speaks mysteriously of hidden revelation (11:25) that is deliberately kept from the undeserving (13:10–17). Tensions continue to mount and to become evident even among Jesus' own townspeople (13:53–58). Only his relationship with his disciples (whom he identifies as his true family, 12:49) seems secure. That, too, will change before this Gospel is done, but the stories that reflect on the failings of those disciples come later in the narrative (16:21–23; 19:13–14; 20:20–24). In this section, the disciples worship Jesus and confess him to be the Son of God (14:33; 16:16); they appear to be almost the only privileged ones (13:11; but see 15:21–28) in whom the message of God's rule is bearing fruit (13:18, 23). Lines are drawn, and Jesus declares, "Whoever is not with me is against me" (12:30).

MATTHEW 11:2–30
A Negative Response

This section of Matthew comes from the Q source, with an added climactic coda (11:28–30) unique to Matthew.

Instead of reports of Jesus being granted acclaim (4:24; 7:28–29; 9:8, 26, 31, 33), we now hear of his identity being questioned, his lifestyle challenged, and his message ignored. Overt persecution, which Jesus has predicted will come upon his followers (10:16–23), is not yet evident, but passive resistance to the good news about God's rule (4:23; 9:35; see also 10:7; 24:14) provokes Jesus' ire and elicits some of his harshest words.

11:2–6. John the Baptist's Question (cf. Luke 7:18–23)

John has been arrested (4:12) and now sends disciples to Jesus to ask whether Jesus is in fact "the one who is to come," that is, the Messiah. The query is prompted by reports that John has heard concerning "what the Messiah was doing," that is, reports of what the one whom John thought was the Messiah was doing (3:14). John, after all, had seemed confident that Jesus was this promised figure (3:14; cf. 3:11). But now John notices a disconnect between what he said that person would do and what he hears Jesus actually is doing. John had publicly declared that the Messiah would execute terrible acts of judgment (3:12), but so far, Jesus has not fulfilled those expectations or prophecies. This is the second time now that disciples of John have questioned Jesus regarding what appear to be anomalies in the program; earlier, they were dumbfounded that this ostensibly godly man did not require more fasting on the part of his followers (9:14–17; cf. 11:18–19). Still, Jesus does not discourage honest inquiry ("Search, and you will find," 7:7), and there is no reason to think that John and his disciples would not be included in the beatitude of 11:6 ("Blessed is anyone who takes no offense at me").

Jesus responds with allusions to Isaiah (29:18–19; 35:5–6; 61:1), indicating that the works being done by him ("the blind receive their sight," 9:27–31; "the lame walk," 9:2–8; "those with a skin disease are cleansed," 8:1–4; "the deaf hear," probably 9:32–34; "the dead are raised," 9:23–25; "the poor have good news brought to them," 6:25–33) and by his followers (10:8) are indeed signs of the messianic age.

He does not, however, indicate that John was wrong with his earlier predictions of a coming Judge (3:11–12). As Jesus will later make clear, those predictions will be fulfilled at the parousia (13:47–50; 24:2–31; 25:31–46). Thus, John's question posed a false alternative. Jesus *is* the one who is to come, but we still must wait for "another," for another *time*, when the Messiah will return as Judge.

11:7–15. The Role of John (cf. Luke 7:24–28; 16:16)

In lofty terms, Jesus now speaks to the crowds about John, essentially proclaiming him the greatest man ever born (11:11). First, he teases the crowds with humorous false descriptions. Whatever one might think of John, no one would call him "a reed" (a weak and vacillating figure) or accuse him of a love for fine things. He hasn't been living in a palace and wearing silk; he has lived in the wilderness and has worn haircloth and leather (3:4). Yes, he is a prophet, Jesus affirms, but more. He is the "messenger" who has come in accord with Scripture to prepare the way for the Messiah (Mal 3:1), the one who fulfills the ancient prophecies (in a nonliteral sense; cf. John 1:21) that Elijah will someday return (Mal 4:5; cf. Matt 17:10–13). Still, Jesus says that the least in the rule of heaven (5:19; 11:11) is greater than John. In that realm of light where the righteous shine like the sun (13:43; cf. Dan 12:3), every child of God will know a glory surpassing that of the greatest person who ever lived on this earth.

Matthew 11:12 is difficult to understand. Most likely, Jesus is referring to persecution, including what John is suffering and what will come upon his own followers in the near future (10:16–23). Godly people (like John) are the treasures of a realm ruled by God; when violent people (like Herod) attack godly people, that sacred realm suffers violence. Thus, Herod's arrest (and eventual murder, 14:1–12) of John not only deprives the earth of one of heaven's treasures but is also viewed as an assault on God's own property.

11:16–19. The Rejection of Wisdom (cf. Luke 7:31–35)

Jesus suddenly castigates not only the powerful people who have attacked John and opposed him, but the common people as well. The entire "generation" of people are depicted as obstinate and unbelieving. He compares them to spoiled or stubborn children who refuse to play, no matter what the game (11:17 probably refers to pretend wedding or funeral pageants that children might put on). They reject John because he seems too strange, and they reject Jesus because he seems too normal. In response, Jesus quotes a proverb that alludes to the personified figure of Wisdom mentioned in such writings as Proverbs 8. At the very least, to say that "Wisdom is vindicated by her deeds" is to affirm that the ultimate course of events always reveals who has made wise decisions (cf. 7:24–27), and Jesus is claiming that the wisdom of his (and John's) actions will be proved right in time. Some interpreters go further and say that Jesus is claiming that he *is* the embodiment or personification of Wisdom. When he speaks of Wisdom, he is speaking of himself in the third person, just as he does in speaking of the Son of Man. In that view, the aphorism in 11:19 means, "I am vindicated by my deeds." The identification of Jesus as the incarnation of Lady Wisdom (the female aspect of God) has been an important element in some feminist Christologies.

The tenor of this assault on the general population, however, is surprising and almost unprecedented. Up to this point in Matthew's narrative, readers would be expected to regard the people as a whole as favorably disposed to Jesus (7:28–29; 9:8, 33; but see 8:10). The opposition has come from religious *leaders* such as scribes and Pharisees (9:3, 11, 34). But now we learn that the generation as a whole has been slandering Jesus, calling him "a glutton and a drunkard" and dismissing him (as did the Pharisees in 9:11) as "a friend of tax collectors and sinners" (11:19). This is new information; with this disclosure, a turning point is reached in the story.

For deeper reflection on the phrase "friend of tax collectors and sinners," see comments on Matthew 9:9–13 and 21:31–32 (and Powell 2015). The first term, "tax collectors," often referred to misfit men (mentally challenged, physically deformed) who were used by unscrupulous revenue agents to extract money that may or may not have been owed by peasants, whose social position did not allow them much recourse for objection. The second term, "sinners," referred primarily (though perhaps not exclusively) to enslaved sex workers, teenage girls who had been sold into servitude by distraught fathers unable to pay their debts (or indeed the taxes they were said to owe). In general, the phrase "tax collectors and sinners" meant something akin to "the dregs of society," poor souls who were unanimously regarded as the most pathetic people on the planet. Of course, they could be pitied, but *friendship* with such people would have been another matter. Within the honor-shame culture of the Greco-Roman world, friendship implied, above all else, a bestowal of honor: to be someone's friend meant, almost definitively, to link one's reputation to that person such that both persons would receive whatever honor or shame was due the other. Accordingly, Matthew tells us that some people in Jesus' day meant to demean him by implying that he had accrued to himself the level of shame accorded those whom they regarded as traitors and harlots. Of course, Matthew's readers would be expected to realize the alternative: tax collectors and sinners have now been accorded whatever honor should accrue from being intentionally befriended by the Messiah of Israel.

11:20–24. Failure to Repent (cf. Luke 10:13–15)

Jesus' castigation of unbelievers continues as he refers to cities where he has performed miracles. Three are singled out: Chorazin, Bethsaida, and Capernaum (4:13; 8:5; 9:1; cf. 17:24). Oddly, no miracles in Chorazin are reported anywhere in the New Testament, and none in Bethsaida are reported in Matthew (cf. Mark 8:22; Luke 9:10). But now these cities are contrasted unfavorably with classic pagan locations: Tyre and Sidon, condemned in Isaiah 23 (cf. Ezek 26–28; Joel 3:4–8); and Sodom, whose destruction is reported in Genesis 18–19. The point of the contrast is to indicate that the present cities have witnessed revelations of God that would have transformed even these evil sites of old. Thus, we learn that the (unreported) miracles were not simply gracious responses to human need (though they *were* that); they were signs that the rule of heaven was near, an affirmation that should have brought repentance (3:2; 4:17). Matthew has told us previously that people were astonished by Jesus' miracles (9:33), that they spread his fame far and wide (4:24; 9:26, 31), that they followed him in great crowds (4:25), that they brought more sick people to him for healing (4:25; 8:16), and that they glorified God for what was being done (9:8). What they have *not* done is what he called them to do in his initial pronouncement: recognize that the rule of heaven is near and *repent* (4:17). It is noteworthy, however, that the condemnations are corporate rather than individual. This is consistent with biblical prophets, who often condemned cities or nations (Isa 13–23; Jer 46–51; Ezek 25–32; Amos 1:3–2:3). Still, such biblical thinking may be foreign to our present milieu, which typically evinces more concern for personal transgressions than for corporate ones and demands repentance of individuals more easily than of communities, nations, or institutions.

11:25–27. Hidden Things (cf. Luke 10:21–22)

Now Jesus turns his attention to the Father, praying to God with public words that his audience is intended to overhear. Surprisingly, he thanks God for the obstinate unbelief that he has encountered, identifying it as God's gracious will. God hides divine truth from "the wise and the intelligent" and reveals it to those who are childlike. Indeed, God allows Jesus himself to be the instrument of such revelation. In context, the wise and intelligent include not only the educated religious leaders of Israel, but also all who think they know what is right and trust in their own understanding (Prov 3:5), those able to give what seem to be good reasons for rejecting the prophetic messages of both John and Jesus (11:16–19). From other references in Matthew, we discern that the "infants" to whom truth is revealed may include Jesus' disciples and others who humble themselves (18:2–4), as well as actual children, who are specially regarded by God because they are helpless and often treated as insignificant (18:5–6, 10, 14; 19:13–15; 21:15–16). By extension, this reference may also apply to others who are helpless and/or treated as "no accounts," such as those mentioned in the first four beatitudes of the Sermon on the Mount (see comments on Matt 5:3–6). This all fits with a motif some find troubling: Matthew's Gospel seems to show a low regard for education, viewing acquisition of knowledge in a manner analogous to acquisition of wealth (see Theme 16 "*Critique of power, wealth, and wisdom*" in the introduction, p. 31). This is undoubtedly because, in his world, education (like wealth) was a major source of power, and Matthew thinks that power is often used to dominate people rather than to serve them (20:25). Readers may judge whether this is still true for us today.

The language of Jesus' prayer in 11:27 is remarkable for the close association it assumes between Jesus as "the Son" and God "the Father." This passage thus serves to develop the meaning of Jesus' identification as the Son of God, which Matthew worked so hard to establish in the first part of his Gospel (1:1–4:16; see Theme 9 "*Jesus as the Son of God*" in the introduction, p. 19). Indeed, 11:27 is sometimes called "the Johannine thunderbolt" because it sounds so similar to what is more commonly found in John's Gospel (see John 3:35; 7:29; 10:14–15;

13:3; 17:2, 25). Jesus is uniquely identified with God to such an extent that no one can know the one without the other.

11:28–30. An Open Invitation (only in Matthew)

After all the harsh talk about judgment (11:20–24) and God hiding the truth from certain people (11:25–27), Jesus concludes this speech to the crowds with a gracious invitation. This is indeed the only passage in the New Testament in which Jesus calls the general population to come to him in the same way that he calls specific disciples to follow him (4:19; the words usually translated "Follow me" can be literally rendered, "Come after me"). Those who are weary and burdened here are the same as those who were described as "harassed and helpless" in 9:36. In both cases, the problem is a dearth of true leadership. But now we hear that the populace is not only aimless because of this lack; they are also burdened. Their leaders have not only failed to provide direction but have also placed unfair and unnecessary demands upon them (cf. 23:4). The principal example of such "burdening" in Matthew is unrealistic interpretation of Torah, as the next two episodes in the narrative illustrate. Still, at first it seems odd to hear Jesus describe *his* yoke as easy and *his* burden as light. At times, Jesus seems to have made even higher demands than do the Pharisees and other religious leaders (5:17–48). The point, then, cannot be that Jesus is more lenient than others; rather, since he interprets the law in accord with God's will, people who follow *his* teaching will live in the will of God and so (no matter how stringent the demands) find rest for their souls (see Jer 6:16). This is in keeping with the almost universal Jewish notion that life within God's will is always delightful and desirable and that the law ought to serve as a reliable guide for discovering this life (Ps 19:7–13).

There are strong parallels here with the role ascribed to Wisdom in many Jewish writings, for example in the book of Sirach, where Wisdom invites people to come to her and learn the way of life (Sir 6:23–31; 24:19; 51:23–27). Thus, Jesus may still be speaking in his role as the personification or embodiment of Wisdom, as indicated above in 11:19. In any case, Jesus' easy yoke is tied specifically to his person. His teaching provides rest precisely because he himself is "gentle and humble in heart." He comes as one who serves (20:28), not as one who lords over others (20:25). Thus, he interprets the law not as a tool for establishing his own authority but for the benefit of those who keep it, in accord with a rule of love (7:12; 22:39–40) and with a hermeneutic that prioritizes mercy (9:13; 12:7; 23:23).

EXCURSUS

"Understanding" and Divine Revelation in Matthew

Matthew's Gospel emphasizes the importance of understanding and offers a somewhat distinctive take on that phenomenon. We may note, first, that understanding is absolutely necessary to bear fruit as people of God. In the parable of the Sower, the good soil that produces fruit stands for "the one who hears the word and *understands* it" (13:23, emphasis added; different from "accepts" in Mark 4:20; Luke 8:15). Likewise, regarding the seed devoured by birds, Jesus says that when anyone hears the message of God's reign "and *does not understand it*, the evil one comes and snatches away what is sown in the heart" (13:19, emphasis added).

Nevertheless, the most significant understanding (of God and of God's reign) must be given through divine revelation. At one point, Jesus prays: "I thank you, Father, Lord of heaven and earth, because you have hidden these things from the wise and the intelligent and have revealed them to infants" (11:25). He also says, "No one knows the Father except the Son and anyone to whom the Son chooses to reveal him" (11:27), and he claims that the reason he speaks in parables is because it has not been given to people in general to understand the mysteries of God's reign (13:10–15 NRSVue, "the secrets of the kingdom"). When Peter identifies Jesus as "the Messiah, the Son of the living God," Jesus indicates that this has been revealed to him not by "flesh and blood" but by the "Father in heaven" (16:16–17).

This relationship between understanding and revelation forms the backdrop for an interesting aspect of the disciples' characterization in this Gospel. Note the following incidents:

- Jesus tells his disciples that it has been given to them to know the mysteries of God's reign (13:11), and he calls them blessed because "many prophets and righteous people longed to see what you see" (13:17).

- After telling several parables, Jesus asks his disciples, "Have you understood all this?" and they answer, "Yes" (13:51).
- The disciples do not understand what Jesus means by "the yeast of the Pharisees," but after he explains it, Matthew notes, "Then they understood" (16:11–12).
- When Jesus tells his disciples that Elijah has already returned, Matthew notes, "Then [they] understood that he was speaking to them about John the Baptist" (17:13).

In all these cases, there is a pattern of the disciples initially lacking understanding but then being given that understanding by Jesus. This is significant because they also lack faith (see Theme 11 "*Disciples as people of little faith*" in the introduction, p. 21) but are never given more faith. Perhaps this is because understanding is the more important quality for mission. The disciples are people of "little faith" in Matthew, yet they are given the Great Commission in 28:18–20 (in spite of their persistent doubt in 28:17). The "Canaanite woman" in 15:21–28 is a person of "great faith," yet she is not given any commission to go and make disciples (likewise for the centurion with remarkable faith in Matt 8:5–13). In spite of their little faith, the disciples can teach people to obey the commandments of Jesus because they have understood the good news about God's reign. It would, of course, be wonderful if the disciples had great faith rather than just a little faith, but the essential quality for mission is *understanding*—and this (rather than faith) is what Jesus gives to those he calls to carry forward the mission of God initiated through his life and work.

MATTHEW 12:1–50
Open Conflict

Matthew edited diverse materials from both Mark and Q to create a fairly coherent stream of material that now constitutes the twelfth chapter of his Gospel. The Sabbath controversies, the Beelzebul accusation, the request for a sign, and the declaration regarding his true family—these all come from Mark. The sayings about good and bad trees, the sign of Jonah, and the return of unclean spirits derive from Q. At the heart of all this, we have unique Matthean material: a long scriptural citation identifying Jesus as the Isaian Servant (12:15–21).

The conflict between Jesus and the religious leaders of Israel has been smoldering throughout the narrative (see Theme 14 "*Religious leaders as enemies of God*" in the introduction, p. 25). It was foreshadowed in the possibly unwitting involvement of chief priests and scribes in Herod's plot to kill Jesus (2:4–5) and in John's rejection of Pharisees and Sadducees as candidates for baptism (3:7–9). Jesus has castigated Israel's so-called leaders as unrighteous (5:20), and we have been told that he views Israel as essentially leaderless (9:36). For their part, the leaders have criticized Jesus for the company he keeps (9:11) and have speculated that he performs miracles through demonic powers (9:34). Now, at last, this conflict bursts into the open with the accusations being made directly. No longer the stuff of "asides" or stray remarks, the conflict between Jesus and the religious leaders becomes the controlling motif for much of the story.

12:1–8. Plucking Grain on the Sabbath (cf. Mark 2:23–28; Luke 6:1–5)

The Pharisees accuse Jesus' disciples of harvesting grain on the Sabbath, which they take to be a violation of one of the Ten Commandments (Exod 20:10; Deut 5:14). At issue is the question of legal interpretation and ultimately of who has the authority to rule on such matters. The principle of "binding and loosing" (16:19; 18:18) is assumed, according to which a determination has to be made regarding the extent of the law's application (see Theme 8 "*Binding-and-loosing commandments*" in the introduction, p. 16). The Pharisees apparently think that plucking just enough grain to satisfy one's hunger (12:1) counts as harvesting; Jesus disagrees and declares his disciples "guiltless" (12:7). The incident illustrates well why Jesus can claim that his yoke is "easy" (11:29–30). He interprets the commandment with a hermeneutic that prioritizes mercy over sacrifice (12:7; see also 9:13): God prefers to see hungry people fed rather than go without food for a day just to demonstrate their fidelity to a rule. Notably, Jesus does not set himself against Scripture; instead, he finds justification for his principle in Scripture, quoting Hosea 6:6 and citing a precedent in which hungry soldiers were allowed to eat holy bread normally reserved for priests (1 Sam 21:1–6; cf. Lev 24:5–9).

In offering such arguments, Jesus sounds remarkably like a rabbi (indeed, a Pharisee), for such claims constitute the point/counterpoint of binding-and-loosing debates. But what he says next changes the tenor of the discussion. He indicates that Sabbath laws don't apply to his disciples any more than they apply to priests who must work in the temple on the Sabbath. Why not? Because the work that he and his disciples are doing constitutes "something greater than the temple" (12:6). Furthermore, he adds that, as the Son of Man, he is "lord of the Sabbath" (12:8) and has divine authority to decide what is right regardless of whether the Pharisees accept the rationale for his decisions. The conflict thus moves to another level. It is no longer just a legal dispute over how to interpret commandments (something on which actual Pharisees would have evinced a spectrum of opinions); it is a christological controversy over fundamental acceptance or rejection of Jesus and his authority.

12:9–14. Healing on the Sabbath (cf. Mark 3:1–6; Luke 6:6–11)

Immediately after claiming to be "lord of the Sabbath" (12:8), Jesus enters a synagogue where the Pharisees test him to see if he will act on this claim in a way that will allow them to discredit him or even charge him with a crime. Since he is known as a healer, they ask him whether he believes it is lawful to practice this profession on the Sabbath—in their eyes clearly a violation of the Mosaic injunction against performing work on the Sabbath (Exod 20:10; Deut 5:14). Jesus takes the bait and heals a man with a withered hand, but first utters words that make them look foolish: since their legal interpretations allow a person to rescue a sheep on the Sabbath, they are apparently more concerned with the health of animals than of people. Readers are not expected to question the logic of this argument, for example, by wondering whether immediate action might be more urgent in the case of the sheep than in that of the man. For the purposes of Matthew's story, the Pharisees are put to shame, and Jesus, instead of being discredited, is vindicated by God through the healing that does occur. The Pharisees are then left to plot against him in other, more dastardly ways: they conspire to destroy him in a manner that begs comparison with the earlier machinations of evil king Herod (2:16, 20). The crowds, however, follow Jesus and continue to be healed by him (see comments on 19:1–2).

This passage is one of the most significant in the Gospel for understanding Matthean ethics, which hinge on the principles of "binding and loosing" spelled out in the introduction (Theme 8 "*Binding-and-loosing commandments*," see p. 16). Both here and in the previous account (12:1–8), Sabbath laws are "loosed," or set aside, as inapplicable for what Jesus regards as exceptional circumstances. Even those who disagree with him (the Pharisees) grant that such laws can sometimes be set aside (loosed) in some circumstances. But the shocking revelation here is that "it is lawful to do good on the Sabbath" (12:12). This justification for setting aside the law sets a sweeping precedent, as did his previous suggestion that sabbath restrictions need not apply to those engaged in the important work that marks his own ministry (12:6). Such declarations have potentially radical implications for ways in which many biblical commandments might be loosed in a variety of instances (as they obviously were in the developing Christian church). Such judgments help to explain why Jesus' ethical demands could be called a "light burden," an "easy yoke" (11:30); they also clarify why some people might say that he has come "to abolish the Law" (5:17).

In terms of narrative flow, this passage represents a climactic turning point in the story. Before now, the religious leaders have criticized Jesus to themselves (9:3), to his disciples (9:11), and to the crowds (9:34)—and they have criticized the disciples to Jesus (12:2)—but this is the first time that they have ever challenged Jesus directly with regard to his own conduct. This acceleration of conflict leads to the first mention in this Gospel of the leaders' plot to kill Jesus (12:14). That plot is not simply prompted by legal arguments but by Jesus' stubborn claim to possess and represent divine authority, to be "lord of the Sabbath" (12:8). Matters of legal interpretation are important to Matthew, and most of the conflicts between Jesus and the religious leaders of Israel concern matters of the law. Still, when the leaders' plot against Jesus finally succeeds, the charge against him will be blasphemy, not heresy (26:65–66; cf. 9:3).

12:15–21. God's Chosen Servant

A citation from Isaiah 42:1–4 interprets Jesus' healing ministry as the work of God's *Servant*, a theme that Matthew has already touched on through his quotation of Isaiah 53:4 in 8:17. Paradoxically, though Jesus has more authority (divine power) than other religious leaders, he exercises this authority in service, for the benefit of God's people.

The focus on the gentiles in this citation, furthermore, points already to the ultimate scope of his ministry: not only to the "lost sheep of the house of Israel" (10:5–6; 15:24), but also to "all nations" (28:19), the whole world (24:14).

12:22–37. The Beelzebul Controversy (cf. Mark 3:22–29; Luke 6:43–45; 11:14–23; 12:10)

Jesus' exorcism of a blind and mute demoniac leads to an extended rant against the religious leaders of Israel when they castigate the healing as the work of Beelzebul. The common people, by contrast, are amazed by the healing and even speculate whether this is the Messiah: "Can this be the Son of David?" (see 22:42). The Pharisees try to dampen this enthusiasm with their suggestion that Jesus derives his power from a satanic rather than godly source (the name Beelzebul, meaning "lord of the flies," was one of several names used for the devil). This is now the second time this accusation has been made (9:32–34; cf. 10:25), though Matthew does not earlier report its being offered to Jesus directly. Once more, Jesus is presented as possessing unusual mental powers: his response to the accusation is based on knowledge of the Pharisees' thoughts (12:25; cf. 9:4; see also 12:15; 16:8; 22:18; 26:10).

The initial response is a simple appeal to logic. Jesus finds it patently ridiculous to suggest that Satan's agents would be ridding the world of demonic influence. Furthermore, the argument that so easily ascribes Jesus' works to the devil could just as easily be turned against the Pharisees, since their own disciples (here referred to metaphorically as "sons"; NRSVue, "exorcists") also take credit for performing exorcisms. No, the logical conclusion is that Jesus is overcoming the spirits of Satan through the spirit of Satan's opponent, the Spirit of God. If this is true, Jesus continues, then his claim that the reign of God has come near (4:17; cf. 3:2; 10:7) must also be true; indeed, if the effects of God's rule are this evident, the reign of God must already be upon them. Again, Jesus uses a simple parable: if someone plunders a strong man's house, you conclude that he must first have bound the strong man, who would not simply let his house be plundered. Likewise, if Jesus is now robbing Satan of some of his prized possessions (the tormented souls that his demons have enslaved), someone (in this case, God) must have tied up the devil.

In commenting on this passage, Martin Luther said that God "has put the devil on a leash" (ever since, Lutherans have felt compelled to add, "though it appears to be a rather long leash").

After thus dispensing with this facetious argument, Jesus turns to a more serious matter. When the Pharisees attribute God's gracious, liberating activity to the devil, they "blaspheme the Holy Spirit" in a way that prevents them from ever benefiting from that activity themselves. The approaching reign of God brings an unprecedented offer: forgiveness of every sin and blasphemy, even those directed against Jesus himself. But if someone rejects even that offer, spurning it as the work of the devil, there can be no hope remaining, in this age or the one to come. That said, 12:30 expresses one of the most unfortunate sentiments in all of Christian Scripture. It seems to be a stray remark, not really related to anything else said here. We should probably dismiss it as an egregious example of what unchecked apocalyptic dualism can generate and be grateful that the sentiment is corrected overtly in other Gospels (Mark 9:40; Luke 9:50) and implicitly in this one (Matt 5:43–45).

The next few verses (12:33–37) are a virulent response to the fact that the Pharisees have offered this, their most nasty assessment of Jesus, behind his back rather than to his face (12:24–25). Normally, a good tree has good fruit, and a bad tree has bad fruit (7:16–20): that's the way it ought to be. But the Pharisees who are characters in Matthew's story of Jesus are hypocrites. They are evil people, a "brood of vipers" (3:7; 23:33); yet somehow they manage to "speak good things," to say things that *appear* to be right and proper (the best example of this is still to come, 22:15–16). It all comes out eventually anyway, Jesus says, and people will be judged on the basis of their careless (literally, "unguarded") words, that is, by what they say when they are not consciously trying to make an impression. This latter point actually plays out in the literary dynamics of Matthew's Gospel. Studies of speech patterns have shown that, in Matthew, words spoken by the religious leaders of Israel only reveal their actual point of view when the discourse is "indirect": they only say what they really think of people when they are talking about those people to others. Notably, Matthew might have simply told us outright that the true character of these leaders is more likely to be revealed by what they say *about* people than by what they say *to* people; by presenting this point as he does (woven into the narrative's rhetoric), he offers his readers practice at learning to detect such duplicity (Powell 1996a).

12:38–42. Request for a Sign (cf. Mark 8:11–12; Luke 11:16, 29–32)

Some of the religious leaders now ask Jesus to give them a sign to verify his claim to divine authority, and he rejects their plea with caustic words (cf. 16:1–4). The request is hypocritical since those who make it have already come together to plot Jesus' murder (12:14). Furthermore, Jesus has just indicated that the exorcisms he performs are an irrefutable sign that the reign of God "has come" to them (12:28). What other sort of sign could they have in mind? Perhaps the kind of omen or wonder that false prophets and false messiahs will be eager to perform in their attempts to lead astray the elect (24:24; cf. 2 Thess 2:9; Rev 13:13–15)? In any case, Jesus dismisses the request as typical thinking for a wicked and adulterous generation so immune to repentance. He then excoriates not only those who have come to him with the request but the entire generation of people they represent. The language is like the judgment oracles of 11:20–24. Jesus brings a greater revelation of God than did Jonah or Solomon, yet those figures generated repentance and attracted a following even among pagan peoples of the earth. How tragic, then, that God's people resist this, the greatest revelation of all!

Embedded in Jesus' response is the curious reference to the one sign that they will be offered, the sign of Jonah. This enigmatic saying comes from Q, and Luke's Gospel probably preserves the more original version: in Luke, the point is that the *person* of Jonah was a sign to the Ninevites, and so, in some parallel fashion, the *person* of the Son of Man will be a sign to the current generation (Luke 11:30). In Matthew, it is the *burial* of Jonah in the belly of the fish that is important: Jesus overtly explains the sign as a reference to the burial (and, we may assume, resurrection) of the Son of Man. Many readers have calculated that Jesus does not spend three days and three nights "in the heart of the earth." He was in a tomb (not underground, much less "in the heart of the earth") and, by the most generous reckoning, the time period was two nights and one full day, with slight portions of two more days. There have been attempts to resolve the problem, but the best explanation is simply that Matthew thought the analogy was close enough and hoped we wouldn't examine it too minutely. In any case, as Matthew's story continues, we will see that the religious leaders do in fact receive the sign of Jonah (as interpreted by Matthew): they hear and know that Jesus is raised from the dead; still they do not repent, but only redouble their efforts to oppose him (28:11–15; see Powell 2007).

12:43–45. Parable of the Unclean Spirit (cf. Luke 11:24–26)

Still speaking to the religious leaders of Israel, Jesus likens them and their generation to a person possessed—and then repossessed—by evil spirits. The comparison is parabolic; he does not mean to indicate that the Pharisees are all literally demon-possessed persons—or else, how would their "sons" be able to perform exorcisms (12:27)? Rather, Jesus means to describe his own ministry to Israel as a time of respite. In driving out the forces of evil, he gives Israel a chance to enact true repentance and become the people of God. If this does not happen, the demons that Jesus is keeping at bay will return, and the condition of Israel will be worse than ever. We should remember that by the time Matthew wrote his Gospel, Israel's capital city, Jerusalem, lay in ruins, destroyed by Roman armies; the parable may have been especially poignant to those Jews and Christians who interpreted that destruction as divine judgment.

12:46–50. The True Family of Jesus (cf. Mark 3:31–35; Luke 8:19–21)

Jesus' mother and brothers (see also 13:55–56) come to speak to him about some unidentified matter. Jesus indicates that his disciples are his true family: everyone who does the will of the Father is his brother, sister, and mother. According to this analogy, God is Father to all people (5:45, 48; 6:26; 23:9), and thus all people are related to each other as part of God's family. Those who do the Father's will (cf. 7:21), however, recognize this standing and acknowledge through their deeds this relationship with God and with each other.

In Matthew, these words are positive, not negative, emphasizing inclusion of disciples in the family of Jesus rather than exclusion of his literal earthly relatives. Matthew's Gospel does not mention the tensions between Jesus and those relatives alluded to elsewhere in the

New Testament (Mark 3:21; John 7:5; but see below on 13:57). Still, the sweeping gesture of Jesus, indicating that *these* (disciples) are his family, does demonstrate that he prioritizes fidelity to God's will over the traditional loyalties of family ties. Hypothetically, at least, he is willing to practice what he preaches, to de-prioritize or even sacrifice family relations for the sake of God's rule in the same way that is sometimes required of others (4:22; 8:21–22; 10:34–39; 19:29).

MATTHEW 13:1–53
The Parable Discourse

This long section of discourse is a Matthean construct, composed of material redacted from Mark and a considerable amount of material unique to Matthew (all of 13:24–30, 36–52).

Most of Matthew 13 is devoted to the third of Jesus' five major speeches (see 5–7; 10; 18; 24–25). It is marked especially by the large number of parables grouped together in one spot. The word *parable* has not been used up to this point in the Gospel, though Jesus has occasionally spoken in ways that seem parabolic (7:24–27; 12:43–45). Now, however, Matthew tells us explicitly that Jesus spoke in parables, and he records seven examples. All these parables, furthermore, concern the main subject of Jesus' preaching, the rule of heaven (4:17; see Theme 2 "*Reign or rule of God/heaven*" in the introduction, p. 8). In this discourse, Jesus alternates between speaking to the crowds (13:2, 34) and to his disciples (13:10, 36). Matthew is careful never to refer to Jesus as *teaching* in parables for, as we shall see, the parables do not necessarily offer instruction. Jesus simply speaks of mysteries, leaving open the question as to who might have ears to hear (13:9, 43).

13:1–9. Parable of the Sower (cf. Mark 4:1–9; Luke 8:4–8)

Jesus begins with an apparently simple story of seed falling onto different types of soil. Most of the seed is wasted. Some of it is eaten by birds before it ever takes root; other seed does begin to grow, but the plants are choked out by thorns or scorched by sun. Nevertheless, the few seeds that do fall onto good soil produce a harvest that more than compensates for seed that did not. There is probably no merit in wondering whether the sower was indiscriminate or careless, or whether a yield of a hundredfold (cf. Gen 26:12) would be considered miraculous or typical. Interpreters have explored all these options, but our knowledge of ancient agricultural practices is limited and the point of the story seems embedded solely in the image of seed being sown with various results. Eventually we learn that Jesus is speaking of what happens with the announcement of God's reign (NRSVue, "the word of the kingdom," 13:19). The proclamation that God's rule has come near (4:17; 10:7) is good news (4:23; 9:35; 24:14) that goes out to all and sometimes has a beneficial outcome. But the crowds will not be privy to that explanation. Still, given the comment in 13:9, they would realize that the story was intended to convey some sort of message: the moral could be "Perseverance pays off!" or even "If at first you don't succeed, try again." But there is more to it than that, as his disciples will discover in 13:18–23.

13:10–17. The Purpose of Parables (cf. Mark 4:10–12; Luke 8:9–10)

Jesus' disciples ask him why he speaks to the crowds in parables instead of just telling them plainly what he wants them to know. In response, he cites Isaiah 6:9 and notes a distinction between the crowds and the disciples themselves (on the role the crowds play as a character in Matthew's narrative, see comments on 19:1–2). The crowds are those for whom the mystery of divine revelation is still an open question; they may or may not have ears to hear (13:9, 43). Jesus has previously said that God hides the truth from some and reveals it to others (11:25). For this reason, he speaks of the secrets or mysteries of God's reign in ways that are only clear to those to whom God grants understanding (see Excursus: "Understanding" and Divine Revelation in Matthew, p. 158). Others hear but do not understand; hence, they do not repent and are not healed. This is justified theologically for Matthew on the presumption that, for some, judgment has already occurred. Some persons, on account of their unrighteousness (5:20) or even lofty status in this world (11:25), are deemed unworthy of receiving the benefits that God's coming reign will bring. The revelation of God's grace and forgiveness and mercy remains hidden from them. This is not arbitrary on God's part, nor is it a matter of simple predestination. It is a preliminary judgment on persons whose hearts are consequently hardened. The thought is expressed well in 13:12: those who have at least a potential receptivity to Jesus' good news about God's reign will hear his parables and understand them; those who lack even this basic orientation to God's will and word (for example, those who blaspheme the Holy Spirit, 12:31) will not gain this understanding and, in fact, will eventually lose whatever it is that they do rely on (pedigree, 3:9; wealth, 19:23–24; etc.). The focus of Jesus' words, however, is primarily positive. He emphasizes that his disciples *do* have ears to hear. God has granted them to know the mysteries of God's rule. Indeed, they are privileged to participate in what many prophets and righteous ones longed to experience.

13:18–23. Explanation of the Sower Parable (cf. Mark 4:13–20; Luke 8:11–15)

Now Jesus explains the parable of the Sower to his disciples. It is an allegory concerning the announcement of God's reign that Jesus (4:17, 23) and his disciples (10:7) have been making to Israel and will eventually bring to the whole world (24:14). The four types of soil illustrate how different people respond to this announcement. Some simply reject it out of hand: these are the ones about whom Jesus has just spoken (13:14–15), whose hearts have been closed to God's word. In Matthew's narrative, the religious leaders of Israel are the best examples of such people (see 15:12–14). Others respond favorably, even with joy, but eventually fall away either because they cannot bear the stress of persecution (24:10) or because they try to serve two masters and become hopelessly entangled in worldly pursuits (see 6:19–24). In Matthew's story, the crowds who are often amazed by Jesus' miracles and follow him in great numbers seem to be the most likely candidates for such a fate (though even Jesus' disciples will temporarily succumb to the fear of persecution; see 26:56, 69–75). Such developments could lead to despair, but Jesus reveals a mystery. Not every seed needs to produce fruit. God is in charge of the harvest, and God has taken opposition and apostasy into account. As has been true throughout the history of Israel, only a remnant is needed, only a handful that will bear fruit, for the fruit they bear will indeed be sufficient to constitute the glorious rule of heaven. The mark of these few, notably, is that they hear the word and *understand* it. Such understanding has nothing to do with mental capacity but, as Jesus has indicated, must be given by God (11:25; 13:11; 16:17; see Excursus: "Understanding" and Divine Revelation in Matthew, p. 158).

Matthew's Gospel uses the metaphor of fruit-bearing several times (3:8, 10; 7:16–20; 12:33; 13:23; 21:43; see also 21:19). In the broadest sense, to "bear fruit" means simply "to do the will of the Father" (see 7:21). But in this parable, fruit-bearing functions as a summary phrase for describing the mission and call of the church, and the decision to describe such activity as "fruit-bearing" is significant. In a basic sense, the phrase means to reproduce what has been sown. Thus the mission of the church is not to be innovative, but to allow the inevitable effects of Jesus' mission on earth to come to pass. To put it differently, the mission of God being accomplished through Jesus continues to be accomplished through the community of his followers (see Theme 3 "*The mission of God*" in the introduction, p. 10). Thus, everything the church does ought to have an obvious coherence with what Jesus did: grape bushes yield grapes, not figs or thorns (7:16). The metaphor may also have both quantitative and qualitative nuances. First, the quality of fruit that is born may identify the bearer as good or evil, since "good trees bear good fruit" (7:16). In that sense, the announcement of God's reign may bear fruit when persons who hear it demonstrate repentance through ethically righteous behavior (see 3:8). But quantity is also important: the person who hears and understands the announcement of God's reign bears *much* fruit, even a hundredfold (13:23). This suggests that persons who hear and understand the word tend to multiply, to increase the community by fulfilling Jesus' initial (4:19) and final (28:19–20) words to his disciples.

13:24–30. Parable of Wheat and Weeds (only in Matthew)

Jesus returns to addressing the crowds (13:34) after a brief hiatus with his disciples (13:10–23). Once again, he tells a parable that he later explains to his disciples in private (13:36–43); again, the image is agricultural: a farmer plants a wheat field, but an enemy comes and sows weeds in it. The man decides to let the wheat and weeds grow together until the harvest rather than risk uprooting some of the wheat while pulling the weeds. Readers are left to imagine what the crowds would have made of this story, lacking Jesus' explanation: all he tells them is that it reveals something significant about the rule of heaven (13:24).

13:31–35. Mustard Seed and Yeast (cf. Mark 4:30–34; Luke 13:18–21)

Before explaining the parable of Wheat and Weeds, Jesus tells two more brief parables with identical meaning, differing only in the images they use. The rule of heaven is like a mustard seed or a measure of yeast, either of which appears tiny but has far more expansive influence than one might anticipate. Jesus has already indicated that the reign of God is evident in his ministry (12:28), so he no doubt intends for these metaphors to be applied to the work that he and his followers are pursuing. A peasant preacher who has nowhere to lay his head (8:20), he has initiated a movement that will reach the whole world (24:14) and transform people from every nation (28:19). The mustard seed is elsewhere used in Matthew as a symbol for the tiny speck of faith required for people to accomplish what would otherwise be impossible (17:20). As such, Matthew may indicate that even the "little faith" of Jesus' disciples (6:30; 8:26; 14:31; 16:8; 17:20; see also 28:17) will be sufficient to facilitate the establishment of God's reign (see Theme 11 "*Disciples as people of little faith*" in the introduction, p. 21). The reference to birds in 13:32 alludes to Daniel 4:12. Matthew elsewhere refers to yeast (16:6, 11–12), but in a context where it is a metaphor for corruption.

A concluding comment in 13:34–35 indicates that Jesus' practice of using parables fulfills an ancient prophecy from Psalm 78:2. The prophecy also reveals the purpose of the parables, as stated above in 13:11. Parables do in fact proclaim the mysteries of God's reign, regardless of whether the audience is enabled to understand this.

13:36–43. Explanation of Wheat and Weeds Parable (only in Matthew)

Alone with his disciples again (cf. 13:10–23), Jesus explains the parable of the Wheat and Weeds. It is an allegory like the parable of the Sower, in a sense picking up where that story left off. Through his ministry, Jesus has sown the word about God's rule, and in some cases (as with his disciples) it has borne fruit. But the devil has sent his minions into the field as well, those who work lawlessness (NRSVue, "evildoers," 13:41; see also 7:23) and cause others to stumble (NRSVue, "causes of sin," 13:41; see also 18:6–7). Elsewhere, Matthew speaks of "false prophets" (7:15) and of people who are just evil (5:39). Jesus' followers need to recognize that the world is so infected, but they also need to resist the impulse to purge it. Under no circumstances are they to try to rid the world of those they would identify as demonic ("children of the evil one," 13:38). Just as God sends rain and sunshine on the good and on the bad, the just and the unjust (5:45), so Jesus' disciples (the field hands) are to let the wheat and weeds grow side by side and leave judgment to God (cf. 7:1). This is the main point of the parable, though it also offers two words of affirmation to those who must live in a world where good and evil are so entwined. First, the devil, not God, is to blame for this situation; the presence of evil is not by God's design. Second, the condition is temporary. In time, the harvest will come, Jesus will send out angels, all causes of sin and all evildoers will be destroyed, and the righteous will "shine like the sun" in a glorious realm where God reigns over all (13:43; cf. Dan 12:3).

As with all parables, the story should not be taken as literally representative of the world. Nowhere else in the Bible is there any indication that the devil has created people or populated the world with human beings who are his minions, and it seems unlikely that either Jesus or Matthew would have believed that this was actually the case. Still, the parable does provide a reasonable paradigm for understanding the fictive world of Matthew's story: in this narrative, some characters are put in the world by the devil (see comments on 15:13).

13:44–46. Parables of the Treasure and the Pearl (only in Matthew)

Still speaking to his disciples, Jesus again tells two short parables that seem to have the same meaning (see also the two parables in 13:31–33). Like a treasure or a pearl, the rule of heaven is of great value, worth sacrificing everything else to obtain (see also 19:27, 29). As typical in Matthew, the phrase "rule of heaven" (NRSVue, "kingdom of heaven") refers not only to a future life beyond death but also to the experience of God's influence and power here and now (see Theme 2 "*Reign or rule of God/heaven*" in the introduction, p. 8). Jesus thus indicates that living in accord with God's will is not burdensome (see 11:28–30). Finding the life that God intends one to live is like discovering a prize of inestimable worth. Life under God's righteous rule is to be sought above anything else (6:33).

13:47–50. Parable of the Dragnet (only in Matthew)

Jesus tells his disciples one more parable and then explains it. The rule of heaven involves judgment, a sorting of good from bad. At the close of the age, angels will separate evil people from the righteous in the same way that fishers sort their catch. The point of the parable is essentially the same as that made in the parable of the Wheat and Weeds (esp. 13:41–43), except that here the injunction for humans to wait on the angels for judgment rather than enacting it ahead of schedule is only implicit. There is also, possibly, another subtle difference. Since Jesus has called his disciples to be "fishers of people" (4:19), the image of sorting fish may signify a judgment of those who have responded to their ministry, of those in the church rather than of those in the world at large (cf. 13:38). The "bad fish" then would not symbolize evildoers in a generic sense (13:41) but false prophets, elsewhere called "wolves . . . in sheep's clothing" (7:15), or anyone who calls Jesus "Lord, Lord" but does not do the will of the Father (7:21–23; see also 18:17; 24:24, 45–51; 25:1–30).

13:51–53. Conclusion (only in Matthew)

As Jesus concludes this series of parables regarding the rule of heaven, his disciples affirm that they have understood all that he said. This confirms his earlier claim that God has granted them to know the mysteries of the reign of God (13:11), and it sustains his hope that, as ones who understand the announcement of that reign, they will bear much fruit (13:23; see Excursus: "Understanding" and Divine Revelation in Matthew, p. 158). Jesus responds to their affirmation with an enigmatic saying that amounts to a bonus, eighth parable. The disciples will be scribes, but of a different sort than those who oppose Jesus throughout this narrative (9:3; 12:38; 15:1–2; 21:15–16; 26:57; 27:41). They will be scribes trained for the rule of heaven, able to view everything from the new perspective that has become imperative now that God's reign has come near (3:2; 4:17; 10:7). As such, they will know how to combine new and old. This is a different metaphor from that used in 9:16–17, where the implication seemed to be that old ways were no longer acceptable. But the thought is consistent with his previous claims: Jesus has insisted that the Law and the Prophets are not to be set aside as long as heaven and earth remain (5:17–19); yet as his own teaching (5:21–48) and practice (9:9–15; 12:1–14) have demonstrated, much that has become traditional needs to be revised. The scribe trained for the rule of heaven (cf. 23:34) will be able to combine the old word of the Law and Prophets with the new word of God's reign.

MATTHEW 13:54–58
Rejection at Nazareth

Matthew took this episode from Mark 6:1–6, redacting it slightly, as noted below.

Jesus comes to his own hometown and teaches in the synagogue. The people are astonished by his wisdom and by reports of his miracles, but they also take offense at him, apparently because he is acting as one above his station. He is the son of a mere construction worker (NRSVue, "carpenter"; the Greek *tektonos* means simply "builder"); his relatives are known to them. But he is behaving like some kind of prophet (cf. John 6:42; 7:15). Jesus responds with a proverb that makes the claim to be a prophet explicit; in fact, their rejection of him only accords with the type of treatment prophets usually receive from their own people. Thus Jesus refrains from doing many miracles there because of their unbelief (a Matthean editing of Mark 6:5, which said he "could do no" miracles there). The reference to being without honor "in [his] own house" is the only hint in Matthew that Jesus' family (mentioned here in 13:55 and also in 12:46–47) might not number among his supporters (cf. Mark 3:21; John 7:5). However, Matthew does not include the phrase "and among their own kin" from Mark 6:4, which made that allegation more explicit. Mark possibly added that phrase to a well-known proverb in order to emphasize the conflict between Jesus and his family (siblings and mother); Matthew, then, simply abbreviated the text to cite the proverb in its traditional form, without implying any overly literal application of the "house" phrase to Jesus' family members. Thus, Matthew does not want to present Jesus' mother and brothers as "enemies" (some of them had become respected persons in the early church); but he wants to retain some motif of Jesus' being rejected by those who might constitute a primary support group: in this way, Jesus himself bears a cost that he says will come upon many of his followers (10:35–37) and he shows that his trust in God transcends the traditional comfort and security of home (see 8:20—also not literally true, since he did have a home in Nazareth and use of a house in Capernaum).

MATTHEW 14:1–12
Murder of John the Baptist

Matthew is following his Markan source, taking this episode from Mark 6:14–29 and abbreviating it in ways that do not significantly alter the meaning.

A wild speculation on the part of Herod the tetrarch (NRSVue, "ruler," 14:1; this is Herod Antipas, a son of Herod the Great, mentioned in Matt 2:1–19) introduces a flashback account that reveals how that ruler had John the Baptist arrested (4:12; 11:2) and subsequently put to death. Only now are we told the reason for that arrest: John objected to Herod's illicit marriage to his half sister Herodias, who earlier was married to another half brother, Philip of Ituraea. Herod Antipas is depicted as a rather pathetic figure, lacking the spine to carry out his plans as his father would have done. He wants to kill John but is afraid of public opinion. Then, after he makes an extravagant promise to Herodias' daughter, who dances for him on his birthday, he is shamed into granting his wife's request to have John beheaded because he apparently fears the opinions of his invited guests (noblemen) even more than those of the populace.

Matthew reports this lurid and gruesome (head on a platter, 14:8) tale without flinching, exposing the cruel culture of paganism for what he thinks it is. In this story, Herod is the prime example of those who dare to plunder a realm that is ruled by God, depriving earth of heaven's gifts (see comments on 11:12). Yet Herod is not daring. Everything he does is motivated by fear, and in the end, he is left worrying that Jesus might be John the Baptist reborn to haunt him (14:2). He illustrates those whom, Jesus says, fear people but not God (10:28). Antipas attacks God's agent without appearing to realize that he thus engages in battling the Lord, who destroys body and soul in hell. Still, it is with a note of sadness that Matthew records the temporal victories of such tyrants. John, the greatest man yet born of woman (11:11), is dead, and his disciples come to collect his body.

The story may be read in light of Matthew's understanding of *coercive power* as definitive of evil (see Theme 16 "*Critique of power, wealth, and wisdom*" in the introduction, p. 31): in Matthew, nearly all persons with power are evil, regardless of whether they are Jewish or gentile, because practically all persons who possess such power use it coercively, to lord it over others rather than to serve (see 20:25–28). Dorothy Jean Weaver has demonstrated, however, that the "power" earthly rulers exercise is ironic since Matthew consistently presents this power as being thwarted in certain respects: Herod the king is tricked by the magi (2:16), Herod the tetrarch is coerced by Herodias (14:6–11), and Pilate is manipulated by the religious leaders and the crowd (27:20–26). In every case, the tyrants act out of fear; in every case, they either fail to accomplish what they want to accomplish or are pressured to issue commands contrary to their own will or desire (see Weaver 2017).

MATTHEW 14:13–36
Feeding of 5,000 and Walking on Water

Still following his Markan source, Matthew derived these stories from Mark 6:22–56, inserting a unique account of Peter (momentarily) walking on water into the account of Jesus doing the same (14:28–31).

Matthew now relates dramatic episodes that present Jesus as one imbued with incredible divine power. There are echoes here of Old Testament heroes, especially Moses and Elijah, but in some ways the stories have even more in common with Greek mythology: Jesus appears to be a god on earth and continues to evoke worship from mortal human beings.

14:13–21. Feeding of 5,000 (cf. Mark 6:32–44; Luke 9:10–17; John 6:1–14

Wary of Herod, Jesus seeks isolation, but his compassion for the crowd (cf. 9:36) moves him to heal those who follow him. Then he miraculously feeds the crowd of well over 5,000 people—since only men are counted, readers would imagine a total crowd of perhaps 20,000 using only five loaves and two fish. A similar miracle will be recounted in 15:32–39 (see also 16:5–12). There are allusions to God providing manna in the wilderness: note the reference to "a deserted place" in 14:15 (cf. Exod 16:1, 3) and the summary statement, "All ate and were filled," in 14:20 (cf. Exod 16:18, "All gathered as much as each of them needed"). But an even closer Old Testament parallel may lie with the story in 2 Kings 4:42–44, in which Elijah miraculously feeds a hundred men with only "twenty loaves of barley" bread and some "fresh ears of grain." In that instance, the prophet works the miracle through an intermediary (his servant), just as Jesus here has the actual multiplication occur through the hands of his disciples (14:19). The story also contrasts with Herod's gruesome banquet (14:6–11) and seems to preview Jesus' Last Supper (26:26–29) and the eucharistic services of the Christian church: references to "taking a loaf," "blessing," "breaking," and "giving it to his disciples" may be found in both 14:19 and 26:26 (also in 15:36). As such, it is often viewed as a preview of the eschatological great banquet at the end of time. But since the focus is more on temporal (and temporary) sustenance, we may do better to read the story as offering illustrations of how God provides for those who are of more value than "the birds of the air" (6:25–26) and of how God answers the prayers that Jesus encourages his disciples to pray in faith (6:11; 7:7–10).

14:22–33. Walking on Water (cf. Mark 6:45–52; John 6:16–21; Matt 14:28–31 only in Matthew)

Jesus walks on water and bids Peter do the same. The latter has some success but must be rescued by Jesus when overtaken by fear. The story is a paradigm for believers in troubled times, depicted through the universal image of a ship in a storm. The boat may even be a symbol of the church since both Peter's call, "Lord, save me" (14:30), and the disciples' confession in 14:33 have a liturgical ring. Jesus previously stilled a storm that had instilled terror in his disciples (8:23–26); now we see that fear is still their enemy (14:27, 30). It may be a natural reaction but, like anxiety (6:25–34), it can be debilitating for people of "little faith." In this story, at least, "little faith" seems to be synonymous with "doubt." Such doubt (*distazō*, used only here and in 28:17) is different from the double-mindedness (*diakrinō*) denounced in James 1:6 or the "refusal to believe" (*apisteō*) attributed to Thomas in John 20:27. The word implies uncertainty or inadequacy, not stubbornness; it means trying to believe with only partial success. Such doubt is the quality of seekers (6:33; 7:7–8); though its deficiency may be lamented, it is never condemned. Jesus does not abandon doubters, and so, in just a few verses, his disciples of little faith move from being terrified of ghosts and storms to worshiping Jesus as "the Son of God" (14:33—a dramatic redactional change from Mark 6:51).

The confession, "Truly you are the Son of God" (14:33), anticipates the celebrated confession of Peter in 16:16, "You are the Messiah, the Son of the living God," which Jesus will claim was given through divine revelation and thus marks Peter as one who will have a special position in the formation of the church (16:17–19). One might wonder why so much will be made of Peter's confession later in the story when all the disciples basically said the same thing two chapters earlier (14:33). My only answer is that Matthew, while somewhat gifted in literary artistry, is ultimately more driven by theology than narratology. The story would frankly work better if 14:33 came somewhere later than 16:16–20. Peter's confession is supposed to be climactic, and Matthew ruined that aspect of the story by inserting the preliminary "Son of God" confession here. But he is driven by theology: specifically, he wants to show that while doubt and "little faith" may prevent believers from walking on water, they do not prevent them from proclaiming Jesus Christ to be God's Son or from worshiping him (on this, see Excursus: Worship in the Gospel of Matthew, p. 51; and comments on 28:17).

14:34–36. Healings at Gennesaret (cf. Mark 6:53–56; John 6:22–25)

In a brief note, we are informed that the healing ministry of Jesus continues unabated and that Jesus is known even in a land he has not previously visited. The reference to the healing power of his garment recalls the story in 9:19–22, where Matthew clarifies that "faith," not magic, is the significant factor.

MATTHEW 15:1–28
Controversy over Defilement and Encounter with a Canaanite Woman

Continuing to follow his Markan source, Matthew has taken this material from Mark 7:1–30, with alterations significant for readers of Jewish background (e.g., the defilement controversy now concerns interpretation of "the tradition of the elders" [15:2], and the gentile woman who seeks his help is specifically a "Canaanite" [15:22]).

The story of Jesus' encounter with the Canaanite woman was already paired with a discussion on defilement in the Gospel of Mark. Matthew retains that pairing, possibly because both evangelists saw a parallel between the claim that purity transcends traditional ideas about diet and the discovery that faith transcends traditional thinking about ethnicity.

15:1–20. Controversy over Defilement (cf. Mark 7:1–23)

When the Pharisees accuse Jesus' disciples of not abiding by "the tradition of the elders," he responds with a countercharge against them and a brief discourse on defilement. The "tradition of the elders" was an oral code of biblical interpretation that generally intensified demands of the law; in Matthean terms, it spelled out occasions for "binding" Torah as applicable to circumstances not explicitly stated (see Theme 8 "*Binding-and-loosing commandments*" in the introduction, p. 16). In this case, the issue is ritual handwashing prescribed before meals. The rationale for such handwashings is not stated, but it seems that the Pharisees' reasoning went something like this: the Torah requires priests to perform ritual handwashing before serving in the temple (actually Tabernacle, Exod 30:17–21); since God is everywhere, every Jewish male may view himself as a priest, serving at the altar of his home table. So, among the deeply pious, a tradition arose according to which the head of a household would pantomime the handwashing associated with temple offerings (not necessarily using any water) as a way of consecrating the meal to God and consuming it as an act of worship. The Pharisees do not claim here that Jesus' disciples are breaking Torah by not doing this (cf. 12:2), but rather that they are deficient in piety, basically the same charge leveled by disciples of John the Baptist with regard to fasting (9:14).

Notably, Jesus does not attack the Pharisees for observing this tradition, but he is upset that they impose their piety upon others and judge others accordingly. Indeed, the incident may serve as this Gospel's most egregious example of hypocrites (15:7) doing what Jesus said not to do in 7:1–5. There, he maintained that those who are quick to judge others are unable to see their own faults. So, Jesus responds to the Pharisees' critique of his disciples' piety by pointing out a far more grievous example in which they break the commandment of God for the sake of their tradition (15:3). Their tradition of the elders allows people to give money to a religious institution that otherwise would have been spent caring for elderly parents. The reasoning for that may have gone something like this: Torah commands one to honor father and mother. Does this apply to providing for parents when they are too old to take care of themselves? Yes, in that regard the law should be bound as applicable—unless someone wants to give the money to God (i.e., the synagogue) instead. Then, the Matthean Pharisees have decided, the law can be loosed since the money will be used for a higher purpose. Jesus claims that their reasoning nullifies the commandment in Exodus 20:12 (cf. Deut 5:16).

Thus, both Jesus and the Pharisees agree that commandments must be bound and loosed: the problem is that the Pharisees who are characters in Matthew's story inevitably bind what should be loosed and loose what should be bound.

Then, on the topic of "defilement," Jesus shifts the focus from ritual purity to moral behavior, insisting that one's conduct rather than one's religious practices are what makes one truly clean or unclean (see also 23:25–26). In saying this, he makes no judgment against Jewish dietary regulations or purity codes (cf. the parenthetical remark in Mark 7:19, missing in Matthew). It is simply a matter of spiritual priority, a common motif in Matthew. Later we will learn that "justice, mercy, and faith" are weightier matters than tithing mint, dill, or cumin—but that does not mean one *shouldn't* tithe the mint, dill, or cumin (Matt 23:23). Likewise, the point here is simply that one can be ritually pure by following dietary and other regulations and still be defiled within—and the inner purity is what is most important. We should note that many Jewish teachers at the time would have agreed with this (but not the ones who are characters in Matthew's story). Paul makes an analogous point with somewhat bizarre imagery when he insists that one can have a circumcised penis and still have an uncircumcised heart (Rom 2:25–29).

The conflict between Jesus and the religious leaders has now reached a fever pitch. He identifies them as plants that the heavenly Father did not plant (15:13), a clear reference back to the parable of Wheat and Weeds (13:24–30, 36–43). The disciples are to regard them as people who were put in the world by the devil, not by God. The angels will cast them into hell when the time comes, but for now Jesus and his followers should simply leave them alone (15:14). Matthew is consistent on this point: John the Baptist deems the religious leaders of Israel ineligible for baptism (3:7), and neither Jesus nor his followers ever call them to repentance or attempt to minister to them, anymore than they would the demons whom Jesus exorcizes. We should note that this is a distinctive feature of Matthew's Gospel that contrasts with what is found elsewhere. In Luke, for example, Jesus tells the religious leaders what benefits they will receive if they change their ways: "do this, and you will live" (10:28); "everything will be clean for you" (11:41); "you will be repaid at the resurrection" (14:14). Nothing like that is ever found in Matthew. This, of course, is a troubling aspect of the narrative, but we should at least realize that Matthew is employing the literary device of using flat characters to personify a value (in this case, evil); such devices are common in fables, parables, and fairy tales, as well as in stories that, like this one, are imbued with a generous dose of apocalyptic dualism. The reader is not supposed to imagine that any actual people in the real world (historically or currently) are being represented (see Theme 14 "*Religious leaders as enemies of God*" in the introduction, p. 25).

15:21–28. Encounter with a Canaanite Woman (cf. Mark 7:24–30)

Traveling to the traditionally pagan region of Tyre and Sidon (see 11:21), Jesus is accosted by a Canaanite woman whose banter so impresses him that he reneges on his usual practice of ministering only to "the lost sheep of the house of Israel" (15:24; see also 10:5–6) and heals her daughter. Her comment about dogs receiving crumbs reveals humble recognition of her position: she deserves nothing from him but nevertheless hopes something good will fall her way. She also calls Jesus "Lord" (15:22, 25, 27), identifies him as the "Son of David" (15:22), and worships him (15:25). She is the only person in the Gospel said to have "great faith," in contrast to the disciples' "little faith" (6:30; 8:26; 14:31; 16:8; 17:20; see also 28:17). The story is similar to that of the gentile centurion in 8:5–13; both accounts prepare for the universal mission charge with which this Gospel concludes (28:19–20).

The exchange between Jesus and the woman expresses divine priorities regarding gentile ministry and the primacy of Israel. Matthew recounts the story as an episode from a bygone era, when the announcement of God's reign was directed primarily to Israel (10:5–6). His readers live in a time when the benefits of God's rule are widely available to gentiles as well (24:14; 28:19). Still, Matthew thinks it is important for the increasingly gentile church to remember that Israel had primacy as God's people, and to recognize that gentiles are now being included among people who already have a history with God. The Canaanite woman is in some sense exemplary of gentiles who "get this."

The proverb Jesus quotes to her assumes a situation where children (Israel) are fed first and household pets (gentiles) get the table scraps (the Greek word for "dog" is *kynarion*, a diminutive of *kynai*, meaning "puppies" or "inside animals" as distinct from street dogs or strays). The analogy is not too different from one offered by Paul, who likened gentiles to a branch from a wild olive tree being grafted into a cultivated tree (Israel). Still, many modern readers have been horrified by the children/dogs analogy, and some are prone to talk about it in ways that accentuate the potential for offense: it is now common for interpreters and preachers to lament that Jesus "calls the woman a dog," though he never actually does that. He simply uses a parabolic analogy in which her position in the current situation is analogous to that of a household pet in a different situation. Such analogies do not usually inspire offense. Paul's gentile readers were probably not offended that he compared them to uncultivated trees, nor do Jesus' disciples seem offended at being compared to sheep (10:16). We might imagine a manager in our own day encouraging her sales team to be proactive with clients because "the early bird gets the worm": would any of them be offended that she compared them to birds (or their clients to worms)? In any case, the Canaanite woman takes no offense at Jesus' remark. She accepts the analogy and goes a step further. Before it is official feeding time, pets *do* get to eat crumbs that fall on the floor—and that's all she's looking for: no need to revise the entire plan of salvation: *Just heal my daughter, will you? Lord, help me!* Here is a gentile who understands what *mercy* means (15:22). She can make no claim on God. She has no right to expect anything from God. Yet she hopes that God will help her anyway. Such nonpresumptive hope is what Jesus calls "great faith" (15:28; see comments on the attitude displayed by the man with a skin disease in 8:2 and by the centurion in 8:8–10).

Still, we must recognize that the story is difficult for modern readers simply because it assumes a value system that most readers today do not espouse (and probably do not want to "pretend to espouse" just so they can understand the story in the way they were expected to understand it). To many modern readers, Jesus comes off here as an authoritative, patriarchal man, lording it over a vulnerable, pleading woman who must humiliate herself to earn his favor. To some extent, these troubling aspects of the text are a given that we cannot ameliorate; but, for what it's worth, I will try to elucidate what I think we are probably supposed to get out of the story (and for what follows, see further, Powell 2001, 122–30). First, as a side note, I need to say that I do *not* think we are expected to read the story as an instance in which the woman "wins an argument with Jesus" or "changes his mind." That interpretation might work for Mark's parallel account (I was one of the first scholars to propose such a reading of Mark 7:24–30), but the Matthean Jesus, unlike the Markan one, is not a character who learns or evolves or develops as the narrative progresses.

Matthew's readers are expected to find this story troubling for reasons different from ours. The story is supposed to be shocking, not because Jesus initially refuses to help this woman, but because he eventually *does* help her and even praises her as a person of great faith. The woman is not just a gentile but indeed a *Canaanite*, a representative of people whom the Scriptures consistently portray in a bad light. Matthew's readers (grounded in those Scriptures) are not expected to have a high opinion of Canaanites; indeed, such people would not even exist if God's will had been done (see Josh 3:9–10; 12:7–8; 17:17–18; Judg 1:1–10, 27–33; 3:1–4). But even apart from ethnicity, Matthew depicts the woman as behaving in a way that shows complete disdain for what readers would be expected to regard as the proper way for a woman to address a man. For a "good example" of such an address, see the mother of James and John in 20:20–21: she comes to Jesus, prostrates herself before him, and refrains from speaking until he asks, "What do you want?" (and she is accompanied by her sons, his disciples, at the time!). This Canaanite woman follows Jesus and his disciples about, *shouting* at them! Modern readers may regard her as daring and heroic, an assertive woman who will not be denied, but Matthew's readers would be expected to think she is rude and obnoxious. We are probably expected to sympathize with the disciples, who plead with Jesus, "Send her away!" But then Jesus praises her and accedes to her demand.

In short, Matthew's readers are expected to be educated (or at least confused) by what happens here. The narrative *presupposes a strong anti-gentile bias* but then challenges and critiques its own presuppositions. It does not necessarily eliminate the bias (one which Matthew himself probably held dear—and one which the historical Jesus might have held as well; see Theme 5 "*Condescending acceptance of gentiles*" in the introduction, p. 12). Rather, it offers a critique from within: God seems to care for these gentiles, whatever we think of them, and God's mercy and power apparently extend to them in unanticipated ways. Likewise, the story *presupposes a patriarchal mindset.* It does not denounce that mindset as such, but it offers something of a critique from within, defying expectations with developments that those who operate with such a mindset would not anticipate (contrasting the "great faith" of an unconventional woman with the "little faith" of twelve much more traditional male apostles). What are the readers expected to make of this? There is no sure answer—my guess is that Matthew himself did not know what to make of it—but those who strive (6:33) and pray (6:10) for the reign of God, where the last are first and the first are last (19:30; 20:16), must expect a degree of disorientation.

MATTHEW 15:29–16:12
Feeding of 4,000 and Discussion on Yeast

Still following his Markan source, Matthew derived this material from Mark 8:1–21, redacting the discussion of yeast in ways that show the disciples as having more potential for the future than seemed evident in Mark's account.

This section features two of Matthew's doublets, where he appears to tell the same, or at least similar, stories twice (cf. stilling a storm in 8:23–27//14:32–33; healing two blind men in 9:27–31//20:29–34; the Beelzebul accusation in 9:32–34//12:22–24). The reason for the doublets is not clear: possibly separate explanations need to be sought for each instance.

15:29–39. Feeding of 4,000 (cf. Mark 8:1–10)

Back in Galilee, Jesus resumes his ministry of healing people with various infirmities (15:29–31). This time, the healings occur on a mountain, a site usually associated with Jesus' teaching (5:1), but a place that is also appropriate for prayer (14:23), epiphany (17:1–9), and a final commissioning (28:16–20). While still on the mountain (apparently), Jesus feeds a multitude of people with a handful of food in a way that closely parallels the account of a similar miracle in 14:13–21.

In this case, Matthew did not create the doublet but inherited it. Mark's Gospel already contained two feeding miracles, probably because one occurred in Jewish territory and the other in predominantly gentile lands. Matthew doesn't seem to have picked up on that, but he may have seen Jesus as imitating the twin feeding miracles attributed to Elijah and Elisha (1 Kgs 17:8–16; 2 Kgs 4:42–44). In any case, because this has happened before, the disciples appear especially obtuse when they are unable to imagine that it can happen again (cf. 16:5–12). The miracle is also one more sign of Jesus' compassion for the crowds (15:32; see also 9:36; 14:14).

16:1–4. Request for a Sign (cf. Mark 8:11–13; Luke 12:54–56)

The religious leaders ask Jesus to show them a sign, as they did before (12:38–42). This time, they specifically request a sign "from heaven," and now the request is explicitly identified as a "test," similar to tests brought by Satan at the beginning of Jesus' ministry (4:1–11, esp. 4:6–7; cf. 19:3; 22:18, 35). The historically unlikely pairing of "Pharisees and Sadducees" (16:1; see also 3:7) is in keeping with

Matthew's desire to portray "the religious leaders of Israel" as a character group in his narrative, basically presenting them as a united front, allied against Jesus in spite of their traditional rivalries (see Theme 14 "*Religious leaders as enemies of God*" in the introduction, p. 25). Jesus responds to their request by indicating that signs are all around them: they just don't know how to read them (cf. 12:28). He then reiterates his prediction of "the sign of Jonah," meaning his burial and resurrection (see comments on 12:39–40).

16:5–12. Yeast of the Pharisees and Sadducees (cf. Mark 8:14–21; Luke 12:1)

The disciples' capacity for incomprehension reaches an all-time high when they misinterpret Jesus' metaphorical warning against "the yeast of the Pharisees and Sadducees" as a literal reference to yeast, required for making bread. This mistake is exacerbated by what Jesus regards as unnecessary anxiety over food (cf. 6:25–27), a concern that should have been obviated by the two miraculous feedings he has performed (14:13–21; 15:32–39). The real danger is not their running out of food, but the teaching of these religious leaders, who are blind guides taking their followers toward a fall (15:14).

This is an episode in which Matthew's redactional changes from Mark are especially noteworthy. In Mark, Jesus launches a vitriolic tirade against his disciples, accusing them of having hearts that have been hardened (Mark 8:17) and lamenting that they still do not understand after all that they have witnessed (8:21). In Matthew, Jesus attributes their obduracy to the "little faith" that is so characteristic of them (16:8; see also 6:30; 8:26; 14:31; 17:20; and Theme 11 "*Disciples as people of little faith*" in the introduction, p. 21). Then, after Jesus explains that he is not talking about literal bread, they *do* understand: once they get that "yeast" is a metaphor, they get the meaning of the metaphor. The significant point for Matthew is that the disciples are capable of growth: they may be a bit slow on the uptake, but eventually they do come to understand (see Excursus: "Understanding" and Divine Revelation in Matthew, p. 158). Matthew's readers are expected to empathize with these disciples and realize that even people they regard as great leaders of the church needed to grow into the role expected of them.

MATTHEW 16:13–20
Confession of Peter at Caesarea Philippi

Continuing to follow his Markan source, Matthew took the gist of this passage from Mark 8:27–30, adding a reference to Jeremiah, expanding Peter's identification of Jesus to include "the Son of the living God," and adding an extravagant blessing of Peter by Jesus (all of 16:17–19 is unique to Matthew).

The question of Jesus' identity is engaged at Caesarea Philippi. The disciples first offer Jesus a sample of opinions regarding him, including a suggestion favored by Herod (14:2). Though these represent high praise, Peter speaks for the Twelve in giving their own evaluation: Jesus is "the Messiah, the Son of the living God" (cf. 14:33; see also 3:17; 17:5). Jesus accepts this acclamation, insisting that it has been revealed to Peter by his Father in heaven; eventually Jesus' refusal to disavow this claim is what will get him crucified (26:63–64). In blessing Peter, Jesus plays on his name (which means "rock"), identifying him as the foundation stone for the church that he will build, against which the gates of Hades will not prevail. Peter will have authority to "bind and loose" the law, to determine on the basis of Scripture the will of God for particular circumstances (see also 18:18). In this sense, he will be given the keys to heaven's rule, the understanding needed to unlock the mysteries of God's will (see 13:11). On the call to secrecy in 16:20, see also 8:4; 9:30; 12:16.

In church history, this text has been central to controversies regarding "the primacy of Peter." Following Luther, Protestant interpreters have tended to argue that when Jesus said "this rock," he was referring to himself, not to Peter, but that seems like theologically motivated special pleading. Surely Matthew's readers would be expected to take the declaration as applying to Peter, though that does not mean they would be expected to hear the words as instituting an ecclesiastical office that would be occupied throughout history by Peter's successors. More likely, they would be expected to regard Peter as serving a preparatory role for the church in a manner analogous to that which John the Baptist served for Christ (see 3:1–12). Ultimately, it is the "church" that will overcome "the gates of Hades" and unlock the rule of God through a communal function of binding and loosing (see 18:15–18), but that church did not spring into existence the day after Easter, and Matthew's readers are urged to realize that Peter was authorized by God to play a special role during the interim. It is possible that this was historically the case in a community like Antioch, where Peter ministered (Gal 2:11) and Matthew's Gospel might have been written. (See further Powell 2006a.)

In a broader sense, this passage is important for understanding Matthew's Christology and ecclesiology. For the first, Matthew's Gospel places special emphasis on the identity of Jesus as the Son of God (see Theme 9 "*Jesus as the Son of God*" in the introduction, p. 19). For the second, Matthew's Gospel is the only one of the four in which Jesus explicitly talks about the church: it makes clear that the church is not some post-Easter human innovation but was established by Jesus himself during his earthly ministry. Through the abiding Christ, the church continues to be the primary locus for God's presence in the world (18:20; see Themes 1 "*The abiding presence of God*" and 13 "*A community called 'the church'*" in the introduction, pp. 7, 23).

In this text, the role of the church is described with three metaphors: (1) the church will be built on a rock; (2) the church will overcome the gates of Hades; (3) the church will be given the keys to the rule of heaven, with which it will bind and loose on earth things that will consequently be bound and loosed in heaven.

The basic meaning of the first metaphor is easy to grasp, especially since Jesus has used it before (7:24–25). A house built on a rock is able to withstand rains and floods and winds that beat upon it; likewise, a church built on a rock will be able to weather storms that inevitably come, to persevere amid trouble and turmoil. Matthew's reader would think at once of the trials and persecutions that Jesus said will come upon his "household" in 10:25 (see also 24:4–14). Less clear is exactly what Matthew's readers would regard as the "rock" that provides the church with such stability—since Peter had been executed twenty years before the Gospel was written. Most likely, they would think that foundation is now to be found in a community of people to whom (like Peter) the Father in heaven has revealed the true identity of Jesus as the Messiah, the Son of the living God. This understanding of Jesus' true identity—and more important, the fact of divine revelation that makes such understanding possible—has become the foundation that continues to keep the church safe and strong throughout perilous times.

The second metaphor is often misunderstood because it is read as an extension of the first and thus taken as a defensive image. Since the church is built on a rock (like a fortress), many have taken the assurance that "the gates of Hades will not prevail against it" as implying a promise of protection: if the gates of Hades attack the church, they will not win. But this demands an unlikely image since gates do not usually attack anything. Normally, they *get* attacked. The image for Matthew is actually one of the church storming the gates of Hades, which must give way before it. The church is on the *offensive* and will overcome the power of death and the devil in this world. This image is parallel to that of Jesus and his followers plundering the devil's house now that this "strong one" has been bound by God (12:28–29). We should not be bothered by any presumed inconsistency between the juxtaposition of two images, one defensive and one offensive: Matthew has no problem employing mixed metaphors (see 7:15–16, which suggests that we may know "wolves in sheep's clothing" by their fruits).

The metaphor of Peter holding the keys to the rule of heaven is misconstrued at a popular level when the word *basilea* (rule) is translated "kingdom" and the phrase "kingdom of heaven" is understood as specifying a location (where God lives with the angels and where people go when they die). Peter has thus been viewed as a kind of doorman, in charge of the keys that open the pearly gates (Rev 21:21), and so he may be viewed as the one authorized to decide who should or should not be admitted. But the phrase *basileia tou ouranou* refers to an *action* rather than a location (see Theme 2 "*Reign or rule of God/heaven*" in the introduction, p. 8). Peter is given the keys for binding and loosing things on earth that will enable people to experience the *rule* of heaven.

What things does he bind and loose? Church leaders of all persuasions have often read Matthew 16:19 as parallel to John 20:22–23 and thought that Peter (and the church) are authorized in Matthew to grant or withhold forgiveness of sins (by which, again, they determine who will enter the heavenly realm upon death). We now know, however, that this interpretation of Matthew 16:19 is almost certainly wrong. As a Jewish Christian (or Christian Jew), Matthew is thinking of the rabbinic practice of binding-and-loosing *commandments* not *sins* (see Theme 8 "*Binding-and-loosing commandments*" in the introduction, p. 16). The issue is moral discernment, determining what sort of behavior constitutes sin, as opposed to determining when sins should or should not be forgiven. According to Matthew, one of the most important things the church does is to tell people when and how they should obey the Bible and when and how they should not obey the Bible. Jesus had the authority to do this (5:21–22, 27–28, 31–32, 33–34, 38–39; 12:8, 12); he gave Peter the authority to do it (16:18–19); and, as we shall see, that authority will ultimately belong to the full community that in Matthew's Gospel is called "the church" (18:15–18).

Part Four of Matthew's Gospel: Journey to Jerusalem

Matthew 16:21–20:34

Once again (see also 4:17), the words "From that time . . ." introduce a major new section of Matthew's narrative. The focus now is on Jesus' journey to Jerusalem and, eventually, on the suffering, death, and resurrection that he will experience there. For the most part, the context for Jesus' teaching shifts from public instruction to training the Twelve. Matthew took the framework for this section of his Gospel from Mark, though he has inserted material from other sources into that framework (notably the Community Discourse in chap. 18). As in Mark, the material is structured around three passion predictions (16:21; 17:22–23; 20:17–19), which are resisted or misunderstood by the disciples, requiring more teaching about the implications of the cross for Christian living.

MATTHEW 16:21–17:27
Looking toward Cross and Glory

Continuing to follow his Markan source, Matthew took all of 16:21–17:23 from Mark 8:31–9:32, with only minor redactional changes. He then appended the unique account regarding payment of the temple tax in 17:24–27.

Jesus redirects his disciples' attention to things that are to come: his death, his resurrection, and his parousia (second coming), summoning them to uncompromising faithfulness in the difficult times ahead and offering three of them a vision of their glorious future in the coming reign of God.

16:21–23. First Passion Prediction (cf. Mark 8:31–33; Luke 9:22)

Following Peter's great confession, Jesus reveals to his disciples for the first time that he is going to be killed and then raised on the third day (see also 17:12, 22–23; 20:17–19; 26:2; 27:63). Ignoring the latter part of this prediction, Peter rebukes him for adopting what he regards as a fatalistic perspective. Jesus, in turn, rebukes Peter with the harshest words ever directed to any of his disciples. He identifies this resistance to suffering and death (cf. 10:39) as a human perspective uninformed by the truth of God, as a point of view that must ultimately be called satanic.

When Jesus tells his disciples that he "must" go to Jerusalem to suffer, be killed, and be raised on the third day, he uses the theologically significant word *dei*, which means something like "it is necessary." The word may be used to identify one's fate or destiny in a generic sense, but in Jewish circles it would always be understood as indicating what God has determined *must* take place. It is the will of God that Jesus suffer, die, and be raised (see 26:39, 42): therefore, it is unavoidable; or, if there is free will, then avoidance should be unthinkable. Many theologians wish that Jesus or Matthew would tell us *why* this is necessary, but that doesn't really happen. We do catch hints later: to provide "a ransom for many" (20:28) or facilitate "forgiveness of sins" (26:28). But Matthew is not interested in atonement theories. It should be sufficient for the disciples (and us) to know that the death and resurrection of Jesus accords with God's will and, indeed, is part of God's plan.

This is not enough for Peter, however. Traditional Jewish thought made no allowance for a *suffering* Messiah (identification of the Messiah with the Servant of Isaiah's songs was a product of Christian exegesis, reflection after-the-fact on what had happened to Jesus). Peter's response to Jesus may seem heartfelt and sensible to modern readers, but it was a fairly serious offense in that culture for a student to rebuke a teacher (we hear of people being put to death for doing so). In any case, Jesus regards his unwelcome counsel as a test, similar to those that Satan laid before him earlier (4:1–11). Peter is being used by the devil to tempt Jesus, appealing to what he no doubt wishes could be true in order to thwart God's plan (26:39). Further, the command "Get behind me!" reminds Peter that he has been called to *follow* Jesus, not lead the way: in Greek, the words *hypage opisō mou* (literally, "Go behind me") in 16:23 are quite similar to the command *deute opisō mou* ("Come behind me"; NRSVue, "Follow me") in 4:19. Then, Jesus' suggestion that Peter is a "stumbling block" (*skandalon*; NRSVue, "hindrance") plays on the name Jesus has given him: *Petros* (Rock). A rock (*petra*) can be a secure foundation upon which something like a church can be built (16:18; cf. 7:24); *or* a rock can be an obstacle in the road, something that causes people to trip and fall. Matthew's readers are expected to see Peter as exemplifying the potential for Christian leaders to be either (or both). We may note an irony: Paul identifies the message of the cross as a *skandalon* (1 Cor 1:23; Gal 5:11; NRSVue: "stumbling block," "offense") to potential believers; here, Peter's *rejection* of that message is deemed to be a *skandalon* to Jesus. For more on the "stumbling block" motif in Matthew, see 17:27 and 18:6 (and Excursus: The "Stumbling Block" Motif in Matthew, p. 210).

16:24–28. The Way of Discipleship (cf. Mark 8:34–9:1; Luke 9:23–27)

Jesus continues voicing an objection to Peter's commitment to saving Jesus' life (16:22) by reiterating the demands of discipleship that he stated previously (10:38–39). The words are more poignant now since he has announced that he himself will suffer and die (16:21). Further, all such suffering must be viewed from the perspective of the future, the imminent parousia, and final judgment, when justice will be done and those who have suffered wrongly will be vindicated. That judgment, however, will not focus on whether people knew the right words to identify Jesus (16:16) but on whether they gave up their lives for his sake (16:25). This is consistent with what was said in 7:21–23.

The last time Jesus talked about bearing the cross and losing one's life for his sake, the implications of this radical demand were spelled out regarding family: devotion to Jesus takes priority even over commitments to one's parents or children (10:37). This time the implication is even closer to home: "If any wish to come after me, let them deny *themselves.*" The point is the same (see comments on 19:27): loving oneself is no more contrary to Christ's message than loving one's parents or children, but following Christ broadens horizons such that a true follower of Jesus will not give priority to what benefits his or her own interests. Self-denial does not mean timid submission or effacement for fear of being thought too forward; it means subordinating one's own will to God's will, renouncing one's rights and privileges when they are maintained at expense to others; and sometimes forgoing legitimate needs for the sake of those whose needs are equally legitimate but more urgent.

Jesus encourages those who are with him to look for the parousia to occur within their own lifetimes (16:28; see also 24:34). Since the Son of Man did not in fact "come with his angels in the glory of his Father" during the lifetime of any of those to whom Jesus spoke these words, interpreters have sought desperate explanations: maybe he was not referring to the parousia but to the transfiguration or to his resurrection? But the text means what it says. Matthew had obviously inherited the teaching and thought it important to include even though, by the time he wrote his Gospel, all those to whom Jesus is represented as speaking were probably gone, and the prediction had not been fulfilled. Still, in a nonliteral way (which is how prophecies are often fulfilled; cf. 17:12–13), those who are standing with Jesus as he speaks are the Gospel's readers: Matthew assumes here, as always, that his readers are empathizing with the disciples and will hear what Jesus says to those disciples as also spoken to them. If Matthew had been overly bothered by the historical nonfulfillment of Jesus' words, he could have simply eliminated this verse (as he did many potentially problematic passages from Mark). Why keep it? Like most writers of the New Testament, he wanted his readers to expect Jesus to return within their own lifetimes. Indeed, the notion that Jesus is coming soon is one of the most pervasive teachings of the New Testament (Rom 13:11–12; 16:20; 1 Cor 7:29; Phil 4:5; 1 Pet 4:7; Heb 10:37; Jas 5:8; Rev 22:7, 12, 20). Of course, we can fudge the data on what "soon" means (2 Pet 3:8), but I take for granted that the authors of all these writings encourage their readers to expect the Lord to come within their own lifetimes (otherwise *soon* would have little existential relevance). An expectation, of course, is not a doctrine. People often get in trouble when they *believe* Jesus is coming soon and base that on some combination of questionable exegesis and supposed fulfillment of prophecies over in Israel (or the like). An expectation is a heartfelt longing, one that Matthew hoped these words of Jesus would stir in the hearts of every generation of readers who would sense that they (like the disciples) were standing with Jesus when he declared that some of them would not taste death before seeing the Son of Man come in power. (On this biblical point, and on the significance of imminent expectation for healthy spirituality, see Powell 2004, 60–69).

17:1–13. The Transfiguration (cf. Mark 9:2–13; Luke 9:28–36)

Jesus appears to be physically transformed in a "vision" (17:9) beheld by three of his disciples on a mountain. His dazzling appearance and the presence of Moses and Elijah offer these disciples a glimpse of life in the heavenly realm beyond death. Why Moses and Elijah? There is no sure rationale, but one common suggestion is that they represent (roughly) "the Law and the Prophets" (see 5:17; 7:12; 11:13; 22:40). Another idea is that both Moses and Elijah were eschatological figures whose appearance would signal the last days: a prophet like Moses would appear (Deut 18:15–19), and Elijah would return (Mal 4:5). Thus, the beatific vision of these two holy ones calls attention to the hidden ways in which the eschatological expectations associated with them are being fulfilled. In any case, the climactic moment comes with God's own affirmation of Jesus as "my Son, the Beloved," in words reminiscent of Jesus' baptism (3:17). The addendum, "Listen to him!" may be directed at Peter, who is still rather foolishly trying to manage Jesus' career (17:4; cf. 16:22). In any case, the vision is to be kept a secret until after the resurrection, but the appearance of Elijah prompts a discussion in which Jesus explains that the ministry of John the Baptist provided metaphorical fulfillment of a prophecy that Elijah would someday resume his work on earth (Mal 4:5; see Matt 11:13–14). Notably, Jesus also insists (in an all-but-forgotten saying) that Elijah "is indeed coming" (Matt 17:11), suggesting that proleptic metaphorical fulfillment of a prophecy need not supplant a subsequent, possibly literal fulfillment. Apparently, some early Christians (including those in Matthew's community) still expected Elijah to come, along with or shortly before the parousia of Jesus.

Many details of the event parallel the biblical account of Moses at Sinai: the six days (17:1) and the bright cloud (17:5) probably allude to Exodus 24:15–18; other features of the story are broadly reminiscent of the revelation of divine glory in the Sinai narrative. But Matthew's claim that Jesus' "clothing became bright [*leuka*] as light" (17:2) also parallels what will later be said of the angel at Jesus' tomb: "his clothes were as white [*leukon*] as snow" (28:3). Further, the note that Jesus' face "shone as the sun" not only recalls Exodus 34:29 but repeats what Matthew has said will be true of all the righteous after the angels have removed evildoers from the earth: they "will shine like the sun" in a realm where God rules over all (13:43; cf. Dan 12:3).

The selection of Peter, James, and John for this special assignment concurs with the role they later play in Gethsemane (26:36–37). Sometimes referred to as an "inner circle" among the Twelve, they were three of the first four disciples called by Jesus, and they are the only ones (other than Judas) to have speech or action attributed to them individually in Matthew (Peter: 8:14; 14:28; 15:15; 16:16, 22; 17:24; 18:21; 19:27; 26:33, 58, 69–75; James and John: Matt 20:20). Granted, they do not come off too well in the present story, but the divine command to "listen" to Jesus is not a sharp rebuke. And their fear in the presence of divine glory (17:6; cf. Exod 34:30) is not in this instance evidence of "little faith" (cf. 14:30–31). It is a standard human response to witnessing God's glory and is completely appropriate since God is indeed fearsome (10:28). People who encounter angels or witness divine manifestations often must be told, "Do not be afraid" (e.g., Luke 1:13, 30; 2:10; 5:10; Rev 1:17; as well as Matt 14:27; 28:5, 10), not because it is wrong for them to be afraid, but because they need to be assured that what is definitely frightening is not at the moment threatening.

Scholars have wondered what *precisely* is wrong with Peter's suggestion to build three booths: is he putting the three figures on equal footing? Or trying to prolong the sojourn on the mountain? I doubt that there is anything wrong with the suggestion as such. The point is that this is an epiphany: a moment for watching and listening. It is a time to *be*, not a time to *do*. But Peter wants to *do* something; indeed, he wants to *build* something. Preachers often take this story and the one that follows (17:14–21) as an example of how Christians may have wonderful "mountaintop experiences" but afterward fail to be useful in the tough work to which they are called. But that's not quite it: the immediate point is *not* that Peter doesn't know how to do work "in the valley below" but that he doesn't know how to have a mountaintop experience. He misses (or almost misses) what could be a defining moment of his life because he doesn't understand that, in order to be a witness for Jesus, he must first witness Jesus. He has been invited to the mountain to listen, not to speak; to receive something he needs, not to offer something he thinks others might need. The drive to be useful derives from a commendable desire to serve Jesus, but Jesus did not come to be served: he came to serve others, including Peter (cf. John 13:8).

It could be noteworthy that the disciples' question in 17:10 is the closest the Matthean disciples ever get to knowing the Scriptures. Never once in this Gospel do they ever evince actual knowledge of anything in the Bible. Now they do know that "Elijah must come first," but apparently they don't know that this teaching comes from Scripture. It is just something that "the scribes say." It is a curious phenomenon that, in Matthew's Gospel, characters who know the Scriptures (including Satan and Israel's religious leaders) are invariably evil and use those Scriptures to thwart what God wants, while those who do not know the Scriptures appear to be included among the "infants" to whom God chooses to reveal wisdom and understanding (11:25; on this critique of education as a frequent marker of worldly power, see Theme 16 "*Critique of power, wealth, and wisdom*" in the introduction, p. 31). A takeaway for modern readers could be the simple realization that knowing the Bible does not equal understanding God's will; those who have opposed what God wants most fervently have often been persons who quote Scripture most passionately.

17:14–21. Healing of an Epileptic (cf. Mark 9:14–29; Luke 9:37–43a)

Jesus exorcizes a demon from a boy who has epilepsy after his disciples' faith proves inadequate to the task (cf. 2 Kgs 4:29–37). His lament regarding the "faithless and perverse generation" with which he must abide is a reflection on the general climate of unbelief (see 13:58) that is now affecting even his own disciples. Indeed, he tells the latter that their chronic "little faith" (see Theme 11 "*Disciples as people of little faith*" in the introduction, p. 21) has now apparently shrunk to a speck even tinier than a mustard seed, since that would be all the faith they need to do whatever extraordinary things God might require. His extreme frustration with the disciples in this instance may be due to the fact that he has specifically granted them authority to cast out demons (10:1) and commissioned them to do so (10:8).

The story serves as a reminder that even devoted leaders fully empowered by Christ sometimes fail in their basic commissions and disappoint Jesus gravely by doing so. Many Christian leaders experience such failures, and Matthew's readers are expected to find some comfort in knowing that even the apostles did not always succeed. With regard to the disciples' paltry faith, furthermore, we note that Jesus never offers any guidance as to what the disciples might do to remedy the situation. Is there any way to increase their faith? Perhaps not. The assumption for this Gospel (and most biblical writings) seems to be that God gives each person a measure of faith and that this is all the faith that they will ever have: faith is a gift from God (Eph 2:8), and there is probably nothing that a person can do to acquire more of it. The disciples, with *less* than a mustard seed of faith, are like the poor guy in a parable Jesus tells who is only given one talent (25:14–30); the Capernaum centurion in 8:10 and the Canaanite woman in 15:28 are like the people with five or ten talents. Still, the important thing is not to bury it in the ground, not to put their dim light under a basket (5:14), but rather to use whatever speck of faith God has given them and to be thankful that they have that much. (For more on implications of "little faith" for spirituality, see Powell 2004, 109–17.)

17:22–23. Second Passion Prediction (cf. Mark 9:30–32; Luke 9:43b–45)

Jesus repeats the prediction he made earlier regarding his impending death and resurrection (16:21; see also 17:12; 20:17–19; 26:2; 27:3). This time he does not use the word *dei* (must//it is necessary), but he does use the theologically loaded *paradidōmi* to indicate that the Son of Man will be "handed over" or "delivered up" to human beings. The NRSVue translates the word "betrayed," probably on an assumption that Jesus is predicting the action of Judas (the word is used with obvious reference to Judas in 10:4 and 26:48). Many scholars disagree, thinking this should be read as a divine passive: God will deliver Jesus into the hands of humans. That thought is expressed elsewhere by Paul: God "did not withhold his own Son but gave him up [*paradidōmi*] for all of us" (Rom 8:32). But, for what it's worth, I think the NRSVue got it right: Matthew means "handed over [by Judas]." Although Jesus' death on a cross is definitely in keeping with God's will for Matthew (26:39, 42), the Matthean Jesus retains the power to call the whole thing off, should he choose to do so (26:53). He is treated as an object (handed over) by humans, but not by God. Further, Matthew uses this word (*paradidōmi*) to establish a triad of guilt, attributing responsibility for Jesus' death to representatives of Christian, Jewish, and pagan communities (see Excursus: Themes in Matthew's Passion Narrative, p. 281). In any case, the disciples who hear what Jesus says refrain from openly challenging him this time (cf. 16:22–23) but remain "greatly distressed." Once again, they appear to hear only the prediction of death, not that of resurrection.

17:24–27. Payment of the Temple Tax (only in Matthew)

Jesus obediently pays a temple tax to avoid conflict with authorities over a peripheral issue, but he lets Peter know that, as the Son of God, he is under no real obligation to do this. Apparently having no cash, both Jesus and Peter must rely on God to supply the money in an unconventional manner: at Jesus' word, Peter catches a fish that has a coin in its mouth equal to the tax owed by two persons (no word about whether or how the other eleven paid).

During the time of Jesus, Exodus 30:13 was used to support payment of an annual tax of two drachma (two denarii//half a shekel) to support the temple in Jerusalem. Payment of the tax was completely voluntary, and many (including the Essenes) advised against paying it. The Pharisees supported it, however, and requested every male over the age of nineteen to make the contribution once a year. The Matthean Jesus acknowledges the temple as the dwelling place of God on earth (23:21) and certainly supports the idea of the temple as a "house of prayer," but he also believes the current institution has been corrupted into "a den of robbers" (21:13, quoting Jer 7:11). We might understand that he would have mixed feelings about supporting the temple under its current leadership.

Besides, he believes that "something greater than the temple" is to be found in his ministry (12:6), so why should money be drawn from support for the greater work to be used for something less? But, as it turns out, all this is beside the point, which in this instance is not to give unnecessary offense—not to place any *skandalon* (stumbling block; see Excursus: The "Stumbling Block" Motif in Matthew, p. 210) in the path of Israelites who might be turned away from his work by what they perceive as a lack of piety. Thus, the story actually encourages compromise, something rare in a book as apocalyptic in perspective as the Gospel of Matthew (but see 5:41). It sets a paradigm for voluntary renunciation of freedom, a hallmark of Christian ethics. Instead of asking, "What are my rights?" the follower of Jesus asks, "How can I avoid offending others?" (cf. Rom 14:13–19). An astute reader might wonder whether similar logic could not have applied to previous controversies: should not the disciples fast more often (Matt 9:14) or practice ritual handwashings (15:1–2) simply to avoid offending others? Hypothetically, the Matthean Jesus might have supported such a conjecture, but in those instances, there was an overriding concern: religious people passing judgment on others (7:1–3). Dismissing those judgmental tendencies was the more urgent matter.

Matthew's Gospel was written after the temple had been destroyed, but that does not mean the subject of the temple tax had become a moot issue. After 70 CE, the "temple tax" was transformed into a mandatory payment of all Jews to the Roman government, construed as war reparations. As with other taxes owed to the emperor (22:15–22), many Jews, including Christian Jews, resisted the imposition. Matthew's counsel seems to be that some things aren't worth fighting (or dying) for: give the emperor his money, but give God what the emperor can never take from you.

MATTHEW 18:1–35
The Community Discourse

As a unit, the eighteenth chapter of Matthew is a thoroughly Matthean construct, but much of the material derives from his various sources. He begins by continuing to follow his Markan source with words from Mark 9:33–47, but omits Mark 9:38–41 since he has already made Jesus an exponent of the opposite point of view expressed there (cf. Matt 12:30 with Mark 9:40). Then, abandoning Mark for a while, he inserts a parable from Q (Matt 18:10–14; cf. Luke 15:3–7) that effectively sets up the rest of the chapter: completely unique material dealing with the question of how the church is to deal with sinners in its midst.

The fourth of Jesus' five major speeches (see also 5–7; 10; 13; 24–25) focuses on the life that his disciples are to have as they seek to live together in the community that Jesus calls "the church" (16:18; 18:17).

18:1–14. Concern for the Little Ones (cf. Mark 9:33–37, 42–47; Luke 15:3–7)

Jesus uses a child to explicate the reversal of values that the rule of heaven brings. The child serves as an example of those whom society regards as unimportant, but with whom Jesus is willing to be identified. Where God rules, those who are otherwise deemed insignificant are most valued, and this is why repentance (18:3) is required to enter the sphere of divine influence that Jesus calls "the rule of heaven" (4:17). The community of God's people is composed of those who not only welcome the insignificant as they would welcome Jesus (18:5; cf. 10:40; 25:40), but also view such persons as role models whom they seek to emulate, even to the point of being regarded as insignificant themselves (18:3). Then, Jesus extrapolates some implications from his claim that children are the greatest of all people ruled by God. The "little ones" are to be treated with special value: they have guardian angels who enjoy immediate access to God (18:10), and severe punishments await any who cause them to stumble (18:6–7). On the other hand, the recovery of a child who has wandered from the way is a concern more pressing than the care of ninety-nine other persons who haven't (18:10–13).

These fourteen verses have a primary literal meaning (regarding children), albeit one that can also have more widespread implications when read in a figurative way (regarding those who "humble themselves" and become like children). Traditional interpretation usually focuses almost exclusively on the latter, a tendency that I think warrants correction. For instance, when Jesus says, "Whoever welcomes one such child in my name welcomes me," he means that what people do to children (actual, physical children), they do to him. Simply put, when you hug a child, you hug Jesus; when you beat a child, you beat Jesus. Likewise, Jesus' famous parable of the Lost Sheep refers primarily to the recovery of endangered children, and his shocking words about cutting off body parts and plucking out one's own eye refer primarily to the drastic measures people should take to ensure the welfare of children: actual, physical children like the child standing in their midst as an object lesson when he offers these teachings.

It helps to trace the logic of the disciples' question and Jesus' response; to do this, we need to appreciate that the phrase *rule of heaven* (NRSVue, "kingdom of heaven") has a range of meaning that allows for ambiguity with regard to time and space (see Theme 2 "*Reign or rule of God/heaven*" in the introduction, p. 8). When the disciples ask, "Who is the greatest in the [rule] of heaven?" (18:1), they are probably using the phrase in a narrow and somewhat pedantic sense to refer to a place called heaven, where God rules in a way that is absolute and unchallenged. Most likely, the Matthean disciples are engaging in theological speculation regarding all the angels that inhabit that sphere. (Note that there is no hint in Matthew [as in Mark 9:34] that the disciples are arguing over which of *them* is the greatest: it would make no sense for them to think any one of them might be the greatest in heaven when none of them are there yet.) Perhaps their curiosity has been aroused by Jesus' earlier comment that "the least in the rule of heaven" is greater than John the Baptist, though John was the greatest man who ever lived on earth (11:11). They apparently think that Jesus is referring to angels, and if the least of the angels is greater than John, then which of the angels is the greatest? There would be many candidates: Gabriel (the messenger), Michael (the warrior), Raphael (the healer), Uriel (who inspires philosophers and artists), the "angel of death" (who figures in the Passover story), and dozens more who are listed in Jewish literature from this period. Which of these is the greatest? Jesus surprises them by placing a child in their midst to indicate that *children* are the greatest in the rule of heaven. He is, of course, using the phrase in its broader sense (as he usually does), to denote the sphere of God's influence, a phenomenon not limited by space or time that becomes real among those with whom God is present. In the rule of heaven, little children are greater than the mightiest angels. Wherever and whenever God rules—including right here, on earth, right now—little children are greater than the mightiest angels. There is logic to this answer: after all, the angels serve children—apparently every child has at least one angel who does this (18:10)—and who is greater? The servant or the one who is served? (cf. Luke 22:27).

Interpreters have sometimes faltered by looking too hard for a rationale: *why* are children the greatest? It has nothing to do with any supposed moral superiority or purity or innocence that might be ascribed to children (often by people who are not parents). Rather, children were exalted by Jesus for one reason only: they were *powerless*. And in Matthew's Gospel, Jesus is always on the side of the powerless (see Theme 16 "*Critique of power, wealth, and wisdom*" in the introduction, p. 31): he says the first will be last, and the last will be first (19:30; 20:16); he blesses the poor in spirit and says the meek will inherit the earth (5:3, 5); he eats with outcasts (9:10–12) and says that enslaved sex workers will enter the reign of God ahead of religious leaders and synagogue rulers (21:31–32); he compares his followers to sheep, rather weak and vulnerable animals in a world filled with wolves (10:16); and he promises that the final judgment will grant reward and punishment based on whether people have been kind and generous to the least of all his siblings: those lacking food, clothing, shelter, or citizenship (25:31–46). The world's wisdom may say, "God helps those who help themselves," but the Matthean Jesus insists that God prioritizes those who cannot help themselves. God helps the helpless, or simply, those who need to play the game of life with a deck of cards that has been stacked against them. Children are a prime example; indeed, they are *the* prime example.

Having observed this much, we do need to confirm that, although these words of Jesus refer primarily to actual children, they also have relevance for those who repent and become "like children," voluntarily accepting the stigma of insignificance that children have thrust upon them (18:3–4; see also the reference to prophets, righteous persons, and disciples as "little ones" in 10:41–42). Again, to become "like children" does not mean to be gullible or naive; it means *to give up power and become vulnerable*. A close parallel may be seen between Jesus telling his disciples that they must become like children and his telling them that they must become like enslaved persons (20:26–27; 23:11): voluntary status reversal characterizes God's reign. A similar point was also made in our interpretation of the two stanzas of the Beatitudes. In Matthew 5:3–6, Jesus emphasizes that God is on the side of the miserable and oppressed people of the earth; but then, in

5:7–10, he indicates that those who are not miserable or oppressed may come into God's favor through identification with those who are, a voluntary identification that approximates what for others is no choice but simple reality.

Jesus once again uses hyperbole to stress the radical commitment expected of those who seek God's reign and God's righteousness (6:33): they will separate themselves from anything that causes children to stumble (18:8–9) or from anything that causes them to become stumbling blocks for little children (18:6–7; on the NRSVue translation of these verses, referring to "sin" rather than "stumbling," see below). Jesus already spoke about the need to cut off one's hand or foot or pluck out one's own eye in Matthew 5:29–30, and what was said about the use of hyperbole in comments on that passage holds here as well. What should not be missed, however, is that now Jesus says one must be willing to take such extreme measures to ensure the safety and security of *children*. To drive the matter home with a contemporary example, we may consider how it is common in English for someone to say, "I would give my right arm" for something (to win the lottery, get a promotion, etc.). Accordingly, Jesus suggests that you might give your right arm (or hand or foot or eye) for one specific thing: to prevent children from stumbling. But what exactly does that mean?

The term used here is *skandalon*, a Matthean favorite (see Excursus: The "Stumbling Block" Motif in Matthew, p. 210). The literal meaning of the word is "stumbling block," and the primary reference is no doubt Leviticus 19:14, which prohibits placing anything in the path of a blind person that would cause that person to fall. Here we may assume that it refers figuratively to doing anything that takes advantage of a child's weaknesses and could cause that child harm (physical, spiritual, emotional). Thus the NRSVue translation of *skandalon* as "cause . . . to sin" is overly precise, in keeping with many English versions that assume the Gospel's concern for people's well-being is exclusively moralistic. Of course, we may allow that teaching or encouraging children to do wrong might be one way of causing them to stumble; but broader application is easily imagined. For meaning in our present day, I suggest that placing stumbling blocks in the path of children might mean traumatizing them or exploiting them, or simply affecting them in ways that blunt their trust, dull their curiosity, quench their enthusiasm, stifle their laughter, or diminish their hope. It means (almost literally) to push them out of the path of being who they are meant to be. Jesus says it is worth giving one's right arm (hand, foot, eye) to keep that from happening.

Then Jesus tells a parable about a man who leaves ninety-nine sheep in the wilderness to search for one that has gone astray. As a segue parable, this story sets up the material that follows regarding recovery of lost sinners in the church. But as 18:14 makes clear, Jesus is still talking primarily about children. The main point of the story (before we get to the subsidiary point in the next section) is that the expectations for the *community* regarding care for children are the same as for individuals. If an individual disciple would risk losing one of her or his members (body parts) to keep a child from harm, then the church must be willing to risk losing ninety-nine members for the sake of just one child: that is how precious these little ones are to God.

18:15–20. Agreement in the Church (only in Matthew)

Now Jesus offers a practical strategy for recovering lost sheep (18:10–14), or at least for identifying those who are in danger of being lost. When a "sibling" (*adelphos*, 18:15) appears to behave in a sinful manner, that person needs to be corrected, preferably in private. If the person persists (probably because he or she does not agree that the behavior is sinful), the whole church will be asked to exercise its authority to bind and loose the Scriptures, to determine what is the will of God (cf. 16:19). The person ought then to accept the ruling of the church and obey (even if under protest). Those who do not obey are to be regarded as gentiles and tax collectors, that is, as candidates for evangelism. They are *not* to be excluded from the community; if anything, the church is to intensify its efforts to keep them in the community (18:10–14), communicating its unqualified forgiveness of the offense no matter how many times it may be repeated (18:21–22). In Matthew, gentiles and tax collectors are typical examples of people whom Jesus wants to have as disciples (9:9–13; 28:19) but who have to be taught to obey his commandments before they can be so regarded (28:20). The ultimate goal is agreement: when the church is united in its understanding of God's will, Jesus is truly present and prayers will be answered (18:19–20).

Granted that Matthew 18:15–20 has implications for church discipline, the text is certainly not intended to be read as a procedure for excommunication, as is so often thought. The focus is clearly on recovery and reconciliation. Indeed, Matthew carefully situates this passage dealing with a potentially recalcitrant sinner between texts indicating that forgiveness must always be unqualified and limitless. He wants to make absolutely certain that no one will ever hear, "Let such a one be to you as a gentile and a tax collector," without *first* hearing, "It is not the will of your Father in heaven that one of these little ones should be lost" (18:14), and *then* hearing that the church's response to persistent sin must always be persistent forgiveness (18:21–22). This intention, however, has been regularly undone by lectionaries and ecclesiastical documents that treat the passage as an isolated, out-of-context pericope. It is cited in numerous church constitutions and governing documents as a checklist to be followed when removing members from fellowship; many church leaders and church bodies have even claimed that 18:18 gives them divine authorization to declare sins unforgiven! Such persons and communities emulate the unforgiving man in the parable Jesus tells as an intentional reflection on this passage (18:35).

Nevertheless, individual believers and the community as a whole are expected to correct what they take to be errant behavior on the part of a potentially wayward member; even if that person's status as someone whose sins are forgiven is not in question, something else is. The person moves from being regarded as a "sibling" (18:15; NRSVue, "brother or sister") to being regarded as "a gentile and a tax collector" (18:18). There are implications to such a change, though, obviously, the church will do everything in its power to ensure that the one now regarded as a gentile and tax collector continues to worship with the community and to benefit from all its ministries. Matthew might understand some analogy to the "court of the gentiles," available in many synagogues of his day. Gentiles who appreciated aspects of Jewish religion but did not "keep Torah" were encouraged to attend the synagogue but to sit in a special section. It is hard to imagine that this did not involve some element of marginalization, but apparently that did not deter gentiles from adopting such a posture. Matthew probably thought that "Christians who do not obey what we consider to be the commands of Jesus" are similar to "gentiles who do not keep a synagogue's understanding of Torah."

A question for modern Christian ecclesiology would be whether such status would disallow one from participating in the community meal, or Eucharist—but we find no answer to that in Matthew, and for modern communities the answer might depend on each sect's understanding of what that meal means.

Matthew 18:15–18 presents the church's ministry of binding and loosing as necessary for the determination of who is to be subject to such reduced status. As explained in the introduction (see Theme 8 "*Binding-and-loosing commandments*," p. 16), this ministry is not to be confused with forgiveness or retention of sins (John 20:23)—especially since, for Matthew, such retention is unthinkable—but rather refers to the Jewish practice of determining the sphere of application that should be accorded biblical commandments (including, for Matthew, commandments of Jesus). Notably, the current text reveals that such ethical discernment will not be the prerogative of one gifted leader (cf. 16:18–19) but will be exercised by the community as a whole. Further, the authority to bind and loose is grounded in Matthew's christological claims: the church possesses such authority because Christ dwells in their midst (18:20; see also 28:20).

Specifically, Matthew 18:15–20 offers us a glimpse of how binding and loosing might function in a conflict situation, where there is disagreement. The sinful sibling in this passage is probably *not* one who stubbornly persists in what he or she acknowledges to be sinful behavior (Matthew's definition of *adelphos* in 12:50 makes that unlikely). An example of a possible situation (albeit an issue never mentioned in Matthew) would be the dispute presented elsewhere in the New Testament regarding the eating of food offered to idols (e.g., Acts 15:29; Rom 14; 1 Cor 8; 10; Rev 2:14, 20). According to the program presented in Matthew 18:15–20, one member of the community might think another is sinning if they are consuming such food. Then the proper procedure would be (a) correct the person privately; (b) if necessary, consult with two or three others; and (c) if there is still no resolution, bring the matter to the community as a whole. The community would then ask, "Is the scriptural prohibition against idolatry applicable to eating food that was once dedicated to idols?" Conceivably, the church might bind or loose the law (siding with either the accuser/s or the accused); in either case, Matthew's Gospel claims that the community speaks with divine authority: "Whatever you bind on earth will be bound in heaven, and whatever you loose on earth will be loosed in heaven." Accordingly, if the church decides against the accused, that person will now need to respect the community's decision and alter her or his behavior—or accept the reduced status of being regarded as a proselyte rather than as a disciple. Otherwise, God will hold the person accountable in the final judgment for having violated the church's ethical standards, which for Matthew is definitive of sin. What such judgment means for people who have been forgiven their sins (by God and the church) is unclear: perhaps it means being put to shame, missing the commendation every true disciple longs to hear (25:21, 23), or simply being one of the least in the reign of God (5:19).

18:21–35. Unlimited Forgiveness (only in Matthew)

Peter finds Jesus' plan for the community to maintain fellowship, even with its most recalcitrant sinful members, to be incredible and asks whether a cap should not be placed on such forgiveness. Though "seven times" may seem generous, Jesus insists that the forgiveness must be infinite. This is implied by a symbolism of numbers (seventy times seven or, possibly, seventy-seven) and explicated further in a parable that serves as an effective commentary on what he said earlier when teaching the Lord's Prayer (6:14–15). There can be no limit to forgiveness for those who experience the limitless grace of God. No follower of Jesus should keep score of another's offenses—unless, of course, they would have no objection to God keeping score of theirs. Furthermore, such forgiveness is to be "from [the] heart" (18:35), not merely for show (cf. 5:8).

As with the Lord's Prayer, the parable of the Unforgiving Enslaved Person uses financial debts as a symbol for sins. The specifics are outlandish: the first enslaved person has incurred a debt of 10,000 talents, a sum that no one would ever be likely to incur under ordinary circumstances. One talent was equivalent to 6,000 denarii (a denarius being a day's wage) and was generally construed as the approximate value of a lifetime's wages—actually, it would have been about twenty years' wages (assuming a six-day work week), but enslaved people and laborers did not have long lifespans. Ten thousand talents would be what this person might earn over ten millennia—only then, provided he saved everything and had no expenses, might he be able to repay the debt, as he promises to do in 18:26. So the image conveys a shocking representation of humanity's deficit before God and caricatures the ludicrous notion that people might, by improved behavior or good intention, reduce that liability in any substantial way.

The second part of the parable parodies the foolishness of any human being, so dependent on mercy, holding grudges, extracting payment, seeking vengeance, or in any other way failing to demonstrate mercy, grace, compassion, and forgiveness toward others. Notably, a debt of 100 denarii would not be trivial; it would be the equivalent of three to four months' wages, and Matthew's audience would think that anyone owed that amount of money would have a right to demand repayment and, indeed, a right to insist on punishment for the debtor if such payment was not made. Still, Matthew wants every Christian claiming to have a legitimate gripe against another to ask, "How can one who has been forgiven 10,000 talents be concerned with a mere 100 denarii?" It is in this light that the troubling coda to the parable (18:34–35) should be read. Obviously, if God literally handed unforgiving people over to torturers, that would diminish the story's claim that God is outrageously merciful, the premise on which everything else rests. It is hardly logical to assume that all sins can be forgiven except the sin of being unforgiving, or to imagine that God takes human beings as role models and mimics their failings (see comments on 7:1–5). The point (as with 6:14–15) is rhetorical: when you are tempted to withhold forgiveness (even for what seem to be valid reasons), ask yourself, "What if God were like this?"

The church has been right to interpret the parable metaphorically as dealing with forgiveness of sins, but it does use cancellation of financial debt as the symbol for such forgiveness. The world in which Jesus lived and that in which Matthew wrote were societies infected with horrendous debt, which kept 95 percent of the population in poverty. Fathers regularly sold some of their children into slavery as partial payments on their unresolvable debts. Jesus' audience would probably have assumed that the two people in the parable had become enslaved for just that reason (see 18:25). The early Christian church seized on teachings of Jesus (Matt 5:42; Luke 6:34–35) and Paul (Rom 13:8; Phlm 1:18) to insist on the moral obligation of believers to cancel literal financial debts owed to them by people unable to pay. Despite vast differences in economic systems and financial strategies, the modern church may still promote debt cancellation as a righteous act, to be practiced and promoted by believers whose experience with grace has taught them the irrelevance of asking whether such clemency is deserved or even appreciated.

EXCURSUS

The "Stumbling Block" Motif in Matthew

Matthew's Gospel uses the terms *skandalon* (stumbling block) and *skandalizō* (to be, create, or place a stumbling block) more times than any other Gospel. The noun is used in 13:41; 16:23; and 18:7 (3×), and the verb in 5:29–30 (2×); 11:6; 13:21, 57; 15:12; 17:27; 18:6–9 (3×); 24:10; 26:31, 33 (3×). This prevalence may be obscured in English translations: the NRSVue, for example, translates the verb with such disparate phrases as "cause to sin," "take offense," and "fall away." The basic concept derives from Torah, which prohibits placing a "stumbling block" in front of a blind person (Lev 19:14). This gave rise to metaphorical application: taking advantage of the gullible, misleading the naive, tempting someone to sin, teaching apostasy. The early Christian tradition offered two innovations, evident in Paul and implicit in Matthew: (1) behavior not intrinsically wrong should be avoided if it could be a stumbling block for someone with inadequate understanding (1 Cor 8:13); and (2) the message of the cross (and its implications) may be a primary reason why people reject the gospel, but this is a "stumbling block" that must not be avoided (1 Cor 1:23; see also Rom 9:33; Gal 5:11).

- Jesus uses hyperbole to indicate that his disciples should take drastic measures ("pluck out an eye," "cut off a hand") to free themselves of stumbling blocks that might cause them to miss out on life and be thrown into hell (5:29–30). The context suggests that this especially applies to whatever might incite one to violate women sexually with their thoughts.
- When John the Baptist wonders if Jesus is really the Messiah, Jesus tells John's disciples that those for whom Jesus is not a stumbling block are blessed (11:6).
- In explaining the parable of the Sower, Jesus indicates that trouble or persecution can be stumbling blocks that prevent a person who has received the announcement of God's reign from bearing fruit (13:21).

- Jesus says that when the Son of Man returns, the angels will seize all people who were stumbling blocks and throw them into the fire (13:41–42).
- Jesus himself is a stumbling block for the people of his hometown since prophets do not receive honor in their own neighborhood (13:57).
- The disciples report that Jesus' denunciation of the Pharisees is a stumbling block for those religious leaders, but Jesus dismisses the critique since they are not to be regarded as God's people (15:12–13; cf. 13:37–39).
- When Peter objects to Jesus' declaration that he (Jesus) is going to be crucified, Jesus calls him Satan and says, "You are a stumbling block to me" (16:23, my trans.).
- Jesus makes a voluntary donation to the temple so that his failure to do so will not become an unnecessary stumbling block for the people of Capernaum who might think such a lapse is impious (17:27).
- Jesus says that stumbling blocks are inevitable but that anyone who places one in the path of a child who believes in him will be harshly judged and punished (18:6–7; cf. Luke 17:1).
- Jesus repeats the hyperbolic warning he gave in 5:29–30, but this time the context suggests the drastic measures to avoid stumbling blocks applies to whatever would cause one to undervalue children as people whom God considers especially important and revered (18:8–10).
- Jesus indicates that in the last days many people will trip over stumbling blocks and end up hating and betraying each other (24:10).
- At the Last Supper, Jesus predicts that his passion will be a stumbling block for all the disciples that night, but Peter insists that he will be the exception (26:31–33).

MATTHEW 19:1–15

Family Matters: Marriage, Divorce, Celibacy, Children

Matthew follows his Markan source, drawing on Mark 10, with some interesting redactional changes (e.g., the addition of an "exception clause" to the divorce saying in 19:9).

As Jesus presses on to Jerusalem, Matthew's narrative increasingly focuses on issues of relationships, including the value of marriage and children.

19:1–2. Jesus Enters Judea (cf. Mark 10:1–2)

As the community discourse ends, Matthew uses his transitional formula, "When Jesus had finished saying these things," to indicate a new section of the narrative (see also 7:28; 11:1; 13:53; 26:1). Jesus proceeds into the region of "Judea beyond the Jordan" (Perea), heading for Jerusalem, where he has predicted he will die (16:21). Large crowds follow him because he continues to heal the sick. Some such movement may have been a historical reality, but the nomadic crowds also serve a literary purpose in Matthew's narrative. In reality, any crowd would have been composed of disparate individuals, and the crowds that appear at different points in the story would have been composed of different individuals. But for literary purposes the entity referred to as "the crowds" in Matthew's story functions as though it were a single character, exhibiting consistent traits and espousing a singular point of view. Thus Matthew's story features three significant "group characters" that demonstrate three different responses to Jesus: the religious leaders of Israel are opposed to him; the disciples are devoted to him; and the crowds are basically neutral, favorably disposed but without real commitment (7:28; 9:33; 12:23; 14:13; 21:45–46). Eventually, however, they will be swayed by the religious leaders to join the opposition (26:47; 27:20).

19:3–12. The Question of Divorce (cf. Mark 10:2–12)

Pharisees ask Jesus whether it is lawful for a man to divorce his wife for any cause, and they challenge his response by reminding him that Moses *did* allow this. Jesus' response, however, had nothing to do with what is permissible but rather with discerning the ideal will of God. Of course, divorce should be allowed: Moses settled that. But this does not mean it is the will of God for those whom God joins in marriage to become separated, except in one circumstance called *porneia* (NRSVue, "sexual immorality," 19:9; see also 5:31–32). This is part of the greater righteousness that Jesus expects of his followers

(5:20): they are not to be satisfied with asking, "What am I allowed to do?" but need to ask, "What does God most want?"

Throughout most of Christian history, church bodies have emulated the Pharisees rather than Jesus on this issue by reading the text as a discussion on when and whether divorce is permissible for a Christian. Most commentaries point out that, at the time of Jesus, there was a debate between the schools of Hillel and Shammai over this very issue: Hillel had followed a broad interpretation of Deuteronomy 24:1, allowing divorce for many different reasons; Shammai had favored a narrow interpretation that recognized only sexual indiscretion as grounds for divorce. Given such a background, Jesus is said to endorse Shammai's interpretation in Matthew (and something even stricter in Mark 10, where the "exception clause" of Matthew 19:9 is missing). This is simply not true. Jesus initially ignores the question of grounds for divorce and then, when pressed, says that Moses permitted it because people are hard-hearted. Such allowance is apparently something Jesus endorses (since he doesn't say otherwise). The answer to the question "Should a man be allowed to divorce his wife for any cause?" is "Yes! Any man who is hard-hearted should be allowed to write his wife a certificate of divorce for any reason—or even for no reason at all." Divorce is always permissible, and no rationale is required beyond being hard-hearted.

Matthew seems to think this much should be obvious—though that did not prove to be the case for communities that would use the text to enforce the legalistic approach to divorce that it actually sought to oppose. Still, the main point is something else: now that God's rule has come near (4:17), there is less cause to be hard-hearted and greater potential for enjoying life (and marriage) as God intends. What perturbs Jesus is that traditional approaches to divorce seem to focus on strategies for ending a marriage in ways that will not constitute a technical violation of Torah. Jesus exposes the fallacy of such strategies: although divorce is always permissible, there would never be any circumstance in which a man might divorce his wife and be able to say, "God's will for our marriage was fulfilled." To suggest that one can get divorced without sinning is tantamount to suggesting that one can commit adultery without sinning (19:9). The sin, of course, is not the termination of the marriage as such but the failure of the marriage that leads to such termination. Divorce, if it occurs, is less commission of sin than confession of sin—and acknowledgment that God's will has not been done.

What then of the "exception clause"? Jesus indicates that divorce for *porneia* (NRSVue, "sexual immorality") qualifies as an exception to what he has just said about divorce and the will or intent of God. On the surface that does not seem to make sense: the issue is not circumstances under which divorce should be allowed (in which case sexual immorality might be one instance, but would it be the only one? Paul cites another in 1 Cor 7:15); rather, the issue is recognizing circumstances that allow a marriage to fulfill God's intention, and it is unclear why a marriage terminated on account of sexual immorality should be recognized as having done this.

There are two possibilities (I favor the latter). The first is that only the divorce episode in Mark 10:2–12 should be interpreted in the manner I suggested for Matthew 19:3–12 in the preceding paragraphs. Matthew, then, would be reckoned as the first in a long line of interpreters who misunderstood the words of Jesus: he himself thought like the Pharisees in the story (and like most ecclesiastical authorities in the centuries since) and believed the value of the pericope to lie in limiting (but not eliminating) the strategies Christians might employ to obtain sinless divorces. So, he basically made Jesus a supporter of the Shammai school: divorce is almost always sinful, but not if your wife cheats on you or does something you regard as a sexual indiscretion (Shammai thought a woman wearing her hair down in public counted as infidelity). In that case, Pharisaic legalism became Matthean legalism, which became Christian legalism, and the point Jesus tried to make was lost. We might, however, wonder why a community that expects people to practice unlimited forgiveness (18:21–35) would think that this one sin should be intolerable.

Another possibility is that the word *porneia* does not refer to "sexual immorality" or infidelity. Research on this matter, though exhaustive, remains inconclusive. There is no doubt, however, that the term can refer to incestuous unions—marriages in the gentile world that, in the minds of Jesus and Matthew, would not count as instances in which God had brought the man and woman together (19:4–6). Matthew (and probably Jesus) would have regarded such so-called marriages (e.g., between brother and sister, or parent and child) as illicit unions that must be separated because they never should have taken place at all. Hence, John the Baptist told Herod he must "divorce" Herodias, who was his half sister (as well as his sister-in-law, 14:3–4). In such cases, termination of a union that had been falsely regarded as a marriage would fulfill God's intention and so would be not only permissible but commendable.

One thing is certain: the notation here and in 5:31–32 that whoever divorces his wife and marries another commits adultery is not to be taken in a pedantic literal sense, as if to imply that the man becomes an adulterer because, despite having obtained a legal divorce, he is still married to his first wife in God's eyes. No; the point is simply that legal niceties do not render his actions pleasing to God. Note that people who lust after women or request signs of the Messiah may also be called adulterous (5:28; 12:39; 16:4); Jesus uses that expression as a term for generic faithlessness. In any case, the envisioned "remarriage" scenario is probably one in which a man replaces his current wife with another (i.e., divorces his wife *in order to* marry another). Nothing in this text takes into account situations where both parties might desire to separate or, indeed, have prospects of better lives if they do so. And certainly, there is no consideration here of abusive situations in which termination of a marriage might represent the only or best option for a person to live safely or securely, to ensure the stability of their emotional or mental health, or to create an environment appropriate for the well-being of children. Still, even in situations where divorce seems necessary or even advisable, Jesus would disagree with the notion that God's will can be fulfilled so long as all is done properly. No. Sin has happened, and those who divorce should do so with frank acknowledgment that what God wanted did not come to pass.

Jesus' disciples respond to his teaching on divorce by asking whether celibacy would not be the better option. Rather than risk disappointing God by committing to a marriage that might fail to fulfill God's intentions, why not be like the Essenes or John the Baptist or Jesus himself (or the apostle Paul) and simply devote oneself to God's mission without the encumbrance of family (see 1 Cor 7:32–34)? They seem to have missed the point that, according to Jesus, it is God who arranges marriages, bringing a man and a woman together in a way that they should not be separated (19:6). Jesus' reply grants that not everyone will be able to accept the standards he has set forth (cf. 26:41b). Thus, he does realize that the reign of God has not been fully established, and people are still hard-hearted. Optimistically, the need for divorce certificates may be reduced for those who receive his announcement of God's rule, but such need will not become nonexistent. Yet, since the disciples mention celibacy, Jesus grants that there are some to whom God has given the capacity to live as eunuchs for the sake of the rule of heaven, which probably means to eschew marriage in favor of a single and celibate lifestyle (19:10–12; cf. 1 Cor 7:25–40). But Jesus' final comment, "Let anyone accept this who can," returns to the acknowledgment that this won't be the case for everyone (cf. 1 Cor 7:7).

Martin Luther made much of Jesus' claim that the celibate life is only for those "to whom it is given" (assuming 19:11 anticipates 19:12). He insisted that God's normative will is for each person to share life with a partner and that celibacy should be viewed as an exceptional calling, dependent upon receiving a "high and supernatural gift" (see "The Sixth Commandment" in The Large Catechism and "Article 23" in Apology of the Augsburg Confession). The church has no right to assume that anyone has received this gift; when it does so in sweeping and cavalier ways, it condemns many to experience life in a way that God says is "not good" (Gen 2:18). Luther was making this point as an argument against requiring celibacy for people with certain religious vocations (perhaps unfairly, if and when such vocations are adopted voluntarily); but since then, Lutherans and others have recognized the relevance of his argument for churches that counsel celibacy as a sweeping and cavalier prescription for anyone born homosexual. For decades, if not centuries, Bible-believing Christians have insisted that a significant portion of the human population should embrace what God in the Bible says is "not good," on the assumption, *contra Jesus*, that celibacy is something anyone can adopt with integrity (i.e., as a meaningful and fulfilling lifestyle), regardless of whether or not it has been given to them to do so.

19:13–15. Jesus and the Children (cf. Mark 10:13–16; Luke 18:15–17)

Jesus welcomes and blesses little children in a manner wholly consistent with what he said earlier, in 18:1–14. His disciples' attempted interference demonstrates an incredible ignorance of values that typify the approaching reign of God. It is as though they did not hear a word he said earlier about the importance of welcoming such children and keeping them safe (see esp. 18:5).

It seems likely that Matthew and his community favored the inclusion of children and young people in the corporate life of the church. This story sets a paradigm for such inclusion, dismissing whatever objections might be offered in terms of children distracting from the interests of (less important) adults. Matthew makes a point of noting the inclusion of children in the two feeding miracles (14:21; 15:38), which foreshadow the church's eucharistic meals, and he emphasizes that children are among those who worship Jesus in Jerusalem (21:15). Indeed, Jesus views infants as paradigms not only for those most likely to receive divine revelation (11:25) but also for those from whom God receives divinely prepared praise (21:16; cf. Ps 8:2). This story of Jesus welcoming and blessing children should be read in light of all these references, which point to a significant participation of children in the life of the early Christian community.

MATTHEW 19:16–20:34
On to the City

Matthew continues to follow his Markan source, taking over the rest of Mark 10 with some expansions: the introduction of James and John's mother to the story in 20:20–28, and the addition of a second blind man in 20:29–34. He also adds the parable of the Day Laborers (20:1–16), which is unique to his Gospel.

Jesus and his disciples are now in Judea, heading for Jerusalem, where he says he will die. As they approach the city, he completes the more-or-less private instruction of the disciples that their journey has afforded him, closing off a section of the Gospel that began broadly in 16:21 and more earnestly in 19:1. The final focus of this instruction is on the inhibiting effect of possessions and on the tendency for God's reign to foster a curious reversal that makes the last to be first and the first to be last.

19:16–27. Jesus and the Rich Man (cf. Mark 10:17–27; Luke 18:18–27)

A discussion concerning the obedience required of those who will enter into eternal life (cf. 7:21–23) comes to focus on the one thing a rich man who has kept God's commandments still needs to do in order "to be perfect" (that is, to be someone who is, or is becoming, the person God wants him to be; see comments on 5:48). He must sell his possessions, give to the poor, and follow Jesus unencumbered. His inability to do this leads Jesus to surmise that it is impossible for God to rule a rich person's life (literally, for "a rich person to enter the rule of God"). The reason would be that, as Jesus has said previously, an individual's heart is always where his or her treasure is (6:21; cf. 19:21). The image of a camel passing through the eye of a needle is a metaphor for something that simply cannot happen, at least in the natural world. Jesus' disciples are shocked at this judgment, wondering aloud that if a rich person cannot be saved, then who can be? They probably assume that rich people (at least Torah-observant ones) are wealthy because they have been supremely blessed by God (see Prov 8:18–21; 22:4). Thus we see the logic behind their question: if people favored and blessed by God cannot enter the reign of God, what hope is there for the rest of us? Jesus does not challenge their erroneous assumption about material wealth and divine blessing, nor does he back down from his declaration. But he does allow that God can accomplish the impossible; so the real point is that it would take a miracle of God for a rich person to follow Jesus with authentic commitment, or to enter into the sphere of God's rule and have a life that accords with God's will. Matthew leaves open the question of whether God ever works such miracles, but later in the story we encounter Joseph of Arimathea, a rich man who had been "discipled" or instructed by Jesus (27:57); perhaps he is an example of one camel whom God squeezed through the needle's eye.

The episode employs five different expressions for the goal that humans desire and only God can grant: "to have eternal life" (19:16), "to enter into life" (19:17), "to enter the kingdom [rule] of heaven" (19:23), "to enter the kingdom [reign] of God" (19:24), and to "be saved" (19:25). Apparently these are synonymous ways of referring to a transformed existence in which the permanent quality of life is as God intended it to be, without the contamination of evil and sin that infects our current world (13:41). Such a reality should not be simply equated with "life after death": eternal life, salvation, and the rule of God are all phenomena that can be experienced proleptically here and now. That said, the future, after-death dimension seems to be in focus here, especially for the rich man and the disciples. The rich man is probably not fundamentally concerned with what he might do to experience the richness of eternal life in his present existence on earth: more likely, he wants to know what he can do now to ensure that he will spend eternity with the righteous in heaven after he dies; likewise, when the disciples ask, "Who can be saved?" they probably mean, saved from hell, from eternal punishment (cf. 25:46). Jesus uses the "rule of heaven/God" language to broaden the focus, but not in a way that removes eschatological implications. Simply put, if the rich man does not have a life ruled by God now, if he is not currently experiencing salvation and eternal life, he will not enjoy those phenomena in the life to come either.

A number of points merit brief comments. First, both Jesus and the rich man agree that keeping God's commandments is how one gains entrance to eternal life (now and in the future). Granted, not all commandments are equally weighted (5:19; 22:37–39; 23:23), but the ones listed here—samples from the Decalogue, plus "Love your neighbor" (added by Matthew to what was in Mark)—are suggestive of the principles that govern the life of one who is on the path to eternal life. Jesus does not dispute the man's claim to have kept all these, and Matthew's readers would not be expected to regard such a claim as presumptuous. The claim does not suggest, "I have never once failed to observe these rules and all that they imply." For Jewish people, then and now, "keeping the commandments" has always meant orienting one's life in accord with these principles, trying to discern their implications for various circumstances, abiding by them to the best of one's ability, and correcting one's behavior and repenting of wrong when the commandments one is keeping reveal inevitable deficits. Christians who do not understand this sometimes claim that it is impossible for anyone to keep the Ten Commandments, much less the love command or other biblical mandates. Neither Jesus nor Matthew would agree: it is absolutely possible to keep the commandments in the only sense that God cares about, and this rich man is someone who has done so.

Still, the rich man knows that he lacks something (19:20). Does he need to perform some extraordinary "good deed" to merit the reward of eternal life? No, that's not it. Jesus identifies what he lacks as a "who," not a "what" (19:17): he is concerned about *what is good* (commandments) but has not been attentive to *the one who is good* (God). This passage, then, can only be fully understood in light of what Jesus says in 22:35–40. What counts most is loving God with all one's heart, soul, and mind: all the other commandments depend on this (and thus are worthless apart from it). This man's devotion to his possessions reveals that he does not love God with an undivided heart. He has another master whom he loves and serves instead (cf. 6:24), He has missed out on this relational aspect of God's rule. When people who love God are moved by that devotion to keep the commandments and live as God asks, they experience salvation, eternal life, and the rule of heaven—now and forever. People who simply keep the commandments because it is what the Bible says to do miss the forest for the trees: their life is defined by obedience to *what is good* rather than by love for *the one who is good.*

Finally, a postscript is needed to clarify that Matthew's Gospel makes a rhetorical point here that is necessarily simplistic. Matthew's dualistic approach to storytelling tends to employ "flat characters" such that he can make points strongly, without the complexity that attaches to real-life contexts (where people are not simply "good" or "evil," where motives may be mixed, and where all sorts of complicating factors intrude). In contemporary society, people with many possessions are not necessarily more devoted to those possessions than are people with fewer ones. And many rich people do love God dearly; some even understand the stewardship of their wealth as a calling from God, as a way of serving God's mission. But does that mean that rich people have now become prevalent in the reign of God? It is hard to say, but some allege that a miracle is required for *anyone* to be saved. The reason the rich man cannot give up his possessions is probably not that he likes them so much: instead, they are his *identity*, and it is not easy for anyone to give up "who they are" in order to receive a new identity as a child of God. Perhaps it is impossible for anyone to do so—impossible, that is, for mortals. Fortunately, "for God all things are possible" (19:26).

19:27–30. Rewards for Discipleship (cf. Mark 10:28–31; Luke 18:28–30)

Continuing the conversation on divestment of possessions, Peter points out that he and the other disciples have done what the rich man could not do: they have left everything and followed Jesus (4:22). So, "What will we have?" he wants to know. Jesus has already answered the question: "treasure in heaven" (19:21). But now he spells that out for Peter's benefit. In broad terms, everyone who gives things up for Jesus' sake will receive those things back again, multiplied a hundredfold—and they will also inherit eternal life. And then, more specifically, the disciples will be elevated to the position of Israelite judges and sit on twelve thrones, receiving honor in a manner reflective of the glory the Son of Man enjoys on his throne. This does not, of course, guarantee a throne for Judas (see 26:24), but reflects Matthew's awareness of an entity known as "the Twelve" that persisted long after Easter (1 Cor 15:5; cf. Acts 1:21–26).

The things that people might need to give up for Jesus' sake include not only material resources like houses and fields, but also family members, revealing perhaps the harsh estrangement that some early Christians suffered as a result of their commitment to Christ (see 8:21–22; 10:21, 34–37; 19:10–12). The restoration of such losses might come by way of belonging to the church, a community in which all members consider themselves to be a family and are willing to share their earthly resources (houses, fields, or whatever) with those who lack. If so, then some benefits of following Jesus are experienced already in the present (see Mark 10:29–30, "now in this age"; Matthew drops the words, but the point may still be implicit). Still, to paraphrase Paul, any losses associated with this present time are not worth comparing with the future glory that awaits the faithful (see Rom 8:18).

The specific promise to the disciples (enthronement) is couched in terms appropriate for their context as Israelites. We might have imagined, given horrific persecution of Christians by gentile authorities, that Matthew's readers would have wanted to see the apostles judging Nero and the other Romans who had tortured and killed so many of them. But no! Vengeance is not what is envisioned here. The word "judge" (*krinō*) in this context does not mean "pass judgment on" but is used with reference to beneficent ruling as in the book of Judges (LXX: Judg 4:4; 10:3; 12:7–14; 15:20). The point is not that the apostles will get a chance to condemn those who rejected them, but rather that they will get a chance to serve those people as their benevolent rulers (cf. 20:25–26). The reward may simply be restoration of honor. When the day of glory comes, they will be seated on thrones, and all of Israel will recognize that the ones they dismissed, derided, or ridiculed were worthy of honor all along. This is, of course, why the promise of rewards segues into Jesus' repeated observation: "Many who are first will be last, and the last will be first" (19:30).

Let us not pass too quickly over the assumption that "the twelve tribes of Israel" will be part of the future reign of God. Although caricatured leaders of Israel serve as literary foils and paragons of evil in Matthew's story, the narrative reflects a generic understanding that the Jewish people as a whole will be saved by their Messiah (see comments on 1:21; 27:25). In a sense, Matthew's insistence that all twelve tribes of Israel will be among the eschatological people of God participating in the "renewal of all things" comports with Paul's assurance that "all Israel will be saved" (Rom 11:25–26)—though in both cases, these affirmations invite questions for which there are no clear answers.

Modern readers sometimes think the concern for rewards is unbecoming of true discipleship; they may regard Peter's desire to know, "What are we going to get out of this?" as crass. Can "giving things up for Jesus" be viewed as an investment strategy rather than as straightforward sacrificial renunciation? Well, we know from prosperity-gospel preachers in our own day that it *can* be so viewed: but *should* it be? God's blessings are never for sale (Acts 8:9–24). Still, Jesus does not reprove Peter for the question he asks, and Matthew does not present the question as inappropriate. Jesus has previously indicated that God rewards faithfulness (6:4, 6, 18); people who believe this should not be faulted for hoping to receive what God has promised. Perhaps some distinction could be made regarding the extent to which rewards motivate faithful behavior. It would be self-serving for someone to do the right thing *only* to gain some desired recompense; but it is quite another matter for those who realize that doing the right thing is costly to be comforted by a promise that there will be remuneration in the end. Personally, I like the divine irony expressed by Jesus in Luke: "Expect . . . nothing in return. Your reward will be great" (Luke 6:35; cf. 14:14).

20:1–16. Parable of Day Workers (only in Matthew)

The preceding discussion of rewards prompts Jesus to tell a parable about persons receiving the same wage even though they are hired at different times of the day. In response to a question from Peter (19:27), Jesus has affirmed that the disciples' sacrifices will be repaid a hundredfold and that they will inherit eternal life. But now, through this parable, he indicates that the same rewards may be given to many who do not suffer and to people who sacrifice considerably less. God is not unfair, only generous (20:15), and it is the very nature of God's rule to reverse standards on which evaluations of worth are usually made. Indeed, an affirmation that the first will be last, and the last first is used twice, as an *inclusio* around this parable (19:30; 20:16, with chiastic inversion of the phrases).

This parable is often read as an apologetic for God's inclusion of gentiles, who as newcomers to the people of God stand to receive the same blessings and rewards as the people of Israel, who offered centuries of (sometimes faltering) obedience and worship. Matthew the evangelist may have preached that sermon, but the parable itself can have broader application. It offers a memorable and extraordinary exposition of a smallness endemic to the human condition, an egotistical absorption that prevents people from rejoicing in the good fortune of others. Even those who have received everything they hoped for can be disgruntled if others are equally blessed. What is it in human nature that makes us so mean? We don't just want our lives to be good; we want them to be *better* than the lives of other people. The parable likewise exposes the folly of envy or of what the Bible sometimes calls "covetousness" (20:15; cf. Rom 1:29; 7:7–8). The tendency toward such indulgence is apparently so prevalent that it had to be condemned twice in the Ten Commandments (Exod 20:17)—and it's not even an enjoyable sin (does anyone desire to be more covetous?).

Most remarkable of all, the parable exposes the reason for this human characteristic that replaces gratitude and satisfaction with grumbling and gloom. Unless they are the immediate beneficiaries, people do not appreciate generosity because (1) they have a strong sense of self-justifying entitlement, and (2) they resist the notion that others are their equals. Presumably, the workers in the parable would be satisfied to receive "what they deserve." The problem is that, when they notice others receiving "more than they deserve" they assume that they are entitled to receive more than they deserve as well. Their complaint is, "You have made them equal to us" (20:11). Elsewhere in Matthew, we see that those who have almost given up on God (the "poor in spirit") are singled out for divine blessing, that Jesus came "not to call the righteous but sinners" (9:13), that a single endangered child warrants more attention than ninety-nine adults (18:10–14), and that tax collectors and enslaved sex workers will be among the first to enter the reign of God (21:32). Even apart from the issue of gentile inclusion, none of this seems *fair*: but the God revealed by the Matthean Jesus is *generous*, which is better than fair. People are wise to prefer a generous God to a merely fair one; the only people who prefer the latter would be poor souls with a deluded notion of what fair treatment might actually mean for them (and others).

In recent decades, William R. Herzog III has sought to interpret many of Jesus' parables (and some of his notable sayings) as codified language that villagers could understand in ways that their oppressors might not (Herzog 1994). This parable, then, is not read as being about God showing mercy to all alike but instead as an exposé of sadistic landowners who torment their day laborers, teasing them into thinking they will receive more than starvation wages for a day's work, only to dash those hopes. Herzog is a remarkable New Testament scholar, and I appreciate his attempts to relate Jesus' ideas to concrete social situations rather than spiritualized religious themes. Nevertheless, his reading of this parable seems desperate in its defiance of an obvious meaning that fits with Jesus' tendency to embrace and then modify traditional Jewish teachings. Several Jewish texts use the motif of workers being paid unexpected wages, usually to make some moral point. For example, a man who works only two hours is paid the same as everyone else because he is diligent and does more in two hours than others who labor all day (a midrash to Leviticus: Sifra Behuqotai pereq [§] 2.262.1.9). Jesus takes up the motif but tells a story in which *need* rather than *merit* determines what is provided: the people who want to work but cannot get hired (20:7) still need a day's wage to feed their families. The landowner in the story seems to know this, and it is hard to fault him for doing what seems to be motivated by simple compassion. Herzog is bothered by the notion that Jesus would use a "wealthy landowner" in a peasant society as a symbol for someone who does good. I do grant that, in Matthew's Gospel, examples of characters who have social power and use that power responsibly are rare (see Theme 16 "*Critique of power, wealth, and wisdom*" in the introduction, p. 31). Still, characters who "stand for" God seem to be an exception to the general rule (see also 18:23–27).

20:17–19. Third Passion Prediction (cf. Mark 10:32–34; Luke 18:31–33)

Once again, Jesus tells his disciples what is going to happen when they reach Jerusalem (16:21; 17:22–23; cf. 26:2; 27:3). This time he offers more detail, explicitly mentioning his crucifixion for the first time in the Gospel (but see 10:38; 16:24). Notably, he assigns ultimate responsibility for this deed to the gentiles, to the Roman government headed by Pontius Pilate. Those powers have not been mentioned previously: the first prediction placed all culpability with the religious leaders of Israel, and the second mentioned only "human hands." With the exception of Herod the baby killer in the opening of the Gospel (2:16), gentiles have seemed favorably disposed to Jesus, with only the Jewish establishment actively opposing him. But the murder of John the Baptist by Herod Antipas (14:1–12) alerted the reader that this may not continue to be the case.

20:20–28. Request for Positions of Honor (cf. Mark 10:35–45; Luke 22:24–27)

Jesus' promise that the Twelve will have thrones alongside that of the Son of Man at the renewal of all things (19:28) prompts the mother of two of his disciples—James and John, the sons of Zebedee (4:21–22)—to ask whether her boys can have the two best seats, the thrones closest to Jesus' throne. She makes the request respectfully (20:20), and nothing Jesus says indicates that she is wrong to ask him for whatever she wants (see 7:7–11). Still, the request can only be granted if it is in keeping with the will of God, and not even Jesus presumes to know God's will in every matter (see 26:39). He then addresses the Zebedee boys themselves, apparently assuming that they have put their mother up to this. Again, he does not rebuke them for making the request or indicate that it was inappropriate to do so. He does, however, warn these ambitious disciples that, if granted, such a request might entail greater demands on them than they realize: suffering and martyrdom similar to what he will experience. It is possible that Matthew's readers would be expected to note an ironic use of the phrase "one at your right hand and one at your left" in 20:21; later, that phrase recurs in 27:38 to describe the location of the two men crucified with Jesus. Unwittingly, the sons of Zebedee may be asking to be "enthroned" with Jesus on crosses; if so, after it becomes clear that this is an option, they renounce the privilege (26:56), giving the lie to their previous confident professions (20:22; 26:35). In a more general sense, the episode is probably informed by an early Christian tradition claiming that only those who suffer with Christ will reign with him (Rom 8:17; 2 Thess 1:5; 2 Tim 2:12).

Jesus' reference to his crucifixion as a "cup" that he must drink foreshadows his prayer in Gethsemane (26:39) as well as the promise that his blood will be "poured out for many for the forgiveness of sins" (26:27–28, offered with reference to the cup at the Last Supper). In the Old Testament, cup imagery can signify God's salvation (Ps 116:13) *or* it can signify the wrath of God, which Israel (Isa 51:17–23) or other nations (Jer 25:15; 49:12) must drink as they experience judgment. Basically, the "cup that one must drink" seems to be a metaphor for one's destiny or lot in life (Ps 16:5), be it good or ill.

In any case, the incident creates strife among the disciples, causing Jesus to remind them that in the reign of God, the greatest is not the one who rules like a tyrant but the one who serves like an enslaved person (20:25–27; see also 19:30; 20:16). In seeking places of honor, the Zebedee boys are actually seeking the lowliest positions, to be greater servants than others. Jesus describes himself as the ultimate example of this great reversal: though Lord of all, he serves all, even to the point of giving his life as a ransom.

Jesus' words regarding how things are among "the gentiles" (in the world at large) offer the Gospel's clearest explication of an ideology that is assumed for the narrative as a whole (see Theme 16 "*Critique of power, wealth, and wisdom*" in the introduction, p. 31). In the story world of Matthew, power is closely correlated with evil: for the most part, the more powerful people are, the more evil they are; the less powerful they are, the less evil they are. This is because power is almost always used coercively, to "lord it over" others rather than to serve them. Matthew allows that it does not need to be that way: Jesus models the noncoercive power of a servant king; there have been godly rulers in the past (David, 12:3; Solomon, 12:42), and the renewal of all things will bring a new era when those on thrones rule justly (19:28). But, in general, Matthew's narrative depicts a world in which representatives of worldly power are aligned with Satan: this includes gentile rulers, Jewish leaders, "great ones" (20:25)—all who are currently first but destined to be last (19:30; 20:16). God's rule, by contrast, is associated with those who lack power or who voluntarily surrender it: enslaved persons (10:24–25; 20:27; 24:45–46); the meek (5:5); children (18:1–4; 19:13–15; 21:15–16; see also 11:25); little ones (10:42; 18:6, 10, 14); the "least" (25:40, 45)—all who are currently last but destined to be first (19:30; 20:16).

In describing himself as one who "came not to be served but to serve" (20:28), Jesus is almost certainly likening himself to the Suffering Servant figure in Isaiah 53, who pours himself out for the sake of others, bearing their sins and iniquities and, possibly (the text is uncertain), being made an offering for sin (53:10–12). At least, Jesus is inspired by the Isaiah figure to view voluntary suffering for the sake of others as preferable to attaining power in order to coerce others. References or allusions to the Isaiah Servant texts are also found at 3:17; 8:17; 12:18–21; 17:5; and 26:28.

The "ransom" language that Jesus uses here has been of great interest to theologians: the word translated ransom (*lytron*) was most commonly used to describe the price that had to be paid for an enslaved person to gain freedom. Matthew inherited this concept from Mark's Gospel (Mark 10:45) and has not developed it significantly. Indeed, up till now, we have heard nothing at all about the purpose of Jesus' death. There have been predictions of his death (16:21; 17:22–23; 20:17–19) and other references or allusions to it (9:15; 12:39–40; 16:4), but no indication of *why* he is going to die or of what purpose that death might serve. Matthew's readers might just assume that Jesus' death is an unfortunate martyrdom (which God quickly corrects through the resurrection) were it not for three verses that point to something more:

- In 1:21, when Jesus is born, we are told, "He will save his people from their sins": at the time, this thought is not connected to his death on a cross, but we are expected to remember that this is what he is destined to do.
- In the present text, 20:28, we learn that his death will be like a "ransom" in that it will result in freedom "for many" people; remembering 1:21, we may assume that this means freedom from sin and its consequences (not from literal, political slavery).
- In 26:28, we find that Jesus' blood is "the blood of the covenant, which is poured out for many for the forgiveness of sins."

Thus, Jesus saves people from their sins by dying on a cross: his death results in forgiveness of sins and, in accord with a new covenant, brings freedom from sin and its consequences. Matthew, however, has no interest in *why* or *how* Jesus' death will have such effects. For the most part, it is enough for him to know that this death is necessary (16:21, using the Greek word *dei*, "must"). It *has* to happen. It is God's will and part of God's plan. Matthew is simply not interested in theological "theories of atonement" that go beyond that affirmation. What does interest him is the model that Jesus' death sets for Christian living: if the Master will serve others to the extent of giving up his life for them, how much more should his followers humble themselves in service and voluntary suffering for the sake of others (cf. Phil 2:1–11; see Theme 3 "*The mission of God*" in the introduction, p. 10; and the discussion on forgiveness of sins in the comments on 6:12, 14–15).

20:29–34. Healing of the Blind (cf. Matt 9:27–31; Mark 10:46–52; Luke 18:35–43)

Motivated by compassion (see also 9:36; 14:14; 15:32; 18:27), Jesus gives sight to two blind men who call out to him as "Son of David" (see also 1:1; 9:27; 12:23; 15:22). This acclamation prepares us for how Jesus will be greeted shortly upon entering Jerusalem (21:9) and helps to set up Jesus' riddle, which identifies the Messiah as both David's "son" (descendant) and David's Lord (22:41–45). The crowd's attempt to hush the blind men is reminiscent of the disciples' shooing away parents who, they think, pester Jesus with children (19:13); it foreshadows the priests' desire to hush a different group of children, who praise Jesus as "the Son of David" in the temple (21:15). In this case, the stern rebukes that the disciples lavish on the blind men reveal an ironic misunderstanding that seeks to protect Jesus from being asked to do what he claims he came to do (11:2–6). The blind men's persistence reminds us of that exhibited by the Canaanite woman in 15:22–25; as in that case, shouting at Jesus seems rude, and Matthew's readers may be expected to sympathize (at least initially) with those who want to silence the offensive supplicants. But, then, the note that these men follow Jesus after being healed highlights the metaphorical potential the story holds for discipleship: Christ removes the spiritual blindness of sinners so that they can follow him in the reign of heaven that has already come near (on "following Jesus," see also 4:18–22; 8:18–22; 9:9; 10:38; 16:24; 19:21).

The story appears to report the same incident as given in Mark 10:46–52, though only one blind man (named Bartimaeus) is mentioned there; on such "doubling" of characters in Matthew, see also 8:28–34 (cf. Mark 5:1–17). Beyond that, the story also appears to be a doublet of a quite similar incident reported in 9:27–31, though that one is set in Galilee. This time, however, the men who are healed are not prohibited from telling anyone what happened. Of course, the miracle is public, but still one senses that, as this phase of the narrative comes to its conclusion, the time for silence is past.

EXCURSUS

"Christ beneath Culture" as a Paradigm for Mission

The Matthean Jesus expects his disciples to carry on the mission of God in a manner similar to what was evident in his own ministry; he instructs them to use whatever power they are given to serve others like enslaved people rather than to rule over others like tyrants (20:25–27; see also 19:30; 20:16). Thus, the Missionary Discourse in Matthew 10 and the Great Commission in 28:16–20 assume an understanding of the relationship between Christ and culture that I believe was missed by H. Richard Niebuhr in his famous work ***Christ and Culture*** (Niebuhr 1951). In that book, Niebuhr outlines five typologies for ways Christians have tried to relate to the world around them. All five are evident in Scripture and in church history. Although Niebuhr's work focuses primarily on the latter, he suggests that Matthew's Gospel evinces a "Christ above Culture" model, according to which the church's knowledge of divine truth grants it a privileged status in society, which implies responsibility for enacting the will of God to the extent that it is able. In my view, what Niebuhr missed is the Gospel's aversion to coercive power.

I suggest that Matthew's Gospel evinces a ***sixth*** typology, distinct from any of those described by Niebuhr. I call this model "Christ beneath Culture" and describe it as follows:

> *The work of Christ is considered to be primarily evident in Christians and Christian institutions that renounce power and approach culture from a position of social inferiority. Christians do have access to superior revelation, but this will always appear as foolishness to the world. Christians are able to enact God's will in society, but they do so only when they emulate Christ in weakness and vulnerability.*

This position is actually an ***inversion*** of what Niebuhr called the "Christ above culture" model. Like that position, it holds that the church is called to do what it can to curb sin in the world at large, but (unlike that model) it recognizes that sin is inextricably caught up with the acquisition of power and with things that offer power (wisdom, status, riches). Therefore, to be effective in its mission, renunciation of any sort of coercive power is necessary. Cultural transformation results from subversion, not by dominance, and the church functions as God's agent in society only so long as it remains powerless. Mission consists of going into the world "like sheep into the midst of wolves" (Matt 10:16) and voluntarily suffering for the sake of a world that is not likely to appreciate the effort.

In the Bible, we find this view primarily in the Gospel of Matthew ("the last will be first," "the meek will inherit the earth," etc.). As such, it may be a minority perspective, but it does have exponents in church history. Some such understanding seems to have informed Francis of Assisi and Martin Luther King Jr. It is sometimes espoused by liberation theologians and has often been the view of martyrs. I suspect that it was the view of the historical Jesus.

Part Five of Matthew's Gospel: Conflict in Jerusalem

Matthew 21:1–26:1

As Jesus at last arrives in Jerusalem, the stage is set for events to play out as he predicted they would (16:21; 17:22–23; 20:17–19). But before the passion story itself commences, Jesus has some final public confrontations with his enemies and he offers a private final testimony to his disciples. After a triumphal entry into the city (21:1–11), Jesus challenges the ruling authorities of Israel in a manner that goes beyond anything we have seen thus far. He closes down the usual commerce of the temple and takes it over as a site for his own ministry of teaching and healing (21:12–17): the teaching, furthermore, consists of a series of parables that present the religious leaders of Israel in a bad light (21:28–22:14). Some of these leaders respond by putting him to a series of three tests, reminiscent of the three temptations with which Satan tested him in 4:1–11 (22:15–40). After besting them in these contests, Jesus denounces the scribes and Pharisees (23:1–36) and then offers the last of his five great discourses, this one focusing on the end times and final judgment (24:1–25:46).

MATTHEW 21:1–22

Confrontation with Temple Authorities

Matthew follows his Markan source closely throughout this section of the Gospel.

The conflict between Jesus and the religious leaders of Israel reaches a new level of intensity as Jesus enters their stronghold and encounters them on their own terms.

21:1–11. Jesus Enters the City (cf. Mark 11:1–11a; Luke 19:28–38; John 12:12–19)

Jesus' disciples and other supporters provide him with a royal welcome as he enters Jerusalem, letting garments and tree branches play the role of a "red carpet" laid out before him. The crowds announce him as "the prophet from Nazareth," but some also acclaim him as "the Son of David," indicating that he could be the Messiah (see 22:42); of course, the identifications of prophet and Messiah were not mutually exclusive (26:68). The procession is peculiar in that Jesus rides not a majestic steed, but a donkey and its colt. This marks him as a humble or gentle king, but a king nonetheless (21:5). This bid to royalty prepares for the passion story, in which Jesus dies on the cross as "the King of the Jews" (27:11, 29, 37, 42; see also 2:2). The scenario was set up intentionally by Jesus, staged to fulfill the prophet Zechariah's proclamation of how Israel's true king (Messiah?) would come (Zech 9:9; see also Isa 62:11). The very procurement of the animals involves divine foresight on his part and the cooperation of strangers who seem unaccountably willing to grant whatever "the Lord" needs (21:2–3). The whole event is a prophetic act or acted parable: Jesus enters Jerusalem in a mock procession, presenting himself as the peasant king of Israel, the true "Son of David," the long-awaited Messiah.

An interesting but not terribly important side note may be offered concerning the animals Jesus rides. First, many are confused by how he sits on two beasts at the same time, but this is not terribly odd. One normally rode a donkey sidesaddle, so if the mother animal had a foal too young to be separated from her, Jesus could have sat on the adult with his legs stretched out over the accompanying colt. Or perhaps he rode only one animal, and the "them" on which he sat refers only to the garments, which were draped over both (21:7). What seems stranger is that the prophecy in Zechariah (quoted by Matthew in 21:5) refers to only one animal, referenced twice as is typical with Hebrew parallelism: the animal is "a donkey" (actually, a *male* donkey in Hebrew), and it is also "a colt, the foal of a donkey." Many scholars think Matthew didn't understand the prophecy and, so, had Jesus ride two beasts in order to fulfill what he thought the prophecy called for. But Matthew almost certainly would have understood Hebrew parallelism, a common device he uses throughout his Gospel (for example, 5:3–10; 6:10–13; 7:7). He seems to be applying the prophecy here in a hyperliteral fashion, ignoring the likely meaning in favor of a sense he considered possible, if unusual. But why would he do that? One guess: he was inspired by Gen 49:10–11. But that hasn't satisfied most interpreters, nor does it offer any help on the larger question of why Matthew doubles characters in other instances: one demoniac in Mark 5:2 becomes two demoniacs in Matthew 8:28; one blind man in Mark 10:46 becomes two blind men in Matthew 20:30. No one has solved this puzzle; for some reason that escapes us, Matthew liked pairs and sometimes seems to have created them just because he could.

On a more substantive note, the Greek word *praüs*, used to describe Jesus in 21:5 (translated "humble" in NRSVue; also in 11:29) is the same word rendered "meek" in the Beatitudes (5:5). As noted in the comments on that passage, the term is normally used in Jewish literature to describe people of low status, especially those who may be considered victims of injustice: the *praüs* are the oppressed or downtrodden people of the earth, those who have been humbled or humiliated by powerful oppressors. Matthew certainly wants to retain the original sense of Zechariah's prophecy, indicating that Jesus does not come as a conquering monarch but as a gentle, pacific king who wishes to serve more than to be served (20:28). But there is also a sense that he comes as one who identifies with the oppressed and downtrodden people of the earth, with the poor, the powerless, the outcasts—all those he will later identify as "the least" of his family members (25:40, 45).

21:12–17. Jesus in the Temple (cf. Mark 11:15–17; Luke 19:45–46; John 2:13–17)

Jesus goes immediately to the temple and disrupts the commerce there, overturning tables in the courtyard where money was changed and animals were bought for the required sacrifices. Apparently he objects to the sacrificial system as practiced by temple goers because it serves to protect people from accountability for their sins (a "den of robbers" is a hideout where criminals are safe from prosecution; see Jer 7:9–11). The temple should be "a house of prayer" (Isa 56:7), where the afflicted find healing and where God can delight to be praised—even (or especially) by children and other supposedly insignificant members of the community (see Ps 8:2). The chief priests, however, want none of this, and they are especially perturbed that this upstart Jesus is being proclaimed "the Son of David," a title with messianic significance (see 22:42).

We must be careful to read the Matthean version of this story without mentally adding details from the other Gospels. Matthew's description of the temple incident takes only two verses, one of which is a Scripture quote. There is no indication that Jesus is angry or that he behaves in a violent manner. He does not make a whip of cords, no animals are mentioned except doves, and Jesus says nothing about people turning the temple into a marketplace. Many of those well-known features derive from John 12:13–17, where the incident might be properly called a "cleansing of the temple": the Johannine Jesus wants to restore reverence to an institution whose practices have become mired in crass materialism. Not in Matthew!

When the Matthean Jesus enters "the temple" in 21:12, he enters the courtyard around the building where sacrifices were to be made. This courtyard contained stalls where sacrificial animals were sold, as well as tables where people could change their Roman coins (with pagan images) into Jewish shekels in order to purchase those animals with more appropriate currency. In Matthew, Jesus does not object to the location of the business operation or to the way in which it is being practiced. We should not imagine, for example, that the moneychangers or dove sellers were cheating people or conducting their business in some inappropriate manner. Jesus does not call *them* thieves nor imply that they or anyone else is robbing people in the temple area itself (thieves do not normally rob people in their den). Further, Jesus drives out the *buyers* as well as the sellers. Then, he turns over some of the tables and quotes a pastiche of Scripture, wedding Isaiah 56:7 to Jeremiah 7:11. Jewish worshipers and Jewish Christian readers of Matthew would have understood. Jeremiah had thought there was something fundamentally wrong with people using the temple system to ensure that their sins would be forgiven, so that they could have a secure place in God's covenant *without actually repenting of their sins!* The fuller context of the Jeremiah quote reads, "Will you steal, murder, commit adultery, swear falsely, make offerings to Baal . . . and then come and stand before me in this house, which is called by my name, and say, 'We are safe!'—only to go on doing all these abominations?" (7:9–10). In this sense the temple is looked upon as a safe haven to which people who commit all sorts of offenses may flee to avoid prosecution, to be assured that their Judge has been appeased and that their sinful acts will have no consequences (for them at least). Matthew presents Jesus, the newly arrived prophet from Nazareth (21:11), as performing a prophetic act, or "acted parable," to indicate that the current leaders of Israel are still guilty of the charges Jeremiah brought against the authorities of *his* day. For what it's worth, historical Jesus scholars think that Matthew's take on the story is probably closest to what actually happened: not a spontaneous tantrum over presumed irreverence in temple practices but a well-planned, deliberate demonstration that only a prophet could perform with immunity—though in the case of Jesus, being a prophet from Nazareth would not provide immunity enough.

Notably, Matthew also emphasizes *positive* roles that the temple serves. It can be "a house of prayer," a place where children sing "Hosanna" to the "Son of David," and a site for healing the blind and the lame (this last part, in 21:14, is unique to Matthew). Some have said Matthew envisions the ideal temple as a big synagogue (or, anachronistically, as a big church). Elsewhere in Matthew, Jesus acknowledges that God dwells in the temple (23:21), and he pays the temple tax to support the institution (17:24–27), though he also indicates that something "greater than the temple" is present in his ministry (12:6). In any case, the theological malpractice that Jeremiah and the Matthean Jesus attributed to temple operatives is not exclusive to Judaism: we can probably assume that Matthew would be unhappy to discover all the ways that *unrepentant* Christians have found for using their religious system to avoid the consequences of sin without actually amending their lives. Indeed, it may be "Christian versions" of the den-of-robbers theme that Matthew wants his readers to see Jesus as addressing. After all, the Jerusalem temple had been destroyed fifteen years before this book was written, and alleged inadequacies of that system would be something of a moot point. Unfortunately, we don't have copies of sermons the evangelist might have preached on texts from his own Gospel, but it is easy to imagine him reading this passage to the congregation and then talking about analogous tendencies he saw developing in communities that bore the Messiah's name.

21:18–22. Cursing the Fig Tree (cf. Mark 11:12–14, 20–24)

A hungry Jesus curses a fig tree that has no fruit, causing it to wither. In church history, this account has often been read as illustrating the humanity of Jesus, presenting him as one who experiences physical hunger and emotional distress. Matthew probably has other interests: note, for instance, that there is no hint of petulance or anger on the part of Jesus in Matthew's version of the story. The event seems staged, with the poor tree simply serving as an object lesson. We may also note that this is the only "negative miracle" in the Gospel; otherwise, Jesus uses his power only to heal, nurture, or save—never to destroy. John Chrysostom suggests that the purpose of the withering was to "furnish the proof of his might in taking vengeance," showing the disciples the destructive power he could unleash if he chose to do so; presumably, they would then be more appreciative of his mercy (*Homilies on Matthew* 67.1). But what did Matthew really intend to teach us with this somewhat absurd tale? In Mark's Gospel, this story was told in two parts, bracketing the temple incident (a literary device called *intercalation*). Matthew simplifies the narration but probably also intends the meaning that was more obvious in Mark. The withering of the fruitless tree is an acted parable, illustrating dramatically the judgment that will come on those who do not bear fruit (3:8–10; 7:16–20; see also 12:33; 13:8, 23). Such a prophetic warning can be generic and universal, but context suggests immediate application to Israel, since both the temple (21:13) and the nation as a whole (21:34) have failed to produce the kind of fruit that God seeks.

On another level, Matthew allows the incident to serve as one more occasion for Jesus to extol the power of faith, demonstrating to his amazed disciples (the people of "little faith," 6:30; 8:26; 14:31; 16:8; 17:20) what is possible for those who do not doubt. The word translated "doubt" in this verse is *diakrinō* (different from *distazō* in 14:31 and 28:17). It normally means "discern" or "discriminate" (as in 16:3)—in other words, "to decide between options." So here, absence of such discrimination implies single-minded focus: to have faith and not doubt means to entertain no other option than what faith demands. The motif of faith that moves mountains has come up before, in 17:20. There, Jesus did not say that faith with no doubt was necessary to accomplish such miracles: indeed, he promised that the tiniest speck of faith (the size of a "mustard seed") was sufficient.

Matthew 21:22 states baldly, "Whatever you ask for in prayer with faith, you will receive." This is one of several "blanket prayer promises" in the Bible that can give way to unfortunate interpretations, inspiring unrealistic hopes among well-intentioned believers or stoking selfish ambition among less well-intentioned ones. Worse, despite obvious failures of existential fulfillment, such promises have become virtual mantras for teachers of the gullible, promoting a popular vision of the Christian God as something akin to a genie who can be forced to grant wishes (answer prayers) if petitioners make their requests correctly. According to this philosophy, the most important requirement in making a request is that the petitioner believes absolutely, with no hint of doubt, that what is requested will come to pass: this is the meaning given to the phrase "with faith" in Matthew 21:22 (cf. Mark 11:24). But both Jesus and Paul pray for things they do not receive (Matt 26:39; 2 Cor 12:7–9), and this does not appear to have been due to a lack of faith or a failure to ask in a more effective manner. The assurance Jesus gives in Matthew 21:22 is offered to persons assumed to understand prayer as a means of discovering and receiving what *God wants to give* rather than as an occult strategy for manipulating divine powers. Indeed, to pray "with faith" means to pray with such a presumed understanding. Further, when Jesus encourages his followers to pray without doubt (21:21), he means that they should have absolute certainty regarding the power of God to accomplish anything; he does not mean that they should have no doubt regarding their personal apprehension of God's will. Confidence in God's power is faith, while confidence that one knows God's will is presumption (see Matt 8:2 and comments on that verse). On the efficacy of prayer, see also 7:7–11; 18:19.

MATTHEW 21:23–22:14
Parables against the Religious Leaders

Matthew basically follows his Markan source for this section of the Gospel, but he adds two parables that make points similar to one already in Mark: a story unique to Matthew (21:28–32) and a story drawn from Q (22:1–10) now bookend the pivotal tale of the rebellious tenants (21:33–46).

Conflict between Jesus and the temple authorities continues to escalate as they directly challenge Jesus concerning his authority and he tells three parables intended to expose their unfaithfulness to God and to God's mission.

21:23–27. Question of Authority (cf. Mark 11:27–33; Luke 20:1–8)

The religious leaders question Jesus about the source of his authority (7:28–29; 9:8; cf. 10:1; 28:18). This time it is the chief priests and elders of the people who challenge him; previously, the scribes and Pharisees (12:38) and then the Pharisees and Sadducees (16:1) posed similar challenges by demanding that he show them a sign (to prove he had divine authorization). Matthew presents all these types of religious leaders as united in their opposition to Jesus, treating them almost as a single character (see Theme 14 "*Religious leaders as enemies of God*" in the introduction, p. 25). This time, the challenge to his authority appears to be prompted by his recent activities in Jerusalem, especially the staged entry procession (21:1–11) and subsequent overturning of tables in the temple courts (21:12–13). The leaders may wonder about his political affiliation, given implicit claims that he is some sort of king (21:5) or prophet (21:11), or even the Messiah (21:9, 15); or they may wonder, as others did (9:34; 12:24), whether the power by which he heals (21:14) and withers (21:18–19) comes from an evil source. In any case, Jesus does not treat the question as sincere since those who ask it lack the integrity either to admit their opposition to John the Baptist or to acknowledge that John was God's servant after all. Jesus regards these authorities as examples of the presumptuous "wise and intelligent" persons to whom God reveals nothing (11:25). Accordingly, he tells them nothing about himself. Instead, he tells three parables that present his evaluation of them.

Matthew does not mean to present Jesus as evasive or as trying to hide his divine identity. Jesus has openly declared the source of his authority throughout his ministry (see, for example, 11:27), but he refuses to play games with hypocrites, knowing full well that these religious leaders do not really care whether he claims to have authority from God or not. The story now can be read at two different levels. At a logical level, we might surmise that these authorities have already made up their minds that Jesus is an impostor (27:63) and that they are simply looking for ways to trap him in blasphemy or expose him as a fraud. Something like that might have been true of some actual Jewish authorities who interacted with Jesus historically. But at another level, the religious leaders who are characters in Matthew's narrative are people who have set themselves against God: they do not oppose Jesus because they fail to recognize that he has authority from God: they oppose him because they *do* recognize this, and they are God's enemies (Powell 1990). It may be difficult for modern readers to follow the latter perspective, but Matthew wants his story to serve as an almost apocalyptic tale of conflict between ultimate powers: he is less interested in a temporal conflict that once occurred between Jesus and some Jewish authorities than he is in the eternal conflict between good and evil, or indeed, between God and Satan. Since Jesus stands for "good" in this rendering, the religious leaders of Israel must be made to stand for "evil." We may regret the casting (I think we should), but we can still follow the story, realizing that what is about to unfold has meaning that transcends historical identifications of the key players (on this aspect of the narrative, see Theme 15 "*Conflict along three plot lines*" in the introduction, p. 29).

21:28–32. Parable of Two Sons (only in Matthew)

While not answering the religious leaders' question about his authority (21:23–27), Jesus does respond to them with a parable that reveals their true plight. Their stubborn refusal to acknowledge that John the Baptist came "in the way of righteousness" (21:32)—as God's agent, whose call to repentance they should heed—marks them as analogous to a boy who only says the right things without actually doing his father's will (cf. 7:21). They will fare worse at the judgment than notorious sinners who believed John the Baptist. The latter may be likened to a boy who at first opposed the father's will but later changed his mind and did as the father wished.

At a basic level, the parable simply affirms that God prefers acknowledged sinners who repent over unacknowledged sinners (hypocrites) who don't. The point would be obvious and only controversial insofar as Jesus identifies Israel's most prominent religious leaders as belonging to the latter group. The matter is complicated by the specific reference to tax collectors and sex workers as prime examples of people who believed John and ultimately did as the father (God) wished. Jesus is almost certainly referring to "the tax collectors and sinners [a euphemism for sex workers]" with whom he has previously been associated and for whom he has previously demonstrated concern. As noted in comments on the earlier passages (9:10–13; 11:19), most tax collectors and probably all sex workers in the world of Jesus were enslaved persons, so we probably should not assume that, once they believed John, they stopped collecting taxes or prostituting themselves. Perhaps some of the tax collectors could find ways of exercising their profession in a less offensive manner (see Luke 3:12–13), but it is hard to imagine how sex workers could do so. In both cases, repentance and faith must have been more a matter of accepting John's promise that God's deliverance was at hand than altering the details of a lifestyle over which they had little control. Jesus might easily have chosen other examples of sinners who responded to John with transformed lives that all would applaud. His choice of *current tax collectors* (not former ones) and *current sex workers* (not former ones) as paradigms of Israelites who believed John in a way that fulfilled all God would demand of them reveals an appreciation for the limited ethical options available to those counted among the last (19:30; 20:16) and least (25:40, 45) in this world.

21:33–46. Parable of Rebellious Tenants (cf. Mark 12:1–12; Luke 20:9–19)

Jesus tells another parable to the religious leaders who question his authority (21:23), one that depicts them as rebels against God. As leaders of Israel, they ought to be faithful stewards of God's vineyard (Isa 5:1–7), but they have not led Israel in such a way as to produce the fruit of repentance (Matt 3:8) that God seeks. Indeed, they have mistreated the prophets whom God sent to them, requesting this fruit (cf. 23:29–36), and now they are prepared to kill Jesus himself, God's own Son. The problem is not that they don't know his source of authority or the source of John the Baptist's authority (21:25–27). Rather, they oppose him precisely *because* he is God's Son, the representative of their enemy, against whom they have rebelled (Powell 1990). Put this way, their fate is obvious, and Jesus traps them into declaring it (21:41) before they realize that the parable applies to them (21:45). If, indeed, their opposition to Jesus is borne of enmity against God, they have no hope of winning such a conflict; they will be broken and crushed, and the benefits of God's rule will pass to others, to people who *will* bear the fruit that God demands (see 3:7–10; 7:15–20; 12:33; 13:1 9; 21:19).

Jesus cites the same psalm that crowds sang when he entered the city the previous day (21:9; cf. Ps 118:25–26); now he suggests that he is the stone that, according to that psalm, becomes the cornerstone despite having been rejected (Ps 118:22–23; cf. Acts 4:11; 1 Pet 2:7). A negative response to Jesus means losing everything (10:33). The religious leaders fully understand the terms that Jesus has set forth in these parables (21:28–44). Leaders specifically mentioned include the chief priests and Pharisees, a pairing that seems unlikely historically but fits well with Matthew's literary intention of portraying all of Israel's disparate authorities as a united front that functions as a single character in the narrative (see Theme 14 "*Religious leaders as enemies of God*" in the introduction, p. 25). In any case, these religious leaders realize that Jesus is accusing them of being not merely misguided, but rebellious stewards, stubbornly unrepentant hypocrites who talk about obedience (21:30) but are actually at war with God. Realizing this, they want to move against him but fear the public opinion of the crowds, who think he is a prophet (21:46; cf. 14:5; 21:26).

Throughout history, Matthew 21:43 has been read as a key text for supersessionism, the notion that the Christian church has *replaced* Jewish Israel as the chosen people of God. Matthew does not understand the matter that way: he views the Christian movement as a phenomenon occurring *within* Judaism, such that even gentile believers belong to an expanded Israel rather than to some emerging new religion. What Matthew envisions is a change in leadership: the apostles and other faithful followers of the Messiah will lead Israel in a manner that the chief priests and Pharisees failed to do. From a modern perspective, of course, traditional Judaism being transformed into a messianic movement led by followers of Jesus may seem a lot like Judaism being superseded by Christianity. Still, we should at least recognize that the author of this Gospel did not imagine that a new religion would replace an old one but rather that a particular expression of the one true religion would emerge as the most prolific and authentic variety. Whatever we make of that vision, we can at least defer from labeling it "anti-Semitic" since Matthew had probably never met any Christian leaders who were not Semites and he no doubt assumed that the people who produce the fruits of the reign of God (21:43) would be a people led by Jews (albeit Jews who believe that Jesus is their Messiah). Of course, we must acknowledge that for centuries this text was used by anti-Semitic Christians to support atrocities against Jewish people; but let the blame for that fall on generations of (mis-)interpreters rather than on the Gospel author himself.

Having said that, we still might want to fault Matthew for giving us a narrative in which the religious leaders of Israel function as generic "bad guys." In reality, it seems extremely unlikely that there were chief priests and Pharisees in Jerusalem around 33 CE who knew Jesus was the Son of God but sought to kill him anyway because they were God's enemies. Indeed, I think it unlikely that Matthew himself thought this about those actual historical persons. Rather, Matthew portrays the chief priests and Pharisees who are characters in his story in that manner for the rhetorical purpose of turning a historical account into an apocalyptic one. Historically, there may have been conflict between Jesus and a few Jewish authorities in the capital city, but Matthew wants to tell a grander tale of conflict between God and Satan, between the Son of God and Satan's minions, between ultimate Good and ultimate Evil (see Theme 15 "*Conflict along three plot lines*" in the introduction, p. 29). As such, the story may be compelling and meaningful, but it is unfortunate that actual historical people had to be caricatured unfairly in order for it to work the way it does.

On another level, more pastoral than strictly exegetical, this parable serves as a paradigmatic statement of what is meant in the church by *stewardship* (see Excursus: Stewardship and the Gospel of Matthew, p. 245). The basic problem here is not that the tenants are poor caretakers, but that they act as though the vineyard belongs to them. This, Jesus indicates, is the fundamental problem with rebellious Israel (or sinful humanity): presuming we are owners when we are only stewards. There are many takeaways for the modern church. One is this: Christian ecological concern will certainly raise the question "Are we doing a good job of taking care of our planet?" but it does not start there. It starts with a frank acknowledgment: it is not our planet (Ps 24:1).

22:1–14. Parable of the Wedding Banquet (cf. Luke 14:16–24)

Jesus tells yet another parable to the religious leaders, one that expands upon his comment that the reign of God will pass from them to people who will produce the fruits that ought to come when God rules, especially the fruit of repentance (21:43; see 3:8). God's reign is a celebration, like a wedding banquet with the king's own son as the bridegroom (cf. 9:15). Having ignored the gracious invitation to participate in this celebration, the religious leaders of Israel will miss out; worse, they will be horribly punished for not only neglecting the invitation but also for mistreating the prophets and agents of God who brought that invitation (cf. 23:29–36). God's reign will come to include people not initially invited, such as those from all nations who are made disciples of Jesus (28:19). But there is a word of warning for them as well: anyone not clothed with the righteousness that the reign of God requires (5:20) will suffer the same fate as those who did not produce the fruit of repentance (i.e., eschatological judgment; cf. 22:13 with 25:46). Living under God's rule implies repentance and righteousness; those who do not do the will of God will be excluded (7:21).

Thus far, this interpretation of the parable of the Wedding Banquet is fairly standard and would be widely accepted. But numerous details merit further comment; with some of these, our insights become more speculative. It is possible that the king's dispatch of an army to burn the city of those who killed his messengers (22:7) is an allusion to the destruction of Jerusalem under Titus in 70 CE. Many have observed that the parable actually reads better when verses 6 and 7 are omitted: they suggest that those verses may have been inserted at some point in the story's tradition history. As is, the banquet, for which food was prepared and all was ready, has to be postponed until after a short war.

Interpretation may also focus on the note that the king who represents God in this story is throwing a wedding banquet for his son (who would be Jesus). Early Christianity sometimes represented the eschatological consummation as a wedding between Christ and the church (see Rev 19:7; 21:2, 9; 22:17; cf. John 3:29; Eph 5:31–32). Matthew 9:15 and 25:1–12 may indicate familiarity with that tradition. In any case, attendance at a royal wedding would have been considered a social obligation in Matthew's world, and few (if any) excuses for absenting oneself would have been deemed acceptable. To shun an invitation to such a wedding would be a prominent and public affront to the honor of the wedding couple and an insult against the dignity of the host. Similarly, those who do not want to celebrate Christ (and the church) are spurning God's invitation to live under the rule of heaven.

More attention has focused on the parable as illustrating the theological paradox "Many are called, but few are chosen" (22:14). Most likely this affirms Matthew's understanding that justification by grace does not obviate a need for subsequent sanctification. Or, to use less Pauline terminology, God graciously invites all to participate in God's reign, but that participation has an inevitably transformative effect. Thus, "both good and bad" are welcome to attend the banquet, but the bad are not expected to remain unchanged once they are there. At the risk of overinterpretation, some scholars suggest that a banquet host would have been happy to provide guests with wedding robes if they required them, so we are to regard the man in 22:11 as a recalcitrant who declined that offer. Perhaps—but evidence for this is slight, and it may be best not to press details. Parables in general, and especially allegorical parables, are not always concerned with logical consistency. We should not worry that the host asks, "How did you get in here without a wedding robe?" (22:12) when he is the one who ordered that the man be brought in from the streets (22:9–10). The point is simply that one can (but shouldn't) respond to the gospel's invitation without heeding its demands or experiencing its effects. In any case, the man remains "speechless" (22:12) because he has no excuse. He stands for those who misinterpret God's gracious favor as indifference to righteousness or who try to take advantage of a gracious God by exploiting such benevolence to justify obstinate disobedience. Such persons would resemble those who treat the temple as a safe haven for robbers (see comments on

21:13) or the hypothetical opponents of Paul who ask, "Should we continue in sin in order that grace may increase?" (Rom 6:1).

EXCURSUS

Stewardship and the Gospel of Matthew

The theme of Christian stewardship, with all its myriad expressions (and indeed, secular applications), derives ultimately from a series of "stewardship parables" that Jesus tells in the Gospel of Matthew (21:33–46; 24:45–51; 25:14–30; the first of these derives from Mark and the latter two from Q, but in all instances the Matthean versions have become the most influential in ecclesiastical teaching). Although those parables make diverse points (and even allow for allegorical interpretations), the basic concept is that human beings are understood to be "stewards" of what ultimately belongs to God.

Simply put, *stewards* are people who live in a place that is not their own and are allowed to make generous use of property and accoutrements that do not belong to them in return for taking care of the owner's possessions. I have explained this with a contemporary example of inviting a student to live in my house while I travel overseas: the student may sleep in my bed, eat at my table, watch my television, read my books, use my dishes, and so forth, all while keeping the house maintained and in better condition than if it were left vacant.

Stewardship parables often make one or, possibly, two points. First, there is the question of whether the steward is responsible and does a good job: in Jesus' parables, we have instances of bad stewards, who don't take good care of what has been entrusted to them. Following my contemporary example, we might imagine a student who throws wild parties, breaks the china, stains the carpet, soils the furniture, and so forth. By analogy, Christian preachers and teachers may ask whether we are being responsible stewards of our finances, our time, our families, our physical bodies, our planet. God has entrusted all these things to us, and we are caretakers. Are we being good stewards or bad stewards?

But a second point is more profound. All of the above is predicated on the notion that we are in fact stewards (be it good ones or bad ones). We are not owners! A basic biblical principle holds that everything we are and everything we have belongs to God (Pss 24:1; 100:3; 1 Chr

29:14; 1 Cor 3:21–23; 6:19–20). We bring nothing into this world and take nothing out of it (Job 1:21; see also Gen 3:19). Accordingly, the basic problem with the bad stewards in at least two of Jesus' parables (21:33–46; 24:45–51) is that they seem to deny this premise. They think they are owners—or, at least, they act as though they think this. To return to my contemporary analogy, imagine if I were to return from travels to find that the student had changed the locks on the house, sold off many of the possessions, and claimed that everything that remained was his! That would be a problem of an entirely different order. And that, Jesus indicates, is a fundamental problem with humanity: the problem isn't just that we should be better stewards than we are (do a better job of caring for what God has entrusted to us); the problem is that we deny or defy our identification as stewards altogether. We think we are *owners*: we think in terms of what we might do with *our* money and *our* time: how we might care for *our* bodies, *our* families, *our* planet.

This fundamental insight from Matthew's Gospel informs thousands of books and sermons on Christian stewardship, primarily by changing the question. It makes a difference whether I ask, "How much of *my* money should I give to the church?" or "How much of the money God has *entrusted* to me should be given to the church?" It makes a difference whether I ask, "How much of *my* time should I spend with *my* family?" or "How much of the time God has *allotted* me should be spent with the family God has *entrusted* to my care?" And so on (see further Powell 2006b).

MATTHEW 22:15–45
A Series of Tests

Matthew follows his Markan source closely for this section of his Gospel; the most severe redactional changes are found in 22:34–40, where a friendly scribe from Mark 12:28–34 is transformed into an opponent who tests Jesus; this is consistent with Matthew's rhetorical use of "the religious leaders of Israel" as a monolithic entity opposed to Jesus in particular and to God's purposes in general.

Conflict between Jesus and the religious leaders of Israel continues and escalates. After a controversial entry into the city of Jerusalem (21:1–11) and an even more controversial demonstration in the temple (21:12–13), Jesus was challenged by the religious leaders to identify by what authority he did such things (21:23–27). Dismissing their question as insincere, Jesus told three parables against the religious leaders of Israel, identifying them as hypocrites opposed to God. Now they come back at him, albeit in a less direct manner. Rather than criticizing him outright, they pose three questions designed to "test" him, to trap him into saying things that will turn the common people against him. In all three cases, the leaders do not actually care about Jesus' answers; their intention is to entice him into taking an unpopular stand, to make him look foolish, or simply to put him in a position that allows for no answer that cannot be easily contested. The questions with which these leaders test (*peirazō*) Jesus (22:18, 35) are almost certainly intended to parallel the series of three challenges with which the devil tempted (*peirazō*) Jesus at the outset of his ministry (4:1–11). Thus, the rhetorical structure of the Gospel underscores one of Matthew's most consistent themes: the religious leaders of Israel who are characters in his story function as agents of Satan, the supreme enemy of God (see Theme 14 "*Religious leaders as enemies of God*" in the introduction, p. 25). After frustrating all their attempts to undermine him, Jesus responds with a simple question of his own that stymies his opponents and puts them to shame.

22:15–22. Question of Taxes to the Emperor (cf. Mark 12:13–17; Luke 20:20–26)

In the first of three tests put to Jesus by religious leaders, Pharisees try to entangle him in his speech. They feign sincerity and ask him a question that they suppose will present him with the same sort of dilemma he foisted upon the chief priests (21:24–26): he must either lose favor with the populace by supporting oppressive Roman taxation or incur the ire of the Herodians (22:16) by opposing it. But Jesus has more integrity than the priests and answers without fear. His point is made subtly by asking whose image (*eikōn*) is on the coin: since the coin bears the emperor's image, he reasons that it belongs to the emperor. Readers familiar with the Septuagint would no doubt recall that people are made in the image (*eikōn*) of God (Gen 1:27); by the same logic, they must belong to God. Jesus' position is, basically, "Give the emperor what is made in the emperor's image [coins], and give God what is made in God's image [yourselves]." Unfortunately, this point is obscured in the NRSVue, which translates *eikōn* as "head" in 22:19.

Jesus supports the payment of Roman taxes for the same reason that he agreed to pay taxes to the corrupt temple (17:24–27; 21:13) and counseled his disciples to travel a second mile for an oppressor who forces them to go one mile (5:41). Whether the tax is just or unfair is not the point. Those who give to God what is God's (22:21)—their heart, soul, and mind (22:37)—are able to love even their enemies and to bless those who oppress them (5:44). With hearts fixed on their treasure in heaven, they are not overly concerned with the loss of money in this life (6:20–21; 19:21). So, sure, Jesus says: give the emperor his worthless coins, and give God everything that counts.

Many interpreters have objected to this rather straightforward interpretation by suggesting that Jesus was actually counseling resistance to Roman taxation, albeit in a clever way that the Romans would not understand, or at least in a veiled or coded manner that would not give them sufficient grounds for action against him. The usual form of this argument claims that since all things belong to God, including the coins and the land over which the emperor claims sovereignty, the second part of Jesus' answer actually deconstructs the first part: "Give to the emperor the things that are the emperor's" = "Give nothing to the emperor because nothing is his." The goal of such interpretations is to present Jesus as a social revolutionary who would never have counseled acquiescence to systemic injustice. In a different book, we might discuss the merits of these arguments relative to the historical Jesus; against them, we would need to weigh evidence that Jesus stood in a prophetic tradition often deemed treasonous by nationalists (Jer 26:8–9; 27:6–22; 29:4–9; Ezek 8–9). But that would be a different book. Here we are concerned with the Matthean Jesus and I think it is unlikely that Matthew wanted to present Jesus to his Diaspora community of Jews and gentiles as an early proponent of the Jewish resistance movement that had ended so disastrously for his homeland fifteen years before he wrote his Gospel. Rather, Matthew wants to assure his congregation that paying taxes to the emperor need not involve any compromise to their faith: followers of Jesus can and will be persecuted for many reasons (10:16–18; 24:9), but holding on to their money should not be one of them. Of course, the taxes are unjust and paying them is egregious, but money is just not that important, not worth dying for. The Matthean Jesus, at least, has no need for coins (note how he must ask for one in 22:19) and counsels his followers to emulate him in this respect (10:8–9).

22:23–33. Question of Marriage in the Resurrection (cf. Mark 12:18–27; Luke 20:27–40)

A second test is put to Jesus by the religious leaders of Israel. This time it is Sadducees who present him with a quandary that they think will expose the doctrine of life after death as inane (thus humiliating him in front of the crowds). With whom will a woman spend eternity if she has had seven legitimate husbands in this life (see Deut 25:5)? Jesus upbraids the Sadducees for trivializing God's power. They assume that life in a new age would be a continuation of this one rather than a more glorious existence, in which people will be like angels who "neither marry nor are given in marriage" (22:30). Then Jesus affirms that the doctrine of resurrection is grounded in Scripture since God continues to speak of the dead as though they are living (cf. Exod 3:6).

Jesus' comment about resurrection life has been the subject of much discussion since it is one of the only passages in the Bible that describes what life beyond death will be like and because its meaning is not completely clear. The comment that people will be "like angels in heaven" in the realm beyond death has led to a popular notion that people become angels after they die—though that is clearly not what Jesus said, and such thinking has no support elsewhere in Scripture. More likely he means that bodies of the resurrected dead will be similar to the bodies of angels: people will no longer have physical bodies of flesh and blood but imperishable and immortal "spiritual bodies" (cf. Paul's comments in 1 Cor 15:35–56). Given this, the logic of Jesus' argument would turn on an assumption that people with spiritual bodies do not marry each other, just as angels do not marry each other. That much seems sound, since nowhere in the Bible or in any other extant Jewish literature do we hear of married angels (though Gen 6:1–4 presents a curious anomaly); nor do we hear of baby angels (contra all those cute cherubs in artwork and on Christmas cards). Extrapolating from this insight, interpreters have often supposed Jesus to be implying that resurrected people are no longer male or female in heaven. Many angels have masculine names (Gabriel, Michael), but they are never said to be male beings (assuming, again, that the "sons of god" in Gen 6:1–4 represent entities distinct from the "angels in heaven" to which Jesus refers). The assumptions may be that spiritual bodies do not have genitals, that sex and sexuality are features of mortal existence, that reproduction is unnecessary and impossible for the imperishable, and that the sexual pleasures that seem so significant in this life would be of no consequence for those enjoying permanent and unimaginable bliss on the spiritual plane. This was not the only imagined scenario. Some Jewish works from this period (belonging to the Pseudepigrapha) speak of the afterlife as a time when women will no longer have pain in childbirth (*2 Baruch* 73:7), or even as a time when every woman will give birth to hundreds or thousands of sons (*1 Enoch* 10:17). But the Matthean Jesus (and probably the historical Jesus) accepted the more common tradition.

So: no marriage in heaven, no sex in heaven, and quite possibly no gender in heaven. If this is what Jesus means, his description of resurrection life could be disappointing for many. For one thing, many people want to be reunited with their spouses in heaven, and here Jesus says that when that happens, the person will no longer be their spouse. The point of Jesus' comment, however, is to emphasize addition, not subtraction: we will experience a new level of unlimited intimacy in heaven, such that we will be unconditionally close to all people, not just the one purchased with a dowry or the one to whom our father sold us. Thus, the woman will not need to choose between her seven husbands: they will all be ineffably compatible and close to one another, and to all others, without hint of envy, jealousy, or any of the other dysfunctions that limit our relationships in this life. Basically, we will be more in love with our spouses than ever before, but also equally in love with everyone else (including our exes).

This interpretation is fairly traditional as an exposition of how Matthew's readers were probably expected to understand the somewhat oblique saying of Jesus in 22:30. Being "like angels" implies no marriage (certainly), no sex (probably), and no gender (possibly). I'll add two caveats. First, I think we now know that gender is not an exclusively biological or anatomical phenomenon; accordingly, people with spiritual bodies might indeed retain their gender in a different manner than was understood in Matthew's day. Second, since Matthew's Gospel allows that these angel-like bodies are capable of eating (8:11) and drinking (26:29), I wouldn't be too quick to assume that they cannot do other things associated with physical existence. But all of this is guesswork, and if this vision of the afterlife still seems incredible (or even undesirable), we should at least admit that we lack imagination. Paul did say that no human heart has yet conceived what God has prepared for those who love God (1 Cor 2:9). No one who enters resurrection life will be disappointed that things are not what they expected.

22:34–40. Question of the Greatest Commandment (cf. Mark 12:28–34; Luke 10:25–28)

Again, one of the Pharisees attempts to put Jesus to the test (see also 22:18) by asking a question that he assumes to be inherently problematic. Jesus, however, has no problem identifying two commandments that share equal billing as the greatest in the law: first, loving God (Deut 6:5); second, loving neighbor (Lev 19:18; cf. Matt 19:19). The enumeration implies no ranking since the second is like the first. Ideally, each assumes the other, and together they form the basis on which everything else depends. Jesus indicates, further, that the whole of Scripture may be understood as an exposition of these twin commandments (cf. 7:12). Miss these, and you've missed it all; keep these, and you will do everything God wants.

This combination of the two Mosaic commands forms the basis for Christian ethics. Originally, the two mandates were completely independent and tied to different contexts. The pairing of the two seems obvious after the fact, but few prophets or teachers appear to have done this prior to Jesus. He is not totally unique in that regard (see *Testament of Issachar* 5:2, "Love the Lord and your neighbor"), but no one before him seems to have identified the conjunction of the two love commands as expressing the whole of the law. The closest we get to that is a tradition that ascribes a version of the Golden Rule to Jesus' Galilean predecessor, Hillel (see comments on 7:12). In any case, Christian tradition would take Jesus' affirmation that "on these two commandments hang all the Law and the Prophets" (22:40) as providing a hermeneutical key for interpreting Scripture to determine God's will. In most expressions of Christianity (at least the enduring ones), it is not sufficient simply to quote a Bible verse as definitive proof that conduct is right or wrong: one must also demonstrate that interpreting Scripture to prescribe or proscribe behaviors coheres with an authentic expression of love for God and love for one's neighbors. Of course, acceptance of that standard has not always resolved arguments, but almost all ethical disputes in Christianity eventually come down to discussion of which position is the most loving.

That is certainly how Matthew understood Jesus' declaration as this text would be crucial for his program of binding and loosing that we have discussed elsewhere (see Theme 8 "*Binding-and-loosing commandments*" in the introduction, p. 16; and comments on 5:21–48; 16:19; 18:18). Moral discernment is an extremely important motif in this Gospel; for Matthew, such discernment begins with a recognition that scriptural mandates sometimes need to be interpreted as applicable to matters they do not explicitly address and, at other times, need to be interpreted as *not* applicable to matters that some people think they do address. The church has the authority and the responsibility for making such determinations; they will often do so based on the Golden Rule (7:12) and the twofold love command (22:37–39; see also 9:13; 12:7; 23:23).

22:41–46. Question of the Messiah's Sonship (cf. Mark 12:35–37; Luke 20:41–44)

Now that Jesus' enemies have put three questions to him (22:17, 28, 36), he turns the tables and presents them with a difficult query: quoting Psalm 110:1 (which all parties assumed was written by David), he asks how the Messiah can be both the son of David and the Lord of David? They are unable to answer, either because they do not know or will not admit something known to Matthew's readers: Jesus the Messiah, who is (of course) the son of David, is also the Son of God, and in the latter capacity he may be identified as David's Lord.

The episode is significant for Matthean Christology since it brings together two of the most significant titles for Jesus in this Gospel: Jesus is the son of David (1:1; 9:27; 12:23; 15:22; 20:30–31; 21:9, 15; cf. 1:20) and the Son of God (4:3, 6; 8:29; 14:33; 16:16; 26:63; 27:40; see also 3:17; 11:27; 17:5). It is generally thought that

Matthew actually preferred the latter title, and this pericope might be intended to assert that preference as representative of a higher understanding. The acclamation "Son of David" could be misunderstood in political and militaristic terms: a warrior king who would drive out the Romans. But for Matthew, at least, the acclamation "Son of God" seems to imply the one who embodies the promise of "Emmanuel," the one through whom God is with us (1:23).

In terms of narrative flow, this episode brings to a close the repartee between Jesus and the religious leaders that began in 21:23. Cultural anthropologists read much of 21:23–22:46 (esp. 22:15–46) as a series of "honor challenges." Jesus has bested his opponents in every instance, putting them to shame and achieving greater honor for himself. This sets up the blistering attacks upon the religious leaders that Jesus, as victor in the contest, will deliver in the next chapter (23:1–34, esp. 13–34).

MATTHEW 23:1–39
Condemnation of the Scribes and Pharisees

Matthew crafted chapter 23 of his Gospel with great originality and relatively slight reliance on his sources. He appears to have combined a brief notation from Mark 12:38–39 with a prophetic "doom oracle" and a lament over Jerusalem that he found in Q (cf. Luke 11:39–52; 13:34–35); then he added a considerable amount of material without parallel in the Gospel tradition and reworked everything to form a coherent harangue in the tradition of Israel's more caustic prophets.

The polemical parables and witty banter of the previous two chapters now give way to outright condemnation as Jesus speaks first to his disciples about the religious leaders of Israel and then to those leaders themselves, cursing them as he did the fig tree that bore no fruit (21:18–19).

23:1–12. Warning to Disciples (cf. Mark 12:38–39; Luke 11:46; 20:45–46; Matthew 23:7–12 is unique)

Just as Jesus has warned his disciples not to emulate the sort of authority exemplified by political tyrants (20:25–26), so now he warns them not to follow the example set by Israel's religious leaders either. Here the Matthean "scribes and Pharisees" (a character group that personifies evil in this story; see Theme 14 "*Religious leaders as enemies of God*" in the introduction, p. 25) are charged with three offenses:

1. They do not practice the teaching of Moses that they themselves are charged with delivering (23:3; more on this in the next paragraph).
2. They interpret Torah in ways unnecessarily burdensome and offer no assistance to those oppressed by the superfluous demands (23:4). This alludes to the practice of "binding and loosing" so important to Matthean ethics (see Theme 8 "*Binding-and-loosing commandments*" in the introduction, p. 16): the Pharisees bind what should be loosed, ignoring God's preference for mercy over sacrifice (9:13; 12:7) and failing to recognize the primacy of the command to love (22:37–40; cf. 7:12).
3. They are enamored of prestige and pretend to an inauthentic piety in their quest for public acclaim (23:5–7; cf. 6:1–6, 16–18).

Picking up the latter charge, Jesus calls his followers to eschew the Pharisees' love of position and power and, like Jesus, strive to exercise authority as humble servants (18:4; 20:25–28). In fact, the community of Jesus' followers should be an egalitarian association in which no one is called "rabbi" or "father," but all are viewed as students of the Messiah and children of God.

Matthew 23:2–3 has often been a puzzle in Matthean interpretation. A fairly literal translation of the Greek would have Jesus telling his disciples to do (*poieō*) and keep (*tēreō*) what the scribes and Pharisees say (*legō*) because they "sit on Moses' seat," but not to do (*poieō*) the works (*erga*) of these leaders. In a common interpretation (apparently endorsed by the NRSVue, which mistranslates *legō* as "teach" two times in 23:3), Jesus grants that the scribes and Pharisees are the authorized interpreters of Moses and that, accordingly, his disciples should follow their teaching even though, ironically, those scribes and Pharisees are such hypocrites that they don't follow this teaching themselves. The basic counsel would be, "Do as they say but not as they do!" The verses could mean that, taken on their own, but almost any Matthew scholar would point out that, elsewhere in this Gospel, Jesus insists that the scribes and Pharisees *misinterpret* Moses to such an extent that their teaching is perverse and dangerous (15:1–2; 16:12; 23:15). Their words reflect their evil nature as clearly as their deeds (12:34; see also 9:4; 12:39, 45; 16:4; 22:18). The Matthean Jesus does not think the Pharisees would be fine if they only followed their own teaching: the teaching *itself* is what's wrong, and the problem is that they *do* follow their own misguided interpretations. So, how do we understand this passage?

In 1995, I proposed a fairly simple solution to the quandary, a proposal that has been accepted by several other scholars and, to my knowledge, has not been rejected outright by any (Powell 1995). Everyone has always agreed that to "sit on Moses' seat" is a metaphor for "fulfilling the role or function of Moses in the community." My suggestion is that the scribes and Pharisees fulfill this role or function not necessarily by being authorized *interpreters* of Moses but first and foremost by being persons who know the content of Torah. They have access to Torah scrolls, they have read and studied Torah, and they generally know what it says (something to which Matthew's Gospel attests). So, when Jesus counsels his disciples to follow what the scribes and Pharisees *say*, he means for them to follow *the words of Torah* that they hear the scribes and Pharisees speak, and when he says that they should not follow what they *do,* he means that they should repudiate *what the scribes and Pharisees do with those words.* What they *do* includes their interpretation of Scripture, such that the disciples are to reject both the teaching and the conduct of these errant religious leaders. I think this makes sense of the Matthean text and fits well with the rest of the Gospel. It also allows an intriguing glimpse into the context of the early Jesus movement and, possibly, the Matthean community. We must imagine a world in which most people were illiterate and in which Torah scrolls were not plentiful. Thus synagogue rulers were the primary possessors of the relatively few copies of Torah extant in any given region, and educated scribes were the primary persons capable of reading those documents. In short, many early Christians did not have Bibles. If they wanted to obey Moses (as Jesus had instructed them to do), they may have been dependent upon synagogue leaders (scribes and Pharisees) to tell them what Moses said on any given subject. So, the message is, hear the words of Moses from them if you must, but do not think as they think, speak as they speak, teach as they teach, or act as they act.

Matthew 23:4–7 assumes a decidedly Jewish context that may seem foreign to modern gentile readers. As indicated above, the "burdens" that Jesus refers to in 23:4 are interpretations of the law that make life unnecessarily harsh. We should not assume that these would include dietary restrictions or Sabbath regulations or other aspects of Jewish piety that might seem cumbersome to gentiles but continue to be meaningful to many Jewish people today. Indeed, such observances appear to have been part of the piety practiced by many Christians within Matthew's community, and this Gospel presents Jesus as insisting on the continuing validity of every letter and "stroke of a letter" of the Mosaic law (5:17–19). The Matthean Jesus' argument with the Matthean Pharisees centers not on the legitimacy of such regulations in themselves but on an uncompromising stance that puts *adherence to a code ahead of human need* (see 12:1–8, 9–13; 15:5).

The "phylacteries" mentioned in 23:5 were small boxes containing Scripture verses that pious Jews wore on their hands or foreheads in literal emulation of Deuteronomy 6:8. The "fringes" that Jesus mentions were probably the tassels of a prayer cloth. We suspect from Matthew 9:20–21 that Jesus wore such a cloth himself, and there is no good reason to doubt that he also wore a phylactery (if not, it likely would have been an issue of controversy). So again, he does not repudiate the pious observances themselves, but in this case the ostentatious manner in which some persons sought to advertise their piety so as to make a favorable impression (cf. 6:1). I imagine today a person wearing a large gold-plated, diamond-encrusted WWJD ("What Would Jesus Do?") bracelet; the first thing Jesus would do might be to tell the person, "Get rid of the bracelet!"

A literalistic reading of 23:8–10 would challenge the very existence of educational and familial systems, but this does not seem to have been Matthew's intent. The verses should probably be construed as employing a figure of speech called "relative negation." The essential meaning, then, would be, "Do not *ultimately* regard anyone on earth as your teacher or father." An analogy may be found in Matthew 9:13, where the sense seems to be, "I have not come to call *primarily* the righteous but *also*, or even *especially*, sinners" (for other examples, see John 6:32; Acts 5:4; Rom 9:11–12; 1 Cor 1:17; 1 Thess 4:8). Jesus does intend, however, to challenge the power structures that are definitive of all relationships in the world at large. Where the reign of God has taken effect, no one is allowed to "lord it over" anyone else (see Matt 20:25–27). Feminist scholars have rightly recognized that the identification of God as Father (which no one at this point had thought to question) is here construed as a basis for *challenging* patriarchy rather than for affirming it.

Redaction critics have long contended that Matthew's immediate concern is not with belittling the Jewish leaders of Jesus' day or even those of his own era (in "the synagogue down the street," as it was often put). Rather, Matthew uses his caricatured portraits of Pharisees as a foil for addressing problems within the Christian community. It is church leaders who need to hear Jesus' words about burdensome legalism, greed, and ego-driven power trips. In extreme cases, the Matthean Jesus would identify some church leaders as "false teachers" and call them "wolves in sheep's clothing" (7:15–16). The case here may be less extreme. Control freaks and self-promoters are not necessarily false prophets; still, "all who exalt themselves will be humbled" (23:12). A reader looking for a bit of good news in all this polemic may find it in the latter half of the just-cited aphorism: "All who humble themselves will be exalted." This positive corollary to the negative judgment (which both Jesus and Matthew emphasize) touches on a promise of the gospel that is also a prevalent theme in Matthew (5:1–12; 19:29–30).

23:13–36. Woes upon the Scribes and Pharisees (cf. Luke 11:39–52; Matt 23:15–22 only in Matthew)

Jesus turns his ire on the scribes and Pharisees themselves, speaking to them in the second person and voicing condemnations in line with what he has said about them to others. I have elsewhere developed charts for "phraseology" in Matthew that reveal a remarkable correspondence between what Jesus says *about* people and what he says *to* them (Powell 1996a); by contrast, there is virtually no correspondence between what the religious leaders say *about* people and what they say *to* people. Thus, the very rhetoric of the narrative reveals what it means to be honorable (Jesus) or hypocritical (the religious leaders).

Jesus delivers seven "Woes" upon Israel's leaders (23:13, 15, 16, 23, 25, 27, 29). The "woe" formula, derived from prophets (e.g., Isa 5:8–22), introduces a judgment oracle that essentially places the recipient under a divine curse (see also 11:21; 18:7; 24:19; 26:24). Notably, in Matthew, Jesus condemns only the leaders of Israel and not the Jewish people themselves, whom he has come to save (1:21;

see below on 27:25). The root problem is simply that the leaders are evil (9:4; 12:34, 39, 45; 16:4; 22:18), a "brood of vipers" (3:7; 12:34; 23:33), plants that the heavenly Father did not plant (15:13; see 13:37–43). But this evil shows up in sundry ways related to the two traits emphasized here: *hypocrisy*, by which they deceive others into thinking they are righteous (23:13, 15, 23, 25, 27, 28, 29; cf. 6:2, 5, 16; 15:7; 22:18; 24:51); and *blindness*, by which they are so deprived of revelation that they become deceived themselves (23:16, 17, 19, 24, 26; cf. 15:14; see Theme 14 "*Religious leaders as enemies of God*" in the introduction, p. 25).

Here are the seven condemnations:

Woe 1. They lock people out of the rule of heaven (23:13). This might mean that their opposition to Jesus and others who proclaim the nearness of God's reign (3:2; 4:17; 10:7) prevents people from participating in eschatological salvation now and in the future. Or, since the Matthean Jesus has previously spoken of the keys to the rule of heaven as the authority to discern God's will by properly binding and loosing the law (16:19; 18:18), he might mean that Israel's leaders do not interpret Scripture in ways that show people how to live in God's will, thus preventing them from experiencing heaven's rule over their lives. The two options are not mutually exclusive.

Woe 2. They lead people to perdition by converting them to become disciples of teachers whose true allegiance is to hell, not to heaven (23:15). This is the only reference in the Bible (or anywhere else) to Pharisees being evangelistic missionaries, traveling throughout the Roman Empire the way Christian missionaries did in the decades after Easter. If that was actually the case historically, we may wonder whether Paul the Pharisee was such a missionary before his momentous transformation—in which case his "call" (Gal 1:15–16) would have involved a change in message, not vocation.

Woe 3. They demonstrate warped priorities by maintaining that oaths sworn by "the gold of the sanctuary" or "the gift on the altar" are more binding than oaths sworn by the sanctuary itself or the altar itself (23:16–22). Jesus has elsewhere counseled his disciples against swearing oaths altogether (5:33–37).

Woe 4. They are paragons of casuistry, obsessing over details of ritual observance while ignoring "weightier matters" that truly affect human lives (23:24). Devout Jews often tithed their agricultural crops, donating a tenth of the yield to the poor, or to the temple, or to the synagogue. Here, Jesus alleges that the Pharisees want to appear super-righteous by tithing not only crops but even tiny amounts of spices grown in personal gardens. He indicates that there is nothing wrong with such piety in and of itself but contrasts the attention to (almost) inconsequential matters, with complete neglect of justice and mercy and faith, things that matter a great deal (Mic 6:8). Neglect of mercy has come up before (9:13; 12:7; 23:4). Jesus' claim that some religious matters are "weightier" than others has been influential in Christian ethics, leading to concern for ethical triage: it is important to distinguish what is merely worthwhile from what is absolutely essential, and to make certain that attention to the former does not distract from the latter. The memorable accusation that people who fail to do this "strain out a gnat but swallow a camel!" (23:24) is typical of the humorous hyperbole that Jesus seems to have frequently employed (5:29–30; 6:3; 7:3; 17:20; 19:24).

Woe 5. They are hypocrites whose concern for righteousness extends only to appearances (23:25–26). They want to appear "clean" to others but are actually filled with greed and self-indulgence that others do not see. Jesus describes such hypocrisy with a memorable metaphor: it is like offering someone a drink from a filthy cup that has only been washed on the outside. On the concern for internal purity, see also 15:11, 17–20.

Woe 6. The previous point is repeated with a different metaphor (23:27–28): they are like tombs that have been whitewashed on the outside to appear pretty and clean, but inside they are actually full of death and decay. In this case, instead of saying they are filled with "greed and self-indulgence," Jesus says they are filled with "hypocrisy and lawlessness." At base here is a concern for authenticity, which has been a common concern in the teachings of Jesus: wolves should not disguise themselves as sheep (7:15); bad trees should not bear seemingly good fruit (12:33); disobedient sons should not deceive their fathers regarding their intentions (21:30).

Woe 7. They are hypocrites insofar as they honor prophets and righteous persons from Israel's past, yet they actually are the spiritual descendants of those who opposed and murdered those heroes (23:29–31; see also 21:34–36; 22:3–6).

Throughout the woes, Jesus questions the intrinsic nature of these religious leaders by challenging their heritage: they are "child[ren] of hell" (23:15); offspring of "vipers" (23:33; see also 3:7; 12:34); and descendants of prophet killers (23:31). This fits with what was said previously: elsewhere in Matthew, we hear that the religious leaders of Israel are incapable of doing good (12:34–35) and that they have been put into the world by the devil rather than by God (15:13; cf. 13:37–43). In Matthew's story, the religious leaders of Israel are evil *by nature*, human analogues to the demons that Jesus exorcises. Their fate is assured: they will not enter the rule of heaven, from which they have tried to exclude others (23:13; cf. 5:20); they will be condemned to hell (23:33; cf. 13:41–42, 49–50; 15:13; 21:43–44; and see Theme 17 "*Divine judgment and condemnation in Matthew*" in the introduction, p. 34). The specific reference to "all the righteous blood shed on earth" coming upon these Jewish leaders (23:35) begs comparison with the later revelation that the (saving) blood of Jesus will come upon the Jewish people in general. (On the development of this ironic motif in Matthew, see Excursus: Themes in Matthew's Passion Narrative, p. 281; for a fuller discussion of the motif, see comments on 27:25).

Once again we must state (since people do not often read commentaries sequentially) that Matthew probably did not intend for readers to view the religious leaders who are characters in his narrative as accurate depictions of actual historical people; and even if he did intend that, we should vehemently reject such an understanding. The Matthean religious leaders are to Second Temple Judaism what Elmer Gantry is to American Protestantism (see the 1962 novel by Sinclair Lewis). They are fictive caricatures presented outlandishly for rhetorical effect. The primary effect, I suggest, is to provide Jesus with the sort of opposition necessary for the narrative to work as a tale of apocalyptic conflict. Matthew is not just telling a story about how his hero Jesus outargued and humiliated rival Jewish leaders in Judea fifty years ago. He is telling a story about how Jesus the Son of God overcame the forces of ultimate evil, minions of the devil. On another level, I suspect (as do most Matthean scholars) that the criticisms of Jewish leaders in chapter 23 (and the woes directed to them) were supposed to be read as warnings to leaders in the Christian movement who may have been exhibiting signs of casuistry, greed, self-indulgence, hypocrisy, lawlessness, and so on. Earlier, the critique of the leaders' vainglory in 23:5–7 served to set up instruction regarding how humble servant leaders in the Christian community ought to act. So, Matthew may now dwell on the Jewish leaders' failings so that his readers will know what should not be evident in the Christian community—and he may dwell on the assurance of the leaders' condemnation, not so his readers would know that a previous generation of Pharisees got what was coming to them, but so that contemporary church leaders would take stock of themselves and realize what awaits them if they emulate these characters.

23:37–39. Lament for Jerusalem (cf. Luke 13:34–35)

The mood of the narrative changes somewhat when Jesus turns his attention to the city of Jerusalem, which has followed its leaders in their murderous opposition to God's prophets and will share in the judgment that comes upon them (23:34–36; cf. 22:3–8). But Jesus takes no delight in that judgment. He would give his own life to spare this city, just as a mother hen will sit unprotected on her chicks rather than seek shelter and leave them to a predator. In Matthew, Jesus the Son of God speaks consistently of God as Father; in this capacity, God blesses the whole earth (5:45; 6:26) while also determining who is and isn't worthy of receiving rewards and forgiveness (e.g., 6:1, 4, 6, 15, 18). Jesus will do the same in the spirit and "glory of his Father" (16:27)—but here, for a moment, we catch him wishing he could fill the absent role of Mother to his people instead, offering them inexplicable and undeserved protection from the terror they are bringing upon themselves. He may be inspired by various Scripture references that employ feminine imagery to depict God as a mother eagle sheltering people under her wings (Pss 17:8; 36:7; 63:7; 91:4). Jesus looks forward to a day when all Jerusalem will welcome him as pilgrims did earlier in the week, when he entered the city (21:9), and the house will be desolate no longer (see Jer 12:7; 22:5). Thus, even though no hope remains for the religious leaders of Israel (Matt 23:34–36), Jesus does imply that the people who have been so poorly led by them (9:36; 15:14–15) will one day return to their God (23:39).

It seems likely that Matthew regarded 23:38 as an allusion to the devastation of Jerusalem and destruction of the temple (see 24:2) by the Romans in 70 CE. As such, he apparently understood those events as divine judgment on a faithless and unrepentant nation, but notably the destruction of Jerusalem is *not* interpreted as judgment on the Jews for rejecting or crucifying Jesus. Rather, the judgment is that Israel in general and Jerusalem in particular have regularly rejected and killed prophets and refused to repent. In this regard, Matthew was in agreement with most Jewish authorities of his day: the Roman destruction of the temple was often interpreted by post-70 Jewish leaders as divine judgment against a people who had somehow failed to maintain their covenant loyalty with God. Matthew probably thought that Jewish involvement in the murder of Jesus and Jewish persecution of Christians (10:17) could be listed as examples of the sort of things that merited God's wrath, but they would be only that: fresh instances of the kind of thing many prophets had tried to address—and, again, the Jewish opposition to Christ and Christians is not actually singled out as something that will occasion God's judgment. Further, Matthew's Gospel betrays no delight in what occurred in Judea. The rift between Christian Jews and all other Jews was no doubt hardening into something irreparable, but Matthew and his church still viewed the temple as God's house (21:12–13), as a place where God had dwelt on earth (23:21). The lament is just that: they view what happened in 70 CE with tremendous sadness and remember that Jesus was likewise saddened by his foreknowledge of what was to come.

MATTHEW 24:1–26:1
Eschatological Discourse

The fifth and last of Jesus' five great speeches is a Matthean expansion of what is often called Mark's Little Apocalypse (Mark 13), an idiosyncratic portion of the second Gospel containing material that Mark apparently copied from one or, more likely, two apocalyptic tracts extant in the 60s. Matthew adds some material from Q (24:37–51; 25:14–30) that may be older than what came from Mark, and appends two pericopes that have no parallel elsewhere (25:1–13, 31–46).

The last of Jesus' five great speeches in Matthew (see also 5–7; 10; 13; 18; Theme 10 "*Jesus as the new Moses*" in the introduction, p. 19) focuses on events leading up to the coming of the Son of Man, on the final judgment he will execute, and on the need for all to be prepared for that day. The audience for the entire two chapters (Matt 24–25) is the twelve disciples: no crowds or religious leaders are privy to this privileged instruction (cf. 13:11).

24:1–2. Prediction of the Temple's Destruction (cf. Mark 13:1–4; Luke 21:5–6)

When his disciples are impressed by the apparently magnificent temple buildings, Jesus says that the complex will be completely destroyed. In this way, he indicates more explicitly what he meant earlier when he said that Jerusalem's "house" would be "left . . . desolate" (23:38).

24:3–28. Coming Tribulations (cf. Mark 13:3–23; Luke 21:7–24; 17:23–24, 37)

Jesus' disciples ask him two questions (24:3): (1) they want to know when the destruction of the temple (to which he has just referred, 24:1–2) will occur, and (2) they want to know what will be the sign of his parousia and the end of the age. In 24:4–28, Jesus responds to the first question; later, in 24:29–44, he will respond to the second. Notably, Matthew records the first response (in 24:4–28) in a way that creates temporal dissonance between his readers and the disciples, with whom those readers typically identify: within the narrative, Jesus' disciples hear his words as referring to the future; but in the world outside the story, readers are invited to hear the words as referring to past events (24:15).

So, readers learn that the disciples were told to be prepared for trouble, typical and extraordinary. War, disasters, persecution, apostasy, heresy, lovelessness—all these would take their toll on the world and on the church, but still the good news of God's reign would be proclaimed, and those who endured would be saved. Nevertheless, for Jerusalem, the days were numbered: a new abomination similar to that mentioned in Daniel 9:27 would defile the very temple itself, initiating a time of terrible suffering. Followers of Jesus would know to flee to the mountains, though Jesus realized this might be hard (e.g., for pregnant women or nursing mothers), unconscionable (e.g., if the day fell on a Sabbath, when major travel was not allowed), or even impossible (e.g., if it occurred in winter, when snow was in the mountains). Thus, more important than fleeing was being on guard against any who would lead them astray (note the repeated warnings in 24:4–5, 11, 23–24). Opportunists always try to take advantage of troubled times, like vultures surrounding a corpse (24:28).

Specifically, disciples were warned not to believe any claims that the Messiah had already come. When Jesus does return (see also 16:27), his entrance will be unmistakable (like lightning flashing from east to west): no one need worry about missing it.

As indicated, Matthew wrote his Gospel fifteen years after these cataclysmic events in Judea (70 CE). The note "Let the reader understand" in 24:15 is an invitation to members of his church to realize that Jesus foresaw and predicted the horrors that have now happened. Matthew's readers are expected to know about the persecutions that occurred, to have heard about the difficulties that many experienced when they tried to get away, and to have received news of false prophets and outright traitors, who made the intolerable situation even worse. But they are also expected to be aware of the "chosen ones" (NRSVue, "the elect") who, through God's intervention, somehow survived (24:22)—though even some of these may have later been lost (24:24). In the wake of such a disaster, there can hardly be any words of comfort, but Matthew's readers are expected to find some reassurance in the words "Take note, I have told you beforehand" (24:25). The foreknowledge of Jesus means that *even this was taken into account*. God's rule is being established, and what God wants will ultimately prevail. The main point, then, is that suffering will not have the last word: the worst tribulation on earth is only temporal and does not derail the mission or plan of God. The end (of tribulation) "will come" (24:13–14)!

24:29–44. Coming of the Son of Man (for 24:29–36, cf. Mark 13:24–32; Luke 21:25–33; for 24:37–44, cf. Luke 17:26–27, 34–35; 12:39–40)

As noted in the previous section, Jesus' disciples asked him two questions in 24:3, and he responded to the first of these in 24:4–28. Now, in 24:29–44, Jesus responds to the second question, concerning the sign of his parousia and the end of the age. The temporal dissonance that attended the first response (Matthew addressing readers in the present / Jesus addressing disciples in the past) is resolved: both the disciples in the story and the readers of Matthew's Gospel in the real world now hear Jesus' words as referring to the future.

That Jesus will return with power and great glory to rescue his chosen ones is certain (10:23; 13:40–43; 26:64): But *when* will he come? And what will be the sign that this is about to happen? Jesus' answer to this query has posed numerous questions and problems for interpretation, but at a basic level it is easy to understand. He will return in power and glory immediately after the suffering that attends the Roman destruction of Jerusalem (24:29–31). When a fig tree puts forth leaves, people know summer is near; so also, when the temple in Jerusalem is destroyed, the faithful will know that the parousia is at hand (24:32–33): the generation that witnesses that destruction (even from afar) will also be on hand for the return of Christ in glory (24:34). Thus, those who look back on the temple's destruction as a past event should look for the sign of the Son of Man to appear in the sky at any moment (24:30). Yet they must be ready at all times for that sign does not serve as advance warning that the time is near (the destruction of the temple did that). No, when the sign appears, he will already be coming in the clouds, and any who are not ready will need to mourn that it is now too late (24:30). Just as the destructive flood in the days of Noah came in the midst of normal activities, so the return of Jesus will be unexpected, interrupting daily routines (24:37–41). And his coming will bring instantaneous judgment. Two men will be working in a field: one will be taken and the other left. Two women will be working at a mill: one will be taken and the other left (24:40–41). In recent church history, the latter passage has been read in light of 1 Thessalonians 4:17 as describing a "rapture" of faithful believers to be with Christ in heaven. Paul does seem to envision some such rapture at the moment of Christ's return to earth (though not some years prior, as popular rapture theology erroneously imagines). For Matthew, the situation could be reversed, some taken in judgment, swept away as in the flood. Maybe the references to one being "taken" in 24:40–41 expand upon 24:31, indicating that the ones taken are among the elect to be gathered from the four winds. But previously Jesus has said that when the Son of Man returns, he will send out his angels to collect sinners and deposit them in a furnace of fire (13:41–42)—in which case, believers should hope to be left behind! Either way, Jesus stresses that this will happen without warning: Jesus will come like a thief, at an hour when he is not expected (24:44).

Many scholars think that two distinct traditions lie behind the material presented here and behind what is found in Mark 13. The theory is that (1) some early Christians held that the return of

Christ was imminent and that the Roman desecration of the temple would signify to those in the know that the hour was at hand; but (2) other Christians maintained that the timing of Christ's return was unknowable and that there would be no signs or other predictors to give the unprepared advance notice. Presumably these were conflicting ideas, but Matthew found a way to preserve both notions without contradiction. For Matthew, the *exact* timing of the parousia is unknowable, but the general time frame (within a generation of the temple's destruction) *is* knowable. Many readers have wondered how the analogy of the fig tree in 24:32–34 is relevant if indeed no one but the Father knows the time of Christ's return (24:36). But for Matthew's original readers, this made perfect sense. Before the Romans sacked Jerusalem, the end of the age was not imminent: Christian missionaries and church leaders could focus on their mission with no heightened sense of urgency. But once the temple was destroyed, all that changed: now believers know they are living in the last days. Jesus will definitely return within their lifetimes (barring premature death). They know that much; they just don't know *when* he will come within that short time frame. Thus, the temple destruction was like the fig tree putting forth its leaves to indicate the time is near, but now there will be no further "sign" until the one that appears in heaven when the moment arrives. Matthew wants his readers to regard the return of Christ and the end of the age as imminent, events that will happen soon, but also as events that will occur suddenly, with no (further) advance notice.

The problem for modern readers, of course, is that it did not happen. Thus, some modern Christians maintain that Jesus (in Matt 24) was not talking about the destruction of the temple that existed in his day, but rather the destruction of some future temple that might be built in Jerusalem hundreds of years later (in our time): the parousia will occur within a generation of *that* temple's destruction. Most critical scholars think this involves an absurd level of special pleading that ignores the clear intention of the Matthean evangelist. A more honest approach may be simply to grant that Matthew got it wrong: he wrote his Gospel for a distressed community experiencing a surge of apocalyptic fervor and passed along questionable traditions that supported what he and his people desperately wanted to be true. But I think there is another option.

The real puzzle, I think, is that by the time Matthew wrote his Gospel, he would have known that some predictions he attributes to Jesus had not come to pass. Here are three examples:

1. Jesus previously told his twelve disciples that the Son of Man would come before they completed a mission tour of Israel (10:23), but obviously mission work in Israel by the original twelve disciples had ceased long before Matthew's Gospel was written—and the Son of Man had not come.
2. Jesus told his twelve disciples that some of them would not taste death before they saw the Son of Man coming to reign (16:28), but it is unlikely that any of those twelve were still alive at the time Matthew's Gospel was written—and the Son of Man had not come.
3. Jesus told his twelve disciples that the Son of Man would come with power and glory *immediately* after the suffering associated with the destruction of Jerusalem, but Matthew's Gospel was written at least fifteen years after that suffering—and the Son of Man had not come.

We might try to find some rationale for why Matthew still held out hope on these matters: perhaps an elderly disciple was still alive somewhere, or maybe "immediately" (*eutheōs*, 24:29) can have a broader range of meaning than we realize. But the simpler solution is to recognize that Matthew preserved sayings of Jesus regarding the parousia that he and his readers knew had not been fulfilled literally. Since I take for granted that Matthew did not want to present Jesus as a failed or misguided prophet, I suspect that such sayings may have been valued for reasons other than their potential for *literal* fulfillment. We are dealing with apocalyptic thought couched in the language of apocalyptic literature or, at least, with exhortations based on motifs that characterize and probably derive from apocalyptic texts. The appeal of such literature was always to the imagination, not to the intellect; the intended effects were more affective than cognitive. We are so far removed from the premodern milieu producing such literature that we may never be able to appreciate fully its intentions, but I think it is possible that what look (to us) like prophetic statements served a rhetorical rather than predictive function. Statements with subjunctive meaning may be expressed in the indicative to make them more forceful and urgent. "The Son of Man *will* come" might be a forceful way of saying, "The Son of Man *may* come," with a nuance that encourages the hearer to expect this to happen and to be ready. (If it seems like this suggestion is playing loose with grammar, we can remember that both Greek and English often use the historical-present tense to talk about the past: "Jesus tells his disciples" is a livelier way of saying, "Jesus told his disciples"). In a similar vein, see comments on 16:28 to the effect that the "you" addressed by Jesus might be not only his disciples (within the story) but also the Gospel's readers (outside the story). The same point is made regarding a different topic in the comments on 5:11–12.

Matthew's Gospel knows the language of paradox, so it might be said that his readers are to understand that Jesus is already near (24:33) in the same sense that the rule of heaven is near (4:17). With regard to the rule of heaven, Matthew encourages readers to maintain that it has already arrived (12:28), even as they continue to seek it and pray for it to come (6:10, 33). Even so, Jesus' teaching on the parousia involves a paradox involving *expectation* and *knowledge*: disciples (especially those who experience tribulation) should expect Jesus to come immediately even though, ironically, they know the timing of his coming will defy all their expectations (24:42, 44). Ultimately, more important than expectation or knowledge regarding Christ's return is the necessary preparation for it. Disciples must be "ready" at any and every hour (24:44).

24:45–51. Parable of an Enslaved Person Who Is Wise or Reckless (cf. Luke 12:42–46)

A simple parable illustrates two courses of action in the time before the judgment (cf. 7:24–27). Those who are wise will not try to compute the time that is left but will simply invest themselves in doing what they have been told to do. Those who are reckless may decide that there has been a delay, grow lax, and forget that they will be held accountable for their actions (cf. 16:27). The results are predictable, if harsh (24:47, 51).

The parable explains what it means to be ready for the parousia and does so in terms of stewardship (see Excursus: Stewardship and the Gospel of Matthew, p. 245). The enslaved person in the parable is a steward: he owns nothing but has been put in charge of a great deal (the master's household and property, which includes other enslaved people). If he is a wise steward, he will exercise that responsibility faithfully and have no cause for shame, no matter when his master comes back. A reckless steward, however, will act as though he is not a steward at all but an owner, thinking he can do as he pleases with what has been entrusted to his care. He consumes an excess of resources (food and drink) that the master provided him to share with others. He interprets his position of power as a warrant for mistreating the people over whom he has authority. Basically, he treats his master's possessions as though they were his possessions, apparently forgetting that he will need to give an account of what he has done.

Biblical texts that treat slavery as a normative institution are always troubling, but Matthew's implied readers would not be expected to question the legitimacy of that institution (within the world of the story). Whatever their actual views about slavery in the real world, Matthew's readers would be expected to recognize that in this story the institution goes unchallenged and appears to be simply accepted as an inevitable reality. It is part of the narrative setting for a fictive tale—part of the social fabric of the world in which the story of Matthew's Gospel transpires (or, indeed, in this case, part of the narrative setting for a particular parable). We need to recognize this lest our fully justified objections to the use of slavery as a metaphor for "belonging to God" distract us from grasping the parable's essential meaning, which concerns a point made throughout Scripture: the earth is the LORD's and all that is in it (Ps 24:1); God made us, and we are God's people (100:3), as are all people on earth. We do not ultimately own anything: not our houses nor material goods, not our bank accounts, not our time nor talents nor physical bodies. We certainly do not own other people: not our employees nor spouses nor children. Nor do we truly own our pets or any living things entrusted to our care (see dedication page). Rather, we are stewards of all that God has made, enjoying and caring for all things (and for one another) in ways congruent with the recognition that we are ultimately accountable to God, to whom all material and living things belong.

This parable is relevant for all of us, but Matthew probably intended it primarily for leaders in the church. Pastors and other church leaders are like the enslaved person in charge of the household, entrusted by their Lord to nourish and care for God's people (the other enslaved people). If they misuse their authority, they will need to answer to the one who gave it to them and will likely end up being grouped with the "hypocrites" (24:51), with the scribes and Pharisees against whom Jesus rails through most of chapter 23 (see 23:13, 15, 23, 25, 27, 29). Corrupt leaders of the church will fare no better in judgment than corrupt leaders of Israel, for those who merely call Jesus "Lord" cannot expect any special treatment if they do not do the will of the Father in heaven (7:21–23). This parable suggests that problems of laxity within the church may derive from people thinking the parousia has been delayed (24:48). This no doubt explains why Matthew encourages his readers to expect Jesus to return soon (within a generation of the temple being destroyed, 24:34) and emphasizes that he will come without any advance notice at a time they do not expect (24:36–44).

25:1–13. Parable of Wise and Foolish Bridesmaids (only in Matthew)

Another parable makes essentially the same point as the preceding one. Those who are wise will be ready and waiting when Jesus comes; those who are foolish may fail to prepare for the long haul, or they may mistakenly think that others can be prepared for them (25:8). The wise who are ready will enter the glorious reign of God that extends beyond this life (cf. 13:43); the foolish who are not ready will be shut out. Thus the parable resonates with several of Jesus' other sayings. The contrast between wise and foolish bridesmaids reminds us of the wise and foolish builders in 7:24–27. The bridesmaids' plea, "Lord, lord, open to us," followed by the response, "I do not know you" (25:11–12), are close to the exchange in 7:21–23 that Jesus says he will have with evildoers on judgment day. Further, the cancellation of the bridesmaids' invitation to the banquet recalls the expulsion of an invited guest who lacks a wedding garment in 22:11–14. These analogies suggest that, in this case, being "ready" for the parousia means obeying Jesus' words (not just hearing them), doing the will of the Father in heaven, and being clothed with righteousness.

This parable is based on what was a familiar occurrence at the time. Jewish marriages often featured a procession from the bride's house to that of the groom, where a banquet or some other party was held. We may note, as an interesting aside, that there are no weddings referenced or recounted anywhere in the Bible, if by "wedding," we mean a civil or religious service that formalizes a marriage. We find lots of references to wedding banquets or public celebrations of marriage (Judg 14:1–20; Ps 19:5; Song 3:11; Matt 9:15; 22:2; Luke 14:8; John 2:1–11; Rev 19:9), but none to a wedding proper. A few scholars have speculated that there was nothing comparable to what we would call a wedding today: the groom simply took the bride to his house, they had a party, and started living together in what everyone regarded as a state of matrimony. But this seems unlikely: if certificates were required for divorce (5:31; 19:7; cf. Deut 24:1–4), then surely there must have been formalities associated with marriage (cf. Tob 7:12–14), and a liturgical service would have been natural for a culture that prized ritual. This could also be suggested by references to marriage songs and wedding garments (Ps 78:63; Isa 61:10; Jer 2:32; Matt 22:11–12). In any case, the banquet or party seems to have been what counted most: there are no parables about unfortunates missing a wedding service, only parables about missing the banquet.

The story has often been treated as an allegory in Christian interpretation, but Matthew probably did not intend it as such, except in the loosest of terms. "Bridegroom" is a fairly consistent image for Jesus (Matt 9:15; 22:2; John 3:29; Rev 19:7; 21:9; cf. Eph 5:25–35), just as in the Old Testament, a bridegroom is often an image that represents God (Isa 49:18; 54:5–7; Jer 2:2; Ezek 16:8–14; Hos 2:16–23). Thus, "waiting for the bridegroom" becomes an easy metaphor for waiting for the Lord or, specifically, awaiting the parousia of Christ. Beyond that, however, the details of the story (bridesmaids, oil, lamps, sleep, shopkeepers) simply make it memorable and ought not be pressed in an effort to squeeze more specific sense out of it (e.g., Luther's attempt to identify the oil as "faith" results in an interpretation more Pauline than Matthean). Nevertheless, in general terms, the parable does seem to recognize that problems of readiness may be exacerbated by delay (25:5). Matthew wants his readers to expect Christ to return soon (24:34; see comments on 24:29–44), and he is concerned that, as more time passes, some who were once ready may no longer be alert ("the love of many will grow cold," 24:12).

25:14–30. Parable of Talents (cf. Luke 19:12–27)

Jesus tells a third parable of the last judgment, one more complicated than the previous two. A master goes on a journey and entrusts those whom he regards as his slaves to manage his money, each according to his ability. To one he entrusts five talents, to another two, and to another only one. A talent was worth 6,000 denarii (a day's wage) such that one talent was equivalent to what a typical worker would earn in 20 years of labor. The first two individuals increase the wealth with which they are entrusted, but the third buries the talent in the ground and returns it to the master unused.

The point now is that mere perseverance is not enough. Mission, not maintenance, is expected (cf. 28:18–20). The enslaved person who does *nothing* in this story fares as poorly as the one who behaves abysmally in 24:48–51 (see comments on that text for acknowledgment that slavery is a problematic metaphor for the relationship of humans with God). This person actually preserves what his master entrusts to him and does not lose any of it, yet he is punished and excluded from God's reign. Jesus is indicating that, although the final judgment will take into account what one was given (the person with two talents is not expected to produce *five* more), it will also take into account what one did with what one was given. As in the previous story, every detail of the parable (e.g., investment with bankers) need not have a specific allegorical meaning. The basic point is that faithful discipleship means taking risks. Inactivity is not the safe option it appears to be.

The fact that the three servants are given different amounts (in contrast to Luke 19:13) mirrors Matthew's narrative presentation of persons who operate (faithfully) with varying degrees of faith. In Matthew's story, some people have "great faith" (8:10; 15:28), some have "little faith" (6:30; 8:26; 14:31; 16:8), and some only a smidgen (17:20), but all are called to use whatever they have. Yet faith is just one example of things that Matthew might envision the Lord giving to each "according to [their] ability" (25:15). The same might be said of wisdom or physical strength or educational opportunities or social power or financial resources or artistic gifts: one reason to avoid specific allegorical identifications is that they limit the parable's range of application. The primary expectation is that all of God's people use whatever God has given them, and in some instances, this may be accompanied by an expectation of growth. Thus, Jesus' often obtuse disciples seem to have been given only a little understanding, but it is enough, and they do grow in understanding as the story progresses (13:51; 16:12; 17:13; see Excursus: "Understanding" and Divine

Revelation in Matthew, p. 158). Growth is a significant theme in Matthew, often expressed through Jesus' basic affirmation that those who belong to God are expected to "bear fruit" (7:16; 13:8; 21:43). The rule of heaven itself is likened to a growing seed (13:31–32) or a rising loaf of bread (13:33): its presence and effects in the world are expected to increase. In this sense, the parable of the Talents in Matthew 25:14–30 may be compared with the parable of the Sower in 13:1–8, 18–23). The man who buries his talent in the ground is like seed that is sown but, for various reasons, produces no fruit. Faithful believers are like seed that grows in good soil and does bear fruit, yielding "in one case a hundredfold, in another sixty, and in another thirty" (13:23). There is no suggestion that the one who bears a hundredfold is more faithful than the one who bears sixty; rather, the point is that even the one that bears only thirtyfold is preferred to those that bear no fruit at all.

The negative effect of yielding to fear is also a recurrent Matthean theme. Fear is what stops the risk-taking Peter from completing his stroll across the sea (14:30); its paralyzing effect is well illustrated in 28:4. In this case the source of fear is a desire to safeguard what must not be lost. But when Jesus returns, he does not want to hear his followers declare, "Look, everything is just as it was when you left!" New wine requires new wineskins (9:17). Growth requires change, change involves risk, and risk requires trust.

The parable of the Talents may be read as the third in a series of judgment parables, but it may also be read in tandem with 21:33–41 and 24:45–51 as one of three stories in Matthew that explicitly present faithfulness to God (or readiness for the parousia) in terms of stewardship. Most of the comments regarding stewardship offered on the other two parables apply here and need not be repeated (and see the Excursus: Stewardship and the Gospel of Matthew, p. 245). But here is one difference. In the previous parables, the "bad examples" seem to be people who fail to recognize that they are stewards; they act as though they are owners, using what the true owner entrusted to them as though it were theirs to do with as they please, as though there will be no accountability for their actions. But in the current parable, the negative example is a person who is fully aware of his status as a steward and who knows that he will need to give an account for what he does with what the master entrusted to him. Indeed, it is *fear* of such accountability that prompts him to do nothing at all:

he buries his talent in the ground because he believes his master is a harsh and unjust man (25:24). In doing this, however, he acts solely out of self-interest. There is no scintilla of gratitude that his master has entrusted him with wealth and responsibility, nor any sense of obligation to use that wealth and responsibility to further the master's concerns.

It is tempting to conclude from this parable that failure in stewardship can result from a lack of trust in God, based on a misunderstanding of God's character. But in the parable, the master does not question the condemned man's assessment of his character (25:26); as it turns out, the fear of his displeasure was justified (25:28–30). Matthew probably does not intend to depict the master as an image for what God is truly like, but he may have been willing to grant that God can sometimes appear to be arbitrary and even unjust to human beings. Certainly Matthew grants that God is to be feared (10:28). The point is that fear of God's judgment should prompt one to greater diligence, to at least make an effort toward fulfilling what might seem like God's impossibly high demands. It could turn out that *seeking* the reign of God was all God really expected (6:33).

25:31–26:1. Judgment of the Pagans (only in Matthew)

After telling three parables about the final judgment, Jesus goes on to describe what that event will be like. Here he discusses only judgment of the unbelieving gentiles (*ethnē*, NRSVue, "nations"), people who have not been made disciples of Jesus through baptism and instruction in obedience (28:18–20). The surprising added information is that even among these there will be a separation. Some will be allowed to enter eternal life (25:46) even though they did not become disciples of Jesus. Why? Because they performed acts of kindness *for* those disciples, with whom Jesus himself identified (cf. 10:40–42). Others, however, will face eternal punishment. They not only ignored the good news of God's reign brought by those disciples, but also failed to show them even the basic hospitality that any human being deserves (cf. 10:9–15). Both groups are surprised to learn that they have previously encountered their Judge in these guises, and both address him as "Lord" (25:37, 44); in the case of the "goats," the failure of that acclamation to affect their fate recalls 7:22–23 and 25:11–12. Jesus has previously said that at the last judgment, everyone will be rewarded or punished according to what they have done (16:27). Now he assures his disciples that people will be specifically rewarded or punished for what they have done *to them.* Jesus identifies with his disciples: he calls them his family (12:50), and he takes personally the manner in which they are treated.

Although this interpretation of Matthew 25:31–46 is widely accepted in Matthean studies, it is not entirely in sync with the way the text is popularly understood in the church. Typically, this text is proclaimed as a charge to Christians to practice their faith by caring for the poor and disadvantaged people of the world, for indeed, when they do so they may be unwittingly ministering to Jesus himself (cf. Heb 13:2, which says that those who show hospitality to strangers are sometimes entertaining incognito angels, "without knowing it"). This is probably not what Matthew intended. For one thing, the word translated "nations" (*ethnē*) is never used in Matthew for believers: it usually refers to pagan gentiles (24:9, 14). Some have suggested that *ethnē* can sometimes refer more generally to "all nations," including Israel, but even then it would refer to the church's mission field (28:19), not to members of the church itself. Second, the word that the NRSVue translates "these brothers and sisters of mine" (*adelphoi*) in 25:40 always refers to disciples of Jesus or to members of a close-knit religious community (5:21–24; 7:3–5; 12:49–50; 18:15; 28:10)—unless, of course, it is used for literal family members (e.g., 4:21). It has become popular in some theological circles to claim that Matthew 25:31–46 locates the presence of God in this world in people who are marginalized, poor, or suffering. But such thinking is not congruent with a careful reading of the text or with Matthean theology in general (the closest we might get to such an affirmation in this Gospel is Jesus' claim in 18:5 that whoever welcomes a child in his name welcomes him—or is that only for children who believe in him? [see 18:6]). Of course, Matthew's Gospel identifies vulnerable, marginalized, and oppressed people as recipients of God's blessing and special concern: no text in the Bible does that more effectively than the first four beatitudes (see comments on Matt 5:3–6). But Matthew is fairly consistent in locating the *presence* of God in Christ himself (1:23) and in the community of his followers (e.g., 10:40; 18:20; 28:20; see Theme 1 "*The abiding presence of God*" in the introduction, p. 7). Thus, the scenario envisioned in Matthew 25:31–46 is not a judgment of church members regarding how they have treated needy people in the world at large, but almost the reverse: a judgment of people in the world at large regarding how they have treated needy members of the church.

Fearing that this may spoil the story for some people, I will suggest momentarily that the popular reading may indeed be a faithful and justifiable extrapolation of the passage for our day—but first I think we should make sure we get the message that Matthew intended to convey (we owe him that much). So, in keeping with what was stated above, let me try to lay out how and why Matthew and his original readers found value in these words attributed to Jesus. Matthew envisions the church as a community of missionaries. His readers will recall that, at the start, there was a mission conducted by Jesus' first disciples to the "house of Israel" (10:5–23). Those disciples set out with scant provisions and needed to trust that those to whom they were sent would provide them with food, hospitality, and other necessities. Not everyone would do so, but Jesus promised that those who did would be rewarded (10:41–42). Indeed, he promised that any who showed hospitality to the disciples would be judged as though they had provided such hospitality to him: "whoever welcomes you, welcomes me" (10:40). Then, after Easter, Jesus commissioned his followers for a similar mission to "all nations" (28:19). While no explicit instructions are given, Matthew's readers would assume that, as before, the missionaries would often face hunger, hardship, prison, and other difficulties—and, especially in the early days when there were no Christian communities to support them, they would have to rely on people from the nations to welcome them and nurture them at least in minimal ways befitting human compassion and what all honorable people recognized as reasonable expectations for hospitality. Some must have done this or else the Matthean community would not even exist. Perhaps many of the "pagans" who showed such kindness also accepted the missionaries' message and became converts: they were baptized and taught to obey the commands of Jesus. But what about those who didn't? The members of Matthew's community would be concerned that unbelievers who were kind to needy Christians would suffer the same horrific fate as those who weren't. Not to fear—Jesus reassures them that, just as before (with the first mission to Israel), any unbelievers who "welcomed" members of his family by offering them food, drink, clothing, health care, and other types of support will be treated as though they offered those things to the Judge himself. They will be counted among the righteous, in a manner similar to the Jewish tradition that claimed certain "righteous gentiles" would be included among the chosen people of God when the day of Israel's vindication arrived. But as for those who refused any kindness or hospitality to the Lord's needy representatives—well, they were bound for hell anyway, but Jesus assures his followers that they will be confronted with their offense in advance of their damnation (see also 12:36; on Matthew's near obsession with damnation, see Theme 17 "*Divine judgment and condemnation in Matthew*" in the introduction, p. 34).

There are some takeaways here for modern Christians. First, it is worth noting that Matthew (and probably the historical Jesus) assumed that followers of Jesus would usually be poor. The clear assumption here and most places in the New Testament is that followers of Jesus are far more likely to be people in need of receiving charity than people able to provide such charity to others. It does not necessarily follow that we should be ashamed of ourselves for not being hungry, estranged, and persecuted, but we should at least recognize how different our life circumstances are from what the biblical writers envisioned for us. In saying this, I am imagining life circumstances for likely readers of this commentary. I am aware that within a broader segment of the world's population, a huge percentage of Jesus' followers still are numbered among the economically poor and socially disadvantaged.

Second, the assumption behind Matthew 25:31–46 is that followers of Jesus (including or especially those committed to evangelizing nonbelievers) will be dependent upon people from the nations to whom their ministry is directed. Jesus envisions a future in which his family (the Christians) are helped by nonbelievers, a future in which his followers benefit from the kindness of the world, a future in which followers of Jesus need to depend upon nonfollowers of Jesus for some of life's basic necessities. Let's take a moment to reflect on how that happens for us today. Even if we are not charity cases in need of handouts, we might at least recognize, for instance, that many of the great scientists of our day are not Christians: we use their science anyhow. Much of the world's most magnificent art is created by people who are not Christians: we still partake of the literature, the music, the paintings, and the poetry that they create, and our lives are better for it. It seems to be God's will that we be dependent upon nonbelievers, just as the early disciples of Jesus were dependent upon those to whom they brought good news. Jesus didn't just want his followers to *love* their enemies; he wanted us to *need* them, to be dependent upon people of whom we might not even approve.

But let us turn at last to consider how this text might be read in a world quite different from that for which it was intended. Christians in many communities today will say, "We are not numbered among the most hungry, thirsty, naked, imprisoned, or estranged members of society. Instead, we are people who have the means of caring for those in need. We are not only 'not hungry'; we have enough food to feed those who *are* hungry. We have enough drink, enough clothes—enough and more than enough." It should be obvious that, given such a shift in context, Matthew would want church members to do for others what he had assumed those church members would want done for them (7:12). That would certainly be supported by encouragement to give alms (6:2–4) and to give to everyone who begs (5:42). It would seem to be required of anyone who wishes to be counted among the merciful, whom Jesus declares blessed in 5:7. The principal difference between Matthew's perspective on Christians' helping the needy and the popular understanding evident in many sermons on Matthew 25:31–46 would be that the sermons construe believers as ministering unknowingly *to* Jesus while Matthew would think the Christians are ministering *as* Jesus. Matthew's primary interest is in locating the abiding presence of Jesus in the community of his followers: this identification would hold regardless of whether those followers are the recipients of charity or the dispensers of charity. So, at the final judgment, Jesus will say to people from the nations, "Whatever you did to one of the least of these brothers and sisters of mine, *you did to me*." But it is easy to imagine the corollary: Jesus will also say to the distressed people of this earth, "What was done to you by even the least of these brothers and sisters of mine *was done to you by me*." In a context never envisioned by Matthew—a world where Christians have economic resources and the church has social power—what this text reveals to even the least of those who belong to Jesus' family is a chance to *become Christ to others*, to be vessels of his mercy, instruments of his peace.

A final notation must be made regarding inclusion of "strangers" among the list of needy and disadvantaged members of Christ's family with whom he identifies (25:35, 43). The word thus translated in the NRSVue is *zenos*, actually meaning “foreigner” or “noncitizen”; it is the term that today would be used to refer to an “undocumented immigrant” (or indeed, an “illegal alien”). This term is used elsewhere in the New Testament (Matt 27:7; Acts 17:21; Eph 2:12, 19; Heb 11:13; 3 John 1:5) and in the LXX (Ruth 2:10; 2 Sam 12:4; 15:19; Job 31:32). A brief survey of those passages reveals that the term does not simply mean “a person unknown to us,” but “a person in a foreign land who lacks the legal rights and protections of citizenship.” The apostles and missionaries bringing the gospel of Christ to the nations often had to assume such a status: as such, they were welcomed by some and not welcomed by others. Modern Americans may take note of this (and of Jesus’ words in 25:35, 43) when reflecting on the circumstances of noncitizens in the United States (with consideration of Lev 19:33–34 as well).

In 26:1, the long discourse on the final judgment (Matt 24–25) comes to a close with the formulaic expression, “when Jesus had finished saying all these things” (see also 7:28; 11:1; 13:53; 19:1; cf. Deut 31:1; 32:45).

Part Six of Matthew's Gospel: Passion and Resurrection

Matthew 26:2–28:20

Matthew's story of Jesus' death and resurrection comes as the climax of his Gospel, the point to which the narrative has been leading all along. Through foreshadowing (2:16–19; 14:1–12), allusions (9:15; 17:12), and outright predictions (16:21; 17:22–23; 20:18–19), Matthew's readers have been prepared for this outcome. This is what Jesus has come to do (20:28); this is how he fulfills his destiny and saves his people from their sins (1:21). Still, the denouement of conflict is striking: Jesus is condemned, tortured, and killed; his disciples are scattered; and his enemies are triumphant. Then, a new story begins, one grounded in resurrection, calling new and renewed disciples to an unprecedented mission.

EXCURSUS

Themes in Matthew's Passion Narrative

Several Matthean motifs are developed or completed in chapters 26–27. These may be outlined here for ease of reference when consulting the comments on texts from those chapters.

Jesus Dies as One Abandoned

- Peter, James, and John fall asleep while he prays in the garden (26:36–45).

- Judas betrays him (26:47–50; 27:3–10).
- Disciples forsake him and run away (26:56).
- Jewish leaders mock him as a false Messiah (26:67–68).
- Peter denies him (26:69–75).
- The crowds call for him to be crucified (27:15–23).
- Roman soldiers mock him as a false king (27:27–31).
- Passersby join Jewish leaders in mocking him on the cross (27:39–43).
- Crucified criminals taunt him (27:44).
- Darkness covers the land, and Jesus cries, "My God, my God, why have you forsaken me?" (27:45–46).

For brief discussion of the "abandonment" theme, see especially the comments on 27:45–46.

Jesus Is Innocent of Any Crime Deserving Crucifixion

- Judas says he has sinned by betraying "innocent blood" (27:4).
- Pilate's wife maintains that Jesus is an "innocent man" (27:19).
- Pilate knows that Jesus has been delivered to him "out of jealousy" (27:18) and maintains that Jesus has done nothing wrong (27:23).

This emphasis is not intended to exonerate Roman authorities, but would have been significant for the original readers of Matthew's Gospel, particularly when they were maligned for following a condemned criminal. See comments on 27:11–26.

Blood That Conveys Guilt and/or Forgiveness

- Jesus tells the religious leaders they will be sentenced to hell when "all the righteous blood shed on earth" comes upon them (23:33–36).
- Jesus says that his "blood of the covenant" will be "poured out for many for the forgiveness of sins" (26:28).
- Judas returns the money he was paid for betraying Jesus so that the innocent blood of Jesus will not come upon him (27:3–5).
- The religious leaders cannot put the "blood money" from Judas in the treasury lest the blood of Jesus come upon them (27:6).
- Pilate washes his hands as a public sign that the blood of Jesus will not be on him (27:24).
- The Jewish people as a whole cry, "His blood be on us and on our children!" (27:25).

A sustained discussion of this theme and its significance for the salvation of Israel is included in the comments on 27:11–26 (esp. the comments on 27:24–25).

Jesus Is "Handed Over" by Various Parties Responsible for His Death

Matthew often uses the word *paradidōmi* (to hand over//deliver//betray) to describe what happens to Jesus in the passion story:

- Judas hands Jesus over to the religious leaders of Israel (26:15, 21, 23, 25, 45; see also 17:22; 20:18); Judas is called "the one who handed him over" (26:46, 48; 27:3). In these texts, the NRSVue translates *paradidōmi* as "betray" or "betrayed."
- The religious leaders hand Jesus over to Pilate, the governor (27:2, 18).
- Pilate hands Jesus over to soldiers to be crucified (27:26).

See also 26:2; compare Romans 8:32; the expression also occurs twice in the LXX text of Isaiah 53:12.

Two points are especially significant: (1) Jesus is regarded as more an object than a person, being acted upon rather than acting; (2) Matthew establishes widespread responsibility for the death of Jesus: Judas, the chief priests, and Pilate are all described as handing Jesus over or delivering him up to be crucified. Thus he establishes a triad of guilt for Jesus' death: Christians (followers of Christ), Jews, and pagans share the blame.

Jesus Dies as the Royal Son of God

- Jesus' identity as Son of God is what arouses the most opposition from the religious leaders who want to kill him (26:63–66; see also 21:38–39).
- Jesus' identity as the "King of the Jews" is why gentile rulers want to kill him (27:11, 29, 37; see also 2:2–3).
- When he is on the cross, religious leaders mock Jesus for claiming to be both the "King of Israel" and "God's Son" (27:42–43).
- Ironically, Jesus' death leads gentiles to confess that he is God's Son (27:54).

(On this point, see also Theme 9 "*Jesus as the Son of God*" in the introduction, p. 19.)

Jesus' Death Saves His People from Their Sins

- At his birth, Jesus was identified as the one who would save his people from their sins (1:21).
- Throughout his ministry, Jesus predicted and accepted his passion as the will of God, declaring that he had come to "give his life [as] a ransom for many" (20:28; see also 16:21–23; 17:22–23; 20:17–19; 26:39, 42).
- Jesus speaks of his blood being "poured out for many for the forgiveness of sins" (26:28).
- When Jesus is on the cross, mockers say, "He saved others; he cannot save himself" (27:42), ironically testifying that not saving himself is the means by which he saves others.
- At his death, people rise from the dead, indicating that the power of death has now been broken and life after death is possible (27:52–53).

For discussion of how Matthew relates salvation to Jesus' death, see comments on 20:20–28.

MATTHEW 26:2–56
Jesus' Last Hours with His Disciples

Matthew follows his Markan source closely for this section of his Gospel.

The plot to kill Jesus (12:14) is thrown into high gear; in the events leading up to Jesus' arrest and crucifixion, the reader's attention is drawn to the twelve disciples of Jesus. Those disciples were portrayed favorably in the first part of the Gospel, as persons called by Jesus (4:18–22; 10:1) and privileged to understand the mysteries of God's reign (13:11; see also 11:25; 13:51; 16:16–20). The problem of their "little faith" (6:30; 8:26; 14:31; 16:8) did not seem insurmountable. But then, as the story continued, tensions between Jesus and the disciples increased (16:21–23; 17:14–20; 19:10, 13–15, 23–25; 20:24). Now, in Jesus' last hours, the inadequacies of these disciples render them unable to do what Jesus called them to do (10:28–33, 38–39; 16:24–25). They fail him.

26:2. Reminder of the Crucifixion

Jesus reminds his disciples that he is about to be crucified (see 16:21; 17:22–23; 20:18–19), revealing for the first time that this will happen during the Passover. The timing of the crucifixion was significant to early Christians who associated Jesus' death with the Passover sacrifice of a lamb (John 1:29; 1 Cor 5:7), and that thought may be implicit here.

26:3–5. The Plot against Jesus (cf. Mark 14:1–2; Luke 22:1–2)

Religious leaders of Israel have been plotting to kill Jesus for some time (12:14), but now the conspiracy moves into the courtyard (NRSV, "palace") of the high priest and is approved by the high priest himself. This fulfills what Jesus predicted in parables (21:37–39). The plan not to arrest him during the festival is revised when Judas comes forward to betray his Master (26:14–16). (See Excursus: Jewish Responsibility for the Death of Jesus in Matthew, p. 305.)

26:6–13. The Anointing at Bethany (cf. Mark 14:3–9; John 12:1–8; and cf. Luke 7:36–50)

When an unnamed woman anoints Jesus, his disciples object to the "waste." Jesus regards the act as unusually significant; in the entire New Testament, this woman is the only person other than Jesus (see Luke 22:19; 1 Cor 11:25) whom Christians are told to *remember* in their celebrations of the gospel. Anointing Jesus may imply designating him as Messiah (the word *Messiah* means "anointed one," as does *Christ*, the Greek equivalent). In the biblical world, kings were anointed on the head at their coronation (1 Sam 10:1; 16:13; 1 Kgs 1:39; 2 Kgs 9:6), and many ordinary people had their bodies anointed when they died (see Mark 16:1). This woman pours the ointment on Jesus' head, apparently proclaiming him to be a king: a royal Messiah, "the king of the Jews" (2:2; 27:11, 29, 37; see also 27:42). But Jesus interprets the anointing differently: whatever her intention was (and we cannot tell from the text), the effect of this anointing is to prepare his body for burial (26:12). He is a Messiah destined for death rather than political power.

Matthew 26:11 obviously implies no subordination of concern for the poor: Jesus heartily approves of giving for their assistance (19:21). The point seems to be that when someone does a good work (26:10; NRSVue, "a good service"), they should not be criticized for not having done a different good work. The disciples' description of the woman's costly sacrifice as wasteful seems to assume that devotion to Jesus lacks intrinsic value. Such an assumption could lead to disparagement of liturgy, music, the arts, and other things that lack obvious practical benefit to the social order. The disciples' complaint has inspired the title of a classic text on Christian worship: *A Royal Waste of Time* (Dawn 1999). Religious people of all sorts have discovered that lavish devotion to one who is worthy of praise renews the worshiper in ways that nurture authentic concern for others. Grateful people often become generous people, and people who love Jesus are likely to love the people Jesus loves.

This story (or its Markan parallel) has also inspired the title of a groundbreaking work on feminist biblical theology called *In Memory of Her* (Schüssler Fiorenza 1983); the title is a direct quotation of Jesus' words in 26:13 RSV, which the NRSVue renders, "in remembrance of her." Readers of that book (and this one) are urged to note that Matthew and Mark record Jesus telling his followers to remember a woman whose name they have ironically forgotten. Basically, the Gospel writers report, "Jesus said, whatever you do, be sure to remember . . . *whoever she was!*" Fortunately for church history, John tells us that she was Mary of Bethany, the sister of Martha and Lazarus (John 12:3; cf. 11:1–2).

(On the present-day "absence of Jesus" affirmed in Matthew 26:11, see comments on 9:15; and Excursus: Presence and Absence of Jesus in Matthew, p. 139.)

26:14–16. The Treason of Judas (cf. Mark 14:10–11; Luke 22:3–6)

Judas Iscariot becomes the first of Jesus' disciples to fall, securing an eternal legacy as "the traitor" (10:4; 26:25, 46, 48; 27:3). Exactly what he offers to do for his thirty pieces of silver (cf. Zech 11:12) is not clear, but it probably involves leading Jesus' enemies to him at an opportune time when they can arrest him in a private rather than public setting (cf. 21:46; 26:3–5). Whatever the specifics of the betrayal might have been, the narrative suggests that Judas undertakes this action as an immediate consequence of the previous scene (the woman anointing Jesus in 26:6–13). But why would that incident tip the scales for a disciple who has shown no signs of apostasy previously? The basic idea seems to be that Judas is not going to stick by Jesus if he really is determined to die. Jesus has been predicting his eventual execution for some time (16:21; 17:22–23; 20:17–19), and all the disciples have found this distressing (17:23); recently Jesus has become even more specific in announcing an immediately impending death (26:2); perhaps Jesus' reinterpretation of what appeared (to the disciples) to be royal acclamation (anointed to rule) as preparation for burial was the last straw. Judas gave up his livelihood to follow Jesus, expecting rewards (19:27–29), and now, if the Master is absolutely committed to dying, then the only sensible thing to do is to get out—and perhaps collect some slight remuneration to compensate for his losses. As we will see, none of the other disciples is willing to stick by Jesus either (26:56). All prove unfaithful: is Judas the worst of the bunch, or simply the wisest? For Matthew, those options are not mutually exclusive (11:25). In any case, the specifics of Judas's motivation cannot be determined except in the most general terms (he is disillusioned with Jesus and wants money); we should avoid reading Matthew in light of all the speculative theories that have been advanced in church history and explored dramatically in popular musicals, films, books, and the like (e.g., that he wanted to compel God to act or that he was assisting the plan of salvation). Matthew allows some mystery about the whys of human corruption (cf. Jer 17:9). With that said, we may note how the downfall of Judas connects with other Matthean themes. His desire to save his own life makes him a foil for Jesus' teaching in 10:39 and 16:25. He is also a paradigm for greed, as one who chooses mammon over his Lord (cf. 6:24). The specific desire for silver links him with the deceitful guards in 28:11–15, and his obscene plan to cash in on Jesus' death places him in stark contrast to the woman who anoints Jesus with costly ointment in 26:6–13: she understands the impending passion as an incentive for sacrifice, while he views it as an opportunity for acquisition.

The word that the NRSVue translates "betray" in this passage is *paradidōmi*, which can also be rendered in a more literal sense as "hand over" or "deliver." Elsewhere it is used with reference to the Jewish and Roman authorities' handing Jesus over to be tried and crucified (26:2; 27:2, 18, 26). By applying the same term to an apostle (10:2–4), a member of the community of Jesus' followers, Matthew shows that the responsibility for Jesus' death is shared symbolically though somewhat anachronistically by "the church" (see Excursus: Themes in Matthew's Passion Narrative, p. 281).

26:17–35. The Last Supper (Mark 14:12–31; Luke 22:7–23, 31–34)

After preparations at the home of a somewhat mysterious "certain man" (*ho deina*, an expression used only here in the NT: Matt 26:18), Jesus eats the Passover meal with his disciples. He invests its symbols with new meaning in light of his impending death. By identifying the bread as his body and the wine as his blood—the blood of the covenant poured out for forgiveness of sins (26:28)—he affirms that his death will indeed be a ransom (20:28) by which his people will be saved from their sins (1:21). This promise is especially poignant since it is offered in the midst of a discourse on the imminent apostasy of his disciples. Judas will betray him, Peter will deny him, and the others will desert him. Literally, Jesus says they will all "stumble" or "be scandalized" (*skandalizomai*, NRSVue, "fall away"), because of him (26:31; cf. 26:33; on this, see Excursus: The "Stumbling Block" Motif in Matthew, p. 210). Their universal declaration that they will never fail him in the manner he has predicted (26:33–35) illustrates the biblical insight that "pride goes before destruction and a haughty spirit before a fall" (Prov 16:18). In any case, the disciples will be first and foremost among the many for whom Jesus' blood provides forgiveness of sins: because of that atoning blood, they may yet follow him after he is raised (26:32). The unfortunate fate of Judas, however, appears to be sealed (26:24): at least it will be once he takes care to evade the effects of that blood (see below on 27:3–10). On the thought that it would be better for Judas never to have been born, compare biblical lamentations in Job 3:3–26 and Jeremiah 20:14–18.

A few matters warrant additional explanation. First, Judas is distinguished here from the other disciples in a subtle way: while they all call Jesus "Lord," Judas now addresses Jesus as "Rabbi" (26:22, 25; see also 26:49). While it is certainly not inappropriate to identify

Jesus as "Teacher" or "Rabbi" (23:8), only opponents or outsiders actually do so in Matthew's narrative (12:38; 19:16; 22:16; see also 8:2, 6, 25; 14:28; 15:22; 17:15). Further, when the eleven ask Jesus if they will betray him, he responds in a way that does not rule any of them out, perhaps because, in a sense, they all will do so. But when Judas asks the same question, Jesus responds with an idiomatic expression found three times in Matthew: "You have said so" (*sy eipas*) in 26:25, 64), and "You say so" (*sy legeis*) in 27:11; the difference in tense does not seem significant. Since it is not found elsewhere, the meaning of this expression is uncertain, but context for the three Matthean occurrences suggests the phrase to be affirmative, with a note of judgment leveled against the questioner: the sense could be something like "Yes—and you know it!" or "Your own words point to the truth."

Jesus says his time (*kairos*) is near (26:18). He means the time when he is to be "delivered up," a phrase used repeatedly in Matthew as a broad reference to Jesus' betrayal, arrest, condemnation, and crucifixion (see Excursus: Themes in Matthew's Passion Narrative, p. 281). The fact that there is an appointed time for this to happen concurs with Matthew's notion that the plan of God is now unfolding. For this reason, much of what now transpires has been foretold (or at least foreshadowed) in Scripture (26:24, 54, 56; 27:9). Judas's betrayal allows the Son of Man to go "as it is written of him" (26:24), and the disciples' desertion of Jesus accords with the prophecy of Zechariah 13:7 (cited in Matt 26:31). Jesus' identification of his enemy as a supposed friend who shares his bread alludes to Psalm 41:9 (and intensifies the opprobrium of the treason, as will the kiss in 26:49). Jesus' reference to the "blood of the covenant" (26:28) alludes to Israel's post-Passover/exodus/Sinai covenant ratification described in Exodus 24:7–8; description of that blood being "poured out for many for the forgiveness of sins" evokes Isaiah 53:11–12, where the LXX says the Servant of the Lord "poured himself out" and "bore the sins of many." The Isaiah Servant motif has been prominent in Matthew previously (Matt 8:17//Isa 53:4; Matt 12:18–21//Isa 42:1–4) and will become even more so throughout the passion narrative (see allusions to Isa 50:6 and 53:7, 11–12 in 26:63, 67; 27:12, 14).

Within Matthew's community, Passover meals probably continued to be observed according to the paradigm of Jesus' Last Supper with his disciples. That meal had become a commemoration of

Jesus' death and a recognition of his current and continued absence. This was the new meaning with which Jesus had invested the festival: where a family or religious leader normally would say, "This is the bread of affliction that our ancestors ate" (Deut 16:3), Jesus said, "This is my body" (26:26). Thus, a meal that commemorated the sufferings of Israel that eventuated in freedom from slavery came to commemorate the sufferings of the Messiah that led to freedom from slavery of another kind (captivity to sin). The meaning of the meal derived from the power of metaphor: bread (which sustains life) was broken and torn apart; as worshipers consumed it, they remembered how Jesus' body was broken and mutilated for their sake; wine (which enriches life) was poured out and as worshipers consumed it, they remembered how Jesus' blood was shed for their sake. Some sort of soteriology is assumed by all this, but no specific "doctrine of atonement" can be adduced. For some reason, the crucifixion of Jesus was in accord with God's plan and it facilitated (or ratified) a covenant of forgiveness for sins (26:28). This must be the "ransom" Jesus spoke of earlier (20:28): God's people have been freed from their captors (sin? death? the devil? themselves?), but it cost God something for this to happen.

Such may have been the theological significance of the meal within Matthew's community, but its function at a level of piety may have been of even greater import. The Passover marks Jesus' *last* supper with his followers, the last time he would break bread or drink wine with them until all are reunited in the reign of God, which stretches beyond death (26:29). Thus a primary purpose of the meal's reenactment in the Matthean community would have been to heighten awareness of the absence of Jesus, to accentuate the emotional, spiritual, and indeed theological significance of the obvious fact that Jesus was no longer with them. With regard to the past, for instance, participants in the meal might recall the feeding miracles, which Matthew reports with images of Jesus taking bread, blessing and breaking it, and giving it to his disciples (14:19; 15:36; cf. 26:26). With regard to the future, they might anticipate the day when many will come from east and west and eat with Abraham and Isaac and Jacob in the rule of heaven (8:11). But the present is a time for mourning: the bridegroom has been taken away (9:14–15). Of course, they still experience the presence of Jesus in certain ways, especially when they gather for prayer (18:20) or go out in mission

(28:20). And some kind of mystical or symbolic realization of his presence seems implicit in the partaking of this meal via identification of key elements with his body and blood. Still, it is not the same: Jesus is not with them as he once was or as he will be. Reenacting his *last* supper was supposed to remind everyone of this and to stimulate longing for Jesus' imminent return.

Perhaps at first the Matthean church only observed this meal once a year, at Passover time. But Paul's Letters indicate that other churches observed what he calls "the Lord's Supper" (1 Cor 11:20) on a regular basis, investing participation in the rite with a sort of power that could actually be dangerous to the unworthy (1 Cor 11:29–30). In those settings, the meal seems to have moved beyond an annual commemoration to become a more frequent celebration that involves actual engagement with divine powers. It seems likely that Matthew and his community may have moved in this direction as well, perhaps long before the Gospel was written.

Obviously, many expressions of the Christian church would end up styling some version of this meal as a sacrament, with various and disputed layers of meaning and a strong (ironic) emphasis on participation in the meal as a means of realizing the presence of Christ and receiving his benefits. I consider many if not most of these extrapolations to be well-grounded theologically and profitable spiritually. I do wish the biblical emphasis on recognizing the absence of Christ would not be so neglected (see Excursus: Presence and Absence of Jesus in Matthew, p. 139).

26:36–56. Prayer and Arrest in Gethsemane (cf. Mark 14:32–50; Luke 22:40–53; John 18:3–11)

Retiring to Gethsemane (an olive grove, not a garden), Jesus prays three times that he might somehow be spared the horrible death that he knows awaits him (see 20:22). Nevertheless, he remains unflagging in his commitment to fulfilling his Father's will, whatever that may be. The sleepy disciples exemplify the inevitable weakness of "the flesh" (26:41), a problem that transcends mere physical limitations. Three exhortations for them to "keep watch/stay awake" (26:38, 40, 41) recall what was emphasized in the recent Eschatological Discourse (24:42, 43; 25:13). But Jesus recognizes that even those who are most committed to doing what is right are sometimes unable to fulfill their good intentions (cf. 26:33–35). Then, in an ultimate display of hypocrisy, Judas betrays his Master with a kiss, calling him "Rabbi" (26:49; for the significance of this address, see comments on 26:25). The need for Judas to identify Jesus to the crowd in some such manner implies that none of the arresters actually knows Jesus well enough to make the identification. They come from "the chief priests and the elders of the people" (26:47) to arrest Jesus at night, but apparently none of them has ever seen or heard him teaching in the temple courts day after day (26:55). They also come armed "with swords and clubs," expecting a fight; but in a remarkable demonstration of his own philosophy, Jesus refuses to resist those who are evil (5:39), submits to their violence, and even calls Judas "Friend." Jesus also indicates that the Father would rescue him if he were to make such an appeal, but he is convinced that the will of the Father, as revealed in Scripture, can only be fulfilled by his accepting this "cup" (see 20:22; 26:39, 42). He eschews the human course of violence as self-perpetuating (26:52) and by his peaceful acquiescence shames those who assumed they would need to beat him into submission. This all accords with the message of love and nonviolence with which his ministry began (e.g., "Blessed are the peacemakers," 5:7; "Love your enemies and pray for those who persecute you," 5:44). His disciples, however, are not yet able to practice what Jesus preaches: they desert him, just as he has predicted they would (26:31).

The NRSVue refers to Judas as "the betrayer" in 26:46 and 48 (also 27:3), but the Greek text calls him "the one handing him over" (*ho paradidous*), using the same verb (*paradidōmi*) that is employed elsewhere to describe how Jewish (27:2, 18) and Roman (27:26) leaders hand Jesus over (or deliver him up) to be tortured and killed (for the significance of this Greek word in establishing widespread responsibility for the death of Jesus in Matthew, see Excursus: Themes in Matthew's Passion Narrative, p. 281).

This episode of Matthew's story portrays Jesus somewhat differently than does the rest of the narrative. For one thing, Matthew usually avoids attributing emotions to Jesus; but in Gethsemane, Jesus is presented as anxious and fearful, as "deeply grieved, even to death" (26:37–38). More to the point, the threefold plea for impending events to take a different course "if it is possible" seems out of sync with Jesus' previous announcements that his suffering and death were unavoidable: he stated with absolute assurance that these things *will* happen, indeed, that they *must* happen (16:21; see also 17:22–23; 20:18–19; 26:2). He even indicated that Scripture testified to this (26:24), a point to which he returns when addressing the crowd that comes to arrest him (26:54, 56). Thus, the time of prayer in Gethsemane appears as an anomalous moment in Matthew's story of Jesus, a moment in which his normally clear understanding of God's will is briefly clouded by human emotion, and he experiences a degree of uncertainty (or doubt). His words, "The spirit indeed is willing, but the flesh is weak" (26:41), are intended for his lethargic disciples, yet in this text they could just as well apply to him. This is the only time in Matthew's narrative when such vulnerability or frailty is attributed to Jesus, and it is theologically significant for several reasons. First, this is one of the major indices of Jesus' humanity in a Gospel that often seems to present him as a divine being. Second, Jesus demonstrates obedience to God's will (cf. Phil 2:8; Heb 5:8), something that would seem less significant if God's will did not run counter to his own predilection. In this sense, we may recognize the agony in Gethsemane as one more temptation, akin to those he had to overcome at the outset of his ministry (4:1–11). To be authentic, a temptation must be tempting: avoiding the cup of suffering must be something that Jesus earnestly wants to do and, indeed, something that he can actually choose to do. The latter point seems clear from his comment in 26:53. He does not need to drink this cup of suffering. He could call for twelve thousand angels to come and deliver him, and that would happen (cf. the previous temptation to depend on angelic rescue, in 4:5–7). Through prayer, Jesus emerges from uncertainty with this new realization: it *is* possible for the cup to pass from him; but that is not what God wants to happen (26:39, 42, 44).

MATTHEW 26:57–27:26
Jesus on Trial

Matthew continues to follow his Markan source closely throughout his narration of the passion, inserting unique accounts of Judas's suicide (27:3–10), of Pilate washing his hands (27:24), and of the Jewish people calling Jesus' blood upon themselves (27:25): all these deal with the motif of whose sins will be forgiven through Jesus' blood (see 26:28).

Two trials, one before Jewish authorities and one before the Roman governor, frame the rest of the narrative leading up to Jesus' crucifixion. The narrative of these events is interrupted twice to follow subplots regarding two of Jesus' unreliable disciples, Peter and Judas.

26:57–68. Trial before Caiaphas (cf. Mark 14:53–65; Luke 22:54–55, 63–71; John 18:13–24)

With Peter in tow "at a distance" (26:58), Jesus is brought before the high priest, Caiaphas, and the Jewish council known as the Sanhedrin. The purpose of this hearing is to find some appropriate justification for his execution, though a decision to put him to death has already been made (26:3–4). Jesus gives no response to the suborned perjury of various false witnesses (cf. Isa 53:7), including one mangled account of a metaphorical saying that Matthew's readers might be expected to understand in a way that eludes the Jewish authorities (26:61; cf. John 2:19–22). But when Jesus is asked about his identity, he openly affirms his claim to be the Christ, the Son of God, adding emphatically that he will soon be seated at God's right hand and will return on the clouds in glory (cf. 16:27; 24:30; Ps 110:1; Dan 7:13–14). This alone, they determine, is blasphemy (cf. 9:3), an offense deserving death (see Lev 24:13–15); while "blasphemy" in a narrow sense consisted of reviling or cursing God, the word appears to have acquired a broader application in this period, such that God could be reviled by theological unorthodoxy, that is, by making heretical claims about God or even by disrespecting God's appointed leaders (on this, see Exod 22:28). In any case, the council's judgment against Jesus had no legal standing since (at the time) only Roman rulers had the authority to sentence people to death (see John 18:31); it was merely (but significantly) intended to justify their petition to the Roman governor to take the next step and enact the death penalty that they believed Jesus merited (27:1–2, 22–23). At a superficial level, the Jewish authorities might be viewed as simply carrying out their sworn duty to protect the sanctity of their religion against false prophets (Deut 18:20) and pretend messiahs. Their subsequent abuse of Jesus (cf. Isa 50:6), however, gives the lie to any impression of righteous (though ignorant) indignation they might otherwise have presented (as did the earlier attempt to suborn perjury). Matthew portrays these rulers as dishonest and cruel, not merely as misguided (see comments on 21:33–44; 23:13–36; for more on Matthew's portrayal of Israel's religious leaders as evil, as enemies of God, see Theme 14 "*Religious leaders as enemies of God*" in the introduction, p. 25; and on the specific interest in assigning responsibility for Jesus' death to Jewish authorities, see the Excursus: Jewish Responsibility for the Death of Jesus in Matthew, p. 305). On the idiomatic character of Jesus' response to Caiaphas in 26:64, see comments on 26:25.

26:69–75. Peter Denies Jesus (cf. Mark 14:53–54, 66–72; Luke 22:55–62; John 18:15–18, 25–27)

In stark contrast to Jesus' bold confession before the high priest (26:64), Peter denies three times that he is a disciple. This fulfills Jesus' earlier prediction that he would do this "before the cock crows" (26:34); thus, at the very moment he denies Christ for the third time, Peter hears a rooster crow and is brought to tears at the realization of what he has done. Peter has been highlighted individually throughout Matthew's narrative (see Theme 12 "*Prominence of Peter*" in the introduction, p. 22), but he will not be singled out or mentioned by name again. How tragic that the story's final word regarding Peter as an individual is "he went out and wept bitterly" (26:75)! The bitterness of his tears might owe somewhat to a recall of Jesus' harsh words in 10:32–33; Matthew's readers, however, are also expected to remember the promise of restoration in 26:27–28.

The story of Peter's threefold denial would have been well-known to Matthew's readers, and it would have had special poignancy for them, given the persecution that had come upon many Christians in the empire. Thus, the story is told with realistic (if repugnant) detail. Earlier, Peter has feared wind and waves (14:30); now, he is afraid of servant girls (26:69, 71). He shuns the merest association with Jesus (26:69) and ignores Jesus' teaching (5:34) by swearing an oath to the claim, "I do not know the man!" (26:72, 74). The latter contention reminds readers of the words Jesus will say in judgment regarding evildoers who dare to call him Lord ("I never knew you," 7:23) or the words of the bridegroom in the parable of foolish bridesmaids ("I do not know you," 25:12). Worst of all, the text suggests that Peter even cursed Jesus as proof positive that he could not possibly be one of his followers. The Greek word for "curse" (*katathematizō*) in 26:74 is transitive: the NRSVue reads, "He began to curse," but a better translation would be "He began to curse *him*." Some interpreters have thought this might mean that Peter called down curses upon himself ("Let me be accursed if I'm lying!"), but since swearing the previous oath already implied that, a less redundant and more likely meaning would be "He began to curse Jesus." Matthew's readers would regard this as a very serious matter. Only a few decades after this Gospel was written, Pliny the Younger, the Roman governor of Bithynia, reported to the emperor Trajan that when someone accused of being a Christian denied it, he insisted that they curse Jesus, since no genuine Christian could ever be induced to do this (Pliny the Younger, *Letter to Trajan*, c. 112 CE; cf. 1 Cor 12:3).

Peter's apostasy will be forgiven; after Easter, he will be commissioned along with ten more worshiping doubters to make disciples of all nations (28:16–20). Still, his faithlessness will cost him a legacy he might otherwise have had. Jesus intended for Peter to be the rock upon which his church would be built (16:18); now that honor will pass to women who prove more faithful to Jesus than any of the twelve men he called to be apostles (see comments on 28:1–10). But Matthew's readers also know that about two decades before this Gospel was written, an older and braver Peter died horribly as a martyr in the Neronian holocaust. The seed that appeared to have fallen on rocky ground (13:20–21) found better soil at last and did bear fruit, a harvest beyond imagining (13:23).

27:1–2. Jesus Brought to Pilate (cf. Mark 15:1; Luke 23:1; John 18:28)

In the morning, the religious leaders confer officially and send Jesus to Pilate, in hope that the Roman governor will authorize the death sentence that they have decided Jesus deserves (26:66). Pilate served as prefect of Judea in 26–36 CE, one of the longest tenures for any who held that position. Jewish sources (especially Philo and Josephus) nevertheless portray him as one of the most unpopular of all Roman rulers, noted especially for his cruelty and for his hatred of Jews. He is said to have been deposed at last because of the excessive number of executions (including crucifixions) that took place under his watch. Matthew's reference to Jesus being "handed over" from one party to another accentuates how he (like most victims of injustice) is now being treated as an object rather than as a human being. (For more on this motif, see Excursus: Themes in Matthew's Passion Narrative, p. 281; on Jewish responsibility for the death of Jesus, see Excursus: Jewish Responsibility for the Death of Jesus in Matthew, p. 305.)

27:3–10. Judas and the Blood Money (only in Matthew)

Regretting his betrayal of Jesus, Judas returns the money and confesses that he has "sinned by betraying innocent blood." The response of the religious leaders ("What is that to us? See to it yourself!") is remarkably callous and should probably be read as the prompt that drives Judas to commit suicide. Further, the leaders acknowledge without shame that the returned silver is "blood money"; they say it would not be lawful to put the money in the treasury, and so instead they use the funds to buy a field, unwittingly fulfilling ancient prophecies (Zech 11:12–13; Jer 18:1–3; 19:1–13; 32:6–15). Since these leaders have shown no concern for being "lawful" thus far, we may surmise the real issue is that they fear (as perhaps Judas did) a curse might be attached to money paid for the shedding of innocent blood: they want to avoid the responsibility for such blood coming upon them (cf. 23:29–36), for incurring what the Scriptures refer to as "bloodguilt" (e.g., Exod 22:2–3; Num 35:26–27; Deut 19:10; 21:8; 22:8; 1 Sam 25:26, 33; 2 Sam 21:1). If so, the story is now being told with a terrible irony: Jesus' blood brings not a curse but forgiveness (26:28), and avoiding the effects of his blood assures the condemnation of those who otherwise might have been saved. (For more on this, see the references related to "Blood That Conveys Guilt and/or Forgiveness" in Excursus: Themes in Matthew's Passion Narrative, p. 281; also see comments on 27:25.)

The NRSVue translation of 27:3 is unfortunate since it says that Judas "repented." The Greek word used here (*metamelomai*) is elsewhere translated "changed his mind" (21:29; cf. 21:32) and may be distinguished from the word translated "repent" everywhere else in Matthew (*metanoeō*, 3:2; 4:17; 11:20–21; 12:41). Most scholars think the former word (*metamelomai*) signifies regret or a change in perspective: "he thought twice" or "he saw things differently" would be better than "he repented." For Matthew and most readers (ancient and modern), the word *repent* has a deeper and more specifically religious meaning: a radical transformation or reorientation of one's life toward God. In Matthew's thinking, every sin against the Son of Man (including denying, deserting, or even betraying him) can be forgiven (12:31–32); so genuine repentance on the part of Judas would have brought the same forgiveness and restoration that was eventually granted to the other eleven disciples. The tragedy for Judas is that awareness of his sin and regret for what he did does *not* lead to repentance in any biblical sense of the word, but to terminal despair. In this Gospel at least, Judas is a lost soul: he may well be condemned (26:24), but that will not be for his sin of betraying Jesus so much as for his rejection or evasion of the forgiveness of sins that Jesus offers. Of course, Matthew knows nothing of clinical depression or mental illness or other factors that lead people to take their own lives. Matthew's readers are expected to regard the character of Judas as a coward who chooses the easy "out" of suicide rather than the more difficult path of repentance, and as a fool who bases that choice on self-loathing that avoids trust in the assurance that the one to whom he was faithless would still be faithful to him. Modern readers can read the story that way and still understand that for actual human beings in the real world, suicide is a much more complicated phenomenon: people who cannot perceive options do not make cowardly or foolish choices; they do what they do without awareness of having made any choice at all.

On the identification of Judas in 27:3 as "his betrayer" (or literally, "the one who handed him over") as well as on the motif of Jesus's innocence, see Excursus: Themes in Matthew's Passion Narrative, p. 281.

27:11–26. Trial before Pilate (cf. Mark 15:2–15; Luke 23:2–3, 18–25; John 18:29–40; 19:16; Matt 27:19, 24–25 only in Matthew)

Pilate interrogates Jesus, asking him if he considers himself to be "the King of the Jews" (cf. 27:29, 42), a title that recalls the description of Jesus by the magi (2:2) and anticipates the notice that will be posted on the cross (27:37). Jesus seems to answer in the affirmative, though somewhat ambiguously, but then he goes silent when the religious leaders offer numerous accusations against him (cf. Isa 53:7; Acts 8:32). Pilate realizes that the religious leaders are motivated by jealousy or rivalry: this fits well with the series of "tests" the leaders previously put before Jesus in futile attempts to make him look bad and themselves good (22:15–40). Further, Pilate's own wife warns him that he should have nothing more to do with the matter because she knows from a dream that Jesus is innocent (27:19; on dreams in Matthew, see also 1:20; 2:12, 13, 19, 22). For all these reasons, Pilate tries to find an acceptable way of releasing Jesus, following a custom of letting the populace pick one prisoner to be granted amnesty in celebration of the Passover festival. The crowds, however, have now shifted their allegiance from Jesus (21:45–46) to the religious leaders, even to the point that they call for a notorious criminal named Jesus Barabbas to be released instead of the Jesus who is known as "Messiah" (27:17, 21). The irony of a choice between two men named Jesus (a common name among Jews at this time) is increased when we realize that "Barabbas" is Aramaic for "son of the father": the choice is between Jesus son-of-the-father and Jesus Son of the Father in heaven (cf. 11:27). Further, Matthew's identification of Barabbas as "notorious" (27:16) suggests that readers might be expected to know more about him than what is stated here. We should be careful making such assumptions, but if Matthew's readers know that Barabbas was an infamous rebel, charged with committing murder during an insurrection (cf. Mark 15:7), then they might construe the choice that Pilate offers the crowd in a manner reflective of Matthew's pacifism (26:52): "Do you want the Jesus who will kill for you, or the Jesus who will die for you?" In any case, the crowds are persuaded by their chief priests and elders to insist that Jesus not only be killed, but indeed be *crucified* (27:22–23). Spurning his wife's counsel, Pilate acquiesces to their wishes for fear of a riot, the same fear that previously appeared to be a factor in Jesus' favor (26:3–4).

First, however, Pilate washes his hands in front of all so that he will bear no responsibility for shedding innocent blood (27:24; cf. 23:35; 27:4). The people as a whole agree to this, shouting, "His blood be on us and on our children!" (27:25). Then Jesus is flogged, tortured with a cruel whip that by itself sometimes brought death to the victim. This fulfills his own prediction of what would happen to him (20:19). Finally, Pilate hands Jesus over to Roman soldiers to be crucified; in so doing, he completes a chain of responsibility for Jesus' death: Christians (followers of Christ), Jews, and pagans cooperate maliciously to bring him to the cross (see comments on this "handing over" motif in Excursus: Themes in Matthew's Passion Narrative, p. 281).

This is the second time in Matthew's Gospel that religious and political authorities have collaborated to bring about the death of Jesus. Indeed, Matthew's story of Jesus is framed by two such accounts. In the first instance (2:1–9, 16–18), the political ruler Herod wanted Jesus dead and manipulated religious authorities into helping him (perhaps unwittingly) arrange for the king of the Jews to be killed. Now, we have the reverse: the religious leaders want Jesus dead, and they manipulate the political ruler (Pilate) into helping them arrange for the king of the Jews to be killed. Dorothy Jean Weaver has explored the supreme irony with which both of these political tyrants exercise their supposed authority (see Weaver 2017). Herod and Pilate are ostensibly the most powerful persons in the narrative, but everything they do is motivated by fear, and neither of them is able to bring about what he wants to happen: Herod wants to kill Jesus and fails; Pilate wants to release him and fails. As Weaver shows, the same can also be said of Herod Antipas in 14:1–12. Those who "lord it over" others with coercive power (20:25) are exposed as ultimately ineffectual cowards.

When Pilate asks Jesus if he is the "King of the Jews," he is asking essentially the same question Caiaphas asked ("Are you the Messiah?" in 26:63) but in a manner that betrays specific Roman interest. Notably, Pilate asks Jesus this in all four Gospels (Matt 27:11; Mark 15:2; Luke 23:3; John 18:33). The title Messiah carried both religious and political (royal) implications, but Pilate is only interested in the latter. Jesus' answer is also essentially the same as what he gave earlier: "You say so" (*sy legeis*) to Pilate in 27:11 instead of "You have said so" (*sy eipas*) to Caiaphas in 26:64, and also to Judas in 26:25. The difference in tense does not seem significant. Previously, people took this as a clear and powerful "Yes!" with a hint of judgment against the petitioner for asking (see comments on 26:25). But if Pilate heard the answer this way, he surely would have condemned Jesus for treason immediately, and that would have been the end of the matter. Apparently the expression was a *Jewish* idiom: Matthew expects his readers to know what it means and to enjoy a little chuckle at how Pilate (unlike Judas or Caiaphas) finds the response cryptic and mystifying, unaware that Jesus has committed sedition to his face and probably insulted him in the bargain.

Pilate's washing his hands is one of the most iconic and memorable scenes in biblical literature. Indeed, almost all cultures influenced by Christianity use the expression "to wash one's hands of something" to mean that one disclaims responsibility for a matter because they fear the involvement could create problems or reflect unfavorably upon them. The action was actually a Jewish practice, deriving from Deuteronomy 21:6–7, where the sense is swearing innocence so as not to be held responsible for blood that one did not shed (see Ps 26:6; Isa 1:15–16). The assumption, then, was that the people washing their hands were in fact innocent; if they weren't, the act would provide no magical protection and in fact would only increase their guilt by adding the offense of a false oath to it. Matthew's readers might also recall Jesus' words in another context, indicating that ritual handwashings do not effect, much less guarantee, inner purity (15:1–20; cf. 23:25–26). Pilate, then, is in no way exonerated by Matthew. Instead, he is portrayed as a fool who thinks he can preemptively declare himself innocent of shedding blood, which he then immediately sheds, having Jesus flogged and turning him over to be crucified. Roman and Jewish law alike viewed few offenses as more vile than rulers reneging on their responsibility to uphold justice merely because it was not popular or expedient to do so. Matthew offers no excuse for Pilate's action, which on a certain level (ignoring for the moment apocalyptic underpinnings), is far worse than that of the Jewish authorities: the Jewish leaders believed Jesus was guilty and wanted him killed; Pilate knew Jesus was innocent and actually killed him. Pilate's washing of his hands also plays into the "blood motif" in Matthew, according to which it functions as an ironic rejection of the very blood that could have brought him forgiveness (26:28; see below on 27:25).

The innocence of Jesus seems important to Matthew (see the list of passages addressing this theme provided in Excursus: Themes in Matthew's Passion Narrative, p. 281). Why does Matthew want his readers to know that the Roman governor knew that Jesus was innocent of any crime punishable by Rome? The point cannot be to make the Romans look better (and the Jews worse) since, as indicated above, the effect is the opposite, presenting Pilate as an unconscionable coward and a capricious tyrant. The purpose, rather, is to assure Christians in the gentile world and their potential converts that Jesus was not a rebel against the empire, at least not in the sense of the Zealots who just waged war against the imperial powers (66–70 CE). This is particularly necessary because a good deal in Matthew's Gospel could be read as revolutionary literature: Jesus was in fact the Messiah (1:1; 16:16; 26:63–64) and the "King of the Jews" (2:2; 27:11, 29, 37; see also 27:42); he spoke of the oppressed inheriting the earth (5:5); he spoke of Roman tyranny as the antithesis of leadership that pleases God (20:25); he told his disciples that gentile governors and kings would judge them harshly because of him (10:18; 24:9). Further, Matthew admits that the Roman-backed rulers who knew of Jesus during his time on earth viewed him as a threat (2:1–23; 14:1–2). Add to all this the inescapable fact that Jesus was executed by order of a Roman governor, indeed, executed as a traitor against Rome (i.e., beneath a placard that mockingly identified him as "the King of the Jews," 27:37), and a case could easily be made for viewing Matthean Christianity as insurgency. Matthew does not want to repudiate that understanding completely: the message of his Gospel and the community it sustains *are* countercultural—and in that sense "insurgent"—and Matthew will accept whatever persecution that brings. But he wants to establish beyond doubt that neither Jesus nor his followers were revolutionary in the conventional sense of seeking to overthrow political rulers. The Christian revolution seeks to change society from the bottom up, not from the top down.

The cry of the people in 27:25 demands extensive commentary because it has been so tragically misused and misunderstood. The verse has often been interpreted in anti-Semitic cultures as implying that a curse has come upon all Jewish people as divine punishment or vengeance for their role in calling for Jesus to be crucified. This position has seldom (if ever) found official ecclesiastical endorsement nor has it garnered much support from Christian theologians or exegetes. For one thing, Matthew is clear that Jesus came to save the Jewish people (1:21), and if his life and death resulted in their condemnation instead, that would constitute a rather epic failure of his mission. Still, those inclined toward anti-Semitism have seized upon the verse for divine authentication of their hate, and the consequences have been horrific. And Christians in general bear guilt for not having denounced such ideas more frequently and forcefully. (For further reflection on Jewish responsibility for the death of Jesus in Matthew, see Excursus: Jewish Responsibility for the Death of Jesus in Matthew, p. 305.)

Today, many Christians associate the cry of the people in 27:25 with its memorable function in liturgical readings of the passion story. In many churches, that cry is the only line of the story spoken by the congregation when the passion narrative is performed or read aloud on Good Friday. All of Matthew 26–27 is typically recounted orally, with one lector serving as narrator and others voicing the parts of individual characters. But then when the narrative comes to 27:25, the entire congregation cries out in unison, "His blood be on us and on our children!" In churches where worship is less formal, this ritual may be absent, but the plea is not: the preaching and hymnody of evangelical and pentecostal Christianity often emphasize the importance of being covered with the blood of Jesus. Such a concern derives from Matthew 27:25, together with other biblical texts that speak of being "sprinkled with his blood" (1 Pet 1:2; cf. Heb 12:24).

In his account of the Last Supper, Matthew explicitly connects Jesus' blood with the establishment of a new covenant (26:27–28; cf. Luke 22:20; Heb 12:24; 13:20) and with the forgiveness of sins (cf. Heb 9:22). Elsewhere in the New Testament, we hear that the blood of Christ cleanses from all sin (1 John 1:7) and has freed us from our sins (Rev 1:5). There is atonement by his blood (Rom 3:25), justification by his blood (Rom 5:9), redemption through his blood (Eph 1:7), and reconciliation through the blood of the cross (Col 1:20; cf. Eph 2:13). The believers who composed the intended audience for Matthew's Gospel were no doubt people who thought they had been ransomed "with the precious blood of Christ" (1 Pet 1:18–19; cf. Matt 20:28). Whatever specific language is used, there are few motifs in early Christianity more widespread than the attribution of salvific effects to the blood of Jesus Christ.

It is likely, then, that the line "His blood be on us and on our children!" (27:25) comes from the Christian liturgy, as employed in Matthew's congregation: something congregants prayed at every service, or at least at celebrations of the community meal, where it would have served as a rejoinder to "This is the blood of Christ shed for the forgiveness of sins." Whether or not that was the case, there can be no doubt that Matthew's readers were expected to regard the blood of Christ coming upon people as a most favorable prospect. So, within the context of the passion narrative, the cry of the people in 27:25 implies that the blood of the covenant (spurned by Judas, the religious leaders, and Pilate) comes upon the people of Israel as a whole; the Greek word that the NRSVue translates "the people" in 27:25 is *laos*, which in Matthew always refers to "the Jewish people" and serves as a virtual synonym for "Israel" (1:21; 2:4, 6; 4:16; 15:8; 21:23; 26:3, 5, 47; 27:1, 64). The Jewish people of Jesus' day and their descendants will benefit from the ransom of Jesus' life (20:28). Their sins will be forgiven (26:28) and, in this way, Jesus will fulfill his destiny of saving his people (*laos*) from their sins (1:21).

The story is of course told with magnificent irony: 27:25 marks the culmination of a motif that Matthew has been developing throughout the latter part of his narrative (see the references related to "Blood That Conveys Guilt and/or Forgiveness" in Excursus: Themes in Matthew's Passion Narrative, p. 281). The Jewish people do not know that they are asking for their sins to be forgiven through the blood of the Christ, whose crucifixion they seek. Nor did others know that they were evading salvation when they were careful to ensure that his blood would *not* come upon them. Normally, it was a terrible thing to have innocent or righteous blood come upon someone: it brought condemnation and assurance of vengeance or judgment—note the frequent concern throughout the Old Testament for avoiding "bloodguilt" (e.g., Exod 22:2–3; Num 35:26–27; Deut 19:10; 21:8; 22:8; 1 Sam 25:26, 33; 2 Sam 21:1). Matthew is more aware of this than any other New Testament writer, laying out the theme in 23:30–35 (cf. Luke 11:50). But the blood of Jesus is different, bringing salvation rather than damnation. Matthew's readers know this, though the characters in the story do not. So, for Matthew's readers, the plot unfolds with tragic irony. First, in 27:4, Judas returns the money he was paid for shedding "innocent blood" so that none of that blood will be on him; the blood could have saved him, but having avoided it, he will be damned (cf. 26:24). Next, in 27:6, the religious leaders of Israel are careful not to put the blood money into their treasury, thinking that by so doing they can be sure none of the innocent blood will come upon them; the blood could have saved them; without it, they will be damned. Then, in 27:24, Pilate washes his hands dramatically to ensure that none of Jesus' blood will be on him; the blood could have saved him; without it, he will be damned. But then in a shocking and unexpected twist, the people whom Jesus came to save (1:21) call for his blood to be on them and on their children (27:25): his blood will cover them, and they will be saved!

We might wonder, of course, what it means for "the Jewish people as a whole" to be saved (cf. Paul's assertion that "all Israel will be saved" in Rom 11:26–27). It probably does not mean "every individual Israelite or Jewish person" based on ethnic identity rather than faith or devotion to Torah (cf. 3:8–9). But for Matthew, it is enough to know that Jesus' mission was a success and that his people were saved from their sins, albeit unwittingly. They helped to bring about the death of their Savior—and, in this respect, Matthew (and almost every Christian preacher for the last 2,000 years) would maintain that they are like Christians, whose sins and apostasies sent Jesus to the cross to bring them a salvation they neither sought nor desired. Matthew surely told both the Jewish and gentile members of his church that they could and should identify with the people who in their sin called for Jesus' blood to be shed without any awareness that he was shedding that blood willingly for their sake.

EXCURSUS

Jewish Responsibility for the Death of Jesus in Matthew

Matthew's Gospel is often viewed as accentuating the guilt incurred by Jewish people for their involvement in the crucifixion of Jesus. The book actually establishes widespread responsibility for the death of Jesus (see comments on the "handed over" motif in Excursus: Themes in Matthew's Passion Narrative, p. 281), but Jewish leaders do plot to have Jesus put to death (12:14; 21:45–46; 26:3–5), condemn him as one deserving death in a hearing before the high priest (26:57–68), and insist that he be crucified when the Roman governor wants to release him (27:15–23). Indeed, the Jewish people as a whole take responsibility for the shedding of Jesus' blood (27:25—but see comments on this passage for discussion of how it should be understood).

There can be no doubt that Matthew's passion narrative became a key text in fomenting anti-Semitism in cultures influenced by Christianity. For what it's worth, most scholars would agree that arousing such hostility was not Matthew's intention. He does cast the religious leaders of Israel as evil minions of the devil (in order to present their conflict with Jesus as an apocalyptic contest), but he seems well-disposed toward the

Jewish people themselves, probably believing that he himself and the core of his congregation still number among them. But then why blame Jews for killing Jesus?

We should start with an almost indisputable historical observation: Jesus was crucified as a Jewish victim of Roman violence (not as a Christian victim of Jewish violence). While it is possible that a few high-ranking Jewish authorities may have wanted him dead, it was a *gentile* Roman governor, Pontius Pilate, who condemned him to death and had him tortured and executed by gentile Roman soldiers. Jesus was, indeed, one of thousands of Jews crucified by the Romans during this period. It seems likely that Matthew knew this and that all his readers were expected to know it as well.

Further, Matthew would agree with the traditional contention of Christianity that historical responsibility for the death of Jesus is theologically irrelevant. First-century Christians (including Matthew) did not believe that Jesus was overpowered by hostile Romans or Jews or anyone else. They believed that, whatever the precise circumstances of his execution, he died because it was God's will for him to give his life as an atonement for sin, and he was obedient to that purpose (Phil 2:8). Specifically, for Matthew, Jesus gave his life as a "ransom" that freed people from the effects of sin (20:28). For Matthew, the thought that Jewish (or Roman) enemies should get credit (or blame) for killing Jesus would be patently ridiculous. Jesus could have called on God to send twelve legions of angels to dispense with such petty opponents (26:53). But he didn't because it was God's will that he be crucified, and so, he went to the cross in obedience to the will of God (26:42).

From this it follows that no one is truly responsible for Jesus' death except the sinners on whose behalf he died. And this, I suspect, is what prompted Matthew to emphasize Jewish involvement in Jesus' crucifixion. It seems unlikely that he would want to "let the Romans off the hook," exonerate them for an obvious act of injustice and sadism. More likely, he wanted to insist, rhetorically, that he and his congregation share the guilt and blame for Christ's sacrifice. Matthew is not saying, "*Those Jews* are to blame for killing Jesus." He is saying, "*We Jews* are responsible for killing Jesus. We can't just blame Pilate and the Romans. His blood is also upon us."

Of course, if we are right in surmising this pastoral and theological motive for Matthew's emphasis on Jewish involvement in Jesus' death, we must nevertheless grant that his Gospel has not been read this way in a gentile-dominated anti-Semitic world. Matthew's passion narrative came to be read by gentile Christians not as saying, "*We* crucified Jesus," but as saying, "*They* crucified Jesus." The essential theological meaning of the story was lost, replaced by a political and social interpretation that explained why Jewish people ought to be despised by gentiles. Jews were routinely condemned in such cultures as "Christ killers," and the misfortunes of Jewish people were explained as a consequence of having been cursed by God for their involvement in the crucifixion of Jesus the Messiah. Christians today should, of course, renounce such thinking: they should also acknowledge that, whatever Matthew's intentions might have been, he created a narrative that lent itself all too easily to supporting an ideology responsible for so many atrocities.

MATTHEW 27:27–56
Jesus Is Crucified

Matthew follows his Markan source closely throughout his narration of Jesus' crucifixion, adding only minor details, such as the opening of the tombs and resurrection of saints in 27:51–52.

The story of the crucifixion is told in sparse and brutal language, yet in terms that ironically portray Jesus as a royal figure (27:28–29, 37, 42), indeed, as the very Son of God (27:40, 43, 54).

27:27–31. Mocking of Jesus (cf. Mark 15:16–20; John 19:2–3)

A cohort of the governor's soldiers (usually ca. 600 men) gather around Jesus and mock him in a way that continues to fulfill Jesus' predictions (20:19) and may identify him with the Servant of the Lord described in Isaiah 50:6. They crown his head with a wreath of thorns and place a bamboo rod for flogging prisoners in his hands as a mock scepter, then take it away and beat him with it. The cruel acts recall similar deeds of the supposedly more pious priests (26:67–68; see also 27:39–44) but focus more on his identification as a king (cf. 21:5; 27:11), which the soldiers misinterpret as a political claim. The idea that power is equally abused by both Jewish and Roman figures is consistent with one of the major motifs of this Gospel:

the tendency for people to be evil or righteous has nothing to do with ethnic or religious identity but rather aligns with acquisition and possession of coercive power. In this Gospel, for the most part, the more powerful people are, the more evil they are (tyrants being the worst of all; 20:25); the less powerful people are, the more righteous they are (children and enslaved persons being the greatest of all; 18:1–5; 20:26; 23:11). Jesus is the exception because he possesses power that serves rather than coerces (20:28; see Theme 16 "*Critique of power, wealth, and wisdom*" in the introduction, p. 31). Of course, Matthew's account of the soldiers' mocking abuse is again rife with irony: the readers know that Jesus really is "King of the Jews," and more, the Lord of all, before whom the soldiers will one day bow their knees and beg for mercy (cf. Phil 2:10–11).

27:32–54. The Crucifixion (cf. Mark 15:21–39; Luke 23:26–39a, 44–47; John 19:17–30; Matt 27:51b–53 only in Matthew)

The act of Jesus' crucifixion is simply referenced without being described (27:35), but several matters associated with it are related with rare detail. Every element later becomes significant for Christian memory: Simon the crossbearer (cf. 10:38; 16:24); the morbid name Golgotha, "Place of a Skull"; the cruel offer of wine mixed with bitter gall (cf. Ps 69:21); the dividing of garments and casting of lots (cf. Ps 22:18); the placard with its mocking, yet ironically accurate description (cf. Matt 2:2; 21:5), and the fellowship of criminals (cf. Isa 53:12).

The mocking of Jesus (26:66–67; 27:27–31; cf. 20:19; Ps 22:7–8) continues, with casual passersby and even the rebels crucified with him joining now in the derision (no mention in Matthew of one rebel's conversion, as in Luke 23:39–41). The taunt of the religious leaders (Matt 27:40) eerily recalls the words of Satan earlier in the Gospel (4:3, 6), in the same way that the three tests they earlier laid before Jesus (22:15–40) recalled the devil's activity in 4:1–11.

Finally, three hours of darkness at noon (cf. 24:29; cf. Amos 8:9; Exod 10:22) indicate to Jesus that God has now abandoned him, an apparent necessity for his death to be the ransom that establishes a new covenant (Matt 20:28; 26:28). His so-called cry of dereliction quotes Psalm 22:1 in a way that simultaneously affirms his continued commitment to God ("*My* God") and his continued confusion as to *why* this abandonment to death is necessary (cf. Matt 26:39). When bystanders misunderstand the Hebrew word for "my God" (*Eli;* cf. Aramaic "Eloi" in Mark 15:34) as a call for Elijah, Matthew's readers may be reminded of what Jesus said regarding Elijah earlier (17:12). "Let us see whether Elijah will come!" the bystanders gleefully cry (27:49); but according to Jesus, Elijah has already come (in the person of John the Baptist), and they did to him what they are now doing to the Son of Man. Thus the motif of the abandonment of Jesus continues (see the bulleted points listed in Excursus: Themes in Matthew's Passion Narrative, p. 281). Forsaken or rejected by the religious leaders of Israel, by the Roman government and soldiers, by his own disciples, by the crowds that once followed him, by casual onlookers, by the criminals crucified with him, and now even by God—Jesus dies with a great cry of anguish.

And then, immediately, heaven and earth respond. The ripping of the temple curtain may signify that a new covenant has begun, through which sins are forgiven by virtue of Jesus' blood rather than animal sacrifices (20:28; 21:12–13); or it could signify that God no longer dwells in the temple but will henceforth be "with" people in a more universal and accessible way (cf. 1:23; see Theme 1 "*The abiding presence of God*" in the introduction, p. 7). Another possibility is that the curtain is ripped (*schizō*) for the same reason that a new patch sewn on an old garment results in a rip (*schisma*, 9:16): Jesus' death inaugurates a new reality, a new communal experience of God's rule on earth; this new reality cannot simply be stuck on the old foundation (Second Temple Judaism) but will require a new foundation (the church Jesus will build). The earthquake (note that the rocks are also "split," *schizō*) and the raising of saints indicate that the gates of Hades are falling (16:18) and the power of death has been broken. Some of the soldiers who have mocked Jesus in the courtyard (27:27–31) and nailed him to the cross now confess him to be God's Son, a proleptic testimony to the effect that the gospel message may have when it is proclaimed among gentiles throughout the world (24:14; 26:13; 28:19).

As indicated by many of the parenthetical references in the preceding paragraphs, Matthew follows established Christian tradition in describing the crucifixion with language borrowed from Psalm 22. That psalm relates the lament of an innocent sufferer who continues to hope that a seemingly absent God will bring deliverance. The most obvious contact point may be 22:16, which in the LXX reads, "They pierced/gouged my hands and feet." Whatever that meant for the psalmist, Christians were quick to find an almost literal reference to the mode of Jesus' execution. Given that, many other references seemed apropos: "All who see me, mock me; they hurl insults, shaking their heads, saying, He trusts in the Lord; let the Lord rescue him'" (Ps 22:7–8 LXX); "They divide my clothes among them and cast lots for my garments" (22:18 LXX). Jesus' last words (Matt 27:46) are essentially the name of the psalm, which probably was known by its first line rather than by a number (Ps 22:1). This all fits with a common motif in Matthew, demonstrating how elements of the Jesus story fulfill or at least resonate with the Hebrew Scriptures (Matt 26:24, 54, 56; see Theme 6 "*Fulfillment of prophecy*" in the introduction, p. 14).

Throughout the crucifixion narrative, Matthew emphasizes Jesus' identity as the royal Son of God (see the bulleted points in Excursus: Themes in Matthew's Passion Narrative, p. 281). The placard on the cross is intended as an indictment: he is officially crucified as a claimant to royal authority and thus a rebel against Rome. This is also clear from the comment that the persons crucified with Jesus were "rebels" (*lēstai*) and that when he was arrested, the mob came prepared to seize a rebel (*lēstēs*, 26:55). On one level, this is a grave injustice: Jesus is not laying claim to a throne that Caesar (or even Pilate) occupies, and Pilate himself knows this (27:18). But Matthew's reader knows that Jesus is in fact "the Son of the living God" (16:16) and "the king" who will judge "the nations" (25:31–46). So the accusation is only a "misunderstanding" in a superficial sense. Matthew presents Jesus as someone who *does* claim to have authority over all earthly powers (28:18), and that claim does have political implications (though perhaps not the immediate, temporal ones that Pilate or Caesar would fear). So, a double irony appears: Pilate treats Jesus as though he were dangerous, knowing that he is not, but not knowing that he actually is (in the long run).

Of course, the greatest irony of all (indeed, the paradigmatic instance of irony in the history of literature) is that the narrative's major conflict is now resolved in such a way that the hero loses and the antagonists win—and yet the readers discern that this is necessary for a more significant, though hidden, conflict to be resolved favorably. Jesus loses and the religious leaders win, but God triumphs over Satan (for more on this, see Theme 15 "*Conflict along three plot lines*" in the introduction, p. 29).

The death of Jesus is followed by an auspicious confession by Roman soldiers that echoes the one made by Peter in 16:16. In Matthew (different from Mark) it is not just the centurion who proclaims, "This man was God's Son!" but also "those with him" (27:54). On a rational level, we may surmise that they are simply responding out of fear, noting the darkness and the earthquake as apocalyptic portents. And, of course, historically, "God's Son" would mean something different to Roman soldiers than to Jewish Christians (more "a god's son!" than "the Son of the one true God!"). Still, according to Matthew, no one can know Jesus as Son of God apart from divine revelation (11:27; 16:17), and those who do know this provide the foundation for the church (16:18). Surely, gentile members of Matthew's community would be thrilled to see signs of such faith blossoming at the foot of the cross.

27:55–56. Women as Witnesses (cf. Mark 15:40–41; Luke 23:49; John 19:25)

Only now does Matthew reveal that some of Jesus' followers are present to witness the events of his crucifixion. Although his male disciples have deserted him (26:56), many women are present, and Matthew says that they have followed him from Galilee "and provided for him" (cf. Luke 8:2–3). These women include (1) the mother of the sons of Zebedee (see also 20:20); she is usually thought to be the woman whose name is given as Salome in Mark 15:40; (2) a woman named Mary who has sons named James and Joseph; she is probably the mother of the disciple called "James son of Alphaeus" (10:3; cf. Mark 15:40), though some interpreters have thought that she might be the mother of Jesus himself (cf. 13:55); and (3) Mary Magdalene, who becomes a popular figure in later noncanonical writings, though the Bible has little to say of her (Luke 8:2 is the only reference to her aside from her presence at the cross and tomb, though John 20:1–18 treats the latter extensively). There is no reason to associate her with the sex worker mentioned in Luke 7:36–50 or with the woman taken in adultery in John 8:2–11, but such misidentifications were sometimes made in an era when written texts were few and preachers had to rely on memory. Thus, to the frustration of exegetes and careful Bible readers, Mary Magdalene came to be known as a fallen woman who had been converted by Jesus, drawn to him spiritually and perhaps romantically. None of this finds support in any credible historical source; the notion that Mary Magdalene was once a sex worker is especially absurd since, at the time of Jesus, all sex workers in the provinces were enslaved persons (normally teenagers) and could not quit their profession for religious or any other reasons. Most likely Mary Magdalene was a wealthy businesswoman, possibly a widow, and probably around the age of Jesus' mother. The notation in Luke 8:2 that she and other wealthy women provided for Jesus and his disciples "out of their resources" suggests financial support, which is probably implicit here in Matt 27:55 as well. Of course, persons responsible for financing a mission usually want some oversight of that mission or, at least, to receive reports as to how things are going. This simple observation led to my oft-quoted (but slightly tongue-in-cheek) comment that "Mary Magdalene was not Jesus' girlfriend; more likely, she was his boss." As we will see, the two Marys mentioned in this text are important to Matthew's story because they serve as the primary witnesses to three key events: the death (27:55–56), burial (27:61), and resurrection (28:1) of Jesus (see 1 Cor 15:3–4).

MATTHEW 27:57–28:20
Jesus Is Raised

Matthew takes the basic account of Jesus' being entombed from Mark, along with the story of women finding the tomb empty on the third day. But he has redacted this material heavily, adding unique accounts of the guard at the tomb (before and after the resurrection), of an encounter between the risen Jesus and the fearful women, and of a final "Great Commission" to the eleven remaining disciples.

Matthew's narrative comes at last to the climactic event that he believes changed everything forever. The sign of Jonah (12:39–40; 16:4) is given and, as anticipated, rejected. In some respects, the account of Jesus' burial and resurrection serves as the conclusion to Matthew's Gospel and is absolutely integral to all that has gone before. In another important sense, however, it serves as a new beginning, as the foundation narrative for a story yet to be told. Some things will be the same: the forces of evil will continue to be powerful (28:15), and disciples of Jesus will continue to doubt (28:17). But, behind the scenes, something will be fundamentally different: Jesus has saved his people from their sins, and he is risen from the dead. Thus he is able to initiate a new mission, one that invokes a new name (28:19; cf. 1:21, 23), is grounded in his universal authority (28:18), and is sustained by his abiding presence (28:20).

27:57–61. Entombment of Jesus (cf. Mark 15:42–47; Luke 23:50–56; John 19:38–42)

Joseph of Arimathea acquires Jesus' dead body and seals it in a tomb. The need for him to do this accentuates the absence of Jesus' closest disciples (26:56), who might be expected to do at least this much for their Master (cf. 14:12). Yet Joseph is a "rich man" who "also was himself a disciple of Jesus" or, more accurately, a rich man who had been discipled or instructed by Jesus. Notably, Matthew does not say that Joseph is "a respected member of the council" (Mark 15:43); this is in keeping with his principle that all religious leaders of Israel function as opponents of God's plan in his narrative (see Theme 14 "*Religious leaders as enemies of God*" in the introduction, p. 25). Still, to be both rich *and* a follower of Jesus is almost a contradiction in terms, according to Matthew 19:24; but only *almost*, according to 19:26. Finally, the mention of the women in this passage highlights the faithlessness of the disciples even more. Previously, Matthew has told us that many women, including the ones mentioned here, were present at the crucifixion, watching from a distance (27:55–56). That reference cast into stark relief the fact that the male disciples were *not* present, not even watching "from a distance" to see what would become of their Master. The reference now to the women watching the tomb picks up that thread and carries it forward: the women are *witnesses*, while the male disciples, whom Jesus empowered to be apostles (10:1–4), are not.

27:62–66. Posting of the Guard (only in Matthew)

Chief priests and Pharisees, the two groups that want Jesus dead (12:14; 26:3–4), convince Pilate to let them place a guard at the tomb to prevent any resurrection hoax from being perpetrated by Jesus' disciples. In Matthew's story, both political and religious leaders are evil perpetrators of injustice; whenever they come together, it is for death. Early in the story, the political ruler manipulates religious leaders as he conspires to kill Jesus (2:3–6); later, the religious leaders manipulate the political authority in service of their own plot to have Jesus put to death (26:3–5; 27:1–2, 11–26). Now, the two forces combine in an attempt to preserve that death (or, at least, to prevent any rumor of life).

Here are ironic moments:

First, Jesus' enemies, but apparently not his disciples, remember the promise of a resurrection (16:21; 17:23; 20:19; see also 17:9; 26:32).

Second, the religious leaders characterize others with terminology applicable to themselves: they call Jesus a "deceiver" (27:63, *planos*; NRSVue, "impostor") though, in the story, they themselves are the ones who have acted deceptively (22:15). They also slander Jesus' disciples as persons who would spread false reports about Jesus' resurrection (claiming it occurred when they knew it had not); but as the story continues, the leaders themselves turn out to be the ones who spread false reports about that resurrection (claiming it had not occurred, when they knew that it had; 28:11).

Third, the rationale for the leaders' request is ironic in that it attributes a loyalty to Jesus' disciples that readers know is lacking. The disciples have abdicated responsibility for Jesus' body, not even bothering to recover it or to bury it or even to witness the burial. It hardly seems likely that they would now come to take the body from the tomb and courageously (if deceptively) proclaim him as risen. The leaders' depiction of the disciples is so far off the mark that it serves to remind readers of just how uncommitted to Jesus those errant disciples truly are.

Finally, in making their request for a guard, the leaders also ironically acknowledge the foolishness of what they have done and the negative consequences that it will have for them. They say that if Jesus' disciples begin proclaiming his resurrection, "the last deception [will] be worse than the first" (27:64). This wording closely parallels what Jesus said earlier, in 12:45: the leaders now liken themselves to a man temporarily relieved of one unclean spirit, only to end up possessed by many more. Basically, the leaders are depicted here as acknowledging that if Jesus is said to be risen, they will be worse off than if they had never pushed for his crucifixion in the first place. The reader cannot help but imagine that, if a *false* report of resurrection would render their situation worse than it was before, how much more might a *true* report of a resurrection render that situation intolerable!

28:1–10. Women at the Empty Tomb (cf. Mark 16:1–8; Luke 24:1–12; John 20:1–18)

Like the religious leaders (27:63), the two Marys (see 27:56, 61) apparently remember Jesus' predictions (16:21; 17:23; 20:19), and they come to the tomb early on the third day to see what will happen. Note that in Mark, the women come to anoint the body of Jesus (Mark 16:1): they expect to find a corpse. Matthew omits that detail, suggesting that the women come to see if the resurrection that Jesus announced will actually occur (that the women were present when the predictions were made is suggested by 27:55). Their vigilance is rewarded: a shining angel terrifies the guard and removes the stone, not to let Jesus out, but to show the women that he is already gone. The women are then commissioned to tell his absent disciples what they have missed and to remind them of what Jesus has told them earlier about a reunion in Galilee (28:7; see 26:32). They respond with eager obedience and "with fear and great joy." Then they encounter Jesus himself; they worship him and are commissioned by him to go and tell his "brothers" to go to Galilee, where they will see him.

Matthew portrays the death, burial, and resurrection of Jesus as a single eschatological drama. The earthquake reported here (28:2) recalls what happened at the moment of Jesus' death (27:51–54); on that occasion, tombs were also opened, and some dead "saints" were raised. The appearance of an "angel of the Lord" leaves no doubt that God is directing these affairs, and it also takes us back to the beginning of Matthew's story, when angels were actively involved (1:20; 2:13–14, 19; 4:11). This time, however, the divine manifestation is more dramatic. Previously, God's angels appeared to humans in dreams and guided them through that medium. Now the angel of the Lord is physically active on earth (moving the stone) and visibly present to all onlookers, even the guards, who become "like dead men" (an ironic fate for those entrusted with guarding the dead). And now God's angel speaks directly to people outside the medium of dreams.

The role of the women in this part of the story is especially significant (for the interpretation presented here, see Powell 2009). They are depicted as ideal disciples, foils to the absent and errant male disciples. Their response to the good news, "fear and great joy," represents an ideal combination of elements. In Matthew's Gospel, fear can be debilitating (e.g., 14:30–33), but sometimes it is appropriate (10:28) and can motivate worship (17:6) or even a confession of faith (27:54). Joy, by contrast, is typically a positive quality (2:10; 13:44; 25:21, 23), but it has potential for negative results: it can signify faith that is superficial and unlikely to endure (13:20–21). The mixture of fear and joy, then, allows for a paradoxical compatibility to the benefit of both elements: joy is what turns fear into worship; fear is what prevents joy from being shallow.

Even more important, the women—Mary Magdalene and "the other Mary" (see comments on 27:56, 61)—serve a unique role in this Gospel as witnesses and proclaimers of the gospel. Previously, they have witnessed the crucifixion of Jesus (27:55–56) and his entombment (27:61); now they are witnesses to his resurrection and are commissioned by both an angel and by Jesus himself to proclaim the news of that resurrection. Matthew's readers are probably expected to know that the "Christian gospel" is typically a witness to three things: the death, burial, and resurrection of Jesus Christ (e.g., 1 Cor 15:3–4). In Matthew's narrative, the women become witnesses to these three things; indeed, they become the *only* witnesses to these three things (i.e., to all three). They also become the first people to worship the risen Lord and the first to proclaim the gospel that is to be taken to the world (24:14). Such primacy in worship and mission gives them the role in the church that had originally been offered to Peter (16:18–19). Of course, Jesus' desire for the male disciples to be recovered and his reference to them as his "brothers" (28:10; see also 12:46–50) conveys a strong sense of his faithfulness to them in a way that contrasts sharply with their faithlessness to him. Clearly, they are to be forgiven, welcomed back, and restored to positions of leadership (see 28:16–20), but their apostasy does cost them the legacy that they might otherwise have had. Now, Jesus wills for his church to be founded by women, and the so-called Great Commission, with which the Gospel concludes, will actually be presented as a secondary commission. The unfaithful men cannot be sent to make disciples of all nations until after the faithful women make disciples of them. Indeed, the men's calling to preach the gospel is made conditional on their ability to receive the gospel as proclaimed by women. To put it bluntly: if men are not able to accept women's proclamation of the gospel and submit themselves to it, there will be no mission to the nations (at least no mission carried out by men) and there will be no church (at least no church that includes male believers). The church of Jesus Christ is founded by women, but it may also include men—if the women follow Christ's direction to include men and if the men are willing to accept their inclusion on precisely those terms.

We may be prompted to consider *why* the narrative would develop in this way? Matthew's readers are not expected to espouse modern views concerning the role of women in society, including those informed by feminism. Rather, Matthew's Gospel presupposes a patriarchal mindset, a view that understands the social inequities between men and women not as the result of unfortunate prejudices but as intrinsic reality. Men have power and women do not: that is just the way things are, and Matthew's readers are probably not expected to imagine that anything so basic to human society could or should be different. Nevertheless, Matthew does offer a critique from within the patriarchal mindset regarding how such gender roles might be evaluated. This critique comes through a sweeping claim that *God prefers the powerless to the powerful* (see Theme 16 "*Critique of power, wealth, and wisdom*" in the introduction, p. 31). Thus, women are not exalted as founders of the church and exemplars of faith because they should be considered "equals" with men. They are so exalted precisely because they are not equals. In God's eyes, women are greater than men for the same reason that children are greater than adults (18:1–4): both lack social power and so are diminished in their capacity to manipulate, dominate, and control others. A central motif of Matthew's Gospel is that coercive power is antithetical to God's purposes; those who neither seek nor possess such power are always favored and preferred by God. In this Gospel's vision of the future, women (like children) may be the greatest in the ultimate manifestation of God's rule even if, there, the men are still the ones on the thrones (19:28). This is not feminism, which typically seeks to empower women and sometimes seeks to debunk stereotypical gender roles altogether. But it is a critique of patriarchy *from within*, a critique that the narrative foists upon its readers without any sure resolution of where it might lead or what could happen as a result. Indeed, we might note that it is potentially a critique of feminism as well, a challenge to the basic assumption that the acquisition (or maintenance) of power is a good thing.

28:11–15. Report of the Guard (only in Matthew)

As the women run to tell the disciples what has happened, the guards make a report to Jesus' enemies, who respond by bribing the guards (cf. 26:15; 27:3) to spread a false rumor that Jesus' disciples stole the body while they slept. The guards' commission to spread the false rumor about the theft of Jesus' body parallels the disciples' commission to baptize and teach all nations, given by Jesus in the next few verses (28:16–20). This parallel is amplified by Matthew's use of the verb *didaskō* (teach) in 28:15. By indicating that the guards did as they were "taught" (NRSVue, "directed"), Matthew styles the false rumor regarding the theft of Jesus' body as a "teaching" of the religious leaders (cf. 16:12). In any case, the plan worked, which Matthew thinks explains why many Jews do not know the truth about the resurrection of Jesus, their Messiah (the NRSVue's translation of *Ioudaioi* in 28:15 as "Judeans" instead of as "Jews" is incorrect and absurd—the Matthean evangelist would not have been troubled by or even cognizant of stories that residents of Judea might by telling at the time he was writing his Gospel).

This episode contributes to Matthew's characterization of the religious leaders of Israel and concludes the plotline that traces the conflict between Jesus and those leaders throughout the Gospel. Two matters are especially significant.

First, the episode reveals that the religious leaders are absolutely recalcitrant and exposes the depth of their evil obstinacy and hypocrisy (cf. 13:14–15). They perpetrate the very sort of deception that they attribute to others; *they* become the "impostors" (cf. 27:62), and they do so in an unconscionable manner, lacking any pretense of a righteous rationale. Twice in this narrative, the religious leaders have requested a sign from Jesus, implying (duplicitously) that they would believe in him if only a proper sign were given (12:38; 16:1). Now they reject the sign he has promised (12:40; 16:4); knowing full well that Jesus has risen from the dead, they do not repent; instead, they redouble their efforts to oppose him by spreading a teaching that they know to be untrue (on the religious leaders as "flat characters," serving as representatives of evil in Matthew, see Theme 14 "*Religious leaders as enemies of God*" in the introduction, p. 25).

Second, the episode reveals that the religious leaders are successful. The narrator speaks directly to the reader to say that the false report denying Jesus' resurrection continued to be told, and presumably believed, by Jews in his day (28:15). Plot analysis usually holds that the conflict between Jesus and the religious leaders in Matthew's story can be defined in terms of two threats that those leaders pose to Jesus: (1) they threaten to turn the Jewish people against him, and (2) they threaten to kill him. In the climactic passion narrative, both of those threats succeed. Now the reader is faced with the awful recognition that the resurrection of Jesus has not undone the success of the first threat: even though Jesus is risen from the dead, the religious leaders of Israel continue to turn the people against him. In like manner, I would argue that the second threat is not undone by the resurrection either. Some scholars have suggested that the leaders' plot to kill Jesus fails because Jesus does not stay dead. I think this trivializes the consequences of the crucifixion as presented in this narrative (see Theme 15 "*Conflict along three plot lines*" in the introduction, p. 29).

The persistence and power of evil is a major theme in Matthew's apocalyptic tale, a story in which characters may be classed as "good" or "evil," or as "righteous" or "unrighteous" (5:45). The story world of this narrative may be likened to a field in which wheat (people who belong to God) and weeds (people put there by the devil) must grow side by side until the harvest (13:24–30, 36–43). In 28:11–15, we learn that the resurrection of Jesus has not altered the basic state of affairs: evil continues unabated, with great success. This brief episode serves to establish the context for the story yet to be told, the context in which the commission given in the next scene will have to be carried out. Jesus' disciples will have to conduct their mission in a world where evil remains both unconscionably devious and incredibly powerful.

28:16–20. The Great Commission (only in Matthew)

The disciples are now only eleven: Judas having forfeited his identification as an "apostle" (10:2–4) and, presumably, the throne from which he might have ruled tribes of Israel (19:28). Those who remain are "made disciples" (cf. 28:19) again through the testimony of women who proved to be more faithful than they were. They join Jesus on a mountain to which he has somehow directed them: mountains are often sites for divine revelation in Matthew (5:1; 17:1), recalling the meeting of Moses with God on Sinai. The disciples are still people of "little faith" (6:30; 8:26; 14:31; 16:8; 17:20), a community in which worship and doubt coexist. But their commission now depends on Jesus' authority, not theirs. His claim, "All authority in heaven and on earth has been given to me," is one of the highest christological claims to be found in the Scriptures. It recalls what Jesus said earlier, "All things have been handed over to me by my Father" (11:27). In that instance the context suggested authority to reveal God and all things godly; now, however, the implication is authority to rule: Jesus is not simply Lord to his followers, but has been made "Lord of heaven and earth" (cf. 11:25). Given that commission, the disciples will no longer limit their ministry to Israel (10:5–6; cf. 15:24) but will go out into the whole world with the good news of God's reign that Jesus preached (24:14; 26:13; see also 4:17, 23), making disciples of all nations. And he will be with them always, to the end of the age (28:20, forming an inclusio with the promise of God's presence in 1:23).

The Great Commission itself begins with the significant word "Go" (28:19). Many expressions of Christianity in our modern world apparently believe that they can fulfill Jesus' Great Commission by maintaining that if and when any people from any nation show up at their church desiring to be made disciples, they will baptize and teach those persons in accord with Jesus' wishes. We will not comment on the success rate of "Go-less" evangelism but will only note that, for Matthew, the church is a missionary *movement*, not a static institution.

The Commission also reveals that becoming a disciple involves two steps:

First, it involves being baptized into the community of people who worship Jesus as the Son of God, an affirmation leading that community to call God by a new name: "Father, Son, and Holy Spirit" (28:19). This is the only biblical reference to that triadic name for God—and the fact that it is *a* name (one name, not three names) is theologically significant. Matthew does not evince developed

Trinitarian doctrine in a Nicene sense: he betrays no interest in ontology, or whether the three entities share the same "substance." But we are clearly moving in that direction (for other instances of embryonic Trinitarian expression, see 2 Cor 13:13; Eph 4:4–6; 1 Pet 1:2). Matthew has realized that his favorite metaphor for God is too limited: "Father" isn't enough; one thing Jesus revealed (apparently) is that God is more like a family or a relationship than a solitary parental figure (cf. 11:27). Of course, some may wish the metaphor had been expanded in ways that were less gender specific (or at least less "traditional male role" specific), but Matthew is not thinking in those terms.

Second, becoming a disciple means being trained in obedience to fulfill the will of the Father (cf. 7:21) by living in accord with the commandments as Jesus has taught and interpreted them. Such training assumes the practice of binding-and-loosing commandments (those of Scripture, and those of Jesus himself) in order to discern God's will for varied contexts and in complex circumstances. The Matthean Jesus has demonstrated how this is done and declared that the church will have both the authority and responsibility for continuing to do so in his name (see Theme 8 "*Binding-and-loosing commandments*" in the introduction, p. 16; and comments on 5:21–48; 16:19; 18:18).

The Great Commission lends a final coda to what is probably the principal theme of Matthew's Gospel: the enduring and abiding presence of God in the world (see Theme 1 "*The abiding presence of God*" in the introduction, p. 7). Matthew has indicated that God is present with people through the person of Jesus (1:23) and that Jesus remains present in the world through the life and mission of his followers (confirmed here in 28:20; see also 18:20; 25:37–40). But, as indicated, those followers will be less a sedentary community than a missionary movement, making the presence of God-in-Christ a reality for all those who welcome them and become disciples (10:40). Thus, "making disciples" means recruiting people to carry out the mission, to become agents of God's presence. Baptizing and catechizing people from all nations is the means, not the end. The missional goal is not just for there to be more disciples (more Christians) in the world, but for God's presence to be manifested in ways that effect God's gracious will for all humanity. Making disciples (by teaching the baptized to practice what Jesus has taught) is the means for accomplishing this goal. Such people will be pure in heart, merciful peacemakers who stand in solidarity with the poor in spirit and all who mourn (5:3–8). They will be conspicuous in their good works, bringing flavor and light to a world that for some is dull and dark (5:13–16). They will be slow to anger (5:21–25) and reluctant to judge (7:1–5). They will aspire to be faithful in marriage and respectful of sexual boundaries (5:27–32). They will forgive their friends (5:23–24; 18:21–22) and love their enemies (5:38–45). They will be active in prayer (6:6; 7:7–11) and generous in giving to all in need (5:42), while remaining discreet and avoiding outward displays of piety (6:1–7, 16–18). They will not be anxious (6:25–34) or greedy (6:19–24), but will be people who actively seek the good of others, striving always to treat others as they wish to be treated (7:12). All this (and so much more) is implied by the Great Commission (28:18–20): the mission is to model such behavior and to encourage and train those who are agreeable (declaring this through baptism) to live in such a manner that God's mission of creating a somewhat more godly world might experience moments of fulfillment. (For more on Matthew's notion of God's mission being conducted first through Jesus and then through the church, see Theme 3 "*The mission of God*" in the introduction, p. 10.)

Recent readers of Matthew have had problems with the general tenor of the Great Commission as supportive of worldwide evangelism that, in history, would often imply or encourage colonialism. We should be aware of this, but I think it is safe to assume that Matthew's readers would not be expected to read the text as implying any endorsement of imperialism. The clear assumption is that those who receive and act on the Great Commission will be relatively powerless persons, seeking to enact love, justice, mercy, and faithfulness (22:34–40; 23:23) in a world dominated by purveyors of opposite tendencies. (On this, see Excursus: "Christ beneath Culture" as a Paradigm for Mission, p. 229.)

We may say a little more about the combination of "worship and doubt," which for Matthew are compatible characteristics definitive of the church (for more on "worship in Matthew," see Excursus: Worship in the Gospel of Matthew, p. 51). First, as a minor point, note that the NRSV and many other English translations read, "They worshiped him; but some doubted"; the NRSVue says simply, "They worshiped him, but they doubted." There has been much discussion over this, but I think the NRSVue has definitely translated it right. The word "some" is not in the Greek; nevertheless, many translators have thought that it might be implied, on an assumption that the expression Matthew employs (*hoi de*) is to be taken in the partitive sense it sometimes has in classical Greek. Matthew, however, uses that expression seventeen other times, and in all those instances it refers either to the entire group of people that has just been mentioned (2:9; 4:20, 22; 8:32; 9:31; 22:5; 27:66; 28:15) or to persons within that group whose perspectives are to be taken as representative of the group as a whole (2:5; 14:17; 16:7, 14; 21:25; 27:21, 23). Thus, the meaning is almost certainly "All eleven worshiped him, and all eleven doubted" (see Reeves 1993). The NRSVue is correct. But even if that were not the case (if the NRSV and other translations were right to indicate that only "some" doubted), we would still note that Jesus does not separate out the disciples: he does not commission the worshipers and rebuke the doubters. Rather, Jesus gives the Great Commission (with his promise of abiding presence) to worshipers and doubters alike; or better, he gives the Great Commission to a *community* of disciples in which worship and doubt coexist.

The word used here for doubt (*distazō*) occurs only twice in Matthew (14:31; 28:17) and nowhere else in the New Testament; it carries a sense of uncertainty or a lack of assurance (see comments on 14:31). Matthew does not tell us why the disciples doubted: perhaps they were not sure that Jesus was actually risen, or maybe they were uncertain as to whether he would have them back. In any case, it is interesting to note that in the Gospel of Matthew, Jesus' disciples are only said to worship him twice (14:33; 28:17); also, in Matthew, Jesus' disciples are only said to doubt him twice (14:31; 28:17)—and these are the same two times! In other words, in Matthew the disciples

- never worship Jesus without doubting him; and
- never doubt Jesus without worshiping him.

What does this mean? At least, it means that, while doubt might keep people from walking on water (14:28–33), it does not keep them from worshiping or from being commissioned by Jesus for a mission to the world. But there could be more. The combination of worship and doubt might function like the mixture of fear and joy that allows for a paradoxical compatibility to the benefit of both elements: joy is what turns fear into worship; fear is what prevents joy from being shallow (see comments on 28:8). Worship is obviously a good and desirable thing; but, like joy, it can sometimes be superficial. In Matthew 15:7–9, Jesus tells the Pharisees that they worship God with their lips while their hearts are far from God (quoting Isa 29:13). The Pharisees may have many faults in Matthew's Gospel, but one thing they never do is *doubt*. They are always certain about everything. By contrast, disciples of Jesus worship and doubt at the same time—and Jesus doesn't call *their* worship superficial. So, it may be that just as fear seasons joy, so doubt seasons worship. Joy without fear becomes shallow, and worship without doubt can be self-assured and superficial.

The Great Commission concludes Matthew's Gospel but also serves as the introduction to another story, one filled with continuing conflicts and challenges. The "story yet to be told" will indeed be an account of sheep being sent into the midst of wolves (10:16), of faithful people being flogged in synagogues and dragged before gentiles (10:17–18), of family members betraying one another (10:21), and of disciples being hated for bearing Jesus' name (10:22). Yet it will be a story of fear *and* great joy (28:8), for both those who are made disciples and those who make them disciples will be people who know that Jesus is risen. These disciples become the community that Jesus calls "the church" (16:18; 18:17). It is an inclusive, ethical community of worshiping doubters: a church founded by women (28:1–10), a church that considers little children to be its most important members (18:1–5), a church that specializes in making room for sinners and outcasts (9:10–13), a church that teaches people to love God, their neighbors, and their enemies (22:37–40; 5:44), and to keep Torah primarily by treating other people the way they want to be treated (7:12)—this is the community of people with whom Jesus promises to abide till the end of time.

BIBLIOGRAPHY

For Further Reading

Bauer, David R. *The Gospel of the Son of God: An Introduction to Matthew*. Downers Grove, IL: InterVarsity Press, 2019.

Brown, Jeannine K., and Kyle Roberts. *Matthew*. Two Horizons Commentary. Grand Rapids: Wm. B. Eerdmans Publishing Co., 2018.

Kampen, John. *Matthew within Sectarian Judaism*. New Haven: Yale University Press, 2019.

Keener, Craig S. *A Commentary on the Gospel of Matthew*. Grand Rapids: Wm. B. Eerdmans Publishing Co., 1999.

Kingsbury, Jack Dean. *Matthew as Story*. 2nd ed. Philadelphia: Fortress Press, 1988.

Levine, Amy-Jill. *The Misunderstood Jesus: The Church and the Scandal of the Jewish Jesus*. San Francisco: HarperSanFrancisco, 2006.

Powell, Mark Allan. *Fortress Introduction to the Gospels*. 2nd ed. Minneapolis: Fortress Press, 2019.

———. *God with Us: Toward a Pastoral Theology of Matthew's Gospel*. Minneapolis: Fortress Press, 1995.

Wainwright, Elaine M. *Shall We Look for Another? A Feminist Rereading of the Matthean Jesus*. Maryknoll, NY: Orbis Books, 2000.

Works Cited

Allison, Dale C. 1993. *The New Moses: A Matthean Typology*. Minneapolis: Fortress Press.

Bacon, Benjamin. 1930. *Studies in Matthew*. New York: H. Holt.

Dawn, Marva J. 1999. *A Royal Waste of Time: The Splendor of Worshiping God and Being Church for the World*. Grand Rapids: Wm. B. Eerdmans Publishing Co.

Hare, Douglas R. A. 1993. *Matthew*. Interpretation. Louisville, KY: John Knox Press. New ed., Westminster John Knox Press, 2009.

Herzog, William R., III. 1994. *Parables as Subversive Speech*. Louisville, KY: Westminster John Knox Press.

Kingsbury, Jack Dean. 1975. *Matthew: Structure, Christology, Kingdom*. Philadelphia: Fortress Press.

Niebuhr, H. Richard. 1951. *Christ and Culture*. New York: Harper & Row.

Powell, Mark Allan. 1990. "The Plot to Kill Jesus from Three Different Perspectives: Point of View in Matthew." In *Society of Biblical Literature 1990 Seminar Papers*, edited by David J. Lull, 603–13. Atlanta: Scholars Press.

———. 1992. "The Plot and Subplots of Matthew's Gospel." *New Testament Studies* 39:187–204.

———. 1995. "Do and Keep What Moses Says (Matthew 23:2–7)." *Journal of Biblical Literature* 114:419–35.

———. 1996a. "Characterization on the Phraseological Plane in the Gospel of Matthew." In *Treasures New and Old: Recent Contributions to Matthean Studies*, edited by David R. Bauer and Mark Allan Powell, 161–77. SBL Symposium Series 1. Atlanta: Scholars Press.

———. 1996b. "Matthew's Beatitudes: Reversals and Rewards of the Kingdom." *Catholic Biblical Quarterly* 58:460–79.

———. 2001. *Chasing the Eastern Star: Adventures in Biblical Reader-Response Criticism.* Louisville, KY: Westminster John Knox Press.

———. 2003. "Binding and Loosing: Asserting the Moral Authority of Scripture in Light of a Matthean Paradigm." *Ex Auditu* 19:81–96.

———. 2004. *Loving Jesus.* Minneapolis: Fortress Press.

———. 2006a. "Does the Gospel of Matthew Support the Notion of a Teaching *Magisterium*?" *Lutheran Forum* 40/2 (Summer): 36–44.

———. 2006b. *Giving to God: The Good News of Biblical Stewardship.* Grand Rapids: Wm. B. Eerdmans Publishing Co.

———. 2007. "Echoes of Jonah in the New Testament." *Word and World* 27/2 (Spring): 157–64.

———. 2009. "Literary Approaches to the Gospel of Matthew." In *Methods for Matthew*, 44–82. Edited by Mark Allan Powell. Cambridge: Cambridge University Press.

———. 2015. "Jesus and the Pathetic Wicked: Re-visiting Sanders's View of Jesus' Friendship with Sinners." *Journal for the Study of the Historical Jesus* 13/2–3:188–208.

Reeves, Keith Howard. 1993. *The Resurrection Narrative in Matthew: A Literary-Critical Examination.* Lewiston, NY: Mellen Biblical Press.

Schüssler Fiorenza, Elisabeth. 1983. *In Memory of Her: A Feminist Theological Reconstruction of Christian Origins.* New York: Crossroad.

Stendahl, Krister. 1968. *The School of St. Matthew.* Philadelphia: Fortress.

Weaver, Dorothy Jean. 2017. *The Irony of Power: The Politics of God within Matthew's Narrative.* Eugene, OR: Wipf & Stock.

Wengst, Klaus. 1988. *Humility: Solidarity of the Humiliated.* Philadelphia: Fortress Press.